CIMA

STUDY TEXT

OPERATIONAL LEVEL

PAPER F1

FINANCIAL OPERATIONS

Our Text has a **brand new look** for CIMA's new 2010 syllabus.
In this edition we:

- **Highlight** the **most important elements** in the syllabus and the **key skills** you will need
- **Signpost** how each chapter links to the syllabus and the learning outcomes
- **Provide** lots of **exam alerts** explaining how what you're learning may be tested
- **Emphasise key points** in **section summaries**
- **Test your knowledge** of what you've studied in **quick quizzes**
- **Examine your understanding** in our **exam question bank**
- **Reference all the important topics** in the **full index**

FOR EXAMS IN MAY 2010

BPP LEARNING MEDIA

First edition May 2009

ISBN 9780 7517 7503 7

British Library Cataloguing-in-Publication Data
A catalogue record for this book
is available from the British Library

Published by

BPP Learning Media Ltd
BPP House, Aldine Place
London W12 8AA

www.bpp.com/learningmedia

Printed in the United Kingdom

Your learning materials, published by BPP Learning Media Ltd, are printed on paper sourced from sustainable, managed forests.

We are grateful to the Chartered Institute of Management Accountants for permission to reproduce past examination questions. The suggested solutions in the exam answer bank have been prepared by BPP Learning Media Ltd.

©
BPP Learning Media Ltd
2009

Contents

		Page
Introduction		
How our Study Text can help you pass		iv
Features in our Study Text		v
Streamlined studying		vi
Syllabus and learning outcomes		vii
Old and new syllabuses		xiv
Studying F1		xv
The exam paper		xviii
Part A Regulation and ethics of financial reporting		
1	The regulatory framework	3
2	External audit	31
3	Ethics	51
Part B Single company financial accounts		
4	Presentation of published financial statements	75
5	Reporting financial performance	97
6	Accounting for non-current assets	113
7	Intangible non-current assets	137
8	IAS 17: Leases	155
9	Statements of cash flows	167
10	Miscellaneous standards	185
11	Inventories and construction contracts	201
12	Capital transactions and financial instruments	221
Part C Group financial statements		
13	Introduction to group accounting	243
14	Consolidated statement of financial position	253
15	Consolidated statement of comprehensive income	277
16	Associates	285
Part D Principles of business taxation		
17	General principles of taxation	297
18	Types of taxation	313
19	IAS 12: Income taxes	325
Objective test question bank		345
Objective test answer bank		353
Exam question bank		359
Exam answer bank		373
Index		393
Review form and free prize draw		

How our Study Text can help you pass

Streamlined studying	• We show you the best ways to study efficiently • Our Text has been designed to ensure you can easily and quickly navigate through it • The different features in our Text emphasise important knowledge and techniques
Exam expertise	• **Studying F1** on page xv introduces the key themes of the syllabus and summarises how to pass • We highlight throughout our Text how topics may be tested and what you'll have to do in the exam • We help you see the complete picture of the syllabus, so that you can answer questions that range across the whole syllabus • Our Text covers the syllabus content – no more, no less
Regular review	• We frequently summarise the key knowledge you need • We test what you've learnt by providing questions and quizzes throughout our Text

Our other products

BPP Learning Media also offers these products for the F1 exam:

Practice and Revision Kit	Providing lots more question practice and helpful guidance on how to pass the exam
Passcards	Summarising what you should know in visual, easy to remember, form
Success CDs	Covering the vital elements of the F1 syllabus in less than 90 minutes and also containing exam hints to help you fine tune your strategy
i-Pass	Providing computer-based testing in a variety of formats, ideal for self-assessment
Interactive Passcards	Allowing you to learn actively with a clear visual format summarising what you must know

You can purchase these products by visiting www.bpp.com/mybpp

Features in our Study Text

Section Introductions explain how the section fits into the chapter

Key Terms are the core vocabulary you need to learn

Key Points are points that you have to know, ideas or calculations that will be the foundations of your answers

Exam Alerts show you how subjects are likely to be tested

Exam Skills are the key skills you will need to demonstrate in the exam, linked to question requirements

Formulae To Learn are formulae you must remember in the exam

Exam Formulae are formulae you will be given in the exam

Examples show how theory is put into practice

Questions give you the practice you need to test your understanding of what you've learnt

Case Studies link what you've learnt with the real-world business environment

Links show how the syllabus overlaps with other parts of the qualification, including Knowledge Brought Forward that you need to remember from previous exams

Website References link to material that will enhance your understanding of what you're studying

Further Reading will give you a wider perspective on the subjects you're covering

Section Summaries allow you to review each section

Streamlined studying

What you should do	In order to
Read the Chapter and Section Introductions	See why topics need to be studied and map your way through the chapter
Go quickly through the explanations	Gain the depth of knowledge and understanding that you'll need
Highlight the Key Points, Key Terms and Formulae To Learn	Make sure you know the basics that you can't do without in the exam
Focus on the Exam Skills and Exam Alerts	Know how you'll be tested and what you'll have to do
Work through the Examples and Case Studies	See how what you've learnt applies in practice
Prepare Answers to the Questions	See if you can apply what you've learnt in practice
Revisit the Section Summaries in the Chapter Roundup	Remind you of, and reinforce, what you've learnt
Answer the Quick Quiz	Find out if there are any gaps in your knowledge
Answer the Question(s) in the Exam Question Bank	Practise what you've learnt in depth

Should I take notes?

Brief notes may help you remember what you're learning. You should use the notes format that's most helpful to you (lists, diagrams, mindmaps).

Further help

BPP Learning Media's *Learning to Learn Accountancy* provides lots more helpful guidance on studying. It is designed to be used both at the outset of your CIMA studies and throughout the process of learning accountancy. It can help you **focus your studies on the subject and exam**, enabling you to **acquire knowledge**, **practise and revise efficiently and effectively**.

Syllabus and learning outcomes

Paper F1 Performance Strategy

The syllabus comprises:

Topic and Study Weighting

A	Principles of Business Taxation	25%
B	Regulation and Ethics of Financial Reporting	15%
C	Financial Accounting and Reporting	60%

Learning Outcomes					
Lead		**Component**		**Syllabus content**	
A	**Principles of business taxation (25%)**				
1	Explain the types of tax that can apply to incorporated businesses, their principles and potential administrative requirements.	(a)	Identify the principal types of taxation likely to be of relevance to an incorporated business in a particular country;	(i)	Concepts of direct versus indirect taxes, taxable person and competent jurisdiction.
		(b)	Describe the features of the principal types of taxation likely to be of relevance to an incorporated business in a particular country;	(ii)	Types of taxation, including direct tax on the company's trading profits and capital gains, indirect taxes collected by the company, employee taxation and withholding taxes on international payments, and their features (e.g. in terms of who ultimately bears the tax cost, withholding responsibilities, principles of calculating the tax base).
		(c)	Explain key administrative requirements and the possible enquiry and investigation powers of taxing authorities associated with the principal types of taxation likely to be of relevance to an incorporated business;	(iii)	Sources of tax rules (e.g. domestic primary legislation and court rulings, practice of the relevant taxing authority, supranational bodies, such as the EU in the case of value added/sales tax, and international tax treaties).
		(d)	Explain the difference in principle between tax avoidance and tax evasion;	(iv)	Indirect taxes collected by the company:
		(e)	Illustrate numerically the principles of different types of tax based on provided information.	–	in the context of indirect taxes, the distinction between unit taxes (e.g. excise duties based on physical measures) and ad valorem taxes (e.g. sales tax based on value);

- the mechanism of value added/sales taxes, in which businesses are liable for tax on their outputs less credits for tax paid on their inputs, including the concepts of exemption and variation in tax rates depending on the type of output and disallowance of input credits for exempt outputs.

(v) Employee taxation:

- the employee as a separate taxable person subject to a personal income tax regime;
- use of employer reporting and withholding to ensure compliance and assist tax collection.

(vi) The need for record-keeping and record retention that may be additional to that required for financial accounting purposes.

(vii) The need for deadlines for reporting (filing returns) and tax payments.

(viii) Types of powers of tax authorities to ensure compliance with tax rules:

- power to review and query filed returns;
- power to request special reports or returns;
- power to examine records (generally extending back some years);
- powers of entry and search;
- exchange of information with tax authorities in other jurisdictions.

(ix) The distinction between tax avoidance and tax evasion, and how these vary among jurisdictions (including the difference between the use of statutory general anti-avoidance provisions and case law based regimes).

2	Explain fundamental concepts in international taxation of incorporated businesses.	(a)	Identify situations in which foreign tax obligations (reporting and liability) could arise and methods for relieving foreign tax;	(i)	International taxation: – the concept of corporate residence and the variation in rules for its determination across jurisdictions (e.g. place of incorporation versus place of management); – types of payments on which withholding tax may be required (especially interest, dividends, royalties and capital gains accruing to non-residents); – means of establishing a taxable presence in another country (local company and branch); – the effect of double tax treaties (based on the OECD Model Convention) on the above (e.g. reduction of withholding tax rates, provisions for defining a permanent establishment).
		(b)	Explain sources of tax rules and the importance of jurisdiction.		
3	Prepare corporate income tax calculations.	(a)	Prepare corporate income tax calculations based on a given simple set of rules.	(i)	Direct taxes on company profits and gains: – the principle of non-deductibility of dividends and systems of taxation defined according to the treatment of dividends in the hands of the shareholder (e.g. classical, partial imputation and imputation); – the distinction between accounting and taxable profits in absolute terms (e.g. disallowable expenditure on revenue account, such as entertaining, and on capital account, such as formation and acquisition costs) and in terms of timing (e.g. deduction on a paid basis);

4					– the concept of tax depreciation replacing book depreciation in the tax computation and its calculation based on the pooling of assets by their classes, including balancing adjustments on the disposal of assets; – the nature of rules recharacterising interest payments as dividends (e.g. where interest is based on profitability); – potential for variation in rules for calculating the tax base dependent on the nature or source of the income (scheduler systems); – the need for rules dealing with the relief of losses; – principles of relief for foreign taxes by exemption, deduction and credit. – the concept of tax consolidation (e.g. for relief of losses and deferral of capital gains on asset transfers within a group).
4	Apply the accounting rules for current and deferred taxation.	(a)	Apply the accounting rules for current and deferred taxation, including calculation of deferred tax based on a given set of rules.	(i)	Accounting treatment of taxation and disclosure requirements under IAS 12.
B	**Regulation and ethics of financial reporting (15%)**				
1	Explain the need for and methods of regulating accounting and financial reporting.	(a) (b)	Explain the need for regulation of published accounts and the concept that regulatory regimes vary from country to country; Explain potential elements that might be expected in a national regulatory framework for published accounts;	(i) (ii) (iii) (iv)	The need for regulation of accounts. Elements in a regulatory framework for published accounts (e.g. company law, local GAAP, review of accounts by public bodies). GAAP based on prescriptive versus principles-based standards. The role and structure of the IASB and IOSCO.

		(c)	Describe the role and structure of the International Accounting Standards Board (IASB) and the International Organisation of Securities Commissions (IOSCO);	(v)	The IASB's Framework for the Presentation and Preparation of Financial Statements.
		(d)	Explain the meaning of given features or parts of the IASB's Framework for the Presentation and Preparation of Financial Statements;	(vi)	The process leading to the promulgation of a standard practice.
		(e)	Describe the process leading to the promulgation of an IFRS;	(vii)	Ways in which IFRSs are used: adoption as local GAAP, model for local GAAP, persuasive influence in formulating local GAAP.
		(f)	Describe ways in which IFRSs can interact with local regulatory frameworks;	(viii)	The powers and duties of the external auditors, the audit report and its qualification for accounting statements not in accordance with best practice.
		(g)	Explain in general terms, the role of the external auditor, the elements of the audit report and types of qualification of that report.		
2	Apply the provisions of the CIMA Code of Ethics for Professional Accountants.	(a)	Explain the importance of the exercise of ethical principles in reporting and assessing information;	(i)	Ethical requirements of the professional accountant in reporting and assessing information (the fundamental principles).
		(b)	Describe the sources of ethical codes for those involved in the reporting or taxation affairs of an organisation, including the external auditors;	(ii)	Sources of ethical codes (IFAC, professional bodies, employing organisations, social/religious/personal sources).
		(c)	Apply the provisions of the CIMA Code of Ethics for Professional Accountants of particular relevance to the information reporting, assurance and tax-related activities of the accountant.	(iii)	Provisions of the CIMA Code of Ethics for Professional Accountants of particular relevance to information reporting, assurance and tax-related activities (especially section 220 and Part C).

C	Financial accounting and reporting (60%)				
1	Prepare the full financial statements of a single company and the consolidated statements of financial position and comprehensive income for a group (in relatively straightforward circumstances) .	(a)	Prepare a complete set of financial statements, in a form suitable for publication for a single company;	(i)	Preparation of the financial statements of a single company, as specified in IAS 1 (revised), including the statement of changes in equity.
		(b)	Apply the conditions required for an undertaking to be a subsidiary or an associate of another company;	(ii)	Preparation of the statement of cash flows (IAS 7).
		(c)	Prepare the consolidated statement of financial position (balance sheet) and statement of comprehensive income for a group of companies in a form suitable for publication for a group of companies comprising directly held interests in one or more fully-controlled subsidiaries and associates (such interests having been acquired at the beginning of an accounting period);	(iii)	Preparation of the consolidated statement of financial position (balance sheet) and statement of comprehensive income where: interests are directly held by the acquirer (parent) company; any subsidiary is fully controlled; and all interests were acquired at the beginning of an accounting period. (IFRS 3 and IAS 27, to the extent that their provisions are relevant to the specified learning outcomes).
		(d)	Apply the concepts of fair value at the point of acquisition, identifiability of assets and liabilities, and recognition of goodwill.		
2	Apply international standards dealing with a range of matters and items.	(a)	Apply the accounting rules contained in IFRSs and IASs dealing with reporting performance, non-current assets, including their impairment, inventories, disclosure of related parties to a business, construction contracts (and related financing costs), post-balance sheet events, provisions, contingencies, and leases (lessee only);	(i)	Reporting performance, prior period items, discontinuing operations, and segment reporting (IAS 8 and IFRS 5 and 8). Recognition of revenue (IAS 18) Measurement of profit or loss (IAS 1 (revised))
				(ii)	Property, Plant and Equipment (IAS 16): the calculation of depreciation and the effect of revaluations, changes to economic useful life, repairs, improvements and disposals.

(b)	Explain the accounting rules contained in IFRSs and IASs governing share capital transactions.	(iii)	Research and development costs (IAS 38): criteria for capitalisation.
		(iv)	Intangible Assets (IAS 38) and goodwill: recognition, valuation, amortisation.
		(v)	Impairment of Assets (IAS 36) and Non-Current Assets Held for Sale (IFRS 5) and their effects on the above.
		(vi)	Inventories (IAS 2).
		(vii)	The disclosure of related parties to a business (IAS 24).
		(viii)	Construction contracts and related financing costs (IAS 11 and 23): determination of cost, net realisable value, the inclusion of overheads and the measurement of profit on uncompleted contracts.
		(ix)	Post-balance sheet events (IAS 10).
		(x)	Provisions and contingencies (IAS 37).
		(xi)	Leases (IAS 17) – distinguishing operating from finance leases and the concept of substance over form (from the Framework); accounting for leases in the books of the lessee.
		(xii)	Issue and redemption of shares, including treatment of share issue and redemption costs (IAS 32 and 39), the share premium account, the accounting for maintenance of capital arising from the purchase by a company of its own shares.

Old and new syllabuses

The syllabus for the F1 *Financial Operations* paper is similar to the syllabus for the old syllabus paper P7 *Financial Accounting and Tax Principles*. The main difference is that the section on managing short term finance which was included in P7 under the old syllabus has moved to P1 *Performance Operations* in the new syllabus.

The other three main areas are roughly the same for both the old and new syllabus exams. There have been changes in study weightings and some new topics introduced.

The following topics have been added into the syllabus, with references to the chapter in which they are covered:

- Ethics (2)
- Group accounting (13-16)
- Written down allowances based on the pooling of assets by their classes (17)

Studying F1

1 What's it about

F1 consists of three fairly distinct areas covering:

- Regulation and ethics
- Financial accounting standards and accounts preparation
- Taxation

1.1 Regulation and ethics

In F1 you are expected to know about the regulation of accounts; why regulation is necessary and the processes of establishing and enforcing the rules that accountants are expected to apply when they prepare company accounts. As accountants, you will have to deal with external auditors; this syllabus also therefore requires you to understand the role of external auditors and interpret external audit reports. Finally, you are expected to know the CIMA *Code of Ethics for Professional Accountants* and be able to apply this to a given scenario. Regulation and ethics are covered in Chapters 1 to 3 of this Study Text.

1.2 Financial accounting standards and accounts preparation

The financial accounting part of the syllabus consists of two main areas. The first area is concerned with the preparation of accounts for a single company and is dealt with in Chapters 4 to 12. It is assumed that you know the basic elements of accounts preparation from previous studies. F1 requires more detailed knowledge of the contents of the main financial statements (statement of comprehensive income, statement of financial position and statement of cash flows) and also how accounting standards impact upon the main statements and the notes to the accounts.

The second area you will need to know is how to prepare accounts for a simple group. Chapters 14 and 15 look at how to prepare accounts for a parent plus subsidiary company and then Chapter 16 applies the same principles for an associate.

1.3 Taxation

As F1 is designed to be an international paper you don't need specific knowledge of any individual country's tax regime. Instead the paper focuses on the elements that are common to most of the major tax regimes. F1 aims to give you knowledge of different kinds of taxation, how tax is administered, the role of the taxation authorities and what is regarded as tax avoidance and evasion. As this is an international paper, you also have to be aware of the international tax dimension and how foreign tax obligations can arise. Taxation is covered in Chapters 17 to 19 of this Study Text.

2 What's required

2.1 Knowledge

As the majority of marks are available for questions worth 5 marks or less, the examiner has a lot of opportunity to test your knowledge of the detail of the syllabus, in particular key definitions, the features of tax regimes and the accounting regulatory process. You will also not only have to answer short questions on the requirements of accounting standards, but in addition use your knowledge of the standards to prepare extracts from accounts that comply with those standards.

2.2 Calculations

Calculation questions will be of two types:

- Short calculations for five marks or less, including taxation calculations and calculations that are required by accounting standards
- Longer calculations for which you will have to prepare proformas. The majority of marks in Section C of F1 will be available for these. The proformas you will need to know are those for the main financial accounting statements

3 How to pass

3.1 Study the whole syllabus

All of the marks available to you will be for compulsory questions. This gives the examiner plenty of opportunity to test all major areas of the syllabus on **every** paper, but sadly doesn't give you much opportunity to avoid questions you don't like. In particular you must spend some time on the rules and regulatory background issues as these may be covered in 5 mark, as well as shorter 2 mark, questions.

3.2 Lots of question practice

Our text gives you ample opportunity to practise by providing questions within chapters, quick quiz questions and questions in the exam question bank at the end. In addition the BPP Learning Media Practice and Revision Kit provides lots more question practice. It's particularly important to practise:

- Banks of objective test questions so that you get used to doing a number together
- More complicated shorter calculations. We highlight within the Text calculations that can cause problems and it's worth doing as many of these as possible
- Longer calculations and proformas. You will need to do these to answer the Section C question well.

3.3 Develop time management skills

The examiner has identified time management as being a problem, with some candidates not leaving themselves enough time to do the shorter calculations. Particularly therefore towards the end of your course, you need to practise all types of question, only allowing yourself the time you will be given in the exam.

3.4 Develop business awareness

Although this is not a higher level paper, candidates with good business awareness can score well in a number of areas.

- Reading articles in CIMA's *Financial Management* magazine and the business press will help you understand the practical rationale for accounting standards and make it easier for you to apply accounting requirements correctly
- Looking through the accounts of major companies will familiarise you with the contents of accounts and help you comment on key figures and changes from year-to-year

4 Brought forward knowledge

Paper F1 builds on the knowledge learned in the certificate level paper C02: *Fundamentals of Financial Accounting.*

5 Links with other Operational level exams

Regulation and ethics are part of the **global business environment** which is covered in **Enterprise Operations.**

Your financial accounting studies in this paper will be useful when studying working capital and investment appraisal in P1 **Performance Operations**.

The exam paper

Format of the paper

		Number of marks
Section A:	A variety of compulsory objective test questions, 2 – 4 marks each	20
Section B:	6 compulsory questions, 5 marks each	30
Section C:	1 or 2 compulsory questions	50
		100

Time allowed: 3 hours, plus 20 minutes reading time

Pilot paper

Section A

1 Systems of taxing corporate income, tax framework, changes in accounting policy, IASB *Framework*, issue of IFRS, calculation of deferred taxation, VAT, double taxation relief

Section B

2a Tax avoidance and evasion
2b Corporate income tax calculation
2c External audit
2d IASB *Framework*
2e Revenue recognition
2f Asset recognition

Section C

3 Accounts preparation for a single entity
4 Accounts preparation for a group

REGULATION AND ETHICS OF FINANCIAL REPORTING

Part A

THE REGULATORY FRAMEWORK

Accounting is regulated by local statute (such as company law), by Stock Exchange requirements and by accounting standards.

In this chapter we first examine the role of the International Accounting Standards Board (IASB), the development of International Financial Reporting Standards and some criticism of the IASB. We then spend some time on the IASB's *Framework*. This is a key document, providing the conceptual framework within which International Financial Reporting Standards are formulated. We then learn about IAS 18 *Revenue*, the first of many standards that we will be studying in this text.

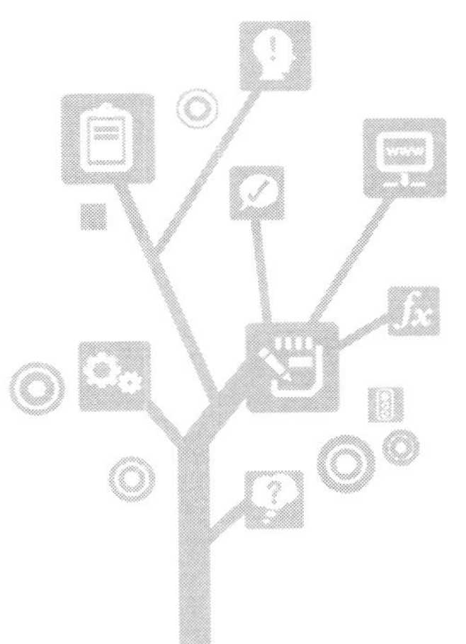

topic list	learning outcomes	syllabus references	ability required
1 The International Accounting Standards Board (IASB)	B1(c)	B1(iv)	comprehension
2 Setting of International Financial Reporting Standards	B1(e)	B1(vi)	comprehension
3 Criticisms of the IASB	B1(f)	B1(vii)	comprehension
4 Conceptual framework and GAAP	B1(a)	B1(i), (iii)	comprehension
5 The IASB Framework	B1(b), (d)	B1(ii), (v)	comprehension
6 IAS 18 *Revenue*	C2(a)	C2(i)	application

1 The International Accounting Standards Board (IASB)

Introduction

In this section we cover the role and structure of the IASB.

1.1 Formation of the IASB

The International Accounting Standards Board is an independent, privately-funded accounting standard setter based in London.

In March 2001 the IASC Foundation was formed as a not-for-profit corporation incorporated in the USA. The IASC Foundation is the parent entity of the IASB.

From April 2001 the IASB assumed accounting standard setting responsibilities from its predecessor body, the International Accounting Standards Committee (IASC). This restructuring was based upon the recommendations made in the *Recommendations on Shaping IASC for the Future.*

1.2 How the IASB is made up

The 14 members of the IASB come from nine countries and have a variety of backgrounds with a mix of auditors, preparers of financial statements, users of financial statements and an academic. The Board consists of 12 full-time members and two part-time members.

1.3 Objectives of the IASB

The formal objectives of the IASB, formulated in its mission statement are:

(a) To develop, in the public interest, a single set of high quality, understandable and enforceable global accounting standards that require transparent and comparable information in general purpose financial statements, and to promote the use and application of these standards.

(b) To co-operate with national accounting standard setters to achieve convergence in accounting standards around the world.

1.4 Structure of the IASB

The structure of the IASB has the following main features.

(a) The IASC Foundation is an independent corporation having two main bodies – the Trustees and the IASB.

(b) The IASC Foundation trustees appoint the IASB members, exercise oversight and raise the funds needed.

(c) The IASB has sole responsibility for setting accounting standards.

(d) There are also two further bodies, the Standards Advisory Council and the International Financial Reporting Interpretations Committee (see below).

The structure can be illustrated as follows.

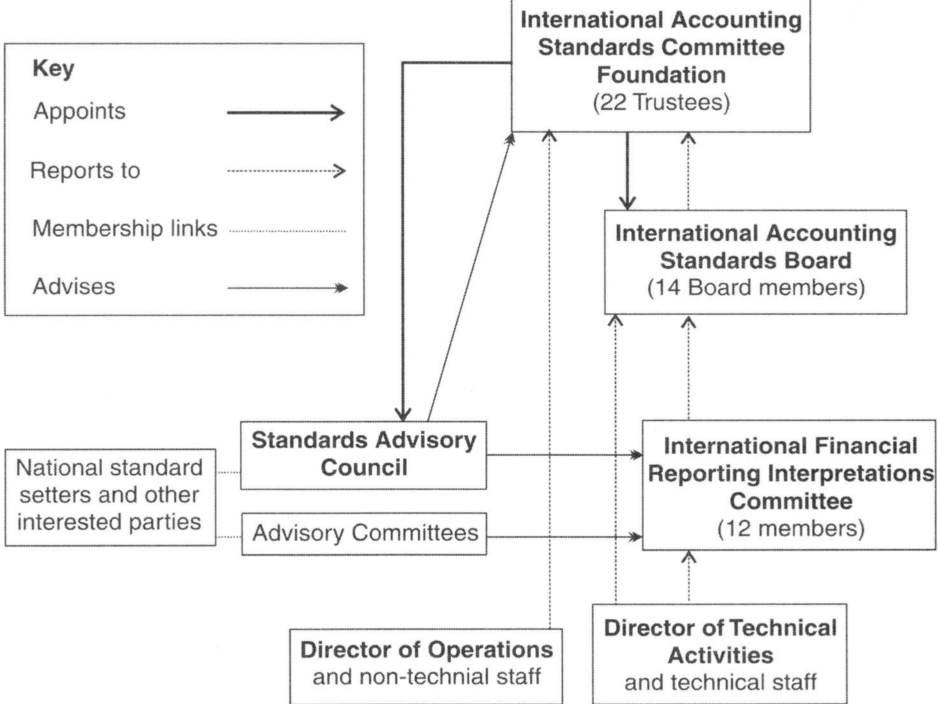

Trustees. The Trustees comprise a group of twenty-two individuals, with diverse geographic and functional backgrounds. The Trustees appoint the Members of the Board, the International Financial Reporting Interpretations Committee and the Standards Advisory Council. In addition to monitoring IASC's effectiveness and raising its funds, the Trustees will approve IASC's budget and have responsibility for constitutional changes. Trustees were appointed so that initially there were six from North America, six from Europe, four from Asia Pacific, and three others from any area, as long as geographic balance is maintained.

(a) The International Federation of Accountants (IFAC) suggested candidates to fill five of the nineteen Trustee seats and international organisations of preparers, users and academics each suggested one candidate.

(b) The remaining eleven Trustees are 'at-large' in that they were not selected through the constituency nomination process.

Standards Advisory Council. The Standards Advisory Council provides a formal vehicle for further groups and individuals with diverse geographic and functional backgrounds to give advice to the Board and, at times, to advise the Trustees. It meets at least three times a year.

International Financial Reporting Interpretations Committee. The IFRIC provides timely guidance on the application and interpretation of International Financial Reporting Standards. It normally deals with complex accounting issues that could give rise to a diversity of accounting treatments. In this way it assists the IASB in setting and improving financial reporting standards. Compliance with IFRS requires compliance with the relevant IFRIC interpretations.

Question 1.1 International harmonisation

Learning outcome B1(a)

In accounting terms what do you think are:

(a) The advantages to international harmonisation?

(b) The barriers to international harmonisation?

1.5 The IASB and current accounting standards

The IASB's predecessor body, the IASC, had issued 41 International Accounting Standards (IASs) and on 1 April 2001 the IASB adopted all of these standards and now issues its own International Financial Reporting Standards (IFRSs). So far eight new IFRSs have been issued.

1.6 The IASB and IOSCO

The International Organisation of Securities Commissions (IOSCO) is the representative of the world's securities markets regulators. High quality information is vital for the operation of an efficient capital market, and differences in the quality of the accounting policies and their enforcement between countries leads to inefficiencies between markets. IOSCO has been active in encouraging and promoting the improvement and quality of IASs over the last ten years. Most recently, this commitment was evidenced by the agreement between IASC and IOSCO to work on a programme of 'core standards' which could be used by publicly listed entities when offering securities in foreign jurisdictions.

The 'core standards' project resulted in fifteen new or revised IASs and was completed in 1999 with the issue of IAS 39 *Financial instruments: recognition and measurement.* IOSCO spent a year reviewing the results of the project and released a report in May 2000 which recommended to all its members that they allow multinational issuers to use IASs, as supplemented by reconciliation, disclosure and interpretation where necessary, to address outstanding substantive issues at a national or regional level.

IASB staff and IOSCO continue to work together to resolve outstanding issues and to identify areas where new IASB standards are needed.

1.7 European Commission and IASs/IFRSs

All listed entities in EU member states were required to report under IFRS in their consolidated financial statements from January 2005.

To this end the IASB undertook an improvements project, dealing with revisions to IAS, for example in the area of materiality, presentation, leases, related parties and earnings per share. This has been matched in, for example, the UK, by a convergence project, bringing UK GAAP into line with IASs where these are better.

Section summary

The IASB replaced the IASC in 2001. It is responsible for setting International Accounting Standards (IASs) and International Financial Reporting Standards (IFRSs). All new standards are now IFRSs.

2 Setting of International Financial Reporting Standards

Introduction

This section looks at the process of developing an IFRS and the impact this has on different countries.

2.1 Due process

The overall agenda of the IASB is initially set by discussion with the Standards Advisory Council. The process for developing an individual standard involves the following steps.

During the early stages of a project, IASB may establish an **Advisory Committee** to give advice on issues arising in the project. Consultation with the Advisory Committee and the Standards Advisory Council occurs throughout the project.

IASB may develop and publish **Discussion Documents** for public comment.

Following the receipt and review of comments, the IASB develops and publishes an **Exposure Draft** for public comment.

Following the receipt and review of comments, the IASB issues a final **International Financial Reporting Standard**.

The period of exposure for public comment is normally 90 days. However, in exceptional circumstances, proposals may be issued with a comment period of 60 days.

2.2 Co-ordination with national standard setters

Close co-ordination between IASB due process and due process of national standard setters is important to the success of the IASB's mandate.

The IASB is exploring ways in which to integrate its due process more closely with national due process. Such integration may grow as the relationship between IASB and national standard setters evolves. In particular, the IASB is exploring the following procedure for projects that have international implications.

(a) IASB and national standard setters would co-ordinate their work plans so that when the IASB starts a project, national standard setters would also add it to their own work plans so that they can play a full part in developing international consensus. Similarly, where national standard setters start projects, the IASB would consider whether it needs to develop a new Standard or review its existing Standards. Over a reasonable period, the IASB and national standard setters should aim to review all standards where significant differences currently exist, giving priority to the areas where the differences are greatest.

(b) National standard setters would not be required to vote for IASB's preferred solution in their national standards, since each country remains free to adopt IASB standards with amendments or to adopt other standards. However, the existence of an international consensus is clearly one factor that members of national standard setters would consider when they decide how to vote on national standards.

(c) The IASB would continue to publish its own Exposure Drafts and other documents for public comment.

(d) National standard setters would publish their own exposure document at approximately the same time as IASB Exposure Drafts and would seek specific comments on any significant divergences

between the two exposure documents. In some instances, national standard setters may include in their exposure documents specific comments on issues of particular relevance to their country or include more detailed guidance than is included in the corresponding IASB document.

(e) National standard setters would follow their own full due process, which they would ideally choose to integrate with the IASB's due process. This integration would avoid unnecessary delays in completing standards and would also minimise the likelihood of unnecessary differences between the standards that result.

2.3 IASB liaison members

Seven of the full-time members of the IASB have formal liaison responsibilities with national standard setters in order to promote the convergence of national accounting standards and International Accounting Standards. The IASB envisages a partnership between the IASB and these national standard setters as they work together to achieve convergence of accounting standards world-wide.

The countries with these liaison members are Australia and New Zealand, Canada, France, Germany, Japan, UK and USA.

In addition all IASB members have contact responsibility with national standards setter not having liaison members and many countries are also represented on the Standards Advisory Council.

2.4 Current IASs/IFRSs

The current list is as follows.

International Accounting Standards/International Financial Reporting Standards		Date of issue
IAS 1 (revised)	Presentation of financial statements	Sept 2007
IAS 2 (revised)	Inventories	Dec 2003
IAS 7 (revised)	Statement of cash flows	Dec 1992
IAS 8 (revised)	Accounting policies, changes in accounting estimates and errors	Dec 2003
IAS 10 (revised)	Events after the reporting period	Dec 2003
IAS 11 (revised)	Construction contracts	Dec 1993
IAS 12 (revised)	Income taxes	Nov 2000
IAS 16 (revised)	Property, plant and equipment	Dec 2003
IAS 17 (revised)	Leases	Dec 2003
IAS 18 (revised)	Revenue	Dec 1993
IAS 19 (revised)	Employee benefits	Nov 2000
IAS 20	Accounting for government grants and disclosure of government assistance	Jan 1995
IAS 21 (revised)	The effects of changes in foreign exchange rates	Dec 2003
IAS 23 (revised)	Borrowing costs	Jan 2008
IAS 24 (revised)	Related party disclosures	Dec 2003
IAS 26	Accounting and reporting by retirement benefit plans	Jan 1995
IAS 27 (revised)	Consolidated and separate financial statements	Jan 2008
IAS 28 (revised)	Investments in associates	Dec 2003

International Accounting Standards/International Financial Reporting Standards		Date of issue
IAS 29	Financial reporting in hyperinflationary economies	Jan 1995
IAS 30	Disclosures in the financial statements of banks and similar financial institutions (not examinable)	Jan 1995
IAS 31 (revised)	Interests in joint ventures	Dec 2003
IAS 32 (revised)	Financial instruments: presentation	Dec 2003
IAS 33 (revised)	Earnings per share	Dec 2003
IAS 34	Interim financial reporting	Feb 1998
IAS 36 (revised)	Impairment of assets	June 1998
IAS 37	Provisions, contingent liabilities and contingent assets	Sept 1998
IAS 38 (revised)	Intangible assets	Sept 1998
IAS 39 (revised)	Financial instruments: recognition and measurement	Dec 2003
IAS 40	Investment property	Dec 2003
IAS 41	Agriculture	Feb 2001
IFRS 1 (revised)	First time adoption of International Financial Reporting Standards	Nov 2008
IFRS 2	Share-based payment	Feb 2004
IFRS 3 (revised)	Business combinations	Jan 2008
IFRS 4	Insurance contracts	Mar 2004
IFRS 5	Non-current assets held for sale and discontinued operations	Mar 2004
IFRS 6	Exploration for and evaluation of mineral resources	Dec 2004
IFRS 7	Financial instruments – disclosure	Aug 2005
IFRS 8	Operating segments	Nov 2006

KEY POINT

Various exposure drafts and discussion papers are currently at different stages within the IFRS process, but these are not of concern to you at this stage of your studies.

2.5 Benchmark and allowed alternative treatment

Many of the old IASs permitted two accounting treatments for like transactions or events. One treatment is designated as the **benchmark treatment** (effectively the **preferred treatment**) and the other is known as the **alternative treatment**. This is no longer the case. The last standard to have a benchmark alternative was IAS 23 which has now been revised to remove the benchmark treatment.

2.6 Scope and application of IFRSs

2.6.1 Scope

Any limitation of the applicability of a specific IFRS is made clear within that standard. IFRSs are **not intended to be applied to immaterial items, nor are they retrospective**. Each individual IFRS lays out its scope at the beginning of the standard.

2.6.2 Application

Within each individual country **local regulations** govern, to a greater or lesser degree, the issue of financial statements. These local regulations include accounting standards issued by the national regulatory bodies and/or professional accountancy bodies in the country concerned.

The IASC **concentrated on essentials** when producing IFRSs. This means that the IASC tried not to make IFRSs too complex, because otherwise they would be impossible to apply on a worldwide basis.

2.7 World-wide effect of IASs and the IASB

The IASB, and before it the IASC, has now been in existence for around 25 years, and it is worth looking at the effect it has had in that time.

As far as **Europe** is concerned, the consolidated financial statements of many of Europe's top multinationals are prepared in conformity with national requirements, EC directives and IFRSs. Furthermore, IFRSs are having a growing influence on national accounting requirements and practices. Many of these developments have been given added impetus by the internationalisation of capital markets.

In **Japan**, the influence of the IASB had, until recently, been negligible. This was mainly because of links in Japan between tax rules and financial reporting. The Japanese Ministry of Finance set up a working committee to consider whether to bring national requirements into line with IFRSs. The Tokyo Stock Exchange has announced that it will accept financial statements from foreign issuers that conform with home country standards.

This was widely seen as an attempt to attract foreign issuers, in particular companies from Hong Kong and Singapore. As these countries base their accounting on international standards, this action is therefore implicit acknowledgement by the Japanese Ministry of Finance of IFRS requirements.

America has been reluctant to accept accounts prepared under IFRS. In 2008, the Securities and Exchange Commission (SEC) proposed its IFRS roadmap. This roadmap set out seven milestones that could lead to the required use of IFRS by 2014 for US issuers. In publishing the roadmap, the SEC commented that it believes the adoption of IFRS overseas has disadvantaged US investors.

However, chief financial officers (CFOs) in American are pushing for the IFRS project to be scrapped due to concerns over the cost of new accounting systems and added confusion during the current financial downturn. The situation at time of going to print (April 2009) is still uncertain.

Section summary

International Financial Reporting Standards (IFRSs) are set in a similar manner to the previous setting of IASs in accordance with the IASB's due process.

3 Criticisms of the IASB

Introduction

This section looks at the difficulties faced by the IASB in developing IFRS.

We will begin by looking at some of the general problems created by **accounting standards**, particularly where they offer a choice of treatment.

3.1 Accounting standards and choice

It is sometimes argued that companies should be given a choice in matters of financial reporting on the grounds that accounting standards are detrimental to the quality of such reporting. There are arguments on both sides.

In favour of accounting standards (both national and international), the following points can be made.

- They **reduce or eliminate confusing variations** in the methods used to prepare accounts.
- They provide a **focal point for debate** and discussions about accounting practice.
- They oblige companies to **disclose the accounting policies** used in the preparation of accounts.
- They are a less rigid alternative to enforcing conformity by means of **legislation**.
- They have obliged companies to **disclose more accounting information** than they would otherwise have done if accounting standards did not exist.

Many companies are reluctant to disclose information which is not required by national legislation. However, the following arguments may be put forward **against standardisation** and **in favour of choice**.

- A set of rules which give backing to one method of preparing accounts might be **inappropriate in some circumstances**. For example, IAS 16 on depreciation is inappropriate for investment properties (properties not occupied by the entity but held solely for investment), which are covered by IAS 40 on investment property.
- Standards may be subject to **lobbying or government pressure** (in the case of national standards). For example, in the USA, the accounting standard FAS 19 on the accounts of oil and gas companies led to a powerful lobby of oil companies, which persuaded the SEC (Securities and Exchange Commission) to step in. FAS 19 was then suspended.
- Unlike IFRSs, many national standards are not based on a **conceptual framework of accounting**.
- There may be a **trend towards rigidity**, and away from flexibility in applying the rules.

3.2 Political problems

Any international body, whatever its purpose or activity, faces enormous political difficulties in attempting to gain **international consensus** and the IASB is no exception to this. How can the IASB reconcile the financial reporting situation between economies as diverse as third-world developing countries and sophisticated first-world industrial powers?

Developing countries are suspicious of the IASB, believing it to be dominated by the **USA.** This arises because acceptance by the USA listing authority, the Securities and Exchange Commission (SEC), of IFRS is seen as the priority. For all practical purposes it is the American market which must be persuaded to accept IFRSs, and a lot of progress has now been made in this direction.

Developing countries have been catered for to some extent by the development of IAS 41 on **agriculture**, which is generally of much more relevance to such countries.

There are also tensions between the **UK/US model** of financial reporting and the **European model**. The UK/US model is based around investor reporting, whereas the European model is mainly concerned with tax rules, so shareholder reporting has a much lower priority.

The break-up of the former USSR and the move in many **Eastern European countries** to free-market economies has also created difficulties. It is likely that these countries will have to 'catch up' to international standards as their economies stabilise.

Section summary

In its attempt to formulate standards which are accepted internationally, the IASB has met opposition over various issues from companies, interest groups and countries.

4 Conceptual framework and GAAP

Introduction

In this section we introduce the idea of a conceptual framework.

4.1 The search for a conceptual framework

KEY TERM

A CONCEPTUAL FRAMEWORK, in the field we are concerned with, is a statement of generally accepted theoretical principles which form the frame of reference for financial reporting.

These theoretical principles provide the basis for the development of new accounting standards and the evaluation of those already in existence. The financial reporting process is concerned with providing information that is useful in the business and economic decision-making process. Therefore a conceptual framework will form the **theoretical basis** for determining which events should be accounted for, how they should be measured and how they should be communicated to the user. Although it is theoretical in nature, a conceptual framework for financial reporting has highly practical final aims.

The **danger of not having a conceptual framework** is demonstrated in the way some countries' standards have developed over recent years; standards tend to be produced in a haphazard and fire-fighting approach. Where an agreed framework exists, the standard-setting body act as an architect or designer, rather than a fire-fighter, building accounting rules on the foundation of sound, agreed basic principles.

The lack of a conceptual framework also means that fundamental principles are tackled **more than once** in different standards, thereby producing **contradictions and inconsistencies** in basic concepts, such as those of prudence and matching. This leads to ambiguity and it affects the true and fair concept of financial reporting.

Another problem with the lack of a conceptual framework has become apparent in the USA. The large number of **highly detailed standards** produced by the Financial Accounting Standards Board (FASB) has created a financial reporting environment governed by specific ru es rather than general principles. This would be avoided if a cohesive set of principles were in place.

A conceptual framework can also bolster standard setters **against political pressure** from various 'lobby groups' and interested parties. Such pressure would only prevail if it was acceptable under the conceptual framework.

4.2 Advantages and disadvantages of a conceptual framework

4.2.1 Advantages

(a) The situation is avoided whereby standards are developed on a patchwork basis, where a particular accounting problem is recognised as having emerged, and resources are then channelled into **standardising accounting practice** in that area, without regard to whether that particular issue was necessarily the most important issue remaining at that time without standardisation.

(b) As stated above, the development of certain standards (particularly national standards) have been subject to considerable **political interference** from interested parties. Where there is a conflict of interest between user groups on which policies to choose, policies deriving from a conceptual framework will be **less open to criticism** that the standard-setter buckled to external pressure.

(c) Some standards may concentrate on the **statement of comprehensive income** whereas some may concentrate on the **valuation of net assets** (statement of financial position).

4.2.2 Disadvantages

(a) Financial statements are intended for a **variety of users**, and it is not certain that a single conceptual framework can be devised which will suit all users.

(b) Given the diversity of user requirements, there may be a need for a variety of accounting standards, each produced for a **different purpose** (and with different concepts as a basis).

(c) It is not clear that a conceptual framework makes the task of **preparing and then implementing** standards any easier than without a framework.

Before we look at the IASB's attempt to produce a conceptual framework, we need to consider another term of importance to this debate: generally accepted accounting practice; or GAAP.

4.3 Generally Accepted Accounting Practice (GAAP)

KEY TERM

GAAP signifies all the rules, from whatever source, which govern accounting..

In individual countries this is seen primarily as a **combination** of:

- National company law
- National accounting standards
- Local stock exchange requirements

Although those sources are the basis for the GAAP of individual countries, the concept also includes the effects of **non-mandatory sources** such as IFRS or statutory requirements in other countries.

In many countries, like the UK, GAAP does not have any statutory or regulatory authority or definition, unlike other countries, such as the USA. The term is mentioned rarely in legislation, and only then in fairly limited terms.

There are different views of GAAP in different countries. The IASB convergence programme seeks to reduce these differences.

GAAP can be based on legislation and accounting standards that are either:

(a) prescriptive; or
(b) principles-based.

The USA operates a **prescriptive** system, where standards are very detailed, attempting to cover all eventualities. Accounts which do not comply in all details are presumed to be misleading. This has the advantage of clear requirements which can be generally understood and it removes any element of judgement.

The IASB *Framework* is a **principles-based** system which does not specify all the details but seeks to obtain adherence to the 'spirit' of the regulations. This does leave room for some element of professional judgement, but it also makes it harder for entities to avoid applying a standard as the terms of reference are broader.

4.3.1 GAAP and a conceptual framework

A conceptual framework for financial reporting can be defined as an attempt to codify existing GAAP in order to reappraise current accounting standards and to produce new standards.

Section summary

A conceptual framework provides the basis for the formulation of accounting standards.

5 The IASB Framework

Introduction

This long section builds on Section 4 and explains the framework developed by the IASB.

5.1 A conceptual framework

In July 1989 the old IASC produced a document, *Framework for the preparation and presentation of financial statements* ('*Framework*'). The *Framework* is, in effect, the **conceptual framework** upon which all IASs and IFRSs are based and hence which determines how financial statements are prepared and the information they contain.

The *Framework* consists of several sections or chapters, following on after a preface and introduction. These **chapters** are as follows.

- The objective of financial statements
- Underlying assumptions
- Qualitative characteristics of financial statements
- The elements of financial statements
- Recognition of the elements of financial statements
- Measurement of the elements of financial statements
- Concepts of capital and capital maintenance

5.2 Preface

The preface to the *Framework* points out the fundamental reason why financial statements are produced worldwide, ie to **satisfy the requirements of external users**, but that practice varies due to the individual pressures in each country.

These pressures may be social, political, economic or legal, but they result in variations in practice from country to country, including the form of statements, the definition of their component parts (assets, liabilities etc), the criteria for recognition of items and both the scope and disclosure of financial statements.

5.3 Introduction

The introduction to the *Framework* lays out the purpose, status and scope of the document. It then looks at different users of financial statements and their information needs. (Note that the Framework refers to the IASC. In practice this now means the IASB.)

5.3.1 Purpose and status

The introduction gives a list of the purposes of the *Framework*.

(a) Assist the Board of the IASC in the **development of future IFRSs** and in its review of existing IFRSs.

(b) Assist the Board of the IASC in **promoting harmonisation** of regulations, accounting standards and procedures relating to the presentation of financial statements by providing a basis for reducing the number of alternative accounting treatments permitted by IFRS.

(c) Assist **national standard-setting bodies** in developing national standards.

(d) Assist **preparers of financial statements** in applying IFRSs and in dealing with topics that have yet to form the subject of an IFRS.

(e) Assist **auditors** in forming an opinion as to whether financial statements conform with IFRS.

(f) Assist **users of financial statements** in interpreting the information contained in financial statements prepared in conformity with IFRS.

(g) Provide those who are interested in the work of IASC with **information** about its approach to the formulation of IFRS.

The *Framework* is not an IFRS and so does not overrule any individual IFRS. In the (rare) cases of conflict between an IFRS and the *Framework*, the **IAS will prevail**. These cases will diminish over time as the *Framework* will be used as a guide in the production of future IFRS. The *Framework* itself will be revised occasionally depending on the experience of the IASB in using it.

5.3.2 Scope

The *Framework* deals with:

(a) The **objective** of financial statements.

(b) The **qualitative characteristics** that determine the usefulness of information in financial statements.

(c) The **definition, recognition and measurement** of the elements from which financial statements are constructed.

(d) Concepts of **capital and capital maintenance**.

The *Framework* is concerned with **'general purpose' financial statements** (ie a normal set of annual statements), but it can be applied to other types of accounts. A complete set of financial statements includes:

(a) A statement of financial position
(b) A statement of comprehensive income
(c) A statement of changes in financial position (eg a statement of cash flows)
(d) Notes, other statements and explanatory material

Supplementary information may be included, but some items are not included, namely commentaries and reports by the directors, the chairman, management etc.

All types of financial reporting entities are included (commercial, industrial, business; public or private sector).

KEY TERM

A REPORTING ENTITY is an entity for which there are users who rely on the financial statements as their major source of financial information about the entity. *(Framework)*

5.3.3 Users and their information needs

We have already looked at the users of accounting information in earlier studies. They consist of investors, employees, lenders, suppliers and other trade creditors, customers, government and their agencies and the public. You should be able to remember enough to do the following question.

Question 1.2 Information needs

Learning outcome B1(a)

Describe the information needs of the users of financial information listed above.

Financial statements cannot meet all these users' needs, but financial statements which meet the **needs of investors** (providers of risk capital) will meet most of the needs of other users.

The *Framework* emphasises that the preparation and presentation of financial statements is primarily the **responsibility of an entity's management**. Management also has an interest in the information appearing in financial statements.

5.4 The objective of financial statements

'The objective of financial statements is to provide information about the **financial position**, **performance** and **changes in financial position** of an entity that is useful to a wide range of users in making economic decisions.' *(Framework)*

Information about **financial position** is mainly provided in the statement of financial position.
Information about **performance** is primarily found in the statement of comprehensive income.
Information about **changes in financial position** is found in the statement of cash flows.

Such financial statements will meet the needs of most users. The information is, however, **restricted**.

(a) It is based on **past events** not expected future events.
(b) It does not necessarily contain **non-financial information**.

The statements also show the results of **management's stewardship**.

5.5 Underlying assumptions

5.5.1 Accruals basis

KEY TERM

ACCRUALS BASIS. The effects of transactions and other events are recognised when they occur (and not as cash or its equivalent is received or paid) and they are recorded in the accounting records and reported in the financial statements of the periods to which they relate. *(Framework)*

Financial statements prepared under the accruals basis show users past transactions involving cash and also obligations to pay cash in the future and resources which represent cash to be received in the future.

5.5.2 Going concern

KEY TERM

GOING CONCERN. The entity is assumed to be a going concern, that is, as continuing in operation for the foreseeable future. It is assumed that the entity has neither the intention nor the need to liquidate or curtail materially the scale of its operations. *(Framework)*

It is assumed that the entity has no intention to liquidate or curtail major operations. If it did, then the financial statements would be prepared on a **different (disclosed) basis.**

5.6 Qualitative characteristics of financial statements

The *Framework* states that qualitative characteristics are the attributes that make the information provided in financial statements useful to users. The four principal qualitative characteristics are **understandability, relevance, reliability and comparability**.

5.6.1 Understandability

Users must be able to understand financial statements. They are assumed to have some business, economic and accounting knowledge and to be able to apply themselves to study the information properly. **Complex matters should not be left out** of financial statements simply due to its difficulty if it is relevant information.

5.6.2 Relevance

The **predictive and confirmatory roles** of information are interrelated.

KEY TERM

RELEVANCE. Information has the quality of relevance when it influences the economic decisions of users by helping them evaluate past, present or future events or confirming, or correcting, their past evaluations. *(Framework)*

Information on financial position and performance is often used to predict future position and performance and other things of interest to the user, eg likely dividend, wage rises. The **manner of showing information** will enhance the ability to make predictions, eg by highlighting unusual items.

The relevance of information is affected by its **nature and materiality**.

KEY TERM

MATERIALITY. Information is material if its omission or misstatement could influence the economic decisions of users taken on the basis of the financial statements. *(Framework)*

Information may be judged relevant simply because of its nature (eg remuneration of management). In other cases, both the nature and materiality of the information are important. Materiality is not a primary qualitative characteristic itself (like reliability or relevance), because it is merely a threshold or cut-off point.

5.6.3 Reliability

Information must also be reliable to be useful. The user must be able to depend on it being a **faithful representation**.

KEY TERM

RELIABILITY. Information has the quality of reliability when it is free from material error and bias and can be depended upon by users to represent faithfully that which it either purports to represent or could reasonably be expected to represent. *(Framework)*

5.6.4 Comparability

Users must be able to compare an entity's financial statements:

(a) **Through time** to identify trends.

(b) **With the financial statements** of other entities to evaluate their relative financial position, performance and changes in financial position.

The consistency of treatment is therefore important across like items over time, within the entity and across all entities.

The **disclosure of accounting policies** is particularly important here. Users must be able to distinguish between different accounting policies in order to be able to make a valid comparison of similar items in the accounts of different entities.

Comparability is **not the same as uniformity**. Entities should change accounting policies if they become inappropriate.

Corresponding information for **preceding periods** should be shown to enable comparison over time.

Exam alert

Make sure you know these qualitative characteristics. They are regularly examined.

5.6.5 True and fair view/fair presentation

The *Framework* does not attempt to define these concepts directly. It does state, however, that the application of the **principal 'qualitative' characteristics** and of **appropriate accounting standards** will usually result in financial statements which show a true and fair view, or present fairly.

5.7 The elements of financial statements

Transactions and other events are grouped together in broad **classes** and in this way their financial effects are shown in the financial statements. These broad classes are the elements of financial statements. The *Framework* lays out these elements as follows.

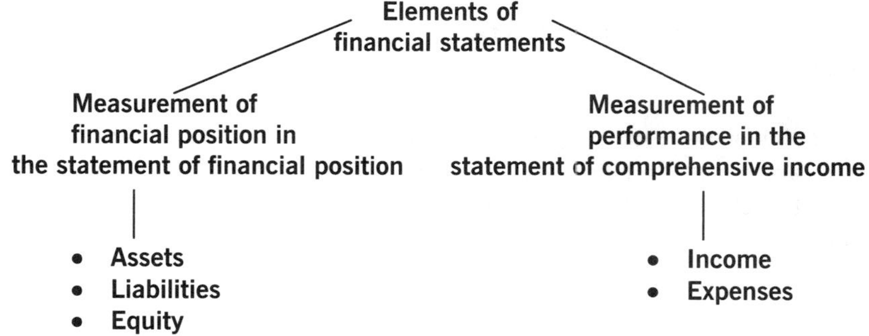

A process of **sub-classification** then takes place for presentation in the financial statements, eg assets are classified by their nature or function in the business to show information in the best way for users to take economic decisions.

5.7.1 Financial position

We need to define the three terms listed under this heading above.

KEY TERMS

ASSET. A resource controlled by an entity as a result of past events and from which future economic benefits are expected to flow to the entity.

LIABILITY. A present obligation of the entity arising from past events, the settlement of which is expected to result in an outflow from the entity of resources embodying economic benefits.

EQUITY. The residual interest in the assets of the entity after deducting all its liabilities.

These definitions are important, but they do not cover the **criteria for recognition** of any of these items, which are discussed in the next section of this chapter. This means that the definitions may include items which would not actually be recognised in the statement of financial position because they fail to satisfy recognition criteria particularly, as we will see below, the **probable flow of any economic benefit** to or from the business.

Whether an item satisfies any of the definitions above will depend on the **substance and economic reality** of the transaction, not merely its legal form.

Exam alert

These definitions should be learnt. You may be asked to define these terms in your exam.

Question 1.3 Assets and liabilities

Learning outcome B1(b)

Consider the following situations. In each case, do we have an asset or liability within the definitions given by the *Framework?* Explain your answer.

(a) Pat Co has purchased a patent for $20,000. The patent gives the company sole use of a particular manufacturing process which will save $3,000 a year for the next five years.

(b) Baldwin Co paid Don Brennan $10,000 to set up a car repair shop, on condition that priority treatment is given to cars from the company's fleet.

(c) Deals on Wheels Co provides a warranty with every car sold.

5.7.2 Equity

Equity is defined above as a **residual**, but it may be sub-classified in the statement of financial position. This will indicate legal or other restrictions on the ability of the entity to distribute or otherwise apply its equity. Some reserves are required by statute or other law, eg for the future protection of creditors. The amount shown for equity depends on the **measurement of assets and liabilities.** It has nothing to do with the market value of the entity's shares.

5.7.3 Performance

Profit is used as a **measure of performance**, or as a basis for other measures (eg EPS). It depends directly on the measurement of income and expenses, which in turn depend (in part) on the concepts of capital and capital maintenance adopted.

The elements of income and expense are therefore defined.

INCOME. Increases in economic benefits during the accounting period in the form of inflows or enhancements of assets or decreases of liabilities that result in increases in equity, other than those relating to contributions from equity participants.

EXPENSES. Decreases in economic benefits during the accounting period in the form of outflows or depletions of assets or incurrences of liabilities that result in decreases in equity, other than those relating to distributions to equity participants. *(Framework)*

5.7.4 Capital maintenance adjustments

A **revaluation** gives rise to an increase or decrease in equity.

KEY TERM

REVALUATION. Restatement of assets and liabilities. *(Framework)*

These increases and decreases meet the definitions of income and expenses. They are **not included** in the statement of comprehensive income under certain concepts of capital maintenance, however, but rather in equity.

5.8 Recognition of the elements of financial statements

Items which meet the definition of assets or liabilities may still not be recognised in financial statements because they must also meet certain **recognition criteria**.

KEY TERM

RECOGNITION. The process of incorporating in the statement of financial position or statement of comprehensive income an item that meets the definition of an element and satisfies the following criteria for recognition:

(a) It is probable that any future economic benefit associated with the item will flow to or from the entity.

(b) The item has a cost or value that can be measured with reliability. *(Framework)*

Regard must be given to **materiality**.

5.8.1 Probability of future economic benefits

Probability here means the **degree of uncertainty** that the future economic benefits associated with an item will flow to or from the entity. This must be judged on the basis of the **characteristics of the entity's environment** and the **evidence available** when the financial statements are prepared.

5.8.2 Reliability of measurement

The cost or value of an item, in many cases, **must be estimated**. The *Framework* states, however, that the use of reasonable estimates is an essential part of the preparation of financial statements and does not undermine their reliability. Where no reasonable estimate can be made, the item should not be recognised, although its existence should be disclosed in the notes, or other explanatory material.

Items may still qualify for recognition **at a later date** due to changes in circumstances or subsequent events.

5.8.3 Recognition of items

We can summarise the recognition criteria for assets, liabilities, income and expenses, based on the definition of recognition given above.

Item	Recognised in	When
Asset	The statement of financial position	It is probable that the future economic benefits will flow to the entity and the asset has a cost or value that can be measured reliably.
Liability	The statement of financial position	It is probable that an outflow of resources embodying economic benefits will result from the settlement of a present obligation and the amount at which the settlement will take place can be measured reliably.
Income	The statement of comprehensive income	An increase in future economic benefits related to an increase in an asset or a decrease of a liability has arisen that can be measured reliably.
Expenses	The statement of comprehensive income	A decrease in future economic benefits related to a decrease in an asset or an increase of a liability has arisen that can be measured reliably.

5.9 Measurement of the elements of financial statements

Measurement is defined as follows.

KEY TERM

MEASUREMENT. The process of determining the monetary amounts at which the elements of the financial statements are to be recognised and carried in the statement of financial position and the statement of comprehensive income. *(Framework)*

This involves the selection of a particular **basis of measurement**. A number of these are used to different degrees and in varying combinations in financial statements. They are:

- **Historical cost**. The amount that was originally paid to acquire an asset.
- **Current cost**. The amount which would be needed at current prices to obtain an equivalent asset.
- **Realisable value**. The net amount expected to be received from selling an asset, or paid to settle a liability.
- **Present value**. The discounted present value of future cash flows that are expected to be received or paid in respect of an asset or liability.

5.10 Concepts of capital and capital maintenance

Most entities use a **financial concept of capital** when preparing their financial statements (see below). The concept of capital selected should be appropriate to the needs of the users of an entity's financial statements.

5.10.1 Concepts of capital maintenance and the determination of profit

First of all, we need to define the different concepts of capital.

KEY TERMS

CAPITAL. Under a **financial concept** of capital, such as invested money or invested purchasing power, the net assets or equity of the entity. The financial concept of capital is adopted by most entities.

Under a **physical concept** of capital, such as operating capability, the productive capacity of the entity based on, for example, units of output per day. *(Framework)*

The definition of profit is also important.

PROFIT. The residual amount that remains after expenses (including capital maintenance adjustments, where appropriate) have been deducted from income. Any amount over and above that required to maintain the capital at the beginning of the period is profit. *(Framework)*

The main difference between the two concepts of capital maintenance is the treatment of the **effects of changes in the prices of assets and liabilities** of the entity. In general terms, an entity has maintained its capital if it has as much capital at the end of the period as it had at the beginning of the period. Any amount over and above that required to maintain the capital at the beginning of the period is profit.

(a) **Financial capital maintenance**: profit is the increase in nominal money capital over the period.

(b) **Physical capital maintenance**: profit is the increase in the physical productive capacity over the period.

Section summary

The *Framework* was produced by the IASC and adopted by the IASB. It provides the conceptual framework within which IASs and IFRSs are formulated. The accruals basis and going concern are underlying assumptions of the *Framework*. The four principal qualitative characteristics are understandability, relevance, reliability and comparability. The *Framework* groups items into the elements of financial statements. These are assets, liabilities, equity, income and expenses.

6 IAS 18 *Revenue*

Introduction

This section explains the recognition and measurement of revenue.

6.1 Introduction to revenue

Accruals accounting is based on the **matching of costs with the revenue they generate**. It is crucially important under this convention that we can establish the point at which revenue may be recognised so that the correct treatment can be applied to the related costs. For example, the costs of producing an item of finished goods should be carried as an asset in the statement of financial position until such time as it is sold; they should then be written off as a charge to the trading account. Which of these two treatments should be applied cannot be decided until it is clear at what moment the sale of the item takes place.

The decision has a **direct impact on profit** since under the prudence concept it would be unacceptable to recognise the profit on sale until a sale had taken place in accordance with the criteria of revenue recognition.

Revenue is generally recognised as **earned at the point of sale**, because at that point four criteria will generally have been met.

- The product or service has been **provided to the buyer**.
- The buyer has **recognised his or her liability** to pay for the goods or services provided. The converse of this is that the seller has recognised that ownership of goods has passed from the seller to the buyer.
- The buyer has indicated **willingness to hand over cash** or other assets in settlement of his or her liability.
- The **monetary value** of the goods or services has been established.

At earlier points in the business cycle there will not in general be **firm evidence** that the above criteria will be met. Until work on a product is complete, there is a risk that some flaw in the manufacturing process will necessitate its writing off; even when the product is complete there is no guarantee that it will find a buyer.

At later points in the business cycle, for example when cash is received for the sale, the recognition of revenue may occur in a period later than that in which the related costs were charged. Revenue recognition would then depend on fortuitous circumstances, such as the cash flow of a company's customers, and might fluctuate misleadingly from one period to another.

However, there are times when revenue is **recognised at other times than at the completion of a sale**. For example, in the recognition of profit on long-term construction contracts. Under IAS 11 *Construction contracts*, contract revenue and contract costs associated with the construction contract should be recognised as revenue and expenses respectively by reference to the stage of completion of the contract activity at the end of the reporting period.

(a) Owing to the length of time taken to complete such contracts, to defer taking profit into account until completion may result in the statement of comprehensive income reflecting, not so much a fair view of the activity of the company during the year, but rather the results relating to contracts which have been completed by the year-end.

(b) Revenue in this case is recognised when production on, say, a section of the total contract is complete, even though no sale can be made until the whole is complete.

6.2 IAS 18 *Revenue*

IAS 18 governs the recognition of revenue in specific (common) types of transaction. Generally, recognition should be when it is probable that **future economic benefits** will flow to the entity and when these benefits can be **measured reliably**.

Income, as defined by the IASB's *Framework* document, includes both revenues and gains. Revenue is income arising in the ordinary course of an entity's activities and it may be called different names, such as sales, fees, interest, dividends or royalties.

Exam skills

In the exam you should be able to apply the IAS, not just describe it.

6.3 Scope

IAS 18 covers the revenue from specific types of transaction or events.

- **Sale of goods** (manufactured products and items purchased for resale)
- **Rendering of services**
- Use by others of entity assets yielding **interest, royalties and dividends**

Interest, royalties and dividends are included as income because they arise from the use of an entity's assets by other parties.

KEY TERMS

INTEREST is the charge for the use of cash or cash equivalents or amounts due to the entity.

ROYALTIES are charges for the use of non-current assets of the entity, eg patents, computer software and trademarks.

DIVIDENDS are distributions of profit to holders of equity investments, in proportion with their holdings, of each relevant class of capital.

The standard specifically **excludes** various types of revenue arising from leases, insurance contracts, changes in value of financial instruments or other current assets natural increases in agricultural assets and mineral ore extraction.

6.4 Definitions

The following definitions are given in the standard.

KEY TERMS

REVENUE is the gross inflow of economic benefits during the period arising in the course of the ordinary activities of an entity when those inflows result in increases in equity, other than increases relating to contributions from equity participants.

FAIR VALUE is the amount for which an asset could be exchanged, or a liability settled, between knowledgeable, willing parties in an arm's length transaction. *(IAS 18)*

Revenue **does not include** sales taxes, value added taxes or goods and service taxes which are only collected for third parties, because these do not represent an economic benefit flowing to the entity. The same is true for revenues collected by an agent on behalf of a principal. Revenue for the agent is only the commission received for acting as agent.

6.5 Measurement of revenue

When a transaction takes place, the amount of revenue is usually decided by the **agreement of the buyer and seller**. The revenue is actually measured, however, as the **fair value of the consideration received,** which will take account of any trade discounts and volume rebates.

6.6 Identification of the transaction

Normally, each transaction can be looked at **as a whole**. Sometimes, however, transactions are more complicated, and it is necessary to break a transaction down into its **component parts**. For example, a sale may include the transfer of goods and the provision of future servicing, the revenue for which should be deferred over the period the service is performed.

At the other end of the scale, **seemingly separate transactions must be considered together** if apart they lose their commercial meaning. An example would be to sell an asset with an agreement to buy it back at a later date. The second transaction cancels the first and so both must be considered together.

6.7 Sale of goods

Revenue from the sale of goods should only be recognised when *all* these conditions are satisfied.

(a) The entity has transferred the **significant risks and rewards** of ownership of the goods to the buyer

(b) The entity retains neither **continuing managerial involvement** to the degree usually associated with ownership, nor effective control over the goods sold

(c) The amount of revenue can be **measured reliably**

(d) It is probable that the **economic benefits** associated with the transaction will flow to the entity

(e) The **costs incurred** or to be incurred in respect of the transaction can be measured reliably

The transfer of risks and rewards can only be decided by examining each transaction. Mainly, the transfer occurs at the same time as either the **transfer of legal title**, or the **passing of possession** to the buyer – this is what happens when you buy something in a shop.

If **significant risks and rewards remain with the seller**, then the transaction is *not* a sale and revenue cannot be recognised, for example if the receipt of the revenue from a particular sale depends on the buyer receiving revenue from his own sale of the goods.

It is possible for the seller to retain only an **'insignificant' risk of ownership** and for the sale and revenue to be recognised. The main example here is where the seller retains title only to ensure collection of what is owed on the goods. This is a common commercial situation, and when it arises the revenue should be recognised on the date of sale.

The probability of the entity receiving the revenue arising from a transaction must be assessed. It may only become probable that the economic benefits will be received when an uncertainty is removed, for example government permission for funds to be received from another country. Only when the uncertainty is removed should the revenue be recognised. This is in contrast with the situation where revenue has already been recognised but where the **collectability of the cash** is brought into doubt. Where recovery has ceased to be probable, the amount should be recognised as an expense, *not* an adjustment of the revenue previously recognised. These points also refer to services and interest, royalties and dividends below.

Matching should take place, ie the revenue and expenses relating to the same transaction should be recognised at the same time. It is usually easy to estimate expenses at the date of sale (eg warranty costs, shipment costs, etc). Where they cannot be estimated reliably, then revenue cannot be recognised; any consideration which has already been received is treated as a liability.

6.8 Rendering of services

When the outcome of a transaction involving the rendering of services can be estimated reliably, the associated revenue should be recognised by reference to the **stage of completion of the transaction** at the end of the reporting period. The outcome of a transaction can be estimated reliably when *all* these conditions are satisfied.

(a) The amount of revenue can be **measured reliably**

(b) It is probable that the **economic benefits** associated with the transaction will flow to the entity

(c) The **stage of completion** of the transaction at the end of the reporting period can be measured reliably

(d) The **costs incurred** for the transaction and the costs to complete the transaction can be measured reliably

The parties to the transaction will normally have to agree the following before an entity can make reliable estimates.

(a) Each party's **enforceable rights** regarding the service to be provided and received by the parties
(b) The **consideration** to be exchanged
(c) The **manner and terms of settlement**

There are various methods of determining the stage of completion of a transaction, but for practical purposes, when services are performed by an indeterminate number of acts over a period of time, revenue should be recognised on a **straight line basis** over the period, unless there is evidence for the use of a more appropriate method. If one act is of more significance than the others, then the significant act should be carried out *before* revenue is recognised.

In uncertain situations, when the outcome of the transaction involving the rendering of services cannot be estimated reliably, the standard recommends a **no loss/no gain approach**. Revenue is recognised only to the extent of the expenses recognised that are recoverable.

This is particularly likely during the **early stages of a transaction**, but it is still probable that the entity will recover the costs incurred. So the revenue recognised in such a period will be equal to the expenses incurred, with no profit.

Obviously, if the costs are not likely to be reimbursed, then they must be recognised as an expense immediately. **When the uncertainties cease to exist**, revenue should be recognised.

6.9 Interest, royalties and dividends

When others use the entity's assets yielding interest, royalties and dividends, the revenue should be recognised on the bases set out below when:

(a) it is probable that the **economic benefits** associated with the transaction will flow to the entity; and

(b) the amount of the revenue can be **measured reliably**.

The revenue is recognised on the following bases.

(a) **Interest** is recognised using the effective interest method set out in IAS 39

(b) **Royalties** are recognised on an accruals basis in accordance with the substance of the relevant agreement

(c) **Dividends** are recognised when the shareholder's right to receive payment is established

6.10 Disclosure

The following items should be disclosed.

(a) The **accounting policies** adopted for the recognition of revenue, including the methods used to determine the stage of completion of transactions involving the rendering of services

(b) The amount of each **significant category of revenue** recognised during the period including revenue arising from:

  (i) The sale of goods
  (ii) The rendering of services

- (iii) Interest
- (iv) Royalties
- (v) Dividends

(c) The amount of revenue arising from **exchanges of goods or services** included in each significant category of revenue

Question 1.4 Revenue recognition

Learning outcome C2(a)

Given that prudence is the main consideration, explain under what circumstances, if any, revenue might be recognised at the following stages of a sale.

(a) Goods are acquired by the business which it confidently expects to resell very quickly.

(b) A customer places a firm order for goods.

(c) Goods are delivered to the customer.

(d) The customer is invoiced for goods.

(e) The customer pays for the goods.

(f) The customer's cheque in payment for the goods has been cleared by the bank.

Section summary

Revenue recognition is straightforward in most business transactions but some situations are more complicated. It is necessary to determine the **substance of each transaction** rather than the legal form.

IAS 18 *Revenue* is concerned with the recognition of revenues arising from:

- the sale of goods
- the rendering of services
- the use by others of equity assets yielding interest, royalties and dividends

Generally revenue is recognised when the entity has transferred to the buyer the **significant risks and rewards of ownership** and when the revenue can be **measured reliably**.

Chapter Roundup

- ✓ The IASB replaced the IASC in 2001. It is responsible for setting International Accounting Standards (IASs) and International Financial Reporting Standards (IFRSs). All new standards are now IFRSs.
- ✓ International Financial Reporting Standards (IFRSs) are set in a similar manner to the previous setting of IASs in accordance with the IASB's due process.
- ✓ In its attempt to formulate standards which are accepted internationally, the IASB has met opposition over various issues from companies, interest groups and countries.
- ✓ A conceptual framework provides the basis for the formulation of accounting standards.
- ✓ The *Framework* was produced by the IASC and adopted by the IASB. It provides the conceptual framework within which IASs and IFRSs are formulated. The accruals basis and going concern are underlying assumptions of the *Framework*. The four principal qualitative characteristics are

understandability, relevance, reliability and comparability. The *Framework* groups items into the elements of financial statements. These are assets, liabilities, equity, income and expenses.

✓ **Revenue recognition** is straightforward in most business transactions but some situations are more complicated. It is necessary to determine the **substance of each transaction** rather than the legal form.

✓ IAS 18 *Revenue* is concerned with the recognition of revenues arising from:

- the sale of goods
- the rendering of services
- the use by others of equity assets yielding interest, royalties and dividends

✓ Generally revenue is recognised when the entity has transferred to the buyer the **significant risks and rewards of ownership** and when the revenue can be **measured reliably**.

Quick Quiz

1 What recent decisions had a beneficial effect on global harmonisation of accounting practices?

2 How many IASs and IFRSs have been published?

3 A conceptual framework is:

A A theoretical expression of accounting standards
B A list of key terms used by the IASB
C A statement of theoretical principles which form the frame of reference for financial reporting
D The proforma financial statements

4 Which of the following are chapters in the IASB *Framework?*

A Subsidiaries, associates and joint ventures
B Profit measurement in financial statements
C The objective of financial statements
D Accounting for interests in other entities
E Recognition of the elements of financial statements
F Presentation of financial information
G Substance of transactions in financial statements
H Qualitative characteristics of financial statements
I Quantitative characteristics of financial statements
J Measurement of the elements of financial statements
K Concepts of capital and capital maintenance
L The elements of financial statements.

5 Which of the following arguments is not in favour of accounting standards?

A They reduce variations in methods used to produce accounts
B They oblige companies to disclose their accounting policies
C They are a less rigid alternative to legislation
D They may tend towards rigidity in applying the rules

6 What five conditions must be satisfied before revenue from the sale of goods can be recognised?

Answers to Quick Quiz

1 The IOSCO endorsement, and the EC requirement that listed companies should use IFRS from 2005.

2 41 IASs and 8 IFRSs

3 C

4 C, E, H, J, K and L.

5 D The other arguments are all in favour of accounting standards.

6
- The entity has transferred the significant risks and rewards of ownership of the goods to the buyer
- The entity retains neither continuing managerial involvement to the degree usually associated with ownership, nor effective control over the goods sold
- The amount of revenue can be measured reliably
- It is probable that the economic benefits associated with the transaction will flow to the entity
- The costs incurred or to be incurred in respect of the transaction can be measured reliably

Answers to Questions

1.1 International harmonisation

(a) Advantages of global harmonisation

The advantages of harmonisation will be based on the benefits to users and preparers of accounts, as follows.

(i) Investors, both individual and corporate, would like to be able to compare the financial results of different companies internationally as well as nationally in making investment decisions.

(ii) Multinational companies would benefit from harmonisation for many reasons including the following.

(1) Better access would be gained to foreign investor funds.

(2) Management control would be improved, because harmonisation would aid internal communication of financial information.

(3) Appraisal of foreign entities for take-overs and mergers would be more straightforward.

(4) It would be easier to comply with the reporting requirements of overseas stock exchanges.

(5) Preparation of group accounts would be easier.

(6) A reduction in audit costs might be achieved.

(7) Transfer of accounting staff across national borders would be easier.

(iii) Governments of developing countries would save time and money if they could adopt international standards and, if these were used internally, governments of developing countries could attempt to control the activities of foreign multinational companies in their own country. These companies could not 'hide' behind foreign accounting practices which are difficult to understand.

(iv) Tax authorities. It will be easier to calculate the tax liability of investors, including multinationals who receive income from overseas sources.

(v) Regional economic groups usually promote trade within a specific geographical region. This would be aided by common accounting practices within the region.

(vi) Large international accounting firms would benefit as accounting and auditing would be much easier if similar accounting practices existed throughout the world.

(b) Barriers to harmonisation

(i) Different purposes of financial reporting. In some countries the purpose is solely for tax assessment, while in others it is for investor decision-making.

(ii) Different legal systems. These prevent the development of certain accounting practices and restrict the options available.

(iii) Different user groups. Countries have different ideas about who the relevant user groups are and their respective importance. In the USA investor and creditor groups are given prominence, while in Europe employees enjoy a higher profile.

(iv) Needs of developing countries. Developing countries are obviously behind in the standard setting process and they need to develop the basic standards and principles already in place in most developed countries.

(v) Nationalism is demonstrated in an unwillingness to accept another country's standard.

(vi) Cultural differences result in objectives for accounting systems differing from country to country.

(vii) Unique circumstances. Some countries may be experiencing unusual circumstances which affect all aspects of everyday life and impinge on the ability of companies to produce proper reports, for example hyperinflation, civil war, currency restriction and so on.

(viii) The lack of strong accountancy bodies. Many countries do not have strong independent accountancy or business bodies which would press for better standards and greater harmonisation.

1.2 Information needs

(a) **Investors** are the providers of risk capital

(i) Information is required to help make a decision about buying or selling shares, taking up a rights issue and voting.

(ii) Investors must have information about the level of dividend, past, present and future and any changes in share price.

(iii) Investors will also need to know whether the management has been running the company efficiently.

(iv) Investors will want to know about the liquidity position of the company, the company's future prospects, and how the company's shares compare with those of its competitors.

(b) **Employees** need information about the security of employment and future prospects for jobs in the company, and to help with collective pay bargaining.

(c) **Lenders** need information to help them decide whether to lend to a company. They will also need to check that the value of any security remains adequate, that the interest repayments are secure.

(d) **Suppliers** need to know whether the company will be a good customer and pay its debts.

(e) **Customers** need to know whether the company can continue producing and supplying goods.

(f) **Government's** interest in a company may be one of creditor or customer, as well as being specifically concerned with compliance with tax and company law, ability to pay tax and the general contribution of the company to the economy.

(g) The **public** at large would wish to have information for all the reasons mentioned above, but it could be suggested that it would be impossible to provide general purpose accounting information which was specifically designed for the needs of the public.

1.3 Assets and liabilities

(a) This is an asset, albeit an intangible one. There is a past event, control and future economic benefit (through cost savings).

(b) This cannot be classified as an asset. Baldwin Co has no control over the car repair shop and it is difficult to argue that there are 'future economic benefits'.

(c) This is a liability; the business has taken on an obligation. It would be recognised when the warranty is issued rather than when a claim is made.

1.4 Revenue recognition

(a) A sale must never be recognised before the goods have even been ordered by a customer. There is no certainty about the value of the sale, nor when it will take place, even if it is virtually certain that goods will be sold.

(b) A sale must never be recognised when the customer places an order. Even though the order will be for a specific quantity of goods at a specific price, it is not yet certain that the sale transaction will go through. The customer may cancel the order, the supplier might be unable to deliver the goods as ordered or it may be decided that the customer is not a good credit risk.

(c) A sale will be recognised when delivery of the goods is made only when:

(i) the sale is for cash, and so the cash is received at the same time; or
(ii) the sale is on credit and the customer accepts delivery (eg by signing a delivery note).

(d) The critical event for a credit sale is usually the despatch of an invoice to the customer. There is then a legally enforceable debt, payable on specified terms, for a completed sale transaction.

(e) The critical event for a cash sale is when delivery takes place and when cash is received; both take place at the same time.

It would be too cautious or 'prudent' to await cash payment for a credit sale transaction before recognising the sale, unless the customer is a high credit risk and there is a serious doubt about his ability or intention to pay.

(f) It would again be over-cautious to wait for clearance of the customer's cheques before recognising sales revenue. Such a precaution would only be justified in cases where there is a very high risk of the bank refusing to honour the cheque.

Now try these questions from the Exam Question Bank

Number	Level	Marks	Time
Q6	Examination	5	9 mins
Q7	Examination	5	9 mins
Q8	Examination	5	9 mins

EXTERNAL AUDIT

Here we look at the role of the external auditor. If you work for an organisation which is audited (internally or externally), try to talk to the auditors about the audit. Because it is the audit of an organisation you know well, you should gain some insight into the role of the auditor.

The CIMA Code provides guidance on the appointment of auditors which we cover in Section 2.

The external auditors are employed to check the good **stewardship** of the directors of the company and the truth and fairness of the financial statements. To enable them to do this they have certain **rights and duties**.

When the audit is completed and the auditors are satisfied with the information and explanations provided, an **audit report** is issued. The audit report is the instrument by which the auditors express an **opinion** on the truth and fairness of the financial statements. In Section 4 we look at the standard audit report and its **qualification** when the auditors are not completely satisfied with the results of the audit.

Although we refer to ISAs, you are **not** required to learn them for the exam.

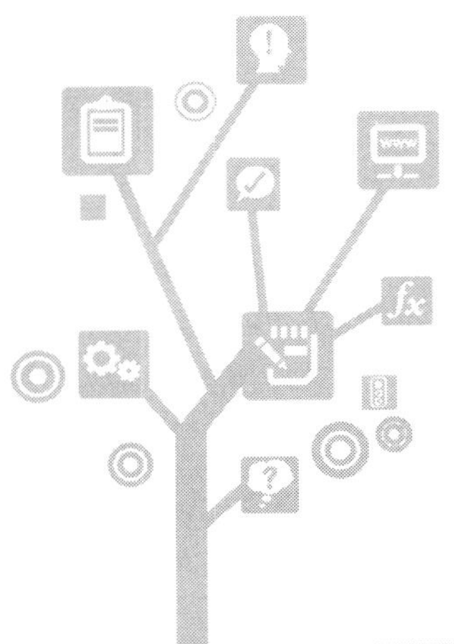

topic list	learning outcomes	syllabus references	ability required
1 External audit	B1(g)	B1(viii)	comprehension
2 Accepting audit appointments	B2(c)	B2(iii)	application
3 Duties and rights of auditors	B1(g)	B1(viii)	comprehension
4 The audit report	B1(g)	B1(viii)	comprehension

1 External audit

Introduction

If you work in an organisation you may have come across the auditors and even been asked questions by them. In this section we look at what an audit is and why it is necessary.

1.1 Why is an audit needed?

In the modern commercial environment, businesses which are operated as companies with limited liability need to produce accounts to indicate how successfully they are performing. However the owners of a business require something more than accounts because the managers responsible for preparing them may, either unintentionally or by deliberate manipulation, produce accounts which are misleading. An independent examination of the accounts is needed so that the owners of the business can assess how well management have discharged their *stewardship*.

1.2 Definition of an audit

The International Auditing and Assurance Standards Board *Glossary of Terms* defines the objective of an audit as follows.

KEY TERM

'The objective of an AUDIT of financial statements is to enable the auditor to express an opinion whether the financial statements are prepared, in all material respects, in accordance with an identified financial reporting framework. The phrases used to express the auditor's opinion are 'give a true and fair view' or 'present fairly, in all material respects', which are equivalent terms. A similar objective applies to the audit of financial or other information prepared in accordance with appropriate criteria.'

We will look at some of the terms used here later on.

First of all, though, we need to look at what an audit is really about. The International Federation of Accountants (IFAC's) International Standard on Auditing (ISA) 200 *Overall objectives of the independent auditor and the conduct of an audit in accordance with international standards on auditing* summarises what audits are all about.

ISA 200

The auditor shall comply with all ISAs relevant to the audit. *Paragraph 18)*

The standard also comments on the auditor's general approach to audit work.

ISA 200

The auditor shall plan and perform an audit with professional scepticism, recognising that circumstances may exist that cause the financial statements to be materially misstated. *Paragraph 15)*

So, for example, the auditor would not simply accept what managers say during the audit of an entity, but would look for supporting evidence.

1.3 Scope of an audit

We talk of the *scope* of an audit here in the sense of the range of audit procedures which are required to achieve the objective of the audit.

ISA 200

To achieve the overall objectives of the auditor, the auditor shall use the objectives stated in relevant ISAs in planning and performing the audit. *Paragraph 15)*

1.4 Limitations of an audit

An audit performed under ISAs should provide **'reasonable assurance'** that the financial statements, taken as a whole, are free from material misstatement (we will look at the definition of 'material' later). Reasonable assurance is concerned with the way evidence is built up throughout the audit, which provides the basis of the auditor's opinion. It therefore reflects the whole audit process.

The definition of the audit given above is comprehensive about what an audit is. The standard also makes it clear that the audit is *not*:

(a) A **guarantee** of the **future viability** of the entity
(b) An **assurance** of **management's effectiveness** and efficiency

The standard points out that there are inherent (ie existing and permanent characteristic or attribute) limitations in an audit which affect the auditor's ability to discover material misstatements. These inherent limitations arise from the following factors.

(a) The nature of financial reporting
(b) The nature of audit procedures
(c) The need for the audit to be conducted within a reasonable period of time and at a reasonable cost

The auditor's **judgement** is also an issue here. Throughout every stage of the audit, the auditor's judgement is brought to bear. In particular, the auditor's judgement has a great impact on:

(a) Materiality and audit risk

(b) The nature, timing and extent of audit procedures

(c) Evaluating whether sufficient, appropriate audit evidence has been obtained

(d) The evaluation of management's judgements in applying the entity's applicable financial reporting framework

(e) The drawing of conclusions based on the audit evidence obtained

1.5 Responsibility for the financial statements

ISA 200 ends by making a very important point, which many non-auditors and members of the public fail to appreciate.

'The financial statements subject to audit are those of the entity, prepared and presented by management of the entity with oversight from those charged with governance. The audit of the financial statements does not relieve management or those charged with governance of those responsibilities.'

1.6 The expectations gap

There are some common misconceptions in relation to the role of the auditors, even among 'financially aware' people, including the following examples.

(a) Many people think that the **auditors report** is to the **directors** of a company, rather than the members.

(b) Some think that a **qualified audit report** is **more favourable** than an unmodified audit report, whereas the converse is true.

(c) There is a perception that it is the auditors' duty to detect fraud, when in fact the detection of fraud is the **responsibility** of the **directors**.

These findings highlight the 'expectations gap' between what auditors do and what people in general think that they do. Add the fact that many 'financially aware' people do not look at the report and accounts of a company they are considering investing in, and you have some sobering facts for the auditors to contemplate!

Public concern at large company failures has highlighted problems with the expectations gap. This has formed part of a general debate on corporate governance (ie how companies are governed) in many countries. Corporate governance developments have aimed to make the role of the auditor clearer and to regulate the relationship between the auditors and the management of the entity being audited.

In most countries, audits are required under national statute in the case of a large number of undertakings, including limited liability companies. Other organisations and entities requiring a statutory audit may include charities, investment businesses, trade unions and so on.

Non-statutory audits are performed by independent auditors because the owners, proprietors, members, trustees, professional and governing bodies or other interested parties want them, rather than because the law requires them.

Auditors may also give an **audit opinion** on **statements** other **than annual accounts**, including:

- Summaries of sales in support of a statement of royalties
- Statements of expenditure in support of applications for government grants
- The circulation figures of a newspaper or magazine

In all such audits the auditors must take into account any regulations contained in the internal rules or constitution of the undertaking. Examples of the regulations which the auditors would need to refer to in such assignments would include:

- The rules of clubs, societies and charities
- Partnership agreements

1.7 Auditor independence

The most important characteristics of the external auditor, and one which must never be compromised, is that he is **independent** of the organisation and its directors. For this reason, audit firms will rotate partners so that the same partner is not continually signing off the audit report for a client. This is intended to prevent the development of a familiarity as a result of which the auditor's independence may be called into question.

Section summary

- An audit is essentially an independent review. External auditors are regulated by statute and by professional bodies.
- The key stages of an audit are to:
  - Carry out procedures to obtain **sufficient appropriate audit evidence**
  - **Evaluate** the **presentation** of accounts
  - Issue a report containing a **clear expression** of **opinion**
- Audits at best give **reasonable assurance** that the accounts are free from **material misstatement**.
- The **expectations gap** is the difference between the work auditors actually carry out and the work non-auditors think they carry out.

2 Accepting audit appointments

Introduction

This section covers the procedures that the auditors must undertake to ensure that their appointment is valid and that they are clear to act.

2.1 Client acceptance

Before a new audit client is accepted, the auditors must ensure that there are **no threats to compliance with the fundamental principles** of the CIMA Code. For example, if the client is known to be involved in money laundering, this could be a threat to integrity or professional behaviour. We will look at the fundamental principles in more detail in Chapter 13.

The significance of any threats to the Code should be evaluated and if necessary the auditors should **apply safeguards** to eliminate them or reduce them to an acceptable level. If this is not possible, the auditors should decline to enter into a relationship with the client.

Appointment decisions should be **periodically reviewed** for recurring audit clients.

2.2 Engagement acceptance

The significance of any threats to the CIMA Code should be evaluated for each specific audit engagement. If necessary, the auditors should apply safeguards to eliminate them or reduce them to an acceptable level. The Code lists the following examples of safeguards that could be applied.

- Acquiring an appropriate understanding of the nature of the client's business, the complexity of its operations, the specific requirements of the engagement and the purpose, nature and scope of the work to be performed
- Acquiring knowledge of relevant industries or subject matters
- Possessing or obtaining experience with relevant regulatory or reporting requirements
- Assigning sufficient staff with the necessary competencies
- Using experts where necessary, bearing in mind their reputation and expertise
- Agreeing on a realistic time frame for the performance of the engagement
- Complying with quality control policies and procedures designed to provide reasonable assurance that specific engagements are accepted only when they can be performed competently.

The auditors must only agree to accept engagements that they are **competent** to perform. A self-interest threat to professional competence and due care is created if the auditors do not posses the required skills for the engagement or are unable to acquire these through further training.

2.3 Changes in a professional appointment

Companies will change their auditors for various reasons such as the audit fee being perceived as too high or that the company's business has expanded beyond the capabilities of the audit firm. There are certain provisions which the CIMA Code requires a new auditor follow before accepting such an engagement.

In particular, the new auditors should **communicate** with the existing auditors to establish the facts and circumstances behind the proposed change. Based on this information, the new auditors can decide whether or not it is appropriate to accept the engagement. For example, if it was discovered that the existing audit firm has not been reappointed because of a serious disagreement with the client, the new auditors may decide not to accept the appointment. The incoming auditor must have **permission** from the audit client before communicating with the existing auditors.

Confidentiality rules require that existing auditors can only communicate with the new auditors when the audit client has given permission. All information should be provided honestly and unambiguously.

2.4 Non-audit engagements

The rules for acceptance of non-audit engagements, for example assurance or tax engagements, are the same as those for auditors.

Section summary

- Before accepting a new client or engagement, the auditors must ensure the correct acceptance procedures have been carried out.

3 Duties and rights of auditors

Introduction

In this section we look at the duties and rights of the auditor under UK law.

3.1 Duties

The auditors should be required to report on every statement of financial position and statement of comprehensive income laid before the company in general meeting.

The auditors may also be required to consider the following.

Compliance with legislation	Whether the accounts have been prepared in accordance with the relevant legislation.
Truth and fairness of accounts	Whether the statement of financial position shows a true and fair view of the company's affairs at the end of the period and the statement of comprehensive income (and a statement of cash flows) show a true and fair view of the results for the period.
Adequate records and returns	Whether adequate accounting records have been kept and proper returns adequate for the audit received from branches not visited by the auditor.
Agreement of accounts to records	Whether the accounts are in agreement with the accounting records.
Consistency of other information	Whether the other information with the accounts is consistent with the accounts.

3.2 Rights

The auditors must have certain rights to enable them to carry out their duties effectively.

The principal rights auditors should have, excepting those dealing with resignation or removal, are set out in the table below, and the following are notes on more detailed points.

Access to records	A right of access at all times to the books, accounts and vouchers of the company.
Information and explanations	A right to require from the company's officers such information and explanations as they think necessary for the performance of their duties as auditors.

Attendance at/notices of general meetings	A right to attend any general meetings of the company and to receive all notices of and communications relating to such meetings which any member of the company is entitled to receive.
Right to speak at general meetings	A right to be heard at general meetings which they attend on any part of the business that concerns them as auditors.
Rights in relation to written resolutions	A right to receive a copy of any written resolution proposed.
Right to require laying of accounts	A right to give notice in writing requiring that a general meeting be held for the purpose of laying the accounts and reports before the company.

Rights to information

It is an offence for a company's officer knowingly or recklessly to make a statement in any form to an auditor which:

(a) Purports to convey any information or explanation required by the auditor
(b) Is materially misleading, false or deceptive

If auditors have not received all the information and explanations they deem necessary, they should state this fact in their report.

Section summary

Auditor's duties generally include the duties to report explicitly on the **reasonableness** of the accounts audited and their **compliance** with legislation. They should also report on whether adequate accounting records have been kept.

Auditor's rights should include the rights of **access to records** and to receive **information** and **explanations**, also rights relating to **attendance** and **speaking** at **general meetings**.

4 The audit report

Introduction

This section looks at the audit report. This is the way that the auditors will report to the shareholders of a company with their findings from the audit. We will look at the structure of the report and the different opinions that the auditor may give.

4.1 Preparing the report

ISA 700 *Forming an opinion and reporting on financial statements* deals with the auditor's responsibility to form an opinion on the financial statements and provides guidance on the form and content of the auditor's report. The auditor's report is the report issued as a result of an audit performed by an independent auditor of the financial statements of an entity.

ISA 700

The auditor shall form an opinion on whether the financial statements are prepared, in all material respects, in accordance with the applicable financial reporting framework. *(Paragraph 10)*

The applicable financial reporting framework could be either IASs or relevant national standards or practices. Auditors may also have to consider whether the financial statements comply with statutory requirements.

ISA 700

The auditor's report shall be in writing *(Paragraph 20)*

4.2 Basic elements of the auditor's report

INDEPENDENT AUDITOR'S REPORT

(APPROPRIATE ADDRESSEE)

Report on the Financial Statements

We have audited the accompanying financial statements of ABC Company, which comprise the statement of financial position as at December 31, 20X1, and the income statement, statement of changes in equity and statement of cash flows for the year then ended, and a summary of significant accounting policies and other explanatory information.

Management's Responsibility for the Financial Statements

Management is responsible for the preparation and fair presentation of these financial statements in accordance with International Financial Reporting Standards,; this includes the design, implementation and maintenance of and for such internal control relevant as management determines is necessary to enable the preparation and fair presentation of financial statements that are free from material misstatement, whether due to fraud or error.

Auditor's Responsibility

Our responsibility is to express an opinion on these financial statements based on our audit. We conducted our audit in accordance with International Standards on Auditing. Those standards require that we comply with ethical requirements and plan and perform the audit to obtain reasonable assurance about whether the financial statements are free from material misstatement.

An audit involves performing procedures to obtain audit evidence about the amounts and disclosures in the financial statements. The procedures selected depend on the auditor's judgment, including the assessment of the risks of material misstatement of the financial statements, whether due to fraud or error. In making those risk assessments, the auditor considers internal control relevant to the entity's preparation and fair presentation of the financial statements in order to design audit procedures that are appropriate in the circumstances, but not for the purpose of expressing an opinion on the effectiveness of the entity's internal control. An audit also includes evaluating the appropriateness of accounting policies used and the reasonableness of accounting estimates made by management, as well as evaluating the overall presentation of the financial statements.

We believe that the audit evidence we have obtained is sufficient and appropriate to provide a basis for our audit opinion.

Opinion

In our opinion, the financial statements present fairly, in all material respects, (or *give a true and fair view of*) the financial position of ABC Company as at December 31, 20X1, and (*of*) its financial performance and its cash flows for the year then ended in accordance with International Financial Reporting Standards.

[Auditor's signature]

[Date of the auditor's report]

[Auditor's address]

4.2.1 Title

ISA 700

The auditor's report shall have a title that clearly indicates that it is the report of an independent auditor. *(Paragraph 21)*

The term 'independent auditor' distinguishes the auditor's report from reports issued by others, such as by officers of the entity.

4.2.2 Addressee

ISA 700

The auditor's report shall be addressed as required by the circumstances of the engagement. *(Paragraph 22)*

The report is ordinarily addressed either to the **shareholders** or **those charged with governance** of the entity whose financial statements are being audited.

4.2.3 Introductory paragraph

ISA 700

The introductory paragraph in the auditor's report shall:

(a) Identify the entity whose financial statements have been audited;

(b) State that the financial statements have been audited;

(c) Identify the title of each statement that comprises the financial statements;

(d) Refer to the summary of significant accounting policies and other explanatory information; and

(e) Specify the date or period covered by each financial statement comprising the financial statements. *(Paragraph 23)*

4.2.4 Management's responsibility for the financial statements

This section of the auditor's report covers the responsibilities of those in charge of preparing the financial statements. This is often the management of an organisation.

The auditor's report must explain that management are responsible for preparing the financial statements in accordance with an applicable financial reporting framework. It must also describe how management are responsible for internal controls which enable the preparation of financial statements which are free from fraud or error.

4.2.5 Auditor's responsibility

ISA 700

The auditor's report shall state that the responsibility of the auditor is to express an opinion on the financial statements based on the audit. *(Para 29)*

The auditor must state that the audit was conducted in accordance with International Standards on Auditing. This section must also contain a description of an audit.

4.2.6 Opinion paragraph

ISA 700

When expressing an unmodified opinion on financial statements ..., the auditor's opinion shall, ..., use one of the following phrases, which are regarded as being equivalent:

(a) The financial statements present fairly, in all material respects, ... in accordance with [the applicable financial reporting framework]; or

(b) The financial statements give a true and fair view of ... in accordance with [the applicable financial reporting framework]. *(Paragraph 35)*

The terms used to express the auditor's opinion are 'give a true and fair view' or 'present fairly, in all material respects', and are **equivalent**. Both terms indicate, amongst other things, that the auditor considers only those matters that are **material** to the financial statements.

The **applicable financial reporting framework** is determined by IASs, rules issued by professional bodies, and the development of general practice within a country, with an appropriate consideration of fairness and with due regard to local legislation. To advise the reader of the context in which 'fairness' is expressed, the auditor's opinion indicates the framework upon which the financial statements are based.

In addition to an opinion of the true and fair view (or fair presentation, in all material respects), the auditor's report may need to include an opinion as to whether the financial statements comply with other requirements specified by **relevant statutes or law**. These other reporting responsibilities must be addressed in a separate section of the auditor's report.

4.2.7 Signature of the auditor

ISA 700

The auditor's report shall be signed. *(Paragraph 40)*

The firm as a whole usually assumes responsibility for the audit, but in some countries an individual partner may be required to take responsibility and sign in his or her own name.

4.2.8 Date of the auditor's report

ISA 700

The auditor's report shall be dated no earlier than the date on which the auditor has obtained sufficient appropriate audit evidence on which to base the auditor's opinion on the financial statements. *(Paragraph 23)*

4.2.9 Auditor's address

ISA 700

The auditor's report shall name the location in the jurisdiction where the auditor practices. *(Paragraph 25)*

4.3 Unmodified audit report

ISA 700

The auditor shall express an *unmodified opinion* when the auditor concludes that the financial statements are prepared, in all material respects, in accordance with the applicable financial reporting framework.

(Paragraph 16)

This section has introduced you to the standard unmodified audit report. The next paragraphs look at how the audit report is affected when problems of varying severity arise in the audit.

Question 2.1 Unmodified audit report

Learning outcome B1(g)

The following is an unmodified audit report, which has been signed by the auditors of Kiln, a limited liability company.

INDEPENDENT AUDITORS' REPORT

TO THE SHAREHOLDERS OF KILN COMPANY

Report on the Financial Statements

We have audited the accompanying financial statements of Kiln Company, which comprise the statement of financial position as at December 31, 20X3, and the income statement, statement of changes in equity and statement of cash flows for the year then ended, and a summary of significant accounting policies and other explanatory information.

Management's Responsibility for the Financial Statements

Management is responsible for the preparation and fair presentation of these financial statements in accordance with International Financial Reporting Standards,; this includes the design, implementation and maintenance of and for such internal control relevant as management determines is necessary to enable the preparation and fair presentation of financial statements that are free from material misstatement, whether due to fraud or error.

Auditor's Responsibility

Our responsibility is to express an opinion on these financial statements based on our audit. We conducted our audit in accordance with International Standards on Auditing. Those standards require that we comply with ethical requirements and plan and perform the audit to obtain reasonable assurance about whether the financial statements are free from material misstatement.

An audit involves performing procedures to obtain audit evidence about the amounts and disclosures in the financial statements. The procedures selected depend on the auditor's judgment, including the assessment of the risks of material misstatement of the financial statements, whether due to fraud or error. In making those risk assessments, the auditor considers internal control relevant to the entity's preparation and fair presentation of the financial statements in order to design audit procedures that are appropriate in the circumstances, but not for the purpose of expressing an opinion on the effectiveness of the entity's internal control. An audit also includes evaluating the appropriateness of accounting policies used and the reasonableness of accounting estimates made by management, as well as evaluating the overall presentation of the financial statements.

We believe that the audit evidence we have obtained is sufficient and appropriate to provide a basis for our audit opinion.

Opinion

In our opinion, the financial statements present fairly, in all material respects, (or *give a true and fair view of*) the financial position of Kiln Company as at December 31, 20X3, and (*of*) its financial performance

and its cash flows for the year then ended in accordance with International Financial Reporting Standards.

AUDITOR

Date of the auditor's report

Auditor's address

Required

Explain the purpose and meaning of the following phrases taken from the above extracts of an unmodified audit report.

(a) '... which comprise the statement of financial position ..., and the income statement, ... and statement of cash flows ... .'
(b) '... in accordance with International Standards on Auditing.'
(c) 'In our opinion ...'

4.4 Matters that affect the auditor's opinion

An auditor cannot express an unmodified opinion when either of the following circumstances exist:

(a) The auditor concludes that, based on the audit evidence obtained, the financial statements as a whole are not free from material **misstatement**

(b) The auditor is **unable to obtain sufficient appropriate audit evidence** to conclude that the financial statements as a whole are free from material misstatement.

There are different types and degrees of modified opinion.

(a) An inability to obtain sufficient appropriate audit evidence may lead to a **qualified opinion** or a **disclaimer of opinion**.

(b) A material misstatement of the financial statements may lead to a **qualified opinion** or an **adverse opinion**.

ISA 705 *Modifications to the opinion in the independent auditor's report* describes these different modified opinions and the circumstances leading to them as follows.

ISA 705

The auditor shall express a **qualified opinion** when:

(a) The auditor, having obtained sufficient appropriate audit evidence, concludes that misstatements, individually or in the aggregate, are material, but not pervasive, to the financial statements; or

(b) The auditor is unable to obtain sufficient appropriate audit evidence on which to base the opinion, but the auditor concludes that the possible effects on the financial statements of undetected misstatements, if any, could be material but not pervasive.

The auditor shall **disclaim** an opinion when the auditor is unable to obtain sufficient appropriate audit evidence on which to base the opinion, and the auditor concludes that the possible effects on the financial statements of undetected misstatements, if any, could be both material and pervasive.

The auditor shall express an **adverse** opinion when the auditor, having obtained sufficient appropriate audit evidence, concludes that misstatements, individually or in the aggregate, are both material and pervasive to the financial statements. *(Paragraphs 7-9)*

When the auditor modifies the opinion on the financial statements, the auditor shall, in addition to the specific elements required by ISA 700 (Redrafted), include a paragraph in the auditor's report that provides a description of the matter giving rise to the modification.

If there is a material misstatement of the financial statements that relates to specific amounts in the financial statements (including quantitative disclosures), the auditor shall include in the basis for modification paragraph a description and quantification of the financial effects of the misstatements, unless impracticable. *(Paragraphs 16-17)*

This description must be set out in a **separate paragraph** immediately before the opinion.

Inability to obtain evidence is not part of the syllabus, so we will concentrate here on misstatement.

Material misstatements may arise in the financial statements in relation to the acceptability of accounting policies selected, the method of their application, or the adequacy of disclosures in the financial statements.

If the auditor believes the accounts to be materially misstated, the auditor will first seek to resolve this with management. Any expected amendments to the audit report should be communicated to with those charged with governance along with the proposed wording of the modification.

ISA 700

If such disagreements are material to the financial statements, the auditor should express a qualified or an adverse opinion. *(Paragraph 45)*

At this point we should look at the concept of **materiality**. A matter is material 'if its omission or misstatement could influence the economic decisions of users taken on the basis of the financial statements' (IASB *Framework*).

The auditor does not report on anything which is not material, but he does have to decide whether something is material or not. He may use guidelines such as treating anything which exceeds 5% of profit as material.

Exam skills

Exam questions will make it clear whether or not an item is material. If this is based on amounts, then immaterial amounts will be far less than 5% of profit and material amounts will be far in excess of 10% of profit.

The following examples are given in ISA 705.

Material misstatement – non-consolidation of a subsidiary – adverse opinion

We have audited ...[as for unmodified].

We conducted our audit in accordance with ... [as for unmodified].

Basis for Adverse Opinion

As explained in Note X, the company has not consolidated the financial statements of subsidiary XYZ Company it acquired during 20X1 because it has not yet been able to ascertain the fair values of certain of the subsidiary's material assets and liabilities at the acquisition date. This investment is therefore accounted for on a cost basis. Under International Financial Reporting Standards, the subsidiary should have been consolidated because it is controlled by the company. Had XYZ been consolidated, many elements in the accompanying financial statements would have been materially affected. The effects on the financial statements of the failure to consolidate have not been determined.

Adverse Opinion

In our opinion, because of the significance of the matter discussed in the Basis for Adverse Opinion paragraph, the consolidated financial statements do not present fairly (or "do not give a true and fair view of") the financial position of ABC Company and its subsidiaries as at December 31, 20X1, and of their financial performance and cash flows for the year then ended in accordance with International Financial Reporting Standards.

Inability to obtain sufficient appropriate audit evidence – single issue – disclaimer of opinion

We have audited ... [as for unmodified].

We conducted our audit in accordance with ... [as for unmodified].

Auditor's Responsibility

Our responsibility is to express an opinion on these financial statements based on conducting the audit in accordance with International Standards on Auditing. Because of the matter described in the Basis for Disclaimer of Opinion paragraph, however, we were not able to obtain sufficient appropriate audit evidence to provide a basis for an audit opinion.

Basis for Disclaimer of Opinion

The company's investment in its joint venture XYZ (Country X) Company is carried at xxx on the company's balance sheet, which represents over 90% of the company's net assets as at December 31, 20X1. We were not allowed access to the management and the auditors of XYZ, including XYZ's auditors' audit documentation. As a result, we were unable to determine whether any adjustments were necessary in respect of the company's proportional share of XYZ's assets that it controls jointly, its proportional share of XYZ's liabilities for which it is jointly responsible, its proportional share of XYZ's income and expenses for the year, and the elements making up the statement of changes in equity and cash flow statement.

Disclaimer of Opinion

Because of the significance of the matter described in the Basis for Disclaimer of Opinion paragraph, we have not been able to obtain sufficient appropriate audit evidence to provide a basis for an audit opinion. Accordingly, we do not express an opinion on the financial statements.

Question 2.2 Audit problems

Learning outcome B1(g)

During the course of your audit of the non-current assets of Eastern Engineering, a listed company, at 31 March 20X4 the following problem has arisen.

The company incurred development expenditure of $25,000 spent on a viable new product which will go into production next year and which is expected to last for ten years. The expenditure has been debited in full to the statement of comprehensive income. The profit before tax is $100,000.

Required

(a) List the general forms of qualified report available to auditors in drafting their report and state the circumstances in which each is appropriate.

(b) State whether you feel that a qualified audit report would be necessary for the circumstances outlined above, giving reasons.

(c) On the assumption that you decide that a qualified audit report is necessary with respect to the treatment of the development expenditure, draft the section of the report describing the matter (the whole report is not required).

(d) Outline the auditors' general responsibility with regard to a statement in the directors' or management report concerning the valuation of land and buildings.

Exam alert

You do not have to memorise the wording of audit reports.

4.5 Emphasis of matter and other matter paragraphs

4.5.1 Emphasis of matter paragraph

KEY TERM

In certain circumstances, an auditor's report may include an EMPHASIS OF MATTER paragraph to highlight a matter appropriately presented or disclosed in the financial statements, that, in the auditor's judgement, is of such importance that it is fundamental to users' understanding of the financial statements.

The addition of such an emphasis of matter **does not affect the auditor's opinion**.

The emphasis of matter paragraph is included immediately after the opinion paragraph and should refer to the fact that the auditor's opinion is not qualified in respect of the matter being emphasised.

ISA 706 *Emphasis of Matter Paragraphs and Other Matter Paragraphs in the Independent Auditor's Report*, states an emphasis of matter paragraph may be necessary under the following circumstances.

(a) Where there is uncertainty relating to the future outcome of litigation or regulatory action

(b) If there has been early application of a new accounting standard that has had a major effect on the financial statements

(c) If there is a major catastrophe that has had, or continues to have, a significant effect on the entity's financial position

The standard also draws attention to paragraphs in other International Standards on Auditing where the auditor is required to include an emphasis of matter paragraph under certain circumstances.

The following example of an emphasis of matter paragraph is given by the ISA, which would be added to the end of the standard unmodified wording given above.

> We draw attention to Note X to the financial statements which describes the uncertainty related to the outcome of the lawsuit filed against the company by XYZ Company. Our opinion is not qualified in respect of this matter.

4.5.2 Other matter paragraph

KEY TERM

The auditor may also include an OTHER MATTER paragraph to report matters not presented or disclosed in the financial statements that in the auditor's judgement are relevant to users' understanding of the audit, the auditor's responsibilities or the audit report.

The placement of an other matter paragraph depends on the nature of the information to be communicated. When an other matter paragraph is included to draw users' attention to a matter relevant to their understanding of the audit of the financial statements, the paragraph is included immediately after the opinion paragraph and any emphasis of matter paragraph. When an other matter paragraph is included for other reasons, it may be included elsewhere. It **does not affect the auditor's opinion**.

An other matter paragraph could be included where laws or regulations exist in a jurisdiction requiring the auditor to elaborate on certain matters. ISA 706 *Emphasis of Matter Paragraphs and Other Matter Paragraphs in the Independent Auditor's Report*, draws attention to paragraphs in other International Standards on Auditing where the auditor is required to include an other matter paragraph under certain circumstances.

4.6 The audit report as a means of communication

Unmodified audit reports may not appear to give a great deal of information. The report says a lot, however, by implication.

The real problem here is that, unfortunately, most users do not know that this is what an unmodified audit report tells them. This issue is also confused by the fact that most users do not understand the responsibilities of either the auditors or the directors in relation to the financial statements.

Different countries have tackled this problem in different ways. The role of auditors has been included in the debate on corporate governance in many Western countries, leading to further rules which are nevertheless voluntary, not mandatory.

Exam alert

This is a small section of the syllabus and is unlikely to give rise to complex questions.

Section summary

- ISA 700 *Forming an opinion and reporting on financial statements* gives guidance on the form and content of audit reports.
- Auditors may modify their audit opinion on the grounds that financial statements are **materially misstated** or an **inability to obtain sufficient appropriate audit evidence**; these may be material or pervasive.
- ISA 705 *Modifications to the opinion in the independent auditor's report* explains the different modified opinions.
- Emphasis of matter and other matter paragraphs **do not** affect the auditor's opinion.

Chapter Roundup

- ✓ An audit is essentially an independent review. External auditors are regulated by statute and professional bodies.
- ✓ The key stages of an audit are to:
  - Carry out procedures to obtain **sufficient appropriate audit evidence**
  - **Evaluate** the **presentation** of accounts
  - Issue a report containing a **clear expression** of **opinion**
- ✓ Audits at best give **reasonable assurance** that the accounts are free from **material misstatement**.
- ✓ The **expectations gap** is the difference between the work auditors actually carry out and the work non-auditors think they carry out.
- ✓ Before accepting a new client or engagement, the auditors must ensure the correct acceptance procedures have been carried out.
- ✓ Auditors' **duties** generally include the duties to report explicitly on the **reasonableness** of the accounts audited and their **compliance** with legislation. They should also report on whether adequate accounting records have been kept.
- ✓ Auditors' rights should include the rights of **access** to **records** and to receive **information** and **explanations**, also rights relating to **attendance** and **speaking** at **general meetings**.
- ✓ ISA 700 *Forming an opinion and reporting on financial statements* gives guidance on the form and content of audit reports.
- ✓ Auditors may modify their audit opinion on the grounds that financial statements are **materially misstated** or an **inability to obtain sufficient appropriate audit evidence**; these may be material or pervasive.
- ✓ ISA 705 *Modifications to the opinion in the independent auditor's report* explains the different modified opinions.
- ✓ Emphasis of matter and other matter paragraphs **do not** affect the auditor's opinion.

Quick Quiz

1. An audit is the work required to enable the .... to express an .... as to whether the .... are prepared, in all material respects, in accordance with an identified ....
2. What is the expectations gap?
3. The main reason why an audit is considered to be necessary is that it gives the financial statements credibility

   True ☐

   False ☐
4. Which of the following is not a statutory right of the auditor?

   A Access to records
   B Right to speak at general meetings
   C Right to amend records
   D Right to receive a copy of any written resolution proposed

5 What are the basic elements of the auditors' report?

6 When will a modified opinion be issued?

Answers to Quick Quiz

1 Auditor, opinion, financial statements, financial reporting standards

2 The **expectations gap** is the difference between the work auditors actually carry out and the work non-auditors think they carry out.

3 True

4 C

5

- The report should be addressed to its recipients and have a title indicating it is the report of an independent auditor
- Introductory paragraph including identification of the financial statements audited
- Separate sections should deal with the responsibilities of management and the responsibility of the auditors
- Opinion paragraph
- Signature of the auditors
- Date of the auditor's report
- Auditor's address

6 When there is an inability to obtain sufficient appropriate audit evidence preventing the auditors from forming an opinion or where there is a material misstatement.

Answers to Questions

2.1 Unmodified audit report

(a) '... which comprise the statement of financial position .... and the income statement, ... and statement of cash flows ... .'

Purpose

The purpose of this phrase is to make it clear to the reader of an audit report the part of a company's annual report upon which the auditors are reporting their opinion.

Meaning

An annual report may include documents such as a five year summary and other voluntary information. However, only the statement of comprehensive income, statement of financial position and associated notes are required to be audited in true and fair terms. IAS 7 also requires a statement of cash flows for the financial statements to show a true and fair view. Page references (for instance, 8 to 20) may be used instead to cover the statement of comprehensive income, statement of financial position, notes to the accounts and statement of cash flows. The directors' report, or any equivalent, although examined and reported on by exception if it contains inconsistencies, is not included in these references.

(b) '...in accordance with International Standards on Auditing ....'

Purpose

This phrase is included in order to confirm to the reader that best practice, as laid down in ISAs, has been adopted by the auditors in both carrying out their audit and in drafting their audit opinion. This means that the reader can be assured that the audit has been properly conducted, and that should he or she wish to discover what such standards are, or what certain key phrases mean, he or she can have recourse to ISAs to explain such matters.

Meaning

Auditing Standards are those auditing standards prepared by the International Auditing and Assurance Standards Board (although local/national standards may be mentioned instead).

These prescribe the principles and practices to be followed by auditors in planning, designing and carrying out various aspects of their audit work, the content of audit reports, both qualified and unmodified and so on. Members of professional accountancy bodies are expected to follow all of these standards.

(c) 'In our opinion ...'

Purpose

Auditors are required to report on every statement of financial position, statement of comprehensive income and statement of cash flows laid before shareholders. In reporting, they are required to state their *opinion* on those accounts. Thus, the purpose of this phrase is to comply with the requirement to report an opinion.

Meaning

An audit report is an expression of opinion by suitably qualified auditors as to whether the financial statements give a true and fair view, and have been properly prepared in accordance with any relevant local legislation. *It is not a certificate*; rather it is a statement of whether or not, in the professional judgement of the auditors, the financial statements give a true and fair view.

2.2 Audit problems

(a) ISA 705 *Modifications to the opinion in the independent auditor's report* suggests that the auditors may need to qualify their audit opinion where they believe the financial statements to be materially misstated.

There can be two 'levels' of qualified opinion:

material but not pervasive, where the misstatements detected are materially individually or in aggregate, but are confined to a specific item that does not represent a substantial proportion of the financial statements and is not fundamental to user's understanding of these financial statements.

(ii) the more serious adverse opinion where the extent of the misstatement is such that it will be *material and pervasive* to the overall view shown by the financial statements.

The general form of qualified report appropriate to each potential situation may be seen by the following table.

Circumstance	*Material but not pervasive*	*Material and Pervasive*
Financial statements are materially misstated	Qualified opinion	Adverse opinion

(b) Whether a modification of the audit opinion would be required in relation to the circumstances described in the question would depend on whether or not the auditors considered them to be material. An item is likely to be considered as material in the context of a company's financial statements if its omission, misstatement or non-disclosure would prevent a proper understanding of those statements on the part of a potential user. Whilst for some audit purposes materiality will be considered in absolute terms, more often than not it will be considered as a relative term.

Development costs debited to the statement of comprehensive income

The situation here is one of misstatement, since best accounting practice, as laid down by IAS 38, requires that development costs should be taken to the statement of comprehensive income over the useful life of the product to which they relate.

This departure from IAS 38 does not seem to be justifiable and would be material to the reported pre-tax profits for the year, representing as it does 22.5% of that figure.

Whilst this understatement of profit would be material to the financial statements, it is not likely to be seen as pervasive and therefore a qualified opinion would be appropriate.

(c) *Basis for Qualified Opinion*

'As explained in note ... development costs in respect of a potential new product have been deducted in full against profit instead of being spread over the life of the relevant product as required by IAS 38; the effect of so doing has been to decrease profits before and after tax for the year by $22,500.

Qualified Opinion

In our opinion, except for the effects of the matter described in the Basis for Qualified Opinion paragraph, the financial statements present fairly, in all material respects, (or "give a true and fair view of") the financial position of Eastern Engineering as at 31 March 20X4, and of its financial performance and its cash flows for the year then ended in accordance with International Financial Reporting Standards.

(d) The auditors' general responsibility with regard to the statement in the directors' report concerning the valuation of land and buildings is to satisfy themselves that this is consistent with the treatment and disclosure of this item in the audited financial statements. If the auditors are not satisfied on the question of consistency then they may have to consider qualifying the opinion in their audit report.

Now try these questions from the Exam Question Bank

Number	Level	Marks	Time
Q9	Examination	5	9 mins
Q10	Examination	5	9 mins

ETHICS

This chapter covers ethical codes, in particular the CIMA *Code of Ethics for Professional Accountants*. It begins by discussing the development of ethical codes in general, before spending time on the CIMA Code.

The ethical matters covered in this chapter are very important. As a CIMA student, you are expected to know and apply the Code in your everyday work.

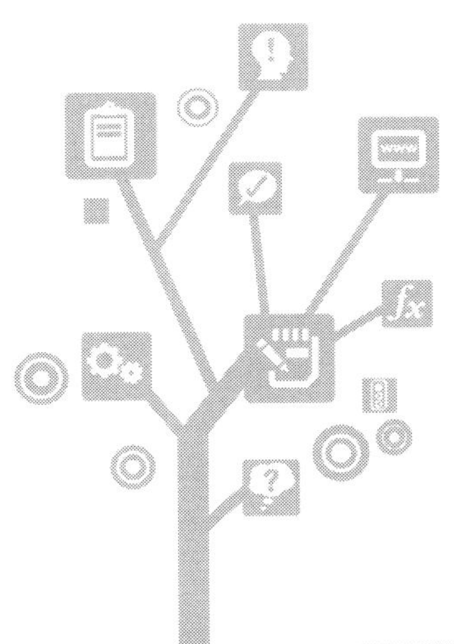

topic list	learning outcomes	syllabus references	ability required
1 The need for an ethical code	B2(b)	B2(ii)	comprehension
2 Sources of ethical codes	B2(b)	B2(ii)	comprehension
3 Rules or principles based guidance?	B2(b)	B2(ii)	comprehension
4 Fundamental principles	B2(a)	B2(i)	comprehension
5 Problems facing accountants in public practice	B2(c)	B2(iii)	application
6 Problems facing accountants in business	B2(c)	B2(iii)	application

1 The need for an ethical code

Introduction

In this section we discuss the reasons why ethical codes are considered necessary.

KEY TERM

ETHICS is a set of moral principles to guide behaviour.

A professional accountant has a responsibility to act in the public interest, not just to satisfy the needs of a particular client or employer. Different **stakeholders**, for example investors, governments and employees, **rely on accountants** and their expertise. If the information produced by professional accountants cannot be relied upon, financial markets will not operate effectively.

Professional accountants must be qualified but also have an additional obligation to act ethically by following an ethical code. This ethical requirement may be above that required by laws or regulations in some jurisdictions. An ethical code helps **maintain the reputation** of the accounting profession.

Ethics and ethical codes are **constantly evolving** to adapt with changes in business and society. Cases such as Enron and WorldCom in the USA resulted in the perceived integrity of accountants becoming increasingly important. The CIMA Code was most recently revised in June 2006.

Question 3.1 — Ethical issues

Learning outcome B2(b)

Briefly explain the main ethical issues that arise in the following situations.

(a) Dealing with a repressive authoritarian government abroad

(b) An aggressive advertising campaign

(c) Employee redundancies

(d) Payments or gifts to officials who have the power to help or hinder the payees' operations

Section summary

A need for an ethical code has developed due to various stakeholders relying on accountants and their reputation. An ethical code must evolve to adapt with changing circumstances.

2 Sources of ethical codes

Introduction

This section covers the variety of sources behind the development of ethical codes.

2.1 Early sources of rules

In prehistoric tribes, there were no laws, no court and no police. Rules would have developed through need. The tribe would have a collective idea of what was right or wrong for the good of the group and would have punished a group member who stepped out of line, for example by taking food from others.

Further sources of rules developed as **society** grew and eventually the first laws were laid down to control the larger populations. **Religion** played a major role in developing the rules for the individual, and many of these rules are still in place today.

Business law is relatively new, and has only developed over the last couple of hundred years with industrialisation and the needs that grew from it. **Professional and corporate codes of conduct** are an even more recent development.

Social attitudes have helped shape ethical codes differently in different countries. For example in some cultures (such as Japan) gifts are regarded as an essential part of civilised negotiation, even in circumstances where to Western eyes they might appear ethically dubious. Globalisation has resulted in a move towards standardisation of ethical codes for accountants across the world.

2.2 IFAC

IFAC (the International Federation of Accountants, of which CIMA is a member) is an international body representing all the major accountancy bodies across the world. Its mission is to develop the high standards in professional accountants and enhance the quality of services they provide. To enable this, the IFAC ethics committee published the *Code of Ethics for Professional Accountants*.

The IFAC Code sets out the five fundamental principles of professional ethics and it provides a conceptual framework for applying those principles. Members must apply this conceptual framework to identify threats to compliance with the five fundamental principles, evaluate their significance and apply appropriate safeguards to eliminate or reduce them so that compliance with the fundamental principles is not compromised.

For further informtion visit www.ifac.org.

2.3 Professional bodies

Professional bodies have their own ethical codes. All CIMA members (and registered students) are required to follow the CIMA *Code of Ethics for Professional Accountants* which is based on the IFAC Code. The CIMA Code has sections which apply to both accountants in business and accountants in public practice.

Although CIMA and IFAC have produced detailed ethical guidance for professional accountants, countries may have their own additional ethical guidance. For example, in the UK, the Auditing Practices Board of the Financial Reporting Council has issued five ethical standards and an ethical standard specific to small entities, which provide an additional source of guidance for UK auditors.

2.4 Employing organisations

Businesses also have ethical values, based on the **norms** and **standards** of **behaviour** that their leaders believe will best help them express their identity and achieve their objectives. Some of these ethical values may be **explicit**, for example, expressed in a mission statement or in employee training programmes. Others may be **unwritten rules and customs** that form part of the organisations' culture.

Business life is a fruitful source of **ethical dilemmas** because its whole purpose is material gain, the making of profit. Success in business requires a constant search for potential advantage over others and business people are under pressure to do whatever yields such advantage.

Organisation systems and targets do have ethical implications. The *Harvard Business Review* reported that the US retailer, Sears Roebuck was deluged with complaints that customers of its car service centre were being charged for unnecessary work. Apparently this was because mechanics had been given targets of the number of car spare parts they should sell.

In recent times, trust in business has fallen and increasingly more evidence is required to demonstrate it. In recent years, the UK has seen a procession of corporate disasters including the names of Barings Bank, Northern Rock and HBOS. The US has seen scandals concerning Worldcom, Enron, AIG and Lehman Brothers. Europe did not escape and has seen its share of problems with Parmalat and in Asia, Mitsubishi Motors and Daewoo have had issues too. All these scandals have severely knocked public confidence and trust in major corporations.

In an attempt to counter this lack of trust, many corporations have developed **ethical strategies** and **policies** to provide **guidance** and **training** for their employees. Increasing numbers of corporations are developing ethical codes for their employees which must be followed during the course of their employment. The strategy is set by the leadership and this will feed into all areas of the business and become part of the culture of the organisation.

Question 3.2 Employee behaviour

Learning outcome B2(b)

How can an organisation influence employee behaviour towards ethical issues?

An ethical strategy is not always visible to outsiders, and many companies now produce **Corporate Responsibility Policies (CRPs)** and **Corporate Responsibility Reports (CRRs)** for their stakeholders to demonstrate their commitment and to manage its relationships in the wider community.

Section summary

Sources of ethical codes include law, religion, social attitudes, IFAC, professional bodies and employing organisations.

3 Rules or principles based guidance?

Introduction

In this section we look at the advantages and disadvantages of principles-based guidance.

The CIMA Code is in the form of a principles-based framework. It contains some rules but in the main it is a flexible guidance. It can be seen as being a framework of principles rather than a set of rules. There are a number of advantages of a framework of principles over a system of ethical rules.

3.1 Advantages of principles-based guidance

(a) A framework of guidance places the onus on the professional to **consider actively** relevant issues in a given situation, rather than just agreeing action with a checklist of forbidden items. It also requires the professional to **demonstrate** that a responsible conclusion has been reached about ethical issues.

(b) The framework prevents professionals interpreting legalistic requirements narrowly to get around the ethical requirements. There is an extent to which rules engender deception, whereas principles encourage compliance.

(c) A framework allows for variations that are found in every individual situation. Each situation is likely to be different.

(d) A framework can accommodate a rapidly changing environment, such as the one in which auditors are.

(e) A framework can contain prohibitions where these are necessary when principles are not enough.

(f) A code prescribes minimum standards of behaviour that are expected.

(g) Codes can include examples to illustrate how the principles are applied.

3.2 Disadvantages of principles-based guidance

(a) As ethical codes cannot include all circumstances and dilemmas, accountants need a very good understanding of the underlying principles.

(b) International codes such as the IFAC Code cannot fully capture regional variations in beliefs and practice.

(c) The illustrative examples can be interpreted mistakenly as rules to follow in all similar circumstances.

(d) Principles– based codes can be difficult to enforce legally, unless the breach of the code is blatant. Most are therefore voluntary and perhaps therefore less effective.

Section summary

The CIMA Code is a principles-based framework. There are advantages and disadvantages of a principles-based framework over a system of rules.

4 Fundamental principles

Introduction

This section explains the fundamental principles in the CIMA Code, threats to those principles and the safeguards which can be applied to counteract those threats.

4.1 CIMA fundamental principles of professional ethics for professional accountants

CIMA's ethical guidelines are available at ***www.cimaglobal.com***. Ensure you read them, especially Section 220 and Part C as these are specifically highlighted in your syllabus.

CIMA's *Code of ethics for professional accountants* was revised in June 2006 so it was more applicable to members across the world and more aligned with IFAC's *Code of ethics for professional accountants*. It sets out the five fundamental principles of professional ethics and provides a conceptual framework for applying those principles.

CIMA members must not only **know** the fundamental principles, but also **apply** them in their everyday work. There are **serious consequences for failing to follow them**, quite apart from the unacceptability of failure. Whenever a complaint is made against a member, failure to follow the contents of the fundamental principles will be taken into account when a decision is made as to whether a *prima facie* case exists of professional misconduct. The code reflects the standards CIMA expects from both its **members** and **students**.

The five fundamental principles are summarised in the table below.

Fundamental principles	
Integrity	A professional accountant should be straightforward and honest in all professional and business relationships.
Objectivity	A professional accountant should not allow bias, conflict of interest or undue influence of others to override professional or business judgments.
Professional competence and due care	A professional accountant has a continuing duty to maintain professional knowledge and skill at the level required to ensure that a client or employer receives competent professional service based on current developments in practice, legislation and techniques. A professional accountant should act diligently and in accordance with applicable technical and professional standards when providing professional services.
Confidentiality	A professional accountant should respect the confidentiality of information acquired as a result of professional and business relationships and should not disclose any such information to third parties without proper and specific authority unless there is a legal or professional right or duty to disclose. Confidential information acquired as a result of professional and business relationships should not be used for the personal advantage of the professional accountant or third parties.
Professional behaviour	A professional accountant should comply with relevant laws and regulations and should avoid any action that discredits the profession.

Exam alert

You may be asked to list and explain the ethical principles in an exam question so make sure you know them.

4.1.1 Integrity

Integrity is the important principle of honesty and requires accountants to be straightforward in all professional and business relationships. Particular care must be taken when reporting figures and statements. Omitting key information, obscuring the facts or making calculations and decisions without due care could result in false or misleading information being produced and integrity being breached.

Integrity goes further than the work an accountant produces. It also requires the accountant to act in a professional, consistent manner. The accountant must treat everyone the same rather than being friendly to some colleagues but cold to others. It also means that they should not back down over their personal or professional values just to avoid a difficult situation.

4.1.2 Objectivity

Objectivity is a combination of impartiality, intellectual honesty and a freedom from conflicts of interest. Accountants should act fairly and not allow prejudice or bias or the influence of others to affect their judgements. It contrasts with subjectivity which means an individual takes matters into consideration which are important to them, eg friendship and loyalty.

Objectivity is the core value that an accountant brings to their organisation. It is often difficult to separate one's personal interest from a decision, but as accountants it is expected.

Circumstances which may leave accountants in particular risk of breaching this principle include accepting excessive hospitality or forming illicit relationships which could cause embarrassment and the risk of blackmail. Where a threat to objectivity exists, it can be reduced or eliminated by withdrawal, terminating the relationship, involving others in the process and discussing the problem with seniors.

4.1.3 Professional competence and due care

Professional competence and due care means accountants should refrain from performing any services that they cannot perform with reasonable care knowledge, competence, diligence and a full awareness of the important issues. There is a duty to remain technically up-to-date and apply appropriate technical and professional standards when providing professional services.

Where others perform work on the accountant's behalf, the accountant must ensure that such staff also have adequate experience, qualification and are supervised. Limitations and problems found should be disclosed to those to whom the accountant is reporting. Fact and opinion should be clearly identified to avoid misunderstandings.

4.1.4 Confidentiality

Accountants have a duty to safeguard the security of information in their possession unless there is a legal or professional right or duty to disclose. Also this means not using information obtained in the course of work for personal advantage or for the benefit of others.

Breaches of confidentiality often occur when information is inadvertently disclosed to friends and family and where the accountant has recently changed employers. Care must be taken to keep confidential all information found in the course of performing a professional duty and where a new job is commenced, prior experience may be used in the new role, but not prior information.

CIMA's code of conduct lists circumstances where confidential information may be disclosed, examples include:

- Disclosure is permitted by law
- Disclosure is authorised by the client or employer
- Disclosure is required by law, such as providing evidence in legal proceedings or assisting public authorities when legal infringements have occurred
- Disclosure is permitted by a professional duty or right, such as complying with technical or ethical requirements, protecting the professional interests of an accountant in a legal action, when dealing with their professional body in an investigation or to comply with a quality review.

4.1.5 Professional behaviour

Professional behaviour means, in essence, not doing anything that might bring discredit to the profession and to comply with all relevant laws and regulations. This is defined by the profession as '*actions which a reasonable and informed third party, having knowledge of all relevant information, would conclude negatively affects the good reputation of the profession.*'

Section summary

The five fundamental principles are integrity, objectivity, professional competence and due care, confidentiality and professional behaviour. Compliance with these principles could be threatened by a wide range of circumstances. The professional accountant should apply safeguards to counteract these threats.

5 Problems facing accountants in public practice

Introduction

This section covers the type of threat that a professional accountant in practice might face and the action that should be taken if such a threat arises. We will first look at some general safeguards and then discuss how to apply these to specific threats and situations.

5.1 Threats to compliance with the fundamental principles for accountants in practice

Accountants in practice carry out a variety of work for their clients. They could be asked to perform an **audit of financial statements** which is a statutory requirement for companies of a certain size in most countries. Accountants in practice also carry out **assurance engagements** where they express a conclusion on a subject matter for one party about another. For example, one company buying another company may seek assurance on the forecasts of the company being purchased. Unlike an audit of financial statements, an assurance engagement is not a statutory requirement. Additionally, accountants in public practice perform **non-assurance engagements** during which clients are provided with specialist services such as tax or IT systems advice.

Compliance with the fundamental principles could be threatened by a wide range of circumstances for accountants in practice. The nature and significance of the threats may differ depending on whether they arise in relation to the provision of services to a financial statement audit client, an assurance client or a non-assurance client.

Threat	Examples
Self-interest	Having a financial interest in a client
Self-review	Auditing financial statements prepared by the firm
Advocacy	Advocating the client's case in a lawsuit
Familiarity	Audit team member having family member employed by the client
Intimidation	Threats of replacement due to disagreement

There are two general categories of safeguard identified in the CIMA guidance. These are:

- Safeguards created by the profession, legislation or regulation
- Safeguards in the work environment

5.1.1 Examples of safeguards created by the profession, legislation or regulation

- Educational training and experience requirements for entry into the profession
- Continuing professional development requirements
- Corporate governance regulations
- Professional standards
- Professional or regulatory monitoring and disciplinary procedures
- External review by a legally empowered third party of the reports, returns, communication or information produced by a professional accountant

5.1.2 Examples of safeguards in the work environment

Work environment safeguards comprise firm-wide safeguards and engagement specific safeguards.

Firm-wide safeguards could include the following.

- Leadership of the firm that stresses the importance of compliance with the fundamental principles and acting in the public interest
- Policies and procedures to implement and monitor quality control of engagements
- Documented policies regarding the identification of threats to compliance with the fundamental principles, the evaluation of the significance of these threats and the identification and the application of safeguards to eliminate or reduce the threats, other than those that are clearly insignificant, to an acceptable level
- Documented internal policies and procedures requiring compliance with the fundamental principles
- Policies and procedures that will enable the identification of interests or relationships between the firm or members of engagement teams and clients
- Policies and procedures to monitor and, if necessary, manage the reliance on revenue received from a single client
- Using different partners and engagement teams with separate reporting lines for the provision of non-assurance services to an assurance client
- Policies and procedures to prohibit individuals who are not members of an engagement team from inappropriately influencing the outcome of the engagement
- Timely communication of a firm's policies and procedures, including any changes to them, to all partners and professional staff, and appropriate training and education on such policies and procedures
- Designating a member of senior management to be responsible for overseeing the adequate functioning of the firm's quality control system
- Advising partners and professional staff of those assurance clients and related entities from which they must be independent
- A disciplinary mechanism to promote compliance with policies and procedures
- Published policies and procedures to encourage and empower staff to communicate to senior levels within the firm any issue relating to compliance with the fundamental principles that concerns them

Engagement specific safeguards could include the following.

- Involving an additional professional accountant to review the work done or otherwise advise as necessary
- Consulting an independent third party, such as a committee of independent directors, a professional regulatory body or another professional accountant
- Discussing ethical issues with those charged with governance of the client
- Disclosing to those charged with governance of the client the nature of services provided and extent of fees charged
- Involving another firm to perform or reperform part of the engagement
- Rotating senior assurance team personnel

Exam skills

Remember in this exam, it is important that you can apply the spirit of the guidance to a given situation rather than just learning and regurgitating the guidance.

5.2 Self-interest threat

The CIMA *Code of Ethics for Professional Accountants* highlights a great number of areas in which a self-interest threat to the fundamental principles might arise.

5.2.1 Financial interests

KEY TERM

FINANCIAL INTERESTS exist where an assurance firm has a financial interest in a client's affairs, for example, the firm owns shares in the client, or is a trustee of a trust that holds shares in the client.

A financial interest in a client constitutes a substantial self-interest threat. **The parties listed below are not allowed to own a direct financial interest or an indirect material financial interest in a client:**

- The **assurance firm**
- **Partners in the same office** as the engagement partner (and their immediate families)
- A **member of the assurance team**
- An **immediate family member of a member of the assurance team**

The following safeguards will therefore be relevant:

- Disposing of the interest
- Removing the individual from the team if required
- Keeping the those charged with governance at the client informed of the situation
- Using an independent partner to review work carried out if necessary

5.2.2 Close business relationships

Examples of when a firm and client have an inappropriately close business relationship include:

- Having a **material financial interest** in a joint venture with the assurance client
- **Arrangements to combine one or more services or products** of the firm with one or more services or products of the assurance client and to market the package with reference to both parties
- **Distribution or marketing arrangements** under which the firm acts as distributor or marketer of the assurance client's products or services or vice versa

Again, it will be necessary to judge the materiality of the interest and therefore its significance. However, unless the interest is **clearly insignificant**, an assurance provider should not participate in such a venture with a client. Appropriate safeguards are therefore to end the assurance provision or to terminate the (other) business relationship.

5.2.3 Employment with assurance clients

It is possible that staff might transfer between a firm and a client, or that negotiations or interviews to facilitate such movement might take place. Both situations are a threat to independence:

- A staff member might be **motivated by a desire to impress a future possible employer** (objectivity is therefore affected)
- A former partner turned Finance Director has **too much knowledge of the assurance firm's systems** and procedures

The extent of the threat to independence depends on various factors, such as the **role** the individual has taken up at the client, the **position of the individual** within the assurance team previously, the length of time that has passed since the individual was a member of the assurance team and the amount of involvement the individual will have with the assurance team.

Various safeguards might be considered:

- Considering **modifying the assurance plan**
- Ensuring the assurance team assigned is of **sufficient experience** in relation to the individual who has joined the assurance client
- Involving an **additional professional accountant** not involved with the engagement to review the work done
- Carrying out a **quality control review** of the engagement

5.2.4 Partner on client board

A partner or employee of an assurance firm should **not serve on the board** of an assurance client. It may be acceptable for a partner or an employee of an assurance firm to perform the role of company secretary for an assurance client, depending on the jurisdiction as this work is mainly administrative.

5.2.5 Family and personal relationships

Family or close personal relationships between assurance firm and client staff could seriously threaten independence. Each situation has to be evaluated individually. Factors to consider are:

- The role of the professional on the assurance team
- The closeness of the relationship
- The role the immediate family member holds with assurance client

When an immediate family member of a member of the assurance team is a **director, an officer or an employee of the assurance client** in a position to exert direct and significant influence over the assurance engagement, the individual should be removed from the assurance team.

The firm should also consider whether there is any threat to independence if an employee who is not a member of the assurance team has a **close family or personal relationship** with a director, an officer or an employee of an assurance client.

A firm should have **quality control policies and procedures** under which staff should disclose if a close family member employed by the client is promoted within the client.

5.2.6 Gifts and hospitality

Unless the value of the gift/hospitality is clearly insignificant, a firm or a member of an assurance team should not accept it.

5.2.7 Loans and guarantees

The advice on loans and guarantees falls into two categories:

- The client is a bank or other similar institution
- Other situations

If a **lending institution client** lends an **immaterial amount to** an assurance firm or member of assurance team on normal commercial terms, there is no threat to independence. If the loan were material it would be necessary to apply safeguards to bring the risk to an acceptable level. A suitable safeguard is likely to be an **independent review** (by a partner from another office in the firm).

Loans to members of the assurance team from a bank or other lending institution client are likely to be **material to the individual,** but provided that they are on normal commercial terms, these do not constitute a threat to independence.

However an assurance firm or individual on the assurance engagement should not enter into any loan or guarantee arrangement with a client that is not a bank or similar institution.

5.2.8 Overdue fees

In a situation where there are overdue fees, the assurance firm runs the risk of, in effect, making a loan to a client, whereupon the guidance above becomes relevant.

Assurance firms should guard against fees building up and being significant by **discussing the issues with the audit committee or others charged with governance,** and, if necessary, the possibility of resigning if overdue fees are not paid.

5.2.9 Percentage or contingent fees

KEY TERM

CONTINGENT FEES are fees calculated on a predetermined basis relating to the outcome or result of a transaction or the result of the work performed.

Ethical guidelines state that a firm should not enter into any fee arrangement for an assurance engagement under which the amount of the fee is contingent on the result of the assurance work or on items that are the subject matter of the assurance engagement. It would also usually be inappropriate to accept a contingent fee for non assurance work from an assurance client.

5.2.10 High percentage of fees

A firm should be alert to the situation arising where when the **total fees generated by an assurance client** represent a **large proportion of a firm's total fees**. Factors such as the **structure of the firm** and the length of time it has been trading will be relevant in determining whether there is a threat to independence. It is also necessary to beware of situations where the fees generated by an assurance client are a large proportion of the revenue of an individual partner.

Safeguards in these situations might include:

- Discussing the issues with the audit committee or others charged with governance
- Taking steps to reduce the dependency on the client
- External quality control reviews
- Consulting a third party such as a professional regulatory body or another professional accountant

5.2.11 Lowballing

When a firm quotes a significantly lower fee level for an assurance service than would have been charged by the predecessor firm, there is a significant self-interest threat. If the firm's tender is successful, the firm must apply safeguards such as:

- Making the client aware of the terms of engagement and, in particular, the basis on which fees are charged and which services are covered by the quoted fee
- Assigning appropriate time and qualified staff

5.2.12 Recruitment

Recruiting senior management for an assurance client, particularly those able to affect the subject matter of an assurance engagement creates may create current or future self-interest, familiarity and intimidation threat for the assurance firm.

Assurance providers must not make management decisions for the client. Their involvement could be limited to reviewing a shortlist of candidates, providing that the client has drawn up the criteria by which they are to be selected.

5.3 Self-review threat

The key area in which there is likely to be a self-review threat is where an assurance firm provides services other than assurance services to an assurance client (providing multiple services).

5.3.1 Recent service with an assurance client

An employee may move from an assurance client to an assurance firm. To include this individual as part of the assurance team may create a self-review threat. For example, the individual may have prepared financial statements at the assurance client which they are required to review as part of the assurance engagement.

For this reason, an individual who has served as a **director or officer of the assurance client** during the period covered by the assurance report, or has been an **employee** in a position to exert **direct and significant influence** over the subject matter information of the assurance engagement should not be a member of the assurance team.

If an individual had been closely involved with the client prior to the period covered by the assurance report, the assurance firm should evaluate the significance of the threats created and apply appropriate safeguards, such as:

- Involving an additional professional accountant to review the work done by the individual as part of the assurance team

- Discussing the issue with those charged with governance, such as the audit committee

5.3.2 Provision of non-assurance services to assurance clients

For assurance clients, accountants are not allowed to:

- Authorise, execute or consummate a transaction
- Determine which recommendation of the firm should be implemented
- Report in a management role to those charged with governance

Having custody of an assurance client's assets, supervising assurance client employees in the performance of their normal duties, and preparing source documents on behalf of the client also pose significant self-review threats which should be addressed by safeguards. These could be:

- Ensuring non assurance team staff are used for these roles
- Involving an independent professional accountant to advise
- Policies and procedures to prohibit staff making management decisions for clients
- Making appropriate disclosures to those charged with governance
- Obtaining acknowledgement from the assurance client of responsibility for the results of work carried out by the firm

5.3.3 Preparing accounting records and financial statements

There is clearly a significant risk of a self-review threat if a firm prepares **accounting records and financial statements** and then audits them. On the other hand auditors routinely assist management with the preparation of financial statements and give advice about accounting treatments and journal entries.

Therefore, audit firms must analyse the risks arising and put safeguards in place to ensure that the risk is at an acceptable level. Safeguards include:

- **Using staff members other than assurance team members** to carry out work
- **Obtaining client approval for any proposed journals entries** or other changes affecting the financial statements

The rules are more stringent when the client is listed. Firms should not prepare accounts or financial statements for listed entities, unless an emergency situation arises.

For any client, audit firms are also not allowed to:

- Determine or change journal entries without client approval
- Authorise or approve transactions
- Prepare source documents

5.3.4 Valuation services

KEY TERM

A VALUATION comprises the making of assumptions with regard to future developments, the application of certain methodologies and techniques, and the combination of both in order to compute a certain value, or range of values, for an asset, a liability or for a business as a whole.

If an audit firm performs a valuation which will be included in financial statements audited by the firm, a self-review threat arises.

Audit firms should not carry out valuations on matters that will be material to the financial statements.

If the valuation is for an immaterial matter, the audit firm should **apply safeguards** to ensure that the risk is reduced to an acceptable level. Matters to consider when applying safeguards are the extent of the audit client's knowledge of the relevant matters in making the valuation and the degree of judgement involved, how much use is made of established methodologies and the degree of uncertainty in the valuation. Safeguards include:

- Second partner review
- Confirming that the client understands the valuation and the assumptions used
- Ensuring the client acknowledges responsibility for the valuation
- Using separate personnel for the valuation and the audit

5.3.5 Taxation services

The **provision of taxation services** is generally not seen to impair independence.

5.3.6 Internal audit services

A firm may provide internal audit services to an audit client in most jurisdictions, but not in America under Sarbanes-Oxley. However, it should ensure that the client **acknowledges its responsibility** for **establishing, maintaining and monitoring the system** of internal controls. It may be appropriate to use safeguards such as ensuring that an employee of the client is designated as responsible for internal audit activities and that the board or internal audit committee approve all the work that internal audit does.

5.3.7 Corporate finance

Certain aspects of corporate finance will create self-review threats that cannot be reduced to an acceptable level by safeguards. Therefore, assurance firms are **not allowed to promote, deal in or underwrite** an assurance client's shares. They are also not allowed to commit an assurance client to the terms of a transaction or consummate a transaction on the client's behalf.

Other corporate finance services, such as assisting a client in defining corporate strategies, assisting in identifying possible sources of capital and providing structuring advice may be acceptable in jurisdictions other than the USA, providing that safeguards are in place, such as using different teams of staff, and ensuring no management decisions are taken on behalf of the client.

5.3.8 Other services

The audit firm might sell a variety of other services to audit clients, such as:

- IT systems services
- Temporary staff cover
- Litigation support services
- Legal services

The assurance firm should consider whether there are any barriers to independence. Examples include the firm being asked to design internal control IT systems, which it would then review as part of its audit, or the firm being asked to provide an accountant to cover the chief accountant's maternity leave. The firm should consider whether the threat to independence could be reduced by appropriate safeguards. Again the rules in the USA are stricter than elsewhere.

5.4 Advocacy threat

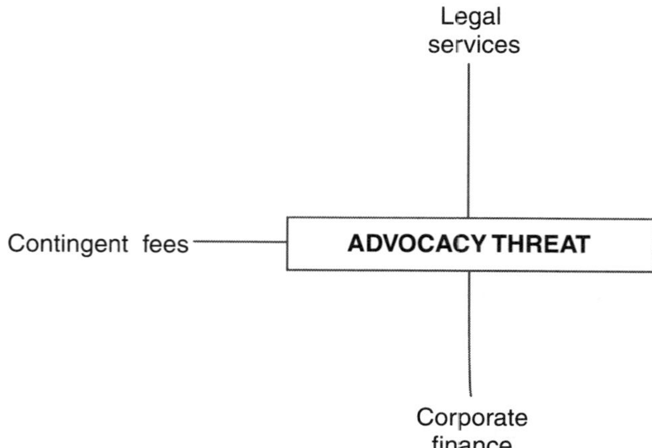

An advocacy threat arises in certain situations where the assurance firm is in a position of **taking the client's part** in a dispute or somehow **acting as their advocate.** The most obvious instances of this would be when a firm offered legal services to a client and, say, defended them in a legal case or provided evidence on their behalf as an expert witness. An advocacy threat might also arise if the firm carried out corporate finance work for the client, for example, if the audit firm was involved in advice on debt reconstruction and negotiated with the bank on the client's behalf.

As with the other threats above, the firm has to appraise the risk and apply safeguards as necessary. Relevant safeguards might be using **different departments** in the firm to carry out the work and making disclosures to the audit committee. Remember, the ultimate option is always to withdraw from an engagement if the risk to independence is too high.

5.5 Familiarity threat

A familiarity threat is where independence is jeopardised by the audit firm and its staff becoming over familiar with the client and its staff. There is a substantial risk of loss of professional scepticism in such circumstances.

We have already discussed some examples of when this risk arises, because very often a familiarity threat arises in conjunction with a self-interest threat.

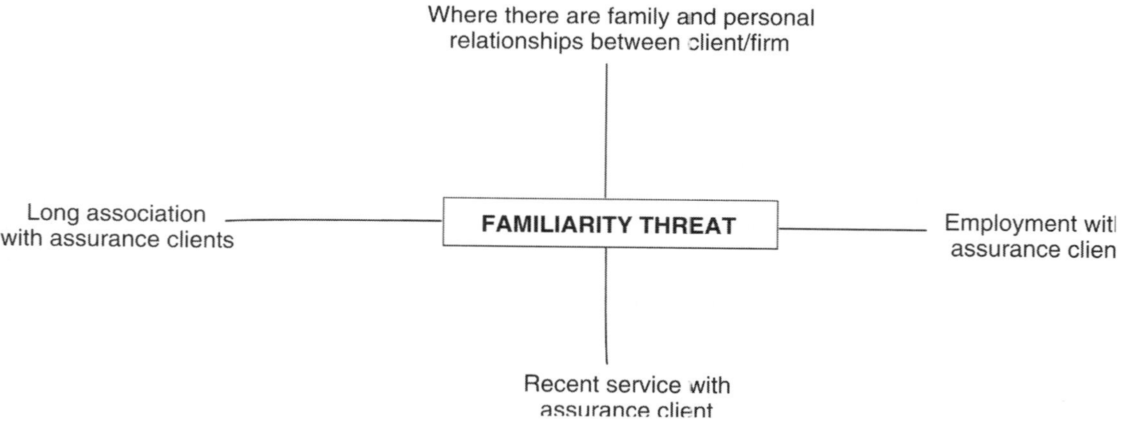

5.5.1 Long association of senior personnel with assurance clients

Senior members of staff at an audit firm having a long association with a client is a significant threat to independence. All firms should therefore monitor the relationship between staff and established clients and use safeguards to independence such as **rotating senior staff off the assurance team**, involving **second partners** to carry out reviews and obtaining independent (but internal) quality control reviews.

The CIMA *Code* sets out specific rules for financial statement audit clients that are listed entities:

- The engagement partner and the individual responsible for the engagement quality control review should be rotated after serving in either capacity, or a combination of the two, for a predefined period, normally no more than **seven years**, and should not return to the engagement until a period of **two years** has elapsed.
- **When an entity becomes a listed entity**, the length of time the staff involved with the audit have been involved should be taken into consideration, but **the engagement partner, or individual responsible for quality control review should only continue in those positions for another two years**.

5.6 Intimidation threat

An intimidation threat arises when members of the assurance team have reason to be intimidated by client staff.

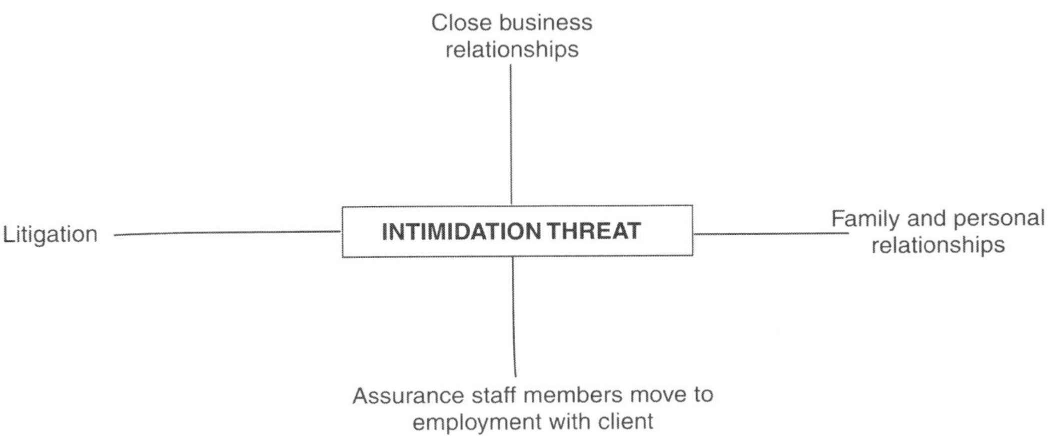

These are also examples of self-interest threats, largely because intimidation may only arise significantly when the assurance firm has something to lose.

5.6.1 Actual and threatened litigation

The most obvious example of an intimidation threat is when the client threatens to sue, or indeed sues, the assurance firm for work that has been done previously. The firm is then faced with the **risk of losing the client, bad publicity** and the **possibility that they will be found to have been negligent,** which will lead to further problems. This could lead for example to the firm being under pressure to produce an unqualified audit report when they have been qualified in the past.

Generally, assurance firms should seek to avoid such situations arising. If they do arise, factors to consider are:

- The materiality of the litigation
- The nature of the assurance engagement
- Whether the litigation relates to a prior assurance engagement

The following safeguards could be considered:

- Disclosing to the audit committee the nature and extent of the litigation
- Removing specific affected individuals from the engagement team
- Involving an additional professional accountant on the team to review work

However, if the litigation is at all serious, it may be necessary to **resign from the engagement**, as the threat to independence is so great.

5.7 Second opinions

There is nothing to stop a company director talking to a second firm of auditors about treatments of matters in the financial statements. However, the firm being asked for a second opinion should be very careful, because it is very possible that the opinion they form could be incorrect anyway if the director has not given them all the relevant information. For that reason, firms giving a second opinion should ensure that they **seek permission** to communicate with the existing auditor and they are appraised of all the facts. If permission is not given, the second auditors should consider whether it is appropriate to comment on the audit opinion.

5.8 Conflicts of interest

Audit firms should take reasonable steps to identify circumstances that could pose a conflict of interest. This is because a conflict of interest could result in the ethical code being breached (for example, if it results in a self-interest threat arising).

A conflict between members' and clients' interests might arise if members compete directly with a client, or have a joint venture or similar with a company that is in competition with the client.

Alternatively, there may be a conflict between the interests of different clients. Assurance firms can have clients who are in competition with each other. However, the firm should ensure that it is **not the subject of a dispute** between the clients. It must also manage its work so that the interests of one client do not adversely affect the other client.

5.8.1 Managing conflicts between clients' interests

When considering whether to accept a client or when there is a change in a client's circumstances, assurance firms should take reasonable steps to ascertain whether there is a **conflict of interest** or if there is likely to be one in the future.

Disclosure is the most important safeguard in connection of conflicts between clients' interests. Safeguards would usually include:

- **Notifying the client** of the interest/activities that may **cause a conflict of interest** and obtaining their consent to act in the circumstances, or
- **Notifying all known relevant parties** that the professional accountant in public practice is **acting for two or more parties** in respect of a matter where their respective interests are in conflict, and obtaining their consent so to act, or
- Notifying the client that the professional accountant in public practice **does not act exclusively for any one client** in the provision of proposed services, and obtaining their consent so to act

Other safeguards

- Using separate engagement teams
- Procedures to prevent access of information (such as special passwords)
- Clear guidelines for the respective teams on issues of security and confidentiality
- The use of confidentiality agreements signed by the partners and staff
- Regular review of the safeguards by an independent senior individual

If a conflict of interest poses a threat to one or more fundamental principles and cannot be eliminated or reduced to an acceptable level through the application of safeguards, the engagement should not be accepted or the accountant should resign from one or more of the conflicting engagements.

Section summary

Accountants in practice may face threats to the fundamental principles in the form of **self-review, self-interest, advocacy, familiarity and intimidation threats**. Appropriate **safeguards** must be put in place to eliminate or reduce such threats to acceptable levels.

6 Problems facing accountants in business

Introduction

This section covers the type of threat that a professional accountant in business might face and the action that should be taken if such a threat arises.

6.1 Conflicts between professional and employment obligations

Ethical guidance stresses that a professional accountant should normally support the legitimate and ethical obligations established by the employer. However the professional accountant may be pressurised to act in ways that threaten compliance with the fundamental principles. These include:

- Acting contrary to law, regulation, technical or professional standards
- Aiding unethical or illegal earnings management strategies
- Misleading auditors or regulators
- Issuing or being associated with a report that misrepresents the facts

If these problems are faced, the accountant should either obtain advice from inside the employer, an independent professional advisor, CIMA, lawyers, or use the formal procedures within the organisation.

6.2 Preparation and reporting of information

As well as complying with financial reporting standards, the professional accountant in business should aim to prepare information that describes clearly the nature of the business transactions, classifies and records information in a timely and proper manner and represents the facts accurately. If the accountant faces pressures to produce misleading information, superiors should be consulted, such as an audit committee. The accountant should not be associated with misleading information, and may need to seek legal advice or report to the appropriate authorities.

6.3 Acting with sufficient expertise

Guidance stresses that the professional accountant should only undertake tasks for which he or she has sufficient specific training or experience. Certain pressures may threaten the ability of the professional accountant to perform duties with appropriate competence and due care:

- Lack of information
- Insufficient training, experience or education
- Lack of time
- Inadequate resources

Whether this is a significant threat will depend on the other people the accountant is working with, the seniority of the accountant and the level of supervision and review of work. If the problem is serious, the accountant should take steps to remedy the situation including obtaining training, ensuring time is available and consulting with others where appropriate. Refusal to perform duties is the last resort.

6.4 Financial interests

Ethical guidance highlights financial interests as a self-interest threat to objectivity and confidentiality. In particular the temptation to manipulate price-sensitive information in order to gain financially is stressed. Financial interests may include shares, profit-related bonuses or share options.

This threat can be countered by the individual consulting with superiors and disclosing all relevant information. Having a remuneration committee composed of independent non-executive directors determining the remuneration packages of executive directors can help resolve the problems at senior levels.

6.5 Inducements

Ethical guidance highlights the possibility that accountants may be offered inducements to influence actions or decisions, encourage illegal behaviour or obtain confidential information.

The guidance points out that threats to compliance may appear to arise not only from the accountant making or accepting the inducement, but from the offer having being made in the first place. It recommends that directors or senior managers be informed, and disclosure may be made to third parties. The accountant should also disclose to senior management whether any close relatives work for competitors or suppliers.

Section summary

The accountant in business may face a variety of difficulties including conflicts between professional and employment obligations, pressure to prepare misleading information, a lack of sufficient expertise, financial interests or inducements.

Chapter Roundup

- ✓ A need for an ethical code has developed due to various stakeholders relying on accountants and their reputation. An ethical code must evolve to adapt with changing circumstances.
- ✓ Sources of ethical codes include law, religion, social attitudes, IFAC, professional bodies and employing organisations.
- ✓ The CIMA Code is a principles-based framework. There are advantages and disadvantages of a principles-based framework over a system of rules.
- ✓ The five fundamental principles are integrity, objectivity, professional competence and due care, confidentiality and professional behaviour. Compliance with these principles could be threatened by a wide range of circumstances. The professional accountant should apply safeguards to counteract these threats.
- ✓ Accountants in practice may face threats to the fundamental principles in the form of **self-review, self-interest, advocacy, familiarity and intimidation threats**. Appropriate **safeguards** must be put in place to eliminate or reduce such threats to acceptable levels.
- ✓ The accountant in business may face a variety of difficulties including conflicts between professional and employment obligations, pressure to prepare misleading information, a lack of sufficient expertise, financial interests or inducements.

Quick Quiz

1 Which of the following is not an advantage of a principles-based ethical code?

A It prevents narrow, legalistic interpretations
B It can accommodate a rapidly-changing environment
C The illustrative examples provided can be followed in all similar situations
D It prescribes minimum expected standards of behaviour

2 Fill in the blank.

.... means that a professional accountant should be straightforward and honest in all business and professional relationships.

3 Give three examples of a familiarity threat.

4 Which of the following is not a legitimate reason to disclose confidential information?

A Disclosure is permitted by law
B To protect the professional interests of an accountant in a legal investigation
C To assist a family member
D To a bank where disclosure is authorised by your employer

5 For a financial statement audit client that is a listed entity, the engagement partner should be rotated after serving in that capacity for two years.

True ☐

False ☐

6 Should a member of an assurance team accept a gift from a client?

Answers to Quick Quiz

1 C Although the examples may be good guides for conduct in many instances, circumstances will vary, so they should not be seen as totally prescriptive.

2 Integrity

3
- Making a business decision that will affect a close family member
- Long association with a business contact
- Acceptance of a gift

4 C Care should be taken not to disclose confidential information to family members.

5 False The engagement partner should be rotated after seven years.

6 No. Unless the value of the gift is clearly insignificant, a member of an assurance team should not accept it.

Answers to Questions

3.1 Ethical issues

(a) Dealing with unpleasantly authoritarian governments can be supported on the grounds that it **contributes to economic growth and prosperity** and all the benefits they bring to society in both countries concerned. It can also be opposed as it is **contributing to the continuation of the regime,** and is **fundamentally repugnant**.

(b) Honesty in advertising is an important problem. Many products are promoted exclusively on image. Deliberately creating the impression that purchasing a particular product will enhance the happiness, success and sex-appeal of the buyer can be attacked as **dishonest.** It can be defended on the grounds that the supplier is actually **selling a fantasy or dream** rather than a physical article.

(c) Dealings with employees are coloured by the **opposing views of corporate responsibility and individual rights**. The idea of a job as property to be defended has now disappeared from labour relations in many countries, but corporate decisions that lead to redundancies are still deplored. This is because of the obvious **impact of sudden unemployment on aspirations and living standards**, even when the employment market is buoyant. Nevertheless businesses have to consider the cost of employing labour as well as its productive capacity.

(d) The main problems with payments or gifts to officials are making distinction between those that should never be made, and those that can be made in certain cultural circumstances.

(i) **Extortion**. Foreign officials have been known to threaten companies with the complete closure of their local operations unless suitable payments are made.

(ii) **Bribery**. This is payments for services to which a company is not legally entitled. There are some fine distinctions to be drawn; for example, some managers regard political contributions as bribery.

(iii) **Grease money**. Multinational companies are sometimes unable to obtain services to which they are legally entitled because of deliberate stalling by local officials. Cash payments to the right people may then be enough to oil the machinery of bureaucracy.

(iv) **Gifts**. In some cultures (such as Japan) gifts are regarded as an essential part of civilised negotiation, even in circumstances where to Western eyes they might appear ethically dubious. Managers operating in such a culture may feel at liberty to adopt the local customs.

3.2 Employee behaviour

Here are some suggestions.

- Recruitment and selection policies and procedures
- Induction and training
- Objectives and reward schemes
- Ethical codes
- Threat of ethical audit

Now try these questions from the Exam Question Bank

Number	Level	Marks	Time
Q11	Examination	5	9 mins

SINGLE COMPANY FINANCIAL ACCOUNTS

Part B

PRESENTATION OF PUBLISHED FINANCIAL STATEMENTS

This chapter covers preparation of the accounts of non-group limited companies. It lays out the IAS 1 (revised) *Presentation of financial statements*, format for the statement of financial position and statement of comprehensive income and the disclosures required in the notes to the accounts. The best way to gain familiarity with these formats and disclosures is by looking through the published accounts of limited companies and by doing practice questions.

You will cover group companies in Part C of this Study Text.

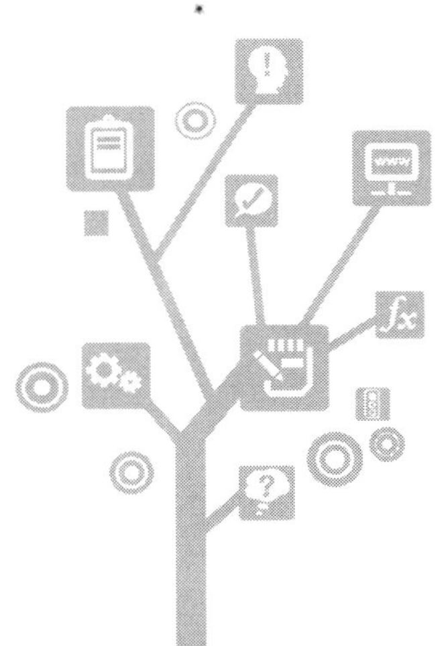

topic list	learning outcomes	syllabus references	ability required
1 Purpose of financial statements	C1(a)	C1(i)	application
2 IAS 1 (revised) *Presentation of financial statements*	C1(a)	C1(i),(iii)	application
3 Statement of financial position	C1(a)	C1(i)	application
4 The current/non-current distinction	C1(a)	C1(i)	application
5 Statement of comprehensive income	C1(a)	C1(i)	application
6 Income statement	C1(a)	C1(i)	application
7 Changes in equity	C1(a)	C1(i)	application
8 Notes to the financial statements	C1(a)	C1(i)	application

1 Purpose of financial statements

Introduction

This section introduces financial statements and discusses fair presentation.

The purpose of financial statements is to provide users with information about the financial position, financial performance and cash flows of an entity. They show the results of managements' stewardship. Per IAS 1, financial statements provide information about an entity's:

(a) assets;
(b) liabilities;
(c) equity;
(d) income and expenses, including gains and losses;
(e) other changes in equity; and
(f) cash flows.

1.1 Fair presentation

Financial statements should **present fairly** the financial position, financial performance and cash flows of an entity. This requires:

- Representing transactions in accordance with the recognition criteria for assets, liabilities, income, expenses and equity set out in the *Framework.*
- Compliance with applicable IFRSs/IASs, and a statement of compliance.
- Selection, application and disclosure of accounting policies in accordance with IAS 8.

In the rare circumstances where management decides that compliance with a standard would not present a true and fair picture, they can depart from that requirements in order to achieve fair presentation. They should disclose:

- that the financial statements are a fair presentation of the entity's position, performance and cash flows
- that is has complied with all other relevant IFRSs
- details of the departure from an IFRS, why it was necessary and the financial impact of the departure

Section summary

Financial statements present the financial position and financial performance of an entity.

2 IAS 1 (revised) *Presentation of financial statements*

Introduction

In this section we look at IAS 1 (revised) *Presentation of financial statements* . This standard gives substantial guidance on the form and content of published financial statements and details the statement of financial position and statement of comprehensive income (the statement of cash flows is covered by IAS 7). It was revised in September 2007.

2.1 Profit or loss for the period

The statement of comprehensive income is the most significant indicator of a company's financial performance. So it is important to ensure that it is not misleading.

The statement of comprehensive income will be misleading if costs incurred in the current year are deducted not from the current year profits but from the balance of accumulated profits brought forward. This presents the current year's results more favourably.

IAS 1 stipulates that all items of income and expense recognised in a period shall be included in profit or loss unless a **Standard** or an **Interpretation** requires otherwise.

Circumstances where items may be excluded from profit or loss for the current year include the correction of errors and the effect of changes in accounting policies. These are covered in IAS 8.

2.2 How items are disclosed

IAS 1 specifies disclosures of certain items in certain ways.

- Some items must appear on the **face** of the statement of financial position or statement of comprehensive income
- Other items can appear in a **note to the financial statements** instead
- **Recommended formats** are given which entities may or may not follow, depending on their circumstances

Obviously, disclosures specified by **other standards** must also be made, and we will mention the necessary disclosures when we cover each statement in turn. Disclosures in both IAS 1 and other standards must be made either on the face of the statement or in the notes unless otherwise stated, ie disclosures cannot be made in an accompanying commentary or report.

2.3 Identification of financial statements

As a result of the above point, it is most important that entities **distinguish the financial statements** very clearly from any other information published with them. This is because all IASs/IFRSs apply *only* to the financial statements (ie the main statements and related notes), so readers of the annual report must be able to differentiate between the parts of the report which are prepared under IFRSs, and other parts which are not.

The entity should **identify each** financial statement and the notes very clearly. IAS 1 also requires disclosure of the following information in a prominent position. If necessary it should be repeated wherever it is felt to be of use to the reader in his understanding of the information presented.

- **Name** of the reporting entity (or other means of identification)
- Whether the accounts cover the **single entity** only or a group of entities
- The **date of the end of the reporting period** or the period covered by the financial statements (as appropriate)
- The **presentation currency**
- The **level of rounding** used in presenting amounts in the financial statements

Judgement must be used to determine the best method of presenting this information. In particular, the standard suggests that the approach to this will be very different when the financial statements are communicated electronically.

The **level of rounding** is important, as presenting figures in thousands or millions of units makes the figures more understandable. The level of rounding must be disclosed, however, and it should not obscure necessary details or make the information less relevant.

2.4 Reporting period

It is normal for entities to present financial statements **annually** and IAS 1 states that they should be prepared at least as often as this. If (unusually) the end of an entity's reporting period is changed, for whatever reason, the period for which the statements are presented will be less or more than one year. In such cases the entity should also disclose:

(a) the **reason(s) why** a period other than one year is used; and
(b) the fact that the comparative figures given **are not in fact comparable**.

For practical purposes, some entities prefer to use a period which **approximates to a year**, eg 52 weeks, and the IAS allows this approach as it will produce statements not materially different from those produced on an annual basis.

2.5 Timeliness

If the publication of financial statements is delayed too long after the reporting period, their usefulness will be severely diminished. The standard states that entities should be able to produce their financial statements **within six months of the end of the reporting period.** An entity with consistently complex operations cannot use this as a reason for its failure to report on a timely basis. Local legislation and market regulation imposes specific deadlines on certain entities.

IAS 1 looks at the statement of financial position and statement of comprehensive income. We will not give all the detailed disclosures as some are outside the scope of your syllabus. Instead we will look at a **'proforma' set of accounts** based on the Standard.

Section summary

IAS 1 covers the **form and content** of financial statements. The main components are:

- Statement of financial position
- Statement of comprehensive income
- Statement of changes in equity
- Statement of cash flows
- Notes to the financial statements

Each component must be **identified clearly**.

3 Statement of financial position

Introduction

First of all we will look at the **suggested format** of the statement of financial position (given in an appendix to the standard) and then at further disclosures required.

Note that the examples given by IAS 1 (revised) are for **group** financial statements. In this chapter we are looking at **single entity** financial statements so some items, such as non-controlling interest, do not apply.

3.1 Statement of financial position example

The example given by IAS 1 revised is as follows.

XYZ GROUP – STATEMENT OF FINANCIAL POSITION AT 31 DECEMBER

	20X9	*20X8*
	$'000	$'000
Assets		
Non-current assets		
Property, plant and equipment		
Goodwill	X	X
Other intangible assets	X	X
Investments in associates	X	X
Available-for-sale financial assets	X	X
	X	X
Current assets	X	X
Inventories	X	X
Trade receivables	X	X
Other current assets	X	X
Cash and cash equivalents	X	X
	X	X
Total assets	X	X
Equity and liabilities		
Equity attributable to owners of the parent		
Share capital	X	X
Retained earnings	X	X
Other components of equity	X	X
	X	X
Non-controlling interest	X	X
Total equity	X	X
Non-current liabilities		
Long-term borrowings	X	X
Deferred tax	X	X
Long-term provisions	X	X
Total non-current liabilities	X	X
Current liabilities		
Trade and other payables	X	X
Short-term borrowings	X	X
Current portion of long-term borrowings	X	X
Current tax payable	X	X
Short-term provisions	X	X
Total current liabilities	X	X
Total liabilities	X	X
Total equity and liabilities	X	X

IAS 1 (revised) specifies various items which must appear on the **face of the statement of financial position** as a minimum disclosure.

(a) Property, plant and equipment
(b) Investment property
(c) Intangible assets
(d) Financial assets (excluding amounts shown under (e), (h) and (i))
(e) Investments accounted for using the equity method
(f) Biological assets
(g) Inventories
(h) Trade and other receivables
(i) Cash and cash equivalents

(j) Assets classified as held for sale under IFRS 5
(k) Trade and other payables
(l) Provisions
(m) Financial liabilities (other than (j) and (k))
(n) Current tax liabilities and assets as in IAS 12
(o) Deferred tax liabilities and assets
(p) Liabilities included in disposal groups under IFRS 5
(q) Non-controlling interests
(r) Issued capital and reserves

Any **other line items**, headings or sub-totals should be shown on the face of the statement of financial position when it is necessary for an understanding of the entity's financial position.

The example shown above is for illustration only (although we will follow the format in this Study Text). The IAS, however, does not prescribe the order or format in which the items listed should be presented. It simply states that they **must be presented separately** because they are so different in nature or function from each other.

Whether additional items are presented separately depends on judgements based on the assessment of the following factors.

(a) **Nature and liquidity of assets and their materiality**. Thus goodwill and assets arising from development expenditure will be presented separately, as will monetary/non-monetary assets and current/non-current assets.

(b) **Function within the entity.** Operating and financial assets, inventories, receivables and cash and cash equivalents are therefore shown separately.

(c) **Amounts, nature and timing of liabilities**. Interest-bearing and non-interest-bearing liabilities and provisions will be shown separately, classified as current or non-current as appropriate.

The standard also requires separate presentation where **different measurement bases** are used for assets and liabilities which differ in nature or function. According to IAS 16, for example, it is permitted to carry certain items of property, plant and equipment at cost or at a revalued amount.

Exam skills

Exam questions usually require you to produce a statement of financial position from a trial balance. Make sure you know the correct format and which items need to appear on the face of the statement of financial position.

3.2 Information presented either on the face of the statement of financial position or by note

Further **sub-classification** of the line items listed above should be disclosed either on the face of the statement of financial position or in the notes. The classification will depend upon the nature of the entity's operations. As well as each item being sub-classified by its nature, any amounts payable to or receivable from any **group company or other related party** should also be disclosed separately.

The sub-classification details will in part depend on the requirements of IFRSs. The size, nature and function of the amounts involved will also be important and the factors listed above should be considered. **Disclosures** will vary from item to item and IAS 1 gives the following examples.

(a) **Property, plant and equipment** are classified by class as described in IAS 16, *Property, plant and equipment*

(b) **Receivables** are analysed between amounts receivable from trade customers, other members of the group, receivables from related parties, prepayments and other amounts

(c) **Inventories** are sub-classified, in accordance with IAS 2 *Inventories,* into classifications such as merchandise, production supplies, materials, work in progress and finished goods

(d) **Provisions** are analysed showing separately provisions for employee benefit costs and any other items classified in a manner appropriate to the entity's operations

(e) **Equity capital and reserves** are analysed showing separately the various classes of paid in capital, share premium and reserves

The standard then lists some **specific disclosures** which must be made, either on the face of the statement of financial position or in the related notes.

(a) **Share capital disclosures (**for each class of share capital)

- (i) Number of shares authorised
- (ii) Number of shares issued and fully paid, and issued but not fully paid
- (iii) Par value per share, or that the shares have no par value
- (iv) Reconciliation of the number of shares outstanding at the beginning and at the end of the year
- (v) Rights, preferences and restrictions attaching to that class including restrictions on the distribution of dividends and the repayment of capital
- (vi) Shares in the entity held by the entity itself or by related group companies
- (vii) Shares reserved for issuance under options and sales contracts, including the terms and amounts

(b) Description of the nature and purpose of **each reserve** within owners' equity

Some types of entity have no share capital, eg partnerships. Such entities should disclose information which is **equivalent** to that listed above. This means disclosing the movement during the period in each category of equity interest and any rights, preferences or restrictions attached to each category of equity interest.

Section summary

IAS 1 suggests a format for the statement of financial position. Certain items are specified for **disclosure on the face of the financial statements**.

4 The current/non-current distinction

Introduction

In this section we will explain the difference between current and non-current assets and liabilities on the statement of financial position.

4.1 The current/non-current distinction

An entity must present **current** and **non-current** assets as separate classifications on the face of the statement of financial position. A presentation based on liquidity should only be used where it provides more relevant and reliable information, in which case all assets and liabilities must be presented broadly **in order of liquidity**.

In either case, the entity should disclose any portion of an asset or liability which is expected to be recovered or settled **after more than twelve months**. For example, for an amount receivable which is due in instalments over 18 months, the portion due after more than twelve months must be disclosed.

The IAS emphasises how helpful information on the **operating cycle** is to users of financial statements. Where there is a clearly defined operating cycle within which the entity supplies goods or services, then information disclosing those net assets that are continuously circulating as **working capital** is useful.

This distinguishes them from those net assets used in the long-term operations of the entity. Assets that are expected to be realised and liabilities that are due for settlement within the operating cycle are therefore highlighted.

The liquidity and solvency of an entity is also indicated by information about the **maturity dates** of assets and liabilities. As we will see later, IFRS 7 *Financial instruments: disclosures* requires disclosure of maturity dates of both financial assets and financial liabilities. (Financial assets include trade and other receivables; financial liabilities include trade and other payables.) In the case of non-monetary assets, eg inventories, such information is also useful.

4.2 Current assets

KEY TERM

An asset should be classified as a CURRENT ASSET when it:

- is expected to be realised in, or is held for sale or consumption in, the normal course of the entity's operating cycle; or
- is held primarily for trading purposes or for the short-term and expected to be realised within twelve months of the end of the reporting period; or
- is cash or a cash equivalent asset which is not restricted in its use.

All other assets should be classified as non-current assets. *(IAS 1)*

Non-current assets includes tangible, intangible, operating and financial assets of a long-term nature. Other terms with the same meaning can be used (eg 'fixed', 'long-term').

The term 'operating cycle' has been used several times above and the standard defines it as follows.

KEY TERM

The OPERATING CYCLE of an entity is the time between the acquisition of assets for processing and their realisation in cash or cash equivalents. *(IAS 1)*

Current assets therefore include inventories and trade receivables that are sold, consumed and realised as part of the normal operating cycle. **This is the case even where they are not expected to be realised within twelve months**.

Current assets will also include **marketable securities** if they are expected to be realised within twelve months after the reporting period. If expected to be realised later, they should be included in non-current assets.

4.3 Current liabilities

KEY TERM

A liability should be classified as a CURRENT LIABILITY when it:

- Is expected to be settled in the normal course of the entity's operating cycle; or
- Is held primarily for the purpose of trading; or
- Is due to be settled within twelve months after the reporting period; or
- The entity does not have an unconditional right to defer settlement of the liability for at least twelve months after the reporting period.

All other liabilities should be classified as non-current liabilities. *(IAS 1)*

The categorisation of current liabilities is very similar to that of current assets. Thus, some current liabilities are part of the **working capital** used in the normal operating cycle of the business (ie trade payables and accruals for employee and other operating costs). Such items will be classed as current liabilities **even where they are due to be settled more than twelve months after the end of the reporting period.**

There are also current liabilities which are not settled as part of the normal operating cycle, but which are due to be settled within twelve months of the end of the reporting period. These include bank overdrafts, income taxes, other non-trade payables and the current portion of interest-bearing liabilities. Any interest-bearing liabilities that are used to finance working capital on a long-term basis, and that are not due for settlement within twelve months, should be classed as **non-current liabilities**.

A **non-current financial liability** due to be **settled within twelve months** of the end of the reporting period should be classified as a **current liability**, even if an agreement to refinance, or to reschedule payments, on a long-term basis is completed after the end of the reporting period and before the financial statements are authorised for issue.

Section summary

You should appreciate the distinction between **current and non-current** assets and liabilities and their different treatments.

5 Statement of comprehensive income

Introduction

The revision of IAS 1 in 2007 introduced a new statement, the statement of comprehensive income. This shows both income statement items and items which would previously have gone to the statement of recognised income and expense. This section looks at the its format.

5.1 Statement of comprehensive income – format

IAS 1 (revised) allows income and expense items to be presented either:

(a) in a single statement of comprehensive income; or
(b) in two statements: a separate income statement and statement of other comprehensive income.

The format for a single statement of comprehensive income is shown as follows in the standard. The section down to 'profit for the year' can be shown as a separate 'income statement' with an additional 'statement of other comprehensive income'.

KEY POINT

In this text where we are dealing with items which only affect the income statement we have referred to the 'income statement'.

XYZ GROUP – STATEMENT OF COMPREHENSIVE INCOME FOR THE YEAR ENDED 31 DECEMBER 20X9

	20X9	*20X8*
	$'000	$'000
Revenue	X	X
Cost of sales	X	X
Gross profit	X	X
Other income	X	X
Distribution costs	X	X
Administrative expenses	X	X
Other expenses	X	X
Finance costs	X	X
Share of profit of associates	X	X
Profit before tax	X	X
Income tax expense	X	X
Profit for the year from continuing operations	X	X
Loss for the year from discontinued operations	X	X
Profit for the year	X	X
Other comprehensive income:		
Available-for-sale financial assets	X	X
Gains on property revaluation	X	X
Share of other comprehensive income of associates	X	X
Income tax relating to components of other comprehensive inccme	X	X
Other comprehensive income for the year, net of tax	X	X
Total comprehensive income for the year	X	X
Profit attributable to:		
Owners of the parent	X	X
Non-controlling interest	X	X
	X	X
Total comprehensive income attributable to		
Owners of the parent	X	X
Non-controlling interest	X	X
	X	X
Earnings per share (in currency units)	X	X

Companies are given the option of presenting this information in two statements as follows:

XYZ GROUP
INCOME STATEMENT FOR THE YEAR ENDED 31 DECEMBER 20X9

	20X9 $'000	*20X8* $'000
Revenue	X	X
Cost of sales	X	X
Gross profit	X	X
Other income	X	X
Distribution costs	X	X
Administrative expenses	X	X
Other expenses	X	X
Finance costs	X	X
Share of profit of associates	X	X
Profit before tax	X	X
Income tax expense	X	X
Profit for the year from continuing operations	X	X
Loss for the year from discontinued operations	X	X
Profit for the year	X	X
Profit attributable to:		
Owners of the parent	X	X
Non-controlling interest	X	X
	X	X

XYZ GROUP STATEMENT OF COMPREHENSIVE INCOME FOR THE YEAR ENDED 31 DECEMBER 20X9

	20X9 $'000	*20X8* $'000
Profit for the year	X	X
Other comprehensive income:		
Available-for-sale financial assets	X	X
Cash flow hedges	X	X
Gains on property revaluation	X	X
Share of other comprehensive income of associates	X	X
Income tax relating to components of other comprehensive income	X	X
Other comprehensive income for the year, net of tax	X	X
Total comprehensive income for the year	X	X
Total comprehensive income attributable to		
Owners of the parent	X	X
Non-controlling interest	X	X
	X	X

Exam skills

In the pilot paper, a question asked for the preparation of a statement of comprehensive income from a trial balance. There was no comprehensive income in the information given so technically this should have asked for an income statement. In exam questions, make sure that you **always call your statement the same name as the statement the examiner asks for in the question**. So, in your answer to the pilot paper question, you would have called your statement a 'statement of comprehensive income', even though there was no comprehensive income.

Section summary

IAS 1 (revised) requires all items of income and expense in a period to be shown in a **statement of comprehensive income**.

6 Income statement

Introduction

In this section we show the possible format for the income statement allowed under IAS 1 (revised).

6.1 Examples of separate income statements

XYZ GROUP
INCOME STATEMENT FOR THE YEAR ENDED 31 DECEMBER 20X9

Illustrating the classification of expenses by function

	20X9	*20X8*
	$'000	$'000
Revenue	X	X
Cost of sales	(X)	(X)
Gross profit	X	X
Other income	X	X
Distribution costs	(X)	(X)
Administrative expenses	(X)	(X)
Other expenses	(X)	(X)
Finance costs	(X)	(X)
Share of profit of associates	X	X
Profit before tax	X	X
Income tax expense	(X)	(X)
Profit for the year	X	X
Attributable to:		
Owners of the parent	X	X
Non-controlling interest	X	X
	X	X

Illustrating the classification of expenses by nature

	20X9	*20X8*
	$'000	$'000
Revenue	X	X
Other operating income	X	X
Changes in inventories of finished goods and work in progress	(X)	X
Work performed by the entity and capitalised	X	X
Raw material and consumables used	(X)	(X)
Employee benefits expense	(X)	(X)
Depreciation and amortisation expense	(X)	(X)
Impairment of property, plant and equipment	(X)	(X)
Other expenses	(X)	(X)
Finance costs	(X)	(X)
Share of profit of associates	X	X
Profit before tax	X	X
Income tax expense	(X)	(X)
Profit for the year	X	X
Attributable to:		
Owners of the parent	X	X
Non-controlling interest	X	X
	X	X

Exam alert

The usual method of presentation is expenses by function and this is the format likely to appear in your exam.

6.2 Information presented in the statement of comprehensive income or separate income statement

The standard lists the following as the **minimum** to be disclosed on the face of the income statement.

(a) Revenue

(b) Finance costs

(c) Share of profits and losses of associates and joint ventures accounted for using the equity method

(d) Pre-tax gain or loss recognised on the disposal of assets or settlement of liabilities attributable to discontinued operations

(e) Tax expense

(f) Profit or loss

The following items must be disclosed in the income statement as allocations of profit or loss for the period.

(a) Profit or loss attributable to non-controlling interest
(b) Profit or loss attributable to owners of the parent

The allocated amounts must not be presented as items of income or expense. (These relate to group accounts, covered later in this text.)

Income and expense items can only be **offset** when, and only when:

(a) It is permitted or required by an IFRS, or

(b) Gains, losses and related expenses arising from the same or similar transactions and events are immaterial, in which case they can be aggregated.

6.3 Information presented either in the statement or in the notes

An analysis of expenses must be shown either in the income statement section (as above, which is encouraged by the standard) or by note, using a classification based on *either* the nature of the expenses or their function. This **sub-classification of expenses** indicates a range of components of financial performance; these may differ in terms of stability, potential for gain or loss and predictability.

6.3.1 Nature of expense method

Expenses are not reallocated amongst various functions within the entity, but are aggregated in the income statement **according to their nature** (eg purchase of materials, depreciation, wages and salaries, transport costs). This is by far the easiest method, especially for smaller entities.

6.3.2 Function of expense/cost of sales method

You are likely to be more familiar with this method. Expenses are classified according to their function as part of cost of sales, distribution or administrative activities. This method often gives **more relevant information** for users, but the allocation of expenses by function requires the use of judgement and can be arbitrary. Consequently, perhaps, when this method is used, entities should disclose **additional information** on the nature of expenses, including staff costs, and depreciation and amortisation expense.

Which of the above methods is chosen by an entity will depend on **historical and industry factors**, and also the **nature of the organisation**. Under each method, there should be given an indication of costs which are likely to vary (directly or indirectly) with the level of sales or production. The choice of method should fairly reflect the main elements of the entity's performance.

6.4 Dividends

IAS 1 also requires disclosure of the amount of **dividends per share** for the period covered by the financial statements. This may be shown either in the income statement or in the statement of changes in equity.

Section summary

IAS 1 offers **two** possible formats for the income statement section or separate income statement - by function or by nature. Classification by function is more common.

7 Changes in equity

Introduction

This section lays out how to produce a statement of changes in equity as per IAS 1 (revised).

7.1 Format

This is the format of the statement of changes in equity as per IAS 1 (revised).

XYZ GROUP – STATEMENT OF CHANGES IN EQUITY FOR THE YEAR ENDED 31 DECEMBER 20X9

	Share capital	*Retained earnings*	*Available for-sale financial assets*	*Revaluation surplus*	*Total*	*Non-controlling interest*	*Total equity*
	$'000	$'000	$'000	$'000	$'000	$'000	$'000
Balance at 1 January 20X8	X	X	X	–	X	X	X
Changes in accounting policy	–	X	–	–	X	X	X
Restated balance	X	X	X	–	X	X	X
Changes in equity							
Dividends	–	X	–	–	X	–	X
Total comprehensive income for the year	–	X	X	X	X	X	X
Balance at 31 December 20X8	X	X	X	X	X	X	X
Changes in equity for 20X9							
Issue of share capital	X	–	–	–	X	–	X
Dividends	–	X	–	–	X	–	X
Total comprehensive income for the year	–	X	X	X	X	X	X
Transfer to retained earnings	–	X	–	X	–	–	–
Balance at 31 December 20X9	X	X	X	X	X	X	X

Note that where there has been a change of accounting policy necessitating a retrospective restatement, the adjustment is disclosed for each period. So, rather than just showing an adjustment to the balance b/f on 1.1.X9, the balances for 20X8 are restated.

Exam alert

In Section C of your exam, you are likely to be asked one or two accounts preparation questions for a total of 50 marks. You must therefore be familiar with the required formats.

Section summary

IAS 1 requires a statement of changes in equity. This shows the movement in the equity section of the statement of financial position. A full set of financial statements includes a statement of changes in equity.

8 Notes to the financial statements

Introduction

In this final section we will learn about notes to the financial statements, including their function and presentation.

8.1 Structure

The notes to the financial statements should perform the following functions.

(a) Provide information about the **basis on which the financial statements were prepared** and which **specific accounting policies** were chosen and applied to significant transactions/events

(b) Disclose any information, not shown elsewhere in the financial statements, which is **required by IFRSs**

(c) Show any additional information that is relevant to understanding which is not shown elsewhere in the financial statements

The way the notes are presented is important. They should be given in a **systematic manner** and **cross referenced** back to the related figure(s) in the statement of financial position, statement of comprehensive income or statement of cash flows.

Notes to the financial statements will amplify the information shown therein by giving the following.

(a) More **detailed analysis** or breakdowns of figures in the statements
(b) **Narrative information** explaining figures in the statements
(c) **Additional information**, eg contingent liabilities and commitments

IAS 1 suggests a **certain order** for notes to the financial statements. This will assist users when comparing the statements of different entities.

(a) Statement of **compliance** with IFRSs

(b) Statement of the **measurement basis** (bases) and accounting policies applied

(c) **Supporting information** for items presented in each financial statement in the same order as each line item and each financial statement is presented

(d) Other disclosures, eg:

(i) Contingent liabilities, commitments and other financial disclosures
(ii) Non-financial disclosures

The order of specific items may have to be varied occasionally, but a systematic structure is still required.

8.2 Presentation of accounting policies

The accounting policies section should describe the following.

(a) The **measurement basis** (or bases) used in preparing the financial statements

(b) The **other accounting policies** used, as required for a proper understanding of the financial statements

This information may be shown in the notes or sometimes as a **separate component** of the financial statements.

The information on measurement bases used is obviously fundamental to an understanding of the financial statements. Where **more than one basis is used**, it should be stated to which assets or liabilities each basis has been applied.

8.3 Other disclosures

An entity must disclose in the notes:

(a) The amount of dividends proposed or declared before the financial statements were authorised for issue but not recognised as a distribution to owners during the period, and the amount per share

(b) The amount of any cumulative preference dividends not recognised

IAS 1 ends by listing some **specific disclosures** which will always be required if they are not shown elsewhere in the financial statements.

(a) The domicile and legal form of the entity, its country of incorporation and the address of the registered office (or, if different, principal place of business)

(b) A description of the nature of the entity's operations and its principal activities

(c) The name of the parent entity and the ultimate parent entity of the group

Question 4.1

Financial statements

Learning outcome C1(a)

The accountant of Wislon Co has prepared the following list of account balances as at 31 December 20X8

	$'000
50c ordinary shares (fully paid)	450
10% debentures (secured)	200
Retained earnings 1.1.X8	242
General reserve 1.1.X8	171
Land and buildings 1.1.X8(cost)	430
Plant and machinery 1.1.X8(cost)	830
Accumulated depreciation	
Buildings 1.1.X8	20
Plant and machinery 1.1.X8	222
Inventory 1.1.X8	190
Sales	2,695
Purchases	2,152
Ordinary dividend	15
Debenture interest	10
Wages and salaries	254
Light and heat	31
Sundry expenses	113
Suspense account	135
Trade accounts receivable	179
Trade accounts payable	195
Cash	126

Notes

(a) Sundry expenses include $9,000 paid in respect of insurance for the year ending 1 September 20X9 Light and heat does not include an invoice of $3,000 for electricity for the three months ending 2 January 20X9 which was paid in February 20X9 Light and heat also includes $20,000 relating to salesmen's commission.

(b) The suspense account is in respect of the following items.

	$'000
Proceeds from the issue of 100,000 ordinary shares	120
Proceeds from the sale of plant	300
	420
Less consideration for the acquisition of Mary & Co	285
	135

(c) The net assets of Mary & Co were purchased on 3 March 20X8 Assets were valued as follows

	$'000
Available-for-sale financial assets	231
Inventory	34
	265

All the inventory acquired was sold during 20X8 The available-for-sale financial assets were still held by Wislon at 31 December 20X8 Goodwill has not been impaired in value.

(d) The property was acquired some years ago. The buildings element of the cost was estimated at $100,000 and the estimated useful life of the assets was fifty years at the time of purchase. As at 31 December 20X8 the property is to be revalued at $800,000.

(e) The plant which was sold had cost $350,000 and had a net book value of $274,000 as on 1 January 20X8. $36,000 depreciation is to be charged on plant and machinery for 20X8.

(f) The management wish to provide for:

(i) Debenture interest due
(ii) A transfer to general reserve of $16,000
(iii) Audit fees of $4,000

(g) Inventory as at 31 December 20X8 was valued at $220,000 (cost).

(h) Taxation is to be ignored.

Required

Prepare the financial statements of Wislon Co as at 31 December 20X8. You do not need to produce notes to the statements.

Section summary

Some items need to be disclosed by way of note.

Chapter Roundup

- ✓ Financial statements present the financial position and financial performance of an entity
- ✓ IAS 1 covers the **form and content** of financial statements. The main components are:
  - Statement of financial position
  - Statement of comprehensive income
  - Statement of changes in equity
  - Statement of cash flows
  - Notes to the financial statements
- ✓ Each component must be **identified clearly**.
- ✓ IAS 1 suggests a format for the statement of financial position. Certain items are specified for **disclosure on the face of the financial statements**.
- ✓ You should appreciate the distinction between **current and non-current** assets and liabilities and their different treatments.
- ✓ IAS 1 (revised) requires all items of income and expense in a period to be shown in a **statement of comprehensive income**.
- ✓ IAS 1 offers **two** possible formats for the income statement section or separate income statement – by function or by nature. Classification by function is more common.
- ✓ IAS 1 requires a statement of changes in equity. This shows the movement in the equity section of the statement of financial position. A full set of financial statements includes a statement of changes in equity.
- ✓ Some items need to be disclosed by way of note.

Quick Quiz

1 Financial statements provide users with information about the financial ...., financial .... and .... of an entity.

2 Which of the following are examples of current assets?

(a) Property, plant and equipment
(b) Prepayments
(c) Cash equivalents
(d) Manufacturing licences
(e) Retained earnings

3 Provisions must be disclosed in the statement of financial position.

True ☐

False ☐

4 Which of the following must be disclosed on the face of the income statement?

(a) Tax expense
(b) Analysis of expenses
(c) Net profit or loss for the period.

5 Where are revaluation gains shown in the financial statements?

Answers to Quick Quiz

1 Position, performance, cashflows

2 (b) and (c) only

3 True

4 (a) and (c) only. (b) may be shown in the notes.

5 In the statement of comprehensive income and the statement of changes in equity.

Answers to Questions

4.1 Financial statements

WISLON CO
STATEMENT OF COMPREHENSIVE INCOME FOR THE YEAR ENDED 31 DECEMBER 20X8

	$'000	$'000
Revenue		2,695
Less cost of sales		
Opening inventory	190	
Purchases (2,152 + 34) (W5)	2,186	
Less closing inventory	(220)	
		2,156
Gross profit		539
Other income (profit on disposal of plant)		26
		565
Administrative expenses		
Wages, salaries and commission (254 + 20) (W2)	274	
Sundry expenses (113 – 6) (W1)	107	
Light and heat (31 – 20 + 3) (W2) (W1)	14	
Depreciation: buildings (W3)	2	
plant	36	
Audit fees	4	
		437
Finance costs		(20)
Profit for the year		108
Other comprehensive income:		
Gain on property revaluation		392
Total comprehensive income for the year		500

Note

The only item of 'other comprehensive income' for the year was the revaluation gain. If there had been no revaluation gain, only an income statement would have been required.

WISLON CO
STATEMENT OF FINANCIAL POSITION AS AT 31 DECEMBER 20X8

	$'000	$'000
Assets		
Non-current assets		
Property, plant and equipment		
Property at valuation		800
Plant: cost (W4)	480	
Accumulated depreciation (W4)	(182)	
		298
Goodwill (W5)		20
Available-for-sale financial assets		231
Current assets		
Inventory	220	
Trade accounts receivable	179	
Prepayments (W1)	6	
Cash	126	
		531
Total assets		1,880

Equity and liabilities		
	$'000	$'000
Equity		
50c ordinary shares	500	
Share premium	70	
Revaluation surplus (W3)	392	
General reserve	187	
Retained earnings	319	
		1,468
Non-current liabilities		
10% loan stock (secured)		200
Current liabilities		
Trade accounts payable	195	
Accrued expenses (W1)	17	
		212
Total equity and liabilities		1,880

WISLON CO
STATEMENT OF CHANGES IN EQUITY
FOR THE YEAR ENDED 31 DECEMBER 20X8

	Share capital	*Share premium*	*Retained earnings*	*General reserve*	*Revaluation Surplus*	*Total*
	$'000	$'000	$'000	$'000	$'000	$'000
Balance at 1.1.X8	450	–	242	171	-	863
Issue of share capital (W6)	50	70				120
Dividends			(15)			(15)
Total comprehensive income for the year			108		392	500
Transfer to reserve			(16)	16		
Balance at 31.12.X8	500	70	319	187	392	1,468

Note that the total comprehensive income is analysed into its components.

Workings

(1) Normal adjustments are needed for accruals and prepayments (insurance, light and heat, debenture interest and audit fees). The debenture interest accrued is calculated as follows.

	$'000
Charge needed in income statement (10% × $200,000)	20
Amount paid so far, as shown in list of account balances	10
Accrual: presumably six months' interest now payable	10

The accrued expenses shown in the statement of financial position comprise:

	$'000
Debenture interest	10
Light and heat	3
Audit fee	4
	17

Prepayment

Insurance (sundry expenses) ($9,000 x 8/12) = $6,000

(2) The misposting of $20,000 to light and heat is also adjusted, by reducing the light and heat expense, but charging $20,000 to salesmen's commission.

(3) Depreciation on the building is calculated as $\frac{\$100,000}{50} = \$2,000$.

The carrying value of the property is then $430,000 – $20,000 – $2,000 = $408,000 at the end of the year. When the property is revalued a reserve of $800,000 – $408,000 = $392,000 is then created.

(4) The profit on disposal of plant is calculated as proceeds $300,000 (per suspense account) less NBV $274,000, ie $26,000. The cost of the remaining plant is calculated at $830,000 – $350,000 = $480,000. The depreciation provision at the year end is:

	$'000
Balance 1.1.X8	222
Charge for 20X8	36
Less depreciation on disposals (350 – 274)	(76)
	182

(5) Goodwill arising on the purchase of Mary & Co is:

	$'000
Consideration (per suspense account)	285
Assets at valuation	265
Goodwill	20

This is shown as an asset in the statement of financial position. The financial assets, being owned by Wislon at the year end, are also shown on the statement of financial position, whereas Mary's inventory, acquired and then sold, is added to the purchases figure for the year.

(6) The other item in the suspense account is dealt with as follows.

	$'000
Proceeds of issue of 100,000 ordinary shares	120
Less nominal value 100,000 × 50c	50
Excess of consideration over par value (= share premium)	70

(7) The transfer to general reserve increases it to $171,000 + $16,000 = $187,000.

REPORTING FINANCIAL PERFORMANCE

This chapter is mainly concerned with the statement of comprehensive income that we covered briefly in the previous chapter. We first look at **IFRS 5** which deals with discontinued operations and non-current assets held for sale. We then move on to cover **IAS 8** which looks at accounting policies. It also examines certain circumstances and transactions which require different treatment to normal profit or loss items.

IFRS 8 on segment reporting requires publicly quoted entities to provide additional information on their results, breaking them down by segment. We cover this in the final part of this chapter.

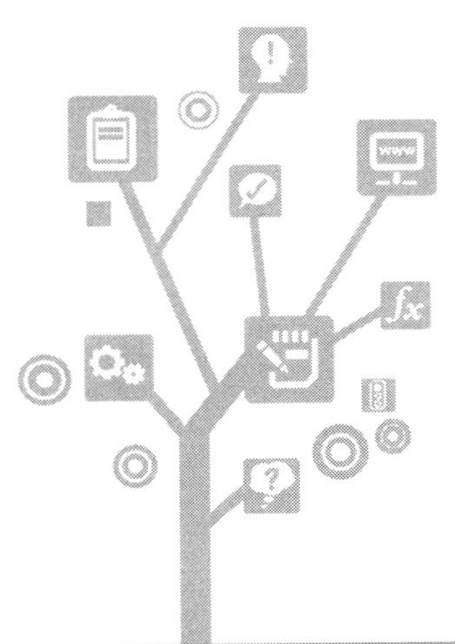

topic list	learning outcomes	syllabus references	ability required
1 IFRS 5 *Non-current assets held for sale and discontinued operations*	C2(a)	C2(i),(v)	application
2 IAS 8 *Accounting policies, changes in accounting estimates and errors*	C2(a)	C2(i)	application
3 Accounting policies	C2(a)	C2(i)	application
4 Changes in accounting policies	C2(a)	C2(i)	application
5 Changes in accounting estimates	C2(a)	C2(i)	application
6 Errors	C2(a)	C2(i)	application
7 Segment reporting	C2(a)	C2(i)	application

1 IFRS 5 *Non-current assets held for sale and discontinued operations*

Introduction

This section looks at IFRS 5 *Non-current assets held for sale and discontinued operations*. We first explore the background to the standard and then move on to examine the necessary presentation and disclosures.

1.1 Background

IFRS 5 is the result of a short-term convergence project with the US Financial Accounting Standards Board (FASB). It replaces IAS 35 *Discontinuing operations*.

IFRS 5 requires assets and groups of assets that are 'held for sale' to be **presented separately** in the statement of financial position and the results of discontinued operations to be presented separately in the statement of comprehensive income. This is required so that users of financial statements will be better able to make **projections** about the financial position, profits and cash flows of the entity.

KEY TERM

DISPOSAL GROUP: a group of assets to be disposed of, by sale or otherwise, together as a group in a single transaction, and liabilities directly associated with those assets that will be transferred in the transaction. (In practice a disposal group could be a subsidiary, a cash-generating unit or a single operation within an entity.) *(IFRS 5)*

IFRS 5 does not apply to certain assets covered by other accounting standards:

(a) Deferred tax assets (IAS 12)

(b) Assets arising from employee benefits (IAS 19)

(c) Financial assets (IAS 39)

(d) Investment properties accounted for in accordance with the fair value model (IAS 40)

(e) Agricultural and biological assets that are measured at fair value less estimated point of sale costs (IAS 41)

(f) Insurance contracts (IFRS 4)

1.2 Classification of assets held for sale

A non-current asset (or disposal group) should be classified as **held for sale** if its carrying amount will be recovered **principally through a sale transaction** rather than **through continuing use**. A number of detailed criteria must be met:

(a) The asset must be **available for immediate sale** in its present condition.
(b) Its sale must be **highly probable** (ie, significantly more likely than not).

For the sale to be highly probable, the following must apply.

(a) Management must be **committed** to a plan to sell the asset.

(b) There must be an active programme to **locate a buyer.**

(c) The asset must be marketed for sale at a **price that is reasonable** in relation to its current fair value.

(d) The sale should be expected to take place **within one year** from the date of classification.

(e) It is unlikely that significant changes to the plan will be made or that the plan will be withdrawn.

An asset (or disposal group) can still be classified as held for sale, even if the sale has not actually taken place within one year. However, the delay must have been **caused by events or circumstances beyond the entity's control** and there must be sufficient evidence that the entity is still committed to sell the asset or disposal group. Otherwise the entity must cease to classify the asset as held for sale.

If an entity acquires a disposal group (eg, a subsidiary) exclusively with a view to its subsequent disposal it can classify the asset as held for sale only if the sale is expected to take place within one year and it is highly probable that all the other criteria will be met within a short time (normally three months).

Question 5.1 Assets held for sale

Learning outcome C2(a)

On 1 December 20X3, a company became committed to a plan to sell a manufacturing facility and has already found a potential buyer. The company does not intend to discontinue the operations currently carried out in the facility. At 31 December 20X3 there is a backlog of uncompleted customer orders. The subsidiary will not be able to transfer the facility to the buyer until after it ceases to operate the facility and has eliminated the backlog of uncompleted customer orders. This is not expected to occur until spring 20X4.

Required

Can the manufacturing facility be classified as 'held for sale' at 31 December 20X3?

1.3 Measurement of assets held for sale

KEY TERMS

FAIR VALUE: the amount for which an asset could be exchanged, or a liability settled, between knowledgeable, willing parties in an arm's length transaction.

COSTS TO SELL: the incremental costs directly attributable to the disposal of an asset (or disposal group), excluding finance costs and income tax expense.

RECOVERABLE AMOUNT: the higher of an asset's fair value less costs to sell and its value in use.

VALUE IN USE: the present value of estimated future cash flows expected to arise from the continuing use of an asset and from its disposal at the end of its useful life.

A non-current asset (or disposal group) that is held for sale should be measured at the **lower of** its **carrying amount** and **fair value less costs to sell**. Fair value less costs to sell is equivalent to net realisable value.

An impairment loss should be recognised where fair value less costs to sell is lower than carrying amount. Note that this is an exception to the normal rule. IAS 36 *Impairment of assets* requires an entity to recognise an impairment loss only where an asset's recoverable amount is lower than its carrying value. Recoverable amount is defined as the higher of net realisable value and value in use. IAS 36 does not apply to assets held for sale.

Non-current assets held for sale **should not be depreciated**, even if they are still being used by the entity.

A non-current asset (or disposal group) that is **no longer classified as held for sale** (for example, because the sale has not taken place within one year) is measured at the **lower of**:

(a) Its **carrying amount** before it was classified as held for sale, adjusted for any depreciation that would have been charged had the asset not been held for sale

(b) Its **recoverable amount** at the date of the decision not to sell

1.4 Presenting discontinued operations

KEY TERMS

DISCONTINUED OPERATION: a component of an entity that has either been disposed of, or is classified as held for sale, and:

(a) Represents a separate major line of business or geographical area of operations

(b) Is part of a single co-ordinated plan to dispose of a separate major line of business or geographical area of operations, or

(c) Is a subsidiary acquired exclusively with a view to resale.

COMPONENT OF AN ENTITY: operations and cash flows that can be clearly distinguished, operationally and for financial reporting purposes, from the rest of the entity.

An entity should **present and disclose information** that enables users of the financial statements to evaluate the financial effects of **discontinued operations** and disposals of non-current assets or disposal groups.

An entity should disclose a **single amount** in the statement of comprehensive income comprising the total of:

(a) The **post-tax profit or loss** of discontinued operations and

(b) The post-tax gain or loss recognised on the **measurement to fair value less costs to sell** or on the disposal of the assets or disposal group(s) constituting the discontinued operation.

An entity should also disclose an **analysis** of this single amount into:

(a) The revenue, expenses and pre-tax profit or loss of discontinued operations

(b) The related income tax expense

(c) The gain or loss recognised on the measurement to fair value less costs to sell or on the disposal of the assets or disposal group(s) constituting the discontinued operation

(d) The related income tax expense

This may be presented either in the statement of comprehensive income or in the notes. If it is presented in the statement of comprehensive income it should be presented in a section identified as relating to discontinued operations, ie separately from continuing operations. This analysis is not required where the discontinued operation is a newly acquired subsidiary that has been classified as held for sale.

An entity should disclose the **net cash flows** attributable to the operating, investing and financing activities of discontinued operations. These disclosures may be presented either on the face of the statement of cash flows or in the notes.

Gains and losses on the remeasurement of a disposal group that is not a discontinued operation but is held for sale should be included in profit or loss from continuing operations.

Exam alert

You may be required to produce an income statement or statement of comprehensive income from a trial balance in an exam question for a company with discontinued operations.

1.5 Illustration

The following amended illustration is taken from the implementation guidance to IFRS 5. Profit for the period from discontinued operations would be analysed in the notes.

XYZ
INCOME STATEMENT
FOR THE YEAR ENDED 31 DECEMBER 20X2

	20X2	*20X1*
Continuing operations	$'000	$'000
Revenue	X	X
Cost of sales	(X)	(X)
Gross profit	X	X
Other income	X	X
Distribution costs	(X)	(X)
Administrative expenses	(X)	(X)
Other expenses	(X)	(X)
Finance costs	(X)	(X)
Profit before tax	X	X
Income tax expense	(X)	(X)
Profit for the year from continuing operations	X	X
Discontinued operations		
Profit for the year from discontinued operations	X	X
Profit for the year	X	X

Note that if there were items of 'other comprehensive income' this would be shown as a full 'statement of comprehensive income' as per the format in the previous chapter.

Question 5.2 Discontinued operation

Learning outcome C2(a)

On 20 October 20X3 the directors of a parent company made a public announcement of plans to close a steel works. The closure means that the group will no longer carry out this type of operation, which until recently has represented about 10% of its total sales revenue. The works will be gradually shut down over a period of several months, with complete closure expected in July 20X4. At 31 December output had been significantly reduced and some redundancies had already taken place. The cash flows, revenues and expenses relating to the steel works can be clearly distinguished from those of the subsidiary's other operations.

Required

How should the closure be treated in the financial statements for the year ended 31 December 20X3?

1.6 Presentation of a non-current asset or disposal group classified as held for sale

Non-current assets and disposal groups classified as held for sale should be **presented separately** from other assets in the statement of financial position. The liabilities of a disposal group should be presented separately from other liabilities in the statement of financial position.

(a) Assets and liabilities held for sale **should not be offset**.

(b) The **major classes** of assets and liabilities held for sale should be **separately disclosed** either in the statement of financial position or in the notes.

1.7 Additional disclosures

In the period in which a non-current asset (or disposal group) has been either classified as held for sale or sold the following should be disclosed.

(a) A **description** of the non-current asset (or disposal group)

(b) A description of the **facts and circumstances** of the disposal

(c) Any **gain or loss** recognised when the item was classified as held for sale

Where an asset previously classified as held for sale is **no longer held for sale**, the entity should disclose a description of the facts and circumstances leading to the decision and its effect on results.

Section summary

IFRS 5 *Non-current assets held for sale and discontinued operations* requires assets 'held for sale' to be presented separately in the statement of financial position. The results of discontinued operations should be presented separately in the statement of comprehensive income.

2 IAS 8 *Accounting policies, changes in accounting estimates and errors*

Introduction

The key definitions in IAS 8 are given in this section. IAS 8 is looked at in more detail in Sections 3 to 6 in this chapter.

2.1 Definitions

The following definitions are given in the standard.

KEY TERMS

ACCOUNTING POLICIES are the specific principles, bases, conventions, rules and practices adopted by an entity in preparing and presenting financial statements.

A CHANGE IN A ACCOUNTING ESTIMATE is an adjustment of the carrying amount of an asset or a liability or the amount of the periodic consumption of an asset, that results from the assessment of the present status of, and expected future benefits and obligations associated with, assets and liabilities. Changes in accounting estimates result from new information or new developments and, accordingly, are not corrections of errors.

MATERIAL: as defined in IAS 1

PRIOR PERIOD ERRORS are omissions from, and misstatements in, the entity's financial statements for one or more prior periods arising from a failure to use, or misuse of, reliable information that:

(a) Was available when financial statements for those periods were authorised for issue, and

(b) Could reasonably be expected to have been obtained and taken into account in the preparation and presentation of those financial statements.

Such errors include the effects of mathematical mistakes, mistakes in applying accounting policies, oversights or misinterpretations of facts, and fraud.

RETROSPECTIVE APPLICATION is applying a new accounting policy to transactions, other events and conditions as if that policy had always been applied.

RETROSPECTIVE RESTATEMENT is correcting the recognition, measurement and disclosure of amounts of elements of financial statements as if a prior period error had never occurred.

PROSPECTIVE APPLICATION of a change in accounting policy and of recognising the effect of a change in an accounting estimate, respectively, are:

(a) Applying the new accounting policy to transactions, other events and conditions occurring after the date as at which the policy is changed; and

(b) Recognising the effect of the change in the accounting estimate in the current and future periods affected by the change.

IMPRACTICABLE. Applying a requirement is impracticable when the entity cannot apply it after making every reasonable effort to do so. It is impracticable to apply a change in an accounting policy retrospectively or to make a retrospective restatement to correct an error if one of the following apply.

(a) The effects of the retrospective application or retrospective restatement are not determinable.

(b) The retrospective application or retrospective restatement requires assumptions about what management's intent would have been in that period.

(c) The retrospective application or retrospective restatement requires significant estimates of amounts and it is impossible to distinguish objectively information about those estimates that: provides evidence of circumstances that existed on the date(s) at which those amounts are to be recognised, measured or disclosed; and would have been available when the financial statements for that prior period were authorised for issue, from other information. *(IAS 8)*

Section summary

IAS 8 deals with the treatment of changes in accounting estimates, changes in accounting policies and errors.

3 Accounting policies

Introduction

In this section we learn about how an entity should develop and apply accounting polices.

3.1 Developing accounting policies

Accounting policies are determined by **applying the relevant IFRS or IAS**.

Where there is no applicable IFRS or IAS management should use its **judgement** in developing and applying an accounting policy that results in information that is **relevant** and **reliable**. Management should refer to:

(a) The requirements and guidance in IFRSs and IASs dealing with **similar** and **related issues**

(b) The definitions, recognition criteria and measurement concepts for assets, liabilities and expenses in the ***Framework***

Management may also consider the most recent pronouncements of **other standard setting bodies** that use a similar conceptual framework to develop standards, other accounting literature and accepted industry practices if these do not conflict with the sources above.

An entity must select and apply its accounting policies for a period **consistently** for similar transactions, other events and conditions, unless an IFRS or an IAS specifically requires or permits categorisation of items for which different policies may be appropriate. If an IFRS or an IAS requires or permits categorisation of items, an appropriate accounting policy must be selected and applied consistently to each category.

Section summary

Accounting policies must comply with accounting standards and be applied **consistently**.

4 Changes in accounting policies

Introduction

This section looks at why companies may need to change their accounting policies. It goes on to cover how these changes should be implemented.

4.1 Making changes

The same accounting policies are usually adopted from period to period, to allow users to analyse trends over time in profit, cash flows and financial position. **Changes in accounting policy will therefore be rare** and should be made only if required by one of three things.

(a) By **statute**

(b) By an **accounting standard setting body**

(c) If the change will result in a **more appropriate presentation** of events or transactions in the financial statements of the entity

The standard highlights two types of event **which do not constitute changes in accounting policy**.

(a) Adopting an accounting policy for a **new type of transaction** or event not dealt with previously by the entity.

(b) Adopting a **new accounting policy** for a transaction or event which has not occurred in the past or which was not material.

In the case of tangible non-current assets, if a policy of revaluation is adopted for the first time then this is treated, not as a change of accounting policy under IAS 8, but as a revaluation under IAS 16 *Property, plant and equipment*. The following paragraphs do not therefore apply to a change in policy to adopt revaluations.

A change in accounting policy **must be applied retrospectively**. **Retrospective application** means that the new accounting policy is applied to transactions and events as if it had always been in use. In other words, at the earliest date such transactions or events occurred, the policy is applied from that date.

Prospective application is **no longer allowed** under the revised IAS 8 unless it is **impracticable** (see Key Terms) to determine the cumulative amount of the adjustment.

An example of a change in accounting policy is where inventory previously valued on a FIFO basis is now to be valued on a weighted average cost basis.

4.2 Adoption of an IAS/IFRS

Where a new IAS or IFRS is adopted, IAS 8 requires any transitional provisions in the new IAS itself to be followed. If none are given in the IAS which is being adopted, then IAS 8 explains the required treatment.

4.3 Other changes in accounting policy

IAS 8 requires **retrospective application**, *unless* it is **impracticable** to determine the cumulative amount of the adjustment. Any resulting adjustment should be reported as an adjustment to the opening balance of retained earnings. Comparative information should be restated unless it is impracticable to do so.

This means that all comparative information must be restated **as if the new policy had always been in force**, with amounts relating to earlier periods reflected in an adjustment to opening reserves of the earliest period presented.

Prospective application is allowed only when it is impracticable to determine the cumulative effect of the change.

Certain **disclosures** are required when a change in accounting policy has a material effect on the current period or any prior period presented, or when it may have a material effect in subsequent periods.

(a) Reasons for the change

(b) Amount of the adjustment for the current period and for each period presented

(c) Amount of the adjustment relating to periods prior to those included in the comparative information

(d) The fact that comparative information has been restated or that it is impracticable to do so

An entity should also disclose information relevant to assessing the **impact of new IFRS** on the financial statements where these have **not yet come into force.**

Section summary

Changes in accounting policy are applied **retrospectively**.

5 Changes in accounting estimates

Introduction

Here we look at accounting estimates. We will discuss their nature and how a change in the estimate should be treated in the financial statements.

5.1 What are estimates?

Estimates arise in relation to business activities because of the **uncertainties inherent within them**. Judgements are made based on the most up to date information and the use of such estimates is a necessary part of the preparation of financial statements. It does *not* undermine their reliability. Here are some examples of accounting estimates.

- A necessary **doubtful debt provision**
- **Useful lives** of depreciable assets
- Provision for **obsolescence of inventory**

The rule here is that the **effect of a change in an accounting estimate** should be included in the determination of net profit or loss in one of:

(a) The period of the change, if the change affects that period only
(b) The period of the change *and* future periods, if the change affects both

Changes may occur in the circumstances which were in force at the time the estimate was calculated, or perhaps additional information or subsequent developments have come to light.

An example of a change in accounting estimate which affects only the **current period** is the doubtful debt estimate. However, a revision in the life over which an asset is depreciated would affect both the **current and future periods**, in the amount of the depreciation expense.

Reasonably enough, the effect of a change in an accounting estimate should be included in the **same expense classification** as was used previously for the estimate. This rule helps to ensure **consistency** between the financial statements of different periods.

The **materiality** of the change is also relevant. The nature and amount of a change in an accounting estimate that has a material effect in the current period (or which is expected to have a material effect in subsequent periods) should be disclosed. If it is not possible to quantify the amount, this impracticability should be disclosed.

Section summary

Changes in accounting estimates are **not** applied retrospectively.

6 Errors

Introduction

This section discusses how prior period errors arise and how they should be treated in the financial statements.

6.1 Prior period errors

Errors discovered during a current period which **relate to a prior period** may arise through:

(a) Mathematical mistakes
(b) Mistakes in the application of accounting policies
(c) Misinterpretation of facts
(d) Oversights
(e) Fraud

A more formal definition is given in the Key Terms at the beginning of this chapter.

Most of the time these errors can be **corrected through net profit or loss for the current period**. Where they fulfil the definition of **material errors**, however, this is not appropriate.

6.2 Accounting treatment

Prior period errors: correct retrospectively. There is no allowed alternative treatment.

This involves:

(a) Either restating the comparative amounts for the prior period(s) in which the error occurred,

(b) Or, when the error occurred before the earliest prior period presented, restating the opening balances of assets, liabilities and equity for that period

so that the financial statements are presented **as if the error had never occurred**.

Only where it is **impracticable** to determine the cumulative effect of an error on prior periods can an entity correct an error **prospectively**.

Various **disclosures** are required.

(a) **Nature** of the prior period error

(b) For each prior period, to the extent practicable, the **amount** of the correction.

 (i) For each financial statement line item affected

 (ii) If IAS 33 applies, for basic and diluted earnings per share

(c) The amount of the correction at the **beginning of the earliest prior** period presented

(d) If **retrospective restatement is impracticable** for a particular prior period, the **circumstances** that led to the existence of that condition and a description of how and from when the error has been corrected. Subsequent periods need not repeat these disclosures

Question 5.3 — Prior period error

Learning outcome C2(a)

During 20X7 Global discovered that certain items had been included in inventory at 31 December 20X6, valued at $4.2m, which had in fact been sold before the year end. The following figures for 20X6 (as reported) and 20X7 (draft) are available.

	20X6	*20X7 (draft)*
	$'000	$'000
Sales	47,400	67,200
Cost of goods sold	(34,570)	(55,800)
Profit before taxation	12,830	11,400
Income taxes	(3,880)	(3,400)
Net profit	8,950	8,000

Reserves at 1 January 20X6 were $13m. The cost of goods sold for 20X7 includes the $4.2m error in opening inventory. The income tax rate was 30% for 20X6 and 20X7.

Required

Prepare the income statement for 20X7, with the 20X6 comparative, and retained earnings.

Section summary

Prior period errors will require **retrospective** correction if they are **material**.

7 Segment Reporting

Introduction

In this section we look at segment reporting. Firstly we discuss why companies need to report by segment before moving on to the disclosures equired by IFRS 8.

7.1 Why segment reporting?

Large entities produce a wide range of products and services, often in several different countries. Further information on how the overall results of entities are made up from each of these operating segments will help the users of the financial statements. This is the reason for **segment reporting**.

(a) The entity's **past performance** will be better understood.
(b) The entity's **risks and returns** may be better assessed.
(c) More **informed judgements** may be made about the entity as a whole.

Risks and returns of a **diversified, multi-national company** can only be assessed by looking at the individual risks and rewards attached to groups of products or services or in different groups of products or services or in different geographical areas. These are subject to differing rates of profitability, opportunities for growth, future prospects and risks.

7.2 IFRS 8 *Operating segments*

IFRS 8 requires an entity to adopt the 'management approach' to reporting on the financial performance of its operating segments. This 'management approach' has two intended advantages:

(a) It allows users of the financial statements to view operations through the eyes of management.

(b) As it is based on information which is being collected anyway, it should not involve too much cost or time to prepare.

In the words of the Standard:

'An entity shall disclose information to enable users of its financial statements to evaluate the nature and financial effects of the business activities in which it engages and the economic environments in which it operates.'

IFRS 8 applies to listed companies only.

7.2.1 Operating segments

KEY TERM

An OPERATING SEGMENT is a component of an entity:

(a) that engages in business activities from which it may earn revenues and incur expenses

(b) whose operating results are regularly reviewed by the entity's chief operating decision maker to make decisions about resources to be allocated to the segment and assess its performance, and

(c) for which discrete financial information is available *IFRS 8*

7.2.2 Determining reportable segments

Information must be reported separately about any segment that meets any of the following criteria

(a) Its revenue is 10% or more of the total revenue of all segments

(b) Its reported profit or loss is 10% or more of the combined profits or losses of all profit-making or loss-making segments

(c) Its assets are 10% or more of the combined assets of all operating segments

7.2.3 Disclosures

An entity must disclose the following for each accounting period:

(a) Factors used to identify reportable segments

(b) Types of products and services from which each reportable segment derives its revenue

(c) Information about reported segment revenue, profit or loss, assets, liabilities and reconciliation of these to the figures in the statement of comprehensive income and statement of financial position

Exam skills

Any question on segment reporting in your exam will probably be fairly simple. You are unlikely to be required to produce a full segmental report.

Here, just for illustration purposes, is a simplified version of the segmental report given in the standard:

	Car parts	*Motor vessels*	*Software*	*Finance*	*Total*
	$'000	$'000	$'000	$'000	$'000
External revenue	3,000	5,000	9,500	5,000	22,500
Intersegment revenue			3,000		3,000
Interest expense	350	600	700		1,650
Interest revenue	450	800	1,000	1,000	3,250
Depreciation	200	100	50	1,100	1,450
Segment profit	200	70	900	500	1,670
Segment assets	2,000	5,000	3,000	57,000	67,000
Expenditure on non-current assets	300	700	500	600	2,100
Segment liabilities	1,050	3,000	1,800	30,000	35,850

Note. The finance segment finances customer purchases of products from the other segments and deals in other financial operations – hence the high level of assets and liabilities.

In addition to the financial information as disclosed above, an entity is also required to disclose:

(a) The types of products and services from which each reportable segment derives its revenues (shown in the above report)

(b) Factors that management used to identify the entity's reportable segments

(c) Geographical information – revenues and non-current assets, based on location of customers

(d) Information about major customers. Identities are not disclosed, but this enables users to see where a large amount of revenue derives from one customer.

Question 5.4 — Segment reporting

Learning outcome C2(a)

A company has three divisions all based in the UK. Their revenues, results and net assets are as below:

	$'000
Division A	
Sales to B	304,928
Other UK sales	57,223
Middle East export sales	406,082
Pacific fringe export sales	77,838
	846,071
Division B	
Sales to C	31,034
Export sales to Europe	195,915
	226,949
Division C	
Export sales to North America	127,003

	Division A	*Division B*	*Division C*
	$'000	$'000	$'000
Profit (loss) before tax	162,367	18,754	(8,303)
Interest costs	3,459	6,042	527
Non-current assets	200,921	41,612	113,076
Current assets	121,832	39,044	92,338
Liabilities	16,959	6,295	120,841

Required

As far as the information permits, prepare the segment information required by IFRS 8.

Section summary

IFRS 8 requires the disclosure of segmental information by listed companies.

Chapter Roundup

- ✓ IFRS 5 *Non-current assets held for sale and discontinued operations* requires assets 'held for sale' to be presented separately in the statement of financial position.
- ✓ The results of discontinued operations should be presented separately in the statement of comprehensive income.
- ✓ IAS 8 deals with the treatment of changes in accounting estimates, changes in accounting policies and errors.
- ✓ Accounting policies must comply with accounting standards and be applied **consistently**.
- ✓ Changes in accounting policy are applied **retrospectively**.
- ✓ Changes in accounting estimates are **not** applied retrospectively.
- ✓ Prior period errors will require **retrospective** correction if they are **material**.
- ✓ IFRS 8 requires the disclosure of segmental information by listed companies.

Quick Quiz

1 How should a prior period error be corrected under IAS 8?

2 Give three circumstances when a change in accounting policy might be required.

3 Accounting standards must be applied ....

4 A non-current asset is classified as held for sale if its carrying amount will be recovered principally through continuing use rather than through a sale transaction

True ☐

False ☐

5 Which of the following is not an accounting estimate?

A Prepaid rent
B Useful lives of depreciable assets
C A doubtful debt provision
D Restructuring provision

6 Prior period errors must be corrected prospectively.

True ☐

False ☐

Answers to Quick Quiz

1 By adjusting the opening balance of retained earnings.

2 (a) By statute
(b) By the IASB
(c) For a more appropriate presentation

3 Consistently

4 False

5 A

6 False

Answers to Questions

5.1 Assets held for sale

The facility will not be transferred until the backlog of orders is completed; this demonstrates that the facility is not available for immediate sale in its present condition. The facility cannot be classified as 'held for sale' at 31 December 20X3. It must be treated in the same way as other items of property, plant and equipment: it should continue to be depreciated and should not be separately disclosed.

5.2 Discontinued operation

Because the steel works is being closed, rather than sold, it cannot be classified as 'held for sale'. In addition, the steel works is not a discontinued operation. Although at 31 December 20X3 the group was firmly committed to the closure, this has not yet taken place and therefore the steel works must be included in continuing operations. Information about the planned closure could be disclosed in the notes to the financial statements.

5.3 Prior period error

INCOME STATEMENT

	20X6	*20X7*
	$'000	$'000
Sales	47,400	67,200
Cost of goods sold (W1)	(38,770)	(51,600)
Profit before tax	8,630	15,600
Income tax (W2)	(2,620)	(4,660)
Profit for the year	6,010	10,940

RETAINED EARNINGS

	20X6	*20X7*
	$'000	$'000
Opening retained earnings		
As previously reported	13,000	21,950
Correction of prior period error (4,200 – 1,260)	–	(2,940)
As restated	13,000	19,010
Profit for the year	6,010	10,940
Closing retained earnings	19,010	29,950

Workings

1 Cost of goods sold

	20X6	*20X7*
	$'000	$'000
As stated in question	34,570	55,800
Inventory adjustment	4,200	(4,200)
	38,770	51,600

2 Income tax

	20X6	*20X7*
	$'000	$'000
As stated in question	3,880	3,400
Inventory adjustment (4,200 × 30%)	(1,260)	1,260
	2,620	4,660

5.4 Segment reporting

Profit, assets and liabilities	*Division A*	*Division B*	*Division C*	*Total*
	$'000	$'000	$'000	$'000
External revenue	541,143	195,915	127,003	864,061
Intersegment revenue	304,928	31,034		335,962
Interest expense	3,459	6,042	527	10,028
Segment profit (loss)	162,367	18,754	(8,303)	172,818
Segment assets	322,753	80,656	205,414	608,823
Segment liabilities	16,959	6,295	120,841	144,095

Information about geographical areas

	UK	*Middle East*	*Pacific fringe*	*Europe*	*N America*	*Total*
	$'000	$'000	$'000	$'000	$'000	$'000
Revenues	57,223	406,082	77,838	195,915	127,003	864,061

Now try these questions from the Exam Question Bank

Number	Level	Marks	Time
Q13	Examination	5	9 mins

ACCOUNTING FOR NON-CURRENT ASSETS

This chapter covers one of the important items on the statement of financial position, non-current assets. Intangible assets are covered later in Chapter 7. This chapter deals with IAS 16, IAS 36 and IAS 23.

IAS 16 should be familiar to you from your earlier studies, as should the mechanics of accounting for depreciation, revaluations of non-current assets and disposals of non-current assets. Some questions are given here for revision purposes.

IAS 36 on impairment is an important and very examinable standard.

IAS 23 deals with the treatment of funds used in self-constructed assets.

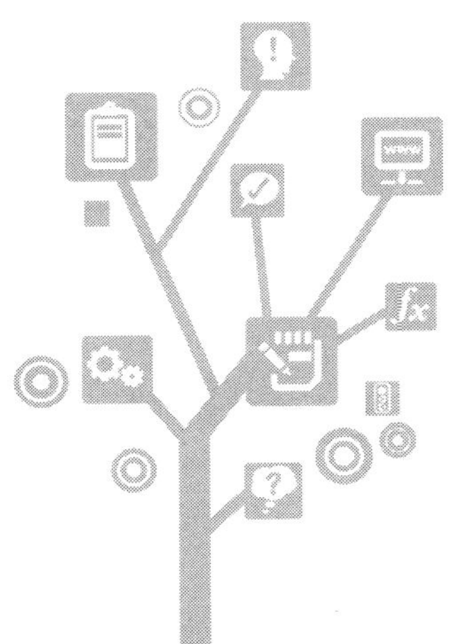

topic list	learning outcomes	syllabus references	ability required
1 Depreciation accounting	C2(a)	C2(ii)	application
2 IAS 16 *Property, plant and equipment*	C2(a)	C2(ii)	application
3 IAS 36 *Impairment of assets*	C2(a)	C2(v)	application
4 IAS 23 *Borrowing costs*	C2(a)	C2(viii)	application

1 Depreciation accounting

Introduction

This section on deprecation of non-current assets should be familiar to you from your earlier studies. Make sure you can answer the questions in this section before moving on.

1.1 Non-current assets

Where assets held by an entity have a **limited useful life** to that entity it is necessary to apportion the value of an asset used in a period against the revenue it has helped to create. If an asset's life extends over more than one accounting period, it earns profits over more than one period. It is a **non-current asset**.

With the exception of land held on freehold or very long leasehold, **every non-current asset eventually wears out over time**. Machines, cars and other vehicles, fixtures and fittings, and even buildings do not last for ever. When a business acquires a non-current asset, it will have some idea about how long its useful life will be, and it might decide what to do with it.

(a) Keep on using the non-current asset until it becomes **completely worn out**, useless, and worthless.

(b) **Sell off** the non-current asset at the end of its useful life, either by selling it as a second-hand item or as scrap.

Since a non-current asset has a cost, and a limited useful life, and its value eventually declines, it follows that a charge should be made in profit or loss to reflect the use that is made of the asset by the business. This charge is called **depreciation**.

1.2 Scope

Depreciation accounting is governed by IAS 16 *Property, plant and equipment* which we will look at in Section 2 of this chapter. However, this section will deal with some of the IAS 16 definitions concerning depreciation.

KEY TERMS

DEPRECIATION is the result of systematic allocation of the depreciable amount of an asset over its useful life.

Property, plant and equipment are tangible items that:

- Are expected to be used during more than one period; and
- Are held for use in the production or supply of goods and service, for rental to others, or for administrative purposes

USEFUL LIFE is one of two things.

- The period over which an asset is expected to be available for use by an entity
- The number of production or similar units expected to be obtained from the asset by the entity.

DEPRECIABLE AMOUNT of a depreciable asset is the cost of an asset or other amount substituted for cost, less its residual value. *(IAS 16)*

An 'amount substituted for cost' will normally be a **current market value** after a revaluation has taken place.

1.3 Depreciation

IAS 16 requires the depreciable amount of a depreciable asset to be allocated on a **systematic basis** to each accounting period during the useful life of the asset. **Every part of an item of property, plant and equipment with a cost that is significant in relation to the total cost of the item must be depreciated separately**.

One way of defining depreciation is to describe it as a means of **spreading the cost** of a non-current asset over its useful life, and so matching the cost against the full period during which it earns profits for the business. Depreciation charges are an example of the application of the accruals assumption.

There are situations where, over a period, an asset has **increased in value**, ie its current value is greater than the carrying value in the financial statements. You might think that in such situations it would not be necessary to depreciate the asset. The standard states, however, that this is irrelevant, and that depreciation should still be charged to each accounting period, based on the depreciable amount, irrespective of a rise in value.

An entity is required to begin depreciating an item of property, plant and equipment when it is available for use and to continue depreciating it until it is derecognised even if it is idle during the period.

1.4 Useful life

The following factors should be considered when **estimating the useful life** of a depreciable asset.

- Expected **physical wear and tear**
- **Obsolescence**
- Legal or other **limits** on the use of the assets

Once decided, the useful life should be **reviewed at least every financial year end** and depreciation rates adjusted for the current and future periods if expectations vary significantly from the original estimates. The effect of the change should be disclosed in the accounting period in which the change takes place.

The assessment of useful life requires **judgement** based on previous experience with similar assets or classes of asset. When a completely new type of asset is acquired (ie through technological advancement or through use in producing a brand new product or service) it is still necessary to estimate useful life, even though the exercise will be much more difficult.

The standard also points out that the physical life of the asset might be longer than its useful life to the entity in question. One of the main factors to be taken into consideration is the **physical wear and tear** the asset is likely to endure. This will depend on various circumstances, including the number of shifts for which the asset will be used, the entity's repair and maintenance programme and so on. Other factors to be considered include obsolescence (due to technological advances/improvements in production/reduction in demand for the product/service produced by the asset) and legal restrictions, eg length of a related lease.

1.5 Residual value

In most cases the residual value of an asset is **likely to be immaterial**. If it is likely to be of any significant value, that value must be estimated at the date of purchase or any subsequent revaluation. The amount of residual value should be estimated based on the current situation with other similar assets, used in the same way, which are now at the end of their useful lives. Any expected costs of disposal should be offset against the gross residual value.

1.6 Depreciation methods

Consistency is important. The depreciation method selected should be applied consistently from period to period unless altered circumstances justify a change. When the method *is* changed, the effect should be quantified and disclosed and the reason for the change should be stated.

Various methods of allocating depreciation to accounting periods are available, but whichever is chosen must be applied **consistently** (as required by IAS 1), to ensure comparability from period to period. Change of policy is not allowed simply because of the profitability situation of the entity.

You should be familiar with the various **accepted methods of allocating depreciation** and the relevant calculations and accounting treatments, which are revised in questions at the end of this section.

1.7 Disclosure

An accounting policy note should disclose the **valuation bases** used for determining the amounts at which depreciable assets are stated, along with the other accounting policies.

IAS 16 also requires the following to be disclosed for each major class of depreciable asset.

- **Depreciation methods** used
- **Useful lives** or the depreciation rates used
- **Gross amount** of depreciable assets and the related accumulated depreciation

1.8 What is depreciation?

The need to depreciate non-current assets arises from the **accruals assumption**. If money is expended in purchasing an asset then the amount expended must at some time be charged against profits. If the asset is one which contributes to an entity's revenue over a number of accounting periods it would be inappropriate to charge any single period (eg the period in which the asset was acquired) with the whole of the expenditure. Instead, some method must be found of spreading the cost of the asset over its useful economic life.

This view of depreciation as a process of allocation of the cost of an asset over several accounting periods is the view adopted by IAS 16. It is worth mentioning here two **common misconceptions** about the purpose and effects of depreciation.

(a) It is sometimes thought that the net book value (NBV) of an asset is equal to its net realisable value and that the object of charging depreciation is to **reflect the fall in value of an asset over its life**. This misconception is the basis of a common, but incorrect, argument which says that freehold properties (say) need not be depreciated in times when property values are rising. It is true that historical cost often give a misleading impression when a property's NBV is much below its market value, but in such a case it is open to a business to incorporate a revaluation into its books, or even to prepare its accounts based on current costs. This is a separate problem from that of allocating the property's cost over successive accounting periods.

(b) Another misconception is that depreciation is provided **so that an asset can be replaced at the end of its useful life**. This is not the case.

   (i) If there is no intention of replacing the asset, it could then be argued that there is no need to provide for any depreciation at all.

   (ii) If prices are rising, the replacement cost of the asset will exceed the amount of depreciation provided.

Question 6.1

Deprecation I

Learning outcome C2(a)

A lorry bought for a business cost $17,000. It is expected to last for five years and then be sold for scrap for $2,000. Usage over the five years is expected to be:

Year 1	200 days
Year 2	100 days
Year 3	100 days
Year 4	150 days
Year 5	40 days

Required

Work out the depreciation to be charged each year under:

(a) The straight line method
(b) The reducing balance method (using a rate of 35%)
(c) The machine hour method

Question 6.2

Depreciation II

Learning outcome C2(a)

(a) What are the purposes of providing for depreciation?

(b) In what circumstances is the reducing balance method more appropriate than the straight-line method? Give reasons for your answer.

Question 6.3

Accounting entries

Learning outcome C2(a)

A business purchased two rivet-making machines on 1 January 20X5 at a cost of $15,000 each. Each had an estimated life of five years and a nil residual value. The straight line method of depreciation is used.

Owing to an unforeseen slump in market demand for rivets, the business decided to reduce its output of rivets, and switch to making other products instead. On 31 March 20X7, one rivet-making machine was sold (on credit) to a buyer for $8,000.

Later in the year, however, it was decided to abandon production of rivets altogether, and the second machine was sold on 1 December 20X7 for $2,500 cash.

Prepare the machinery account, provision for depreciation of machinery account and disposal of machinery account for the accounting year to 31 December 20X7.

Exam alert

Non-current assets are examined regularly.

Section summary

The **cost of a non-current asset**, less its estimated residual value, is allocated fairly between accounting periods by means of depreciation. The provision for depreciation is both:

- Charged against profit
- Deducted from the value of the non-current asset in the statement of financial position

2 IAS 16 *Property, plant and equipment*

Introduction

This section looks at IAS 16 and the rules for recognition, derecognition and measurement. We will also cover what happens when an asset is revalued.

2.1 Application of IAS 16

This standard covers all aspects of accounting for property, plant and equipment. This represents the bulk of items which are **'tangible' non-current assets**.

2.2 Scope

IAS 16 should be followed when accounting for property, plant and equipment *unless* another international accounting standard requires a **different treatment**.

IAS 16 **does not apply** to the following.

(a) Biological assets related to agricultural activity
(b) Mineral rights and mineral reserves, such as oil, gas and other non-regenerative resources

However, the standard applies to property, plant and equipment used to develop these assets.

2.3 Definitions

The standard gives a large number of definitions.

KEY TERMS

PROPERTY, PLANT AND EQUIPMENT are tangible assets that:

- are held for use in the production or supply of goods or services, for rental to others, or for administrative purposes; and
- are expected to be used during more than one period.

COST is the amount of cash or cash equivalents paid or the fair value of the other consideration given to acquire an asset at the time of its acquisition or construction.

RESIDUAL VALUE is the net amount which the entity expects to obtain for an asset at the end of its useful life after deducting the expected costs of disposal.

ENTITY-SPECIFIC VALUE is the present value of the cash flows an entity expects to arise from the continuing use of an asset and from its disposal at the end of its useful life, or expects to incur when settling a liability.

FAIR VALUE is the amount for which an asset could be exchanged between knowledgeable, willing parties in an arm's length transaction.

CARRYING AMOUNT is the amount at which an asset is recognised in the statement of financial position after deducting any accumulated depreciation and accumulated impairment losses.

An IMPAIRMENT LOSS is the amount by which the carrying amount of an asset exceeds its recoverable amount. *(IAS 16)*

Exam skills

These definitions are important. Make sure you know them all for the exam.

2.4 Recognition

In this context, recognition simply means incorporation of the item in the business's accounts, in this case as a non-current asset. The recognition of property, plant and equipment depends on two criteria.

(a) It is probable that **future economic benefits** associated with the asset will flow to the entity
(b) The cost of the asset to the entity can be **measured reliably**

These recognition criteria apply to **subsequent expenditure** as well as costs incurred initially. There are no longer any separate criteria for recognising subsequent expenditure.

Property, plant and equipment can amount to **substantial amounts** in financial statements, affecting the presentation of the company's financial position and the profitability of the entity, through depreciation and also if an asset is wrongly classified as an expense and taken to profit and loss.

2.4.1 First criterion: future economic benefits

The **degree of certainty** attached to the flow of future economic benefits must be assessed. This should be based on the evidence available at the date of initial recognition (usually the date of purchase). The entity should thus be assured that it will receive the rewards attached to the asset and it will incur the associated risks, which will only generally be the case when the rewards and risks have actually passed to the entity. Until then, the asset should not be recognised.

2.4.2 Second criterion: cost measured reliably

It is generally easy to measure the cost of an asset as the **transfer amount on purchase**, ie what was paid for it. **Self-constructed assets** can also be measured easily by adding together the purchase price of all the constituent parts (labour, material etc) paid to external parties.

2.5 Separate items

Most of the time assets will be identified individually, but this will not be the case for **smaller items**, such as tools, dies and moulds, which are sometimes classified as inventory and written off as an expense.

Major components or spare parts, however, should be recognised as property, plant and equipment.

For very **large and specialised items**, an apparently single asset should be broken down into its composite parts. This occurs where the different parts have different useful lives and different depreciation rates are applied to each part, eg an aircraft, where the body and engines are separated as they have different useful lives.

2.6 Safety and environmental equipment

When such assets as these are acquired they will qualify for recognition where they enable the entity to **obtain future economic benefits** from related assets in excess of those it would obtain otherwise. The recognition will only be to the extent that the carrying amount of the asset and related assets does not exceed the total recoverable amount of these assets.

2.7 Initial measurement

Once an item of property, plant and equipment qualifies for recognition as an asset, it will initially be **measured at cost**.

2.7.1 Components of cost

The standard lists the components of the cost of an item of property, plant and equipment.

- **Purchase price**, less any trade discount or rebate
- **Import duties** and non-refundable purchase taxes
- **Directly attributable costs** of bringing the asset to working condition for its intended use, eg:
  - The cost of site preparation
  - Initial delivery and handling costs
  - Installation costs
  - Testing
  - Professional fees (architects, engineers)
- Initial estimate of the cost of dismantling and removing the asset and restoring the site on which it is located

IAS 16 provides **additional guidance on directly attributable** costs included in the cost of an item of property, plant and equipment.

(a) These costs bring the asset to the location and working conditions necessary for it to be capable of operating in the manner intended by management, including those costs to test whether the asset is functioning properly.

(b) These are determined after deducting the net proceeds from selling any items produced when bringing the asset to its location and condition.

The standard also states that income and related expenses of operations that are **incidental** to the construction or development of an item of property, plant and equipment should be **recognised** in profit or loss.

The following costs **will not be part of the cost** of property, plant or equipment unless they can be attributed directly to the asset's acquisition, or bringing it into its working condition.

- Administration and other general overhead costs
- Start-up
- Initial operating losses before the asset reaches planned performance

All of these will be recognised as an **expense** rather than an asset.

In the case of **self-constructed assets**, the same principles are applied as for acquired assets. If the entity makes similar assets during the normal course of business for sale externally, then the cost of the asset will be the cost of its production under IAS 2 *Inventories*. This also means that abnormal costs (wasted material, labour or other resources) are excluded from the cost of the asset. An example of a self-constructed asset is when a building company builds its own head office.

2.7.2 Exchanges of assets

IAS 16 specifies that exchange of items of property, plant and equipment, regardless of whether the assets are similar, are measured at **fair value**, **unless the exchange transaction lacks commercial substance** or the fair value of neither of the assets exchanged can be **measured reliably**. If the acquired item is not measured at fair value, its cost is measured at the carrying amount of the asset given up.

2.7.3 Subsequent expenditure

Expenditure incurred in replacing or renewing a component of an item of property, plant and equipment must be **recognised in the carrying amount of the item**. The carrying amount of the replaced or renewed component must be derecognised. A similar approach is also applied when a separate component of an item of property, plant and equipment is identified in respect of a major inspection to enable the continued use of the item.

2.8 Measurement subsequent to initial recognition

The standard offers two possible treatments here, essentially a choice between keeping an asset recorded at **cost** or revaluing it to **fair value**.

(a) **Cost model.** Carry the asset at its cost less depreciation and any accumulated impairment losses.

(b) **Revaluation model.** Carry the asset at a revalued amount, being its fair value at the date of the revaluation less any subsequent accumulated depreciation and subsequent accumulated impairment losses. The revised IAS 16 makes clear that the **revaluation model is available only if the fair value of the item can be measured reliably**.

2.8.1 Revaluations

The **market value** of land and buildings usually represents fair value, assuming existing use and line of business. Such valuations are usually carried out by professionally qualified valuers.

In the case of **plant and equipment**, fair value can also be taken as **market value**. Where a market value is not available, however, depreciated replacement cost should be used. There may be no market value where types of plant and equipment are sold only rarely or because of their specialised nature (ie they would normally only be sold as part of an ongoing business).

The frequency of valuation depends on the **volatility of the fair values** of individual items of property, plant and equipment. The more volatile the fair value, the more frequently revaluations should be carried out. Where the current fair value is very different from the carrying value then a revaluation should be carried out.

Most importantly, when an item of property, plant and equipment is revalued, **the whole class of assets to which it belongs should be revalued.**

All the items within a class should be **revalued at the same time**, to prevent selective revaluation of certain assets and to avoid disclosing a mixture of costs and values from different dates in the financial statements. A rolling basis of revaluation is allowed if the revaluations are kept up to date and the revaluation of the whole class is completed in a short period of time.

How should any **increase in value** be treated when a revaluation takes place? The debit will be the increase in value in the statement of financial position, but what about the credit? IAS 16 requires the increase to be credited to a **revaluation surplus** (ie part of owners' equity), *unless* the increase is reversing a previous decrease which was recognised as an expense. To the extent that this offset is made, the increase is recognised as income; any excess is then taken to the revaluation surplus.

Example: Revaluation surplus

Binkie Co has an item of land carried in its books at $13,000. Two years ago a slump in land values led the company to reduce the carrying value from $15,000. This was taken as an expense in the income statement. There has been a surge in land prices in the current year, however, and the land is now worth $20,000.

Required

Account for the revaluation in the current year.

Solution

The double entry is:

DEBIT	Asset value (statement of financial position)	$7,000	
CREDIT	Income statement		$2,000
	Revaluation surplus		$5,000

Note: the credit to the revaluation surplus will be shown under 'other comprehensive income'.

The case is similar for a **decrease in value** on revaluation. Any decrease should be recognised as an expense, except where it offsets a previous increase taken as a revaluation surplus in owners' equity. Any decrease greater than the previous upwards increase in value must be taken as an expense in the profit or loss.

Example: Revaluation decrease

Let us simply swap round the example given above. The original cost was $15,000, revalued upwards to $20,000 two years ago. The value has now fallen to $13,000.

Required

Account for the decrease in value.

Solution

The double entry is:

DEBIT	Revaluation surplus	$5,000	
DEBIT	Income statement	$2,000	
CREDIT	Asset value (statement of financial position)		$7,000

There is a further complication when a **revalued asset is being depreciated**. As we have seen, an upward revaluation means that the depreciation charge will increase. Normally, a revaluation surplus is only realised when the asset is sold, but when it is being depreciated, part of that surplus is being realised as the asset is used. The amount of the surplus realised is the difference between depreciation charged on the revalued amount and the (lower) depreciation which would have been charged on the asset's original cost. **This amount can be transferred to retained (ie realised) earnings but *not* through profit or loss.**

Example: Revaluation and depreciation

Crinckle Co bought an asset for $10,000 at the beginning of 20X6. It had a useful life of five years. On 1 January 20X8 the asset was revalued to $12,000. The expected useful life has remained unchanged (ie three years remain).

Required

Account for the revaluation and state the treatment for depreciation from 20X8 onwards.

Solution

On 1 January 20X8 the carrying value of the asset is $10,000 – (2 × $10,000 ÷ 5) = $6,000. For the revaluation:

DEBIT	Asset value	$6,000	
CREDIT	Revaluation surplus		$6,000

The depreciation for the next three years will be $12,000 ÷ 3 = $4,000, compared to depreciation on cost of $10,000 ÷ 5 = $2,000. So each year, the extra $2,000 can be treated as part of the surplus which has become realised:

DEBIT	Revaluation surplus	$2,000	
CREDIT	Retained earnings		$2,000

This is a movement on owners' equity only, not an item in the income statement.

Exam skills

The transfer of excess depreciation to retained earnings is optional. Do not do this unless the question tells you to.

2.9 Depreciation

The standard states:

- The **depreciable amount** of an item of property, plant and equipment should be allocated on a systematic basis over its useful life.
- The **depreciation method** used should reflect the pattern in which the asset's economic benefits are consumed by the entity.
- The **depreciation charge** for each period should be recognised as an expense unless it is included in the carrying amount of another asset.

Land and buildings are dealt with separately even when they are acquired together because land normally has an unlimited life and is therefore not depreciated. In contrast buildings do have a limited life and must be depreciated. Any increase in the value of land on which a building is standing will have no impact on the determination of the building's useful life.

Depreciation is usually treated as an **expense**, but not where it is absorbed by the entity in the process of producing other assets. For example, depreciation of plant and machinery may be incurred in the production of goods for sale (inventory items). In such circumstances, the depreciation is included in the cost of the new assets produced.

2.9.1 Review of useful life

A review of the **useful life** of property, plant and equipment should be carried out at **least each financial year end** and the depreciation charge for the current and future periods should be adjusted if expectations have changed significantly from previous estimates. Changes are changes in accounting estimates and are accounted for prospectively as adjustments to future depreciation.

2.9.2 Review of depreciation method

The **depreciation method** should also be reviewed **at least each financial year end** and, if there has been a significant change in the expected pattern of economic benefits from those assets, the method should be changed to suit this changed pattern. When such a change in depreciation method takes place the change should be accounted for as a **change in accounting estimate** and the depreciation charge for the current and future periods should be adjusted.

2.9.3 Impairment of asset values

An **impairment loss** should be treated in the same way as a **revaluation decrease** ie the decrease should be **recognised as an expense**. However, a revaluation decrease (or impairment loss) should be charged directly against any related revaluation surplus to the extent that the decrease does not exceed the amount held in the revaluation surplus in respect of that same asset.

A **reversal of an impairment** loss should be treated in the same way as a **revaluation increase**, ie a revaluation increase should be recognised as income to the extent that it reverses a revaluation decrease or an impairment loss of the same asset previously recognised as an expense.

2.10 Retirements and disposals

When an asset is permanently **withdrawn from use, or sold or scrapped**, and no future economic benefits are expected from its disposal, it should be withdrawn from the statement of financial position.

Gains or losses are the difference between the net disposal proceeds and the carrying amount of the asset. They should be recognised as income or expense in profit or loss. This applies also to **revalued assets**. The gain or loss on disposal is the difference between the carrying value at the date of disposal and the proceeds.

2.11 Derecognition

An entity is required to **derecognise the carrying amount** of an item of property, plant or equipment that it disposes of on the date the **criteria for the sale of goods** in IAS 18 *Revenue* would be met. This also applies to parts of an asset.

An entity cannot classify as revenue a gain it realises on the disposal of an item of property, plant and equipment.

2.12 Disclosure

The standard has a long list of disclosure requirements, for each class of property, plant and equipment.

(a) **Measurement bases** for determining the gross carrying amount (if more than one, the gross carrying amount for that basis in each category)

(b) **Depreciation methods** used

(c) **Useful lives** or depreciation rates used

(d) **Gross carrying amount** and accumulated depreciation (aggregated with accumulated impairment losses) at the beginning and end of the period

(e) **Reconciliation** of the carrying amount at the beginning and end of the period showing:

- (i) Additions
- (ii) Disposals and assets classified as 'held for sale' in accordance with IFRS 5
- (iii) Acquisitions through business combinations
- (iv) Increases/decreases during the period from revaluations and from impairment losses
- (v) Impairment losses recognised in profit or loss

(vi) Impairment losses reversed in profit or loss
(vii) Depreciation

The financial statements should also disclose the following.

(a) Existence and amounts of **restrictions on title**, and items pledged as security for liabilities
(b) Amount of commitments to **acquisitions**

Revalued assets require further disclosures.

(a) Basis used to revalue the assets

(b) Effective date of the revaluation

(c) Whether an independent valuer was involved

(d) Carrying amount of each class of property, plant and equipment that would have been included in the financial statements had the assets not been revalued.

(e) Revaluation surplus.

The following format (with notional figures) is commonly used to disclose non-current asset movements.

	Total	*Land and buildings*	*Plant and equipment*
	$	$	$
Cost or valuation			
At 1 January 20X4	50,000	40,000	10,000
Revaluation surplus	12,000	12,000	–
Additions in year	4,000	–	4,000
Disposals in year	(1,000)	–	(1,000)
At 31 December 20X4	65,000	52,000	13,000
Depreciation			
At 1 January 20X4	16,000	10,000	6,000
Charge for year	4,000	1,000	3,000
Eliminated on disposals	(500)	–	(500)
At 31 December 20X4	19,500	11,000	8,500
Carrying value			
At 31 December 20X4	45,500	41,000	4,500
At 1 January 20X4	34,000	30,000	4,000

Exam alert

You could be asked to produce a disclosure note for non-current assets in an exam question.

Question 6.4

IAS 16

Learning outcome C2(a)

(a) In a statement of financial position prepared in accordance with IAS 16, what does carrying value represent?

(b) In a set of financial statements prepared in accordance with IAS 16, is it correct to say that the carrying value figure in a statement of financial position cannot be greater than the market (net realisable) value of the partially used asset as at the end of the reporting period? Explain your reasons for your answer.

Section summary

IAS 16 *Property, plant and equipment* provides the basic rules on **depreciation** including important definitions of depreciation, depreciable assets, useful life and depreciable amount.

When a non-current asset is **revalued**, depreciation is charged on the revalued amount.

When a non-current asset is **sold**, there is likely to be a profit or loss on disposal. This is the difference between the net sale price of the asset and its net book value at the time of disposal.

3 IAS 36 *Impairment of assets*

Introduction

There is an established principle that assets should not be carried at above their recoverable amount. An entity should write down the carrying value of an asset to its recoverable amount if the carrying value of an asset is not recoverable in full. IAS 36 was published in June 1998 and was revised in March 2004. It puts in place a detailed methodology for carrying out impairment reviews and related accounting treatments and disclosures. We will look at the standard in this section.

3.1 Scope

IAS 36 applies to all tangible, intangible and financial assets except inventories, assets arising from construction contracts, deferred tax assets, assets arising under IAS 19 *Employee benefits* and financial assets within the scope of IAS 32 *Financial instruments, disclosure and presentation*. This is because those IASs already have rules for recognising and measuring impairment. Note also that IAS 36 does not apply to non-current assets held for sale, which are dealt with under IFRS 5 *Non-current assets held for sale and discontinued operations*.

KEY TERM

IMPAIRMENT: a fall in the value of an asset, so that its 'recoverable amount' is now less than its carrying value in the statement of financial position. *(IAS 36)*

The basic principle underlying IAS 36 is relatively straightforward. If an asset's value in the accounts is higher than its realistic value, measured as its 'recoverable amount', the asset is judged to have suffered an impairment loss. It should therefore be reduced in value, by the amount of the **impairment loss**. The amount of the impairment loss should be **written off against profit** immediately.

The main accounting issues to consider are therefore as follows.

(a) How is it possible to **identify when** an impairment loss may have occurred?
(b) How should the **recoverable amount** of the asset be measured?
(c) How should an 'impairment loss' be **reported in the accounts**?

3.2 Identifying a potentially impaired asset

An entity should assess at the end of each reporting period whether there are any indications of impairment to any assets. The concept of **materiality** applies, and only material impairment needs to be identified.

If there are indications of possible impairment, the entity is required to make a formal estimate of the **recoverable amount** of the assets concerned.

IAS 36 suggests how **indications of a possible impairment** of assets might be recognised. The suggestions are based largely on common sense.

(a) **External sources of information**

(i) A fall in the asset's market value that is significantly more than would normally be expected from passage of time or normal use.

(ii) Significant adverse changes in the technological, market, economic or legal environment in which the entity operates.

(iii) An increase in market interest rates or other market rates of return on investments likely to affect the discount rate used in calculating value in use.

(iv) The carrying amount of the entity's net assets being more than its market capitalisation.

(b) **Internal sources of information**: evidence of obsolescence or physical damage, adverse changes in the use to which the asset is put, or the asset's economic performance

Even if there are no indications of impairment, the following assets must **always** be tested for impairment annually.

(a) An intangible asset with an **indefinite useful life**
(b) **Goodwill** acquired in a business combination

3.3 Measuring the recoverable amount of the asset

What is an asset's recoverable amount?

KEY TERM

The RECOVERABLE AMOUNT of an asset should be measured as the *higher value* of:

(a) the asset's fair value less costs to sell; and
(b) its value in use. *(IAS 36)*

An asset's fair value less costs to sell is the amount net of selling costs that could be obtained from the sale of the asset. Selling costs include sales transaction costs, such as legal expenses.

(a) If there is **an active market** in the asset, the net selling price should be based on the **market value**, or on the price of recent transactions in similar assets.

(b) If there is **no active market** in the assets it might be possible to **estimate** a net selling price using best estimates of what 'knowledgeable, willing parties' might pay in an arm's length transaction.

Net selling price **cannot** be reduced, however, by including within selling costs any **restructuring or reorganisation expenses**, or any costs that have already been recognised in the accounts as liabilities.

The concept of 'value in use' is very important.

KEY TERM

The VALUE IN USE of an asset is measured as the present value of future cash flows expected to be derived from an asset or cash-generating unit.

The cash flows used in the calculation should be **pre-tax cash flows** and a **pre-tax discount rate** should be applied to calculate the present value.

The calculation of **value in use** must reflect the following.

(a) An estimate of the **future cash flows** the entity expects to derive from the asset
(b) Expectations about **possible variations** in the amount and timing of future cash flows
(c) The **time value of money**
(d) The price for bearing the **uncertainty** inherent in the asset, and
(e) **Other factors** that would be reflected in pricing future cash flows from the asset

Calculating a value in use therefore calls for estimates of future cash flows, and the possibility exists that an entity might come up with **over-optimistic estimates** of cash flows. The IAS therefore states the following.

(a) Cash flow projections should be based on **'reasonable and supportable' assumptions**.

(b) Projections of cash flows, normally up to a maximum period of five years, should be based on the most **recent budgets or financial forecasts**.

(c) Cash flow projections beyond this period should be obtained by extrapolating short-term projections, using either a **steady or declining growth rate** for each subsequent year (unless a rising growth rate can be justified). The long term growth rate applied should not exceed the average long term growth rate for the product, market, industry or country, unless a higher growth rate can be justified.

3.3.1 Composition of estimates of future cash flows

These should include the following.

(a) Projections of **cash inflows** from **continuing use** of the asset

(b) Projections of **cash outflows** necessarily incurred to **generate the cash inflows** from continuing use of the asset

(c) **Net cash flows** received/paid on **disposal** of the asset at the end of its useful life

There is an underlying principle that future cash flows should be estimated for the asset in its current condition. Future cash flows relating to restructurings to which the entity is not yet committed, or to future costs to add to, replace part of, or service the asset are excluded.

Estimates of future cash flows should **exclude** the following.

(a) Cash inflows/ outflows from financing activities
(b) Income tax receipts/payments

The amount of net cash inflow/outflow on **disposal** of an asset should assume an arm's length transaction.

Foreign currency future cash flows should be forecast in the currency in which they will arise and will be discounted using a rule appropriate for that currency. The resulting figure should then be translated into the reporting currency at the spot rate at the end of the reporting period.

The **discount rate** should be a current pre-tax rate (or rates) that reflects the current assessment of the time value of money and the risks specific to the asset. The discount should not include a risk weighting if the underlying cash flows have already been adjusted for risk.

3.4 Recognition and measurement of an impairment loss

The rule for assets at historical cost is:

KEY POINT

If the recoverable amount of an asset is lower than the carrying amount, the carrying amount should be reduced by the difference (ie the impairment loss) which should be charged as an expense in profit or loss.

The rule for assets held at a revalued amount (such as property revalued under IAS 16) is:

KEY POINT

The impairment loss is to be treated as a revaluation decrease under the relevant IAS.

In practice this means:

- To the extent that there is a revaluation surplus held in respect of the asset, the impairment loss should be charged to revaluation surplus.
- Any excess should be charged to profit or loss.

The IAS goes into quite a large amount of detail about the important concept of cash generating units. As a basic rule, the recoverable amount of an asset should be calculated for the **asset individually**. However, there will be occasions when it is not possible to estimate such a value for an individual asset, particularly

in the calculation of value in use. This is because cash inflows and outflows cannot be attributed to the individual asset.

KEY TERM

A CASH GENERATING UNIT is the smallest identifiable group of assets for which independent cash flows can be identified and measured.

Question 6.5 Cash-generating unit

Learning outcome C2(a)

Can you think of some examples of how a cash-generating unit would be identified?

Example: Recoverable amount and carrying amount

Fourways Co is made up of four cash-generating units. All four units are being tested for impairment.

(a) Property, plant and equipment and separate intangibles would be allocated to the cash-generating units as far as possible.

(b) Current assets such as inventories, receivables and prepayments would be allocated to the relevant cash-generating units.

(c) Liabilities (eg payables) would be deducted from the net assets of the relevant cash-generating units.

(d) The net figure for each cash-generating unit resulting from this exercise would be compared to the relevant recoverable amount, computed on the same basis.

3.5 Goodwill and the impairment of assets

Goodwill acquired in a business combination does not generate cash flows independently of other assets. It must be **allocated** to each of the acquirer's **cash-generating units** (or groups of cash-generating units) that are expected to benefit from the synergies of the combination.

A cash-generating unit to which goodwill has been allocated is tested for impairment annually. The **carrying amount** of the unit, including goodwill, is **compared with the recoverable amount**. If the carrying amount of the unit exceeds the recoverable amount, the entity must recognise an impairment loss.

The annual impairment test may be performed at any time during an accounting period, but must be performed at the **same time every year**.

3.6 Corporate assets

Corporate assets are group or divisional assets such as a head office building, computer equipment or a research centre. Essentially, corporate assets are assets that do not generate cash inflows independently from other assets, hence their carrying amount cannot be fully attributed to a cash-generating unit under review.

In testing a cash-generating unit for impairment, an entity should identify all the corporate assets that relate to the cash-generating unit. Corporate assets will need to be allocated to cash-generating units on a reasonable and consistent basis.

3.7 Accounting treatment of an impairment loss

If, and only if, the recoverable amount of an asset is less than its carrying amount in the statement of financial position, an impairment loss has occurred. This loss should be **recognised immediately**.

(a) The asset's **carrying amount** should be reduced to its recoverable amount in the statement of financial position.

(b) The **impairment loss** should be recognised immediately in profit or loss (unless the asset has been revalued in which case the loss is treated as a revaluation decrease).

After reducing an asset to its recoverable amount, the **depreciation charge** on the asset should then be based on its new carrying amount, its estimated residual value (if any) and its estimated remaining useful life.

An impairment loss should be recognised for a **cash-generating unit** if (and only if) the recoverable amount for the cash-generating unit is less than the carrying amount in the statement of financial position for all the assets in the unit. When an impairment loss is recognised for a cash-generating unit, the loss should be allocated between the assets in the unit in the following order.

(a) First, to the **goodwill** allocated to the cash-generating unit
(b) Then to all other assets in the cash-generating unit, on a **pro rata basis**

In allocating an impairment loss, the carrying amount of an asset should not be reduced below the highest of:

(a) Its fair value less costs to sell
(b) Its value in use (if determinable)
(c) Zero

Any remaining amount of an impairment loss should be recognised as a liability if required by other IASs.

Example: Impairment loss 1

A company that extracts natural gas and oil has a drilling platform in the Caspian Sea. It is required by legislation of the country concerned to remove and dismantle the platform at the end of its useful life. Accordingly, the company has included an amount in its accounts for removal and dismantling costs, and is depreciating this amount over the platform's expected life.

The company is carrying out an exercise to establish whether there has been an impairment of the platform.

(a) Its carrying amount in the statement of financial position is $3m.

(b) The company has received an offer of $2.8m for the platform from another oil company. The bidder would take over the responsibility (and costs) for dismantling and removing the platform at the end of its life.

(c) The present value of the estimated cash flows from the platform's continued use is $3.3m.

(d) The carrying amount in the statement of financial position for the provision for dismantling and removal is currently $0.6m.

What should be the value of the drilling platform in the statement of financial position, and what, if anything, is the impairment loss?

Solution

Fair value less costs to sell	=	$2.8m
Value in use	=	PV of cash flows from use less the carrying amount of the provision/liability = $3.3m – S0.6m = $2.7m
Recoverable amount	=	Higher of these two amounts, ie $2.8m
Carrying value	=	$3m
Impairment loss	=	$0.2m

The carrying value should be reduced to $2.8m

Example: Impairment loss 2

A company has acquired another business for $4.5m: tangible assets are valued at $4.0m and goodwill at $0.5m.

An asset with a carrying value of $1m is destroyed in a terrorist attack. The asset was not insured. The loss of the asset, without insurance, has prompted the company to estimate whether there has been an impairment of assets in the acquired business and what the amount of any such loss is. The recoverable amount of the business (a single cash-generating unit) is measured as $3.1m.

Solution

There has been an impairment loss of $1.4m ($4.5m – $3.1m).

The impairment loss will be recognised in profit or loss. The loss will be allocated between the assets in the cash-generating unit as follows.

(a) A loss of $1m can be attributed directly to the uninsured asset that has been destroyed.
(b) The remaining loss of $0.4m should be allocated to goodwill.

The carrying value of the assets will now be $3m for tangible assets and $0.1m for goodwill.

3.8 Disclosure

IAS 36 calls for substantial disclosure about impairment of assets. The information to be disclosed includes the following.

(a) For each class of assets, the amount of **impairment losses recognised** and the amount of any **impairment losses recovered** (ie reversals of impairment losses)

(b) For each individual asset or cash-generating unit that has suffered a **significant impairment loss**, details of the nature of the asset, the amount of the loss, the events that led to recognition of the loss, whether the recoverable amount is fair value price less costs to sell or value in use, and if the recoverable amount is value in use, the basis on which this value was estimated (eg the discount rate applied)

Section summary

The main aspects of IAS 36 to consider are:

- Indications of impairment of assets
- Measuring recoverable amount, as net selling price or value in use
- Measuring value in use
- Cash-generating units
- Accounting treatment of an impairment loss, for individual assets and cash-generating units

4 IAS 23 *Borrowing costs*

Introduction

This short section covers borrowing costs and available-for-sale financial assets.

4.1 Definitions

Only two definitions are given by the standard.

KEY TERMS

BORROWING COSTS. Interest and other costs incurred by an entity in connection with the borrowing of funds.

QUALIFYING ASSET. An asset that necessarily takes a substantial period of time to get ready for its intended use or sale. *(IAS 23)*

4.2 Capitalisation

All eligible borrowing costs must be **capitalised**.

Only borrowing costs that are **directly attributable** to the acquisition, construction or production of a qualifying asset can be capitalised as part of the cost of that asset. The standard lays out the criteria for determining which borrowing costs are eligible for capitalisation.

4.2.1 Borrowing costs eligible for capitalisation

Those borrowing costs directly attributable to the acquisition, construction or production of a qualifying asset must be identified. These are the borrowing costs that **would have been avoided** had the expenditure on the qualifying asset not been made. This is obviously straightforward where funds have been borrowed for the financing of one particular asset.

4.2.2 Disclosure

The following should be disclosed in the financial statements in relation to borrowing costs.

(a) Amount of borrowing costs capitalised during the period

(b) Capitalisation rate used to determine the amount of borrowing costs eligible for capitalisation

4.3 Available-for-sale financial assets

The non-current asset section of the statement of financial position includes a category for **available-for-sale financial assets**. These are investments in equity and other shares in other entities, as categorised by IAS 39.

This designation does not mean that they are held for the purpose of selling them. It simply means that they are available for sale. They are carried at fair value, which will probably be open market value.

You are most likely to encounter these assets, if at all, as an item on the statement of financial position in your section C question.

Any increase in the value of these assets should go to the revaluation surplus.

Section summary

IAS 23 looks at the treatment of borrowing costs, particularly where the related borrowings are applied to the **construction of certain assets**.

Chapter Roundup

- ✓ The **cost of a non-current asset**, less its estimated residual value, is allocated fairly between accounting periods by means of depreciation. The provision for depreciation is both:
  - Charged against profit
  - Deducted from the value of the non-current asset in the statement of financial position.
- ✓ IAS 16 *Property, plant and equipment* provides the basic rules on **depreciation**, including important definitions of depreciation, depreciable assets, useful life and depreciable amount.
- ✓ When a non-current asset is **revalued**, depreciation is charged on the revalued amount.
- ✓ When a non-current asset is **sold**, there is likely to be a profit or loss on disposal. This is the difference between the net sale price of the asset and its net book value at the time of disposal.
- ✓ The main aspects of IAS 36 to consider are:
  - Indications of impairment of assets
  - Measuring recoverable amount, as net selling price or value in use
  - Measuring value in use
  - Cash-generating unit
  - Accounting treatment of an impairment loss, for individual assets and cash-generating units
- ✓ IAS 23 looks at the treatment of borrowing costs, particularly where the related borrowings are applied to the **construction of certain assets**.

Quick Quiz

1 Define depreciation.

2 Which of the following elements can be included in the production cost of a non-current asset?

A Purchase price
B Architect's fees
C Import duties
D Installation costs

3 Market value can usually be taken as fair value.

True ☐

False ☐

4 Define impairment.

5 Any increase in the value of available for-sale assets should go to the .... surplus.

Answers to Quick Quiz

1 The result of the systematic allocation of the depreciable amount of an asset over its useful life.
2 All of them.
3 True
4 A fall in value of an asset, so that its 'recoverable amount' is less than its carrying value.
5 Revaluation

Answers to Questions

6.1 Depreciation I

(a) Under the straight line method, depreciation for each of the five years is:

$$\text{Annual depreciation} = \frac{\$(17{,}000 - 2{,}000)}{5} = \$3{,}000$$

(b) Under the reducing balance method, depreciation for each of the five years is:

Year	Depreciation	
1	35% × $17,000	= $5,950
2	35% × ($17,000 – $5,950) = 35% × $11,050	= $3,868
3	35% × ($11,050 – $3,868) = 35% × $7,182	= $2,514
4	35% × ($7,182 – $2,514) = 35% × $4,668	= $1,634
5	Balance to bring book value down to $2,000 = $4,668 – $1,634 – $2,000	= $1,034

(c) Under the machine hour method, depreciation for each of the five years is calculated as follows.

Total usage (days) = 200 + 100 + 100 + 150 + 40 = 590 days

$$\text{Depreciation per day} = \frac{\$(17{,}000 - 2{,}000)}{590} = \$25.42$$

Year	Usage (days)	Depreciation ($) (days × $25.42)
1	200	5,084.00
2	100	2,542.00
3	100	2,542.00
4	150	3,813.00
5	40	1,016.80
		14,997.80

Note. The answer does not come to exactly $15,000 because of the rounding carried out at the 'depreciation per day' stage of the calculation.

6.2 Depreciation II

(a) The accounts of a business try to recognise that the cost of a non-current asset is gradually consumed as the asset wears out. This is done by gradually writing off the asset's cost to profit or loss over several accounting periods. This process is known as depreciation, and is an example of the accruals assumption. IAS 16 *Property, plant and equipment* requires that depreciation should be allocated on a systematic basis to each accounting period during the useful life of the asset.

With regard to the accrual principle, it is fair that the profits should be reduced by the depreciation charge; this is not an arbitrary exercise. Depreciation is not, as is sometimes supposed, an attempt to set aside funds to purchase new non-current assets when required. Depreciation is not generally provided on freehold land because it does not 'wear out' (unless it is held for mining etc).

(b) The reducing balance method of depreciation is used instead of the straight line method when it is considered fair to allocate a greater proportion of the total depreciable amount to the earlier years and a lower proportion to the later years on the assumption that the benefits obtained by the business from using the asset decline over time.

In favour of this method it may be argued that it links the depreciation charge to the costs of maintaining and running the asset. In the early years these costs are low and the depreciation charge is high, while in later years this is reversed.

6.3 Accounting entries

MACHINERY ACCOUNT

		$			$
20X7			*20X7*		
1 Jan	Balance b/f	30,000	31 Mar	Disposal of machinery account	15,000
			1 Dec	Disposal of machinery account	15,000
		30,000			30,000

ACCUMULATED DEPRECIATION OF MACHINERY

		$			$
20X7			*20X7*		
31 Mar	Disposal of machinery account*	6,750	1 Jan	Balance b/f	12,000
1 Dec	Disposal of machinery account**	8,750	31 Dec	Income statement***	3,500
		15,500			15,500

* Depreciation at date of disposal = $6,000 + $750

** Depreciation at date of disposal = $6,000 + $2,750

*** Depreciation charge for the year = $750 + $2,750

DISPOSAL OF MACHINERY

		$			$
20X7			*20X7*		
31 Mar	Machinery account	15,000	31 Mar	Account receivable (sale price)	8,000
1 Dec	Machinery account	15,000	31 Mar	Provision for depreciation	6,750
			1 Dec	Cash (sale price)	2,500
			1 Dec	Provision for depreciation	8,750
			31 Dec	Income statement (loss on disposal)	4,000
		30,000			30,000

You should be able to calculate that there was a loss on the first disposal of $250, and on the second disposal of $3,750, giving a total loss of $4,000.

Workings

1 At 1 January 20X7, accumulated depreciation on the machines will be:

$$2 \text{ machines} \times 2 \text{ years} \times \frac{\$15{,}000}{5} \text{ per machine pa} = \$12{,}000, \text{ or } \$6{,}000 \text{ per machine}$$

2 Monthly depreciation is $\frac{\$3{,}000}{12}$ = $250 per machine per month

3 The machines are disposed of in 20X7.

(a) On 31 March – after 3 months of the year. Depreciation for the year on the machine = 3 months × $250 = $750.

(b) On 1 December – after 11 months of the year. Depreciation for the year on the machine = 11 months × $250 = $2,750

6.4 IAS 16

(a) In simple terms the carrying value of an asset is the cost of an asset less the 'accumulated depreciation', that is all depreciation charged so far. It should be emphasised that the main purpose of charging depreciation is to ensure that profits are fairly reported. Thus depreciation is concerned with the statement of comprehensive income rather than the statement of financial position. In consequence the carrying value in the statement of financial position can be quite arbitrary. In particular, it does not necessarily bear any relation to the market value of an asset and is of little use for planning and decision making.

An obvious example of the disparity between carrying value and market value is found in the case of buildings, which may be worth more than ten times as much as their carrying value.

(b) Carrying value can in some circumstances be higher than market value (net realisable value). IAS 16 *Property, plant and equipment* states that the carrying value of an asset cannot be greater than its 'recoverable amount'. However 'recoverable amount' as defined in IAS 16 is the amount recoverable from further use. This may be higher than the market value.

This makes sense if you think of a specialised machine which could not fetch much on the secondhand market but which will produce goods which can be sold at a profit for many years.

6.5 Cash-generating unit

Here are two possibilities.

(a) A mining company owns a private railway that it uses to transport output from one of its mines. The railway now has no market value other than as scrap, and it is impossible to identify any separate cash inflows with the use of the railway itself. Consequently, if the mining company suspects an impairment in the value of the railway, it should treat the mine as a whole as a cash-generating unit, and measure the recoverable amount of the mine as a whole.

(b) A bus company has an arrangement with a town's authorities to run a bus service on four routes in the town. Separately identifiable assets are allocated to each of the bus routes, and cash inflows and outflows can be attributed to each individual route. Three routes are running at a profit and one is running at a loss. The bus company suspects that there is an impairment of assets on the loss-making route. However, the company will be unable to close the loss-making route, because it is under an obligation to operate all four routes, as part of its contract with the local authority. Consequently, the company should treat all four bus routes together as a cash-generating unit, and calculate the recoverable amount for the unit as a whole.

Now try these questions from the Exam Question Bank

Number	Level	Marks	Time
Q17	Examination	5	9 mins

INTANGIBLE NON-CURRENT ASSETS

We begin our examination of intangible non-current assets with a discussion of a revised IAS on the subject **(IAS 38)**.

Goodwill and its treatment is a controversial area, as is the accounting for items similar to goodwill, such as brands. Goodwill is very important in **group accounts** which we will cover later in this text.

In Section 3 we look in more detail at the IAS 38 provisions covering research and development.

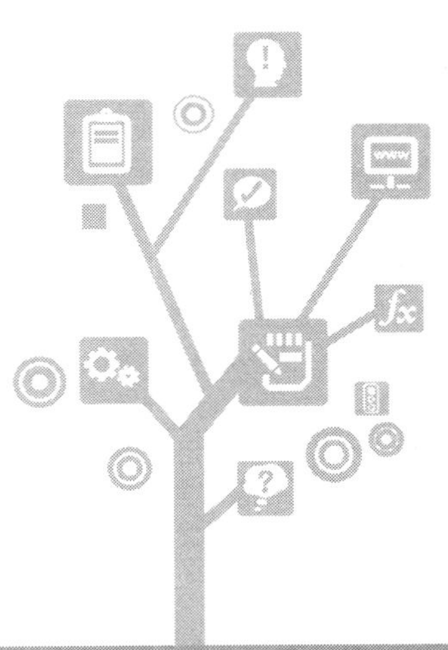

topic list	learning outcomes	syllabus references	ability required
1 IAS 38 *Intangible assets*	C2(a)	C2(iv)	application
2 Goodwill	C2(a)	C2(iv)	application
3 Research and development costs	C2(a)	C2(iii)	application

1 IAS 38 *Intangible assets*

Introduction

This section covers IAS 38 *Intangible assets* which was originally published in September 1998. It has been revised to reflect changes introduced by IFRS 3 *Business combinations.*

1.1 The objectives of the standard

(a) To establish the criteria for when intangible assets may or should be **recognised**
(b) To specify how intangible assets should be **measured**
(c) To specify the **disclosure requirements** for intangible assets

It applies to all intangible assets with certain **exceptions**: deferred tax assets (IAS 12), leases that fall within the scope of IAS 17, financial assets, insurance contracts, assets arising from employee benefits (IAS 19), non-current assets held for sale and mineral rights and exploration and extraction costs for minerals etc (although intangible assets used to develop or maintain these rights are covered by the standard). It does *not* apply to goodwill acquired in a business combination, which is dealt with under IFRS 3 *Business combinations.*

1.2 Definition of an intangible asset

The definition of an intangible asset is a key aspect of the standard, because the rules for deciding whether or not an intangible asset may be **recognised** in the accounts of an entity are based on the definition of what an intangible asset is.

KEY TERM

An INTANGIBLE ASSET is an identifiable non-monetary asset without physical substance. The asset must be:

(a) Controlled by the entity as a result of events in the past, and
(b) Something from which the entity expects future economic benefits to flow.

Examples of items that might be considered as intangible assets include computer software, patents, copyrights, motion picture films, customer lists, franchises and fishing rights. An item should not be recognised as an intangible asset, however, unless it **fully meets the definition** in the standard. The guidelines go into great detail on this matter.

1.3 Intangible asset: must be identifiable

An intangible asset must be identifiable in order to distinguish it from goodwill. With non-physical items, there may be a problem with **'identifiability'**.

(a) If an intangible asset is **acquired separately through purchase**, there may be a transfer of a legal right that would help to make an asset identifiable.

(b) An intangible asset may be identifiable if it is **separable**, ie if it could be rented or sold separately. However, 'separability' is not an essential feature of an intangible asset.

1.4 Intangible asset: control by the entity

Another element of the definition of an intangible asset is that it must be under the control of the entity as a result of a past event. The entity must therefore be able to enjoy the future economic benefits from the asset, and prevent the access of others to those benefits. A **legally enforceable right** is evidence of such control, but is not always a *necessary* condition.

(a) Control over **technical knowledge or know-how** only exists if it is protected by a **legal right**.

(b) The skill of employees, arising out of the benefits of **training costs**, are most unlikely to be recognisable as an intangible asset, because an entity does not control the future actions of its staff.

(c) Similarly, **market share and customer loyalty** cannot normally be intangible assets, since an entity cannot control the actions of its customers.

1.5 Intangible asset: expected future economic benefits

An item can only be recognised as an intangible asset if economic benefits are expected to flow in the future from ownership of the asset. Economic benefits may come from the **sale** of products or services, or from a **reduction in expenditures** (cost savings).

An intangible asset, when recognised initially, must be measured at **cost**. It should be recognised if, and only if **both** the following occur.

(a) It is probable that the **future economic benefits** that are attributable to the asset will **flow to the entity.**

(b) The **cost can be measured reliably**.

Management has to exercise its judgement in assessing the degree of certainty attached to the flow of economic benefits to the entity. External evidence is best.

(a) If an intangible asset is **acquired separately**, its cost can usually be measured reliably as its purchase price (including incidental costs of purchase such as legal fees, and any costs incurred in getting the asset ready for use).

(b) When an intangible asset is acquired as **part of a business combination** (ie an acquisition or takeover), the cost of the intangible asset is its fair value at the date of the acquisition.

IFRS 3 explains that the fair value of intangible assets acquired in business combinations can normally be measured with sufficient reliability to be **recognised separately** from goodwill.

Quoted market prices in an active market provide the most reliable estimate of the fair value of an intangible asset. If no active market exists for an intangible asset, its fair value is the amount that the entity would have paid for the asset, at the acquisition date, in an arm's length transaction between knowledgeable and willing parties, on the basis of the best information available. In determining this amount, an entity should consider the outcome of recent transactions for similar assets. There are techniques for estimating the fair values of unique intangible assets (such as brand names) and these may be used to measure an intangible asset acquired in a business combination.

In accordance with IAS 20, intangible assets acquired by way of government grant and the grant itself may be recorded initially either at cost (which may be zero) or fair value.

1.6 Exchanges of assets

If one intangible asset is exchanged for another, the cost of the intangible asset is measured at fair value unless:

(a) The exchange transaction lacks commercial substance, or
(b) The fair value of neither the asset received nor the asset given up can be measured reliably.

Otherwise, its cost is measured at the carrying amount of the asset given up.

1.7 Internally generated goodwill

KEY POINT

Internally generated goodwill may **not** be recognised as an **asset**.

The standard deliberately precludes recognition of internally generated goodwill because it requires that, for initial recognition, the cost of the asset rather than its fair value should be capable of being measured reliably and that it should be identifiable and controlled. Thus you do not recognise an asset which is subjective and cannot be measured reliably.

1.8 Research costs

Research activities by definition do not meet the criteria for recognition under IAS 38. This is because, at the research stage of a project, it cannot be certain that future economic benefits will probably flow to the entity from the project. There is too much uncertainty about the likely success or otherwise of the project. **Research costs should therefore be written off as an expense as they are incurred**.

1.9 Other internally generated intangible assets

The standard **prohibits** the recognition of **internally generated brands**, **mastheads**, **publishing titles and customer lists** and similar items as intangible assets. These all fail to meet one or more (in some cases all) of the definition and recognition criteria and in some cases are probably indistinguishable from internally generated goodwill.

1.10 Cost of an internally generated intangible asset

The costs allocated to an internally generated intangible asset should be only costs that can be **directly attributed** or allocated on a reasonable and consistent basis to creating, producing or preparing the asset for its intended use. The principles underlying the costs which may or may not be included are similar to those for other non-current assets and inventory.

The cost of an internally operated intangible asset is the sum of the **expenditure incurred from the date when** the intangible asset first **meets the recognition criteria**. If, as often happens, considerable costs have already been recognised as expenses before management could demonstrate that the criteria have been met, this earlier expenditure should not be retrospectively recognised at a later date as part of the cost of an intangible asset.

Question 7.1 — Intangible asset

Learning outcome C2(a)

Doug Co is developing a new production process. During 20X3, expenditure incurred was $100,000, of which $90,000 was incurred before 1 December 20X3 and $10,000 between 1 December 20X3 and 31 December 20X3. Doug Co can demonstrate that, at 1 December 20X3, the production process met the criteria for recognition as an intangible asset. The recoverable amount of the know-how embodied in the process is estimated to be $50,000.

How should the expenditure be treated?

1.11 Recognition of an expense

All expenditure related to an intangible which does not meet the criteria for recognition either as an identifiable intangible asset or as goodwill arising on an acquisition should be **expensed as incurred**. The IAS gives examples of such expenditure.

- Start up costs
- Training costs
- Advertising costs
- Business relocation costs

Prepaid costs for services, for example advertising or marketing costs for campaigns that have been prepared but not launched, can still be recognised as a **prepayment**.

If tangible asset costs have been expensed in previous financial statements, they may not be recognised as part of the cost of the asset.

1.12 Measurement of intangible assets subsequent to initial recognition

The standard allows two methods of valuation for intangible assets after they have been first recognised.

Applying the **cost model**, an intangible asset should be **carried at its cost**, less any accumulated depreciation and less any accumulated impairment losses.

The **revaluation model** allows an intangible asset to be carried at a revalued amount, which is its **fair value** at the date of revaluation, less any subsequent accumulated amortisation and any subsequent accumulated impairment losses.

(a) The fair value must be able to be measured reliably with reference to an **active market** in that type of asset.

(b) The **entire class** of intangible assets of that type must be revalued at the same time (to prevent selective revaluations).

(c) If an intangible asset in a class of revalued intangible assets cannot be revalued because there is **no active market** for this asset, the asset should be carried at its **cost less any accumulated amortisation and impairment losses**.

(d) Revaluations should be made with such **regularity** that the carrying amount does not differ from that which would be determined using fair value at the end of the reporting period.

KEY POINT

This treatment is **not** available for the **initial recognition** of intangible assets. This is because the cost of the asset must be reliably measured.

The guidelines state that there **will not usually be an active market** in an intangible asset; therefore the revaluation model will usually not be available. For example, although copyrights, publishing rights and film rights can be sold, each has a unique sale value. In such cases, revaluation to fair value would be inappropriate. A fair value might be obtainable however for assets such as fishing rights or quotas or taxi cab licences.

Where an intangible asset is revalued upwards to a fair value, the amount of the revaluation should be credited directly to equity under the heading of a **revaluation surplus**.

However, if a revaluation surplus is a **reversal of a revaluation decrease** that was previously charged against income, the increase can be recognised as income.

Where the carrying amount of an intangible asset is revalued downwards, the amount of the **downward revaluation** should be charged as an expense against income, unless the asset has previously been revalued upwards. A revaluation decrease should be first charged against any previous revaluation surplus in respect of that asset.

Question 7.2 Revaluation

Learning outcome C2(a)

An intangible asset is measured by a company at fair value. The asset was revalued by $400 in 20X3, and there is a revaluation surplus of $400 in the statement of financial position. At the end of 20X4, the asset is valued again, and a downward valuation of $500 is required.

Required

State the accounting treatment for the downward revaluation.

When the revaluation model is used, and an intangible asset is revalued upwards, the cumulative revaluation **surplus may be transferred to retained earnings** when the surplus is eventually realised. The surplus would be realised when the asset is disposed of. However, the surplus may also be realised over time as the **asset is used** by the entity. The amount of the surplus realised each year is the difference between the amortisation charge for the asset based on the revalued amount of the asset, and the amortisation that would be charged on the basis of the asset's historical cost. The realised surplus in such case should be transferred from revaluation surplus directly to retained earnings, and should not be taken through profit or loss.

1.13 Useful life

An entity should **assess** the useful life of an intangible asset, which may be **finite or indefinite**. An intangible asset has an indefinite useful life when there is **no foreseeable limit** to the period over which the asset is expected to generate net cash inflows for the entity.

Many factors are considered in determining the useful life of an intangible asset, including: expected usage; typical product life cycles; technical, technological, commercial or other types of obsolescence; the stability of the industry; expected actions by competitors; the level of maintenance expenditure required; and legal or similar limits on the use of the asset, such as the expiry dates of related leases. Computer software and many other intangible assets normally have short lives because they are susceptible to technological obsolescence. However, uncertainty does not justify choosing a life that is unrealistically short.

The useful life of an intangible asset that arises from **contractual or other legal rights** should not exceed the period of the rights, but may be shorter depending on the period over which the entity expects to use the asset.

1.14 Amortisation period and amortisation method

An intangible asset with a finite useful life should be amortised over its **expected useful life**.

(a) Amortisation should start when the asset is **available for use**.

(b) Amortisation should cease at the earlier of the date that the asset is classified **as held for sale** in accordance with IFRS 5 *Non-current assets held for sale and discontinued operations* and the date that the asset is **derecognised**.

(c) The amortisation method used should reflect the **pattern in which the asset's future economic benefits are consumed**. If such a pattern cannot be predicted reliably, the straight-line method should be used.

(d) The amortisation charge for each period should normally be recognised **in profit or loss**.

The **residual value** of an intangible asset with a finite useful life is **assumed to be zero** unless a third party is committed to buying the intangible asset at the end of its useful life or unless there is an active market for that type of asset (so that its expected residual value can be measured) and it is probable that there will be a market for the asset at the end of its useful life.

The amortisation period and the amortisation method used for an intangible asset with a finite useful life should be **reviewed at each financial year-end**.

1.15 Intangible assets with indefinite useful lives

An intangible asset with an indefinite useful life **should not be amortised**. (IAS 36 requires that such an asset is tested for impairment at least annually.)

The useful life of an intangible asset that is not being amortised should be **reviewed each year** to determine whether it is still appropriate to assess its useful life as indefinite. Reassessing the useful life of an intangible asset as finite rather than indefinite is an indicator that the asset may be impaired and therefore it should be tested for impairment.

Question 7.3 — Useful life

Learning outcome C2(a)

It may be difficult to establish the useful life of an intangible asset, and judgement will be needed. Consider how to determine the useful life of a *purchased* brand name.

1.16 Disposals/retirements of intangible assets

An intangible asset should be eliminated from the statement of financial position when it is disposed of or when there is no further expected economic benefit from its future use. On disposal the gain or loss arising from the **difference between the net disposal proceeds and the carrying amoun**t of the asset should be taken to profit or loss as a gain or loss on disposal (ie treated as income or expense).

1.17 Disclosure requirements

The standard has fairly extensive disclosure requirements for intangible assets. The financial statements should disclose the **accounting policies** for intangible assets that have been adopted.

For **each class of intangible assets**, disclosure is required of the following.

- The **method of amortisation** used
- The **useful life** of the assets or the amortisation rate used
- The **gross carrying amount**, the **accumulated amortisation** and the **accumulated impairment losses** as at the beginning and the end of the period
- A **reconciliation of the carrying amount** as at the beginning and at the end of the period (additions, retirements/disposals, revaluations, impairment losses, impairment losses reversed, amortisation charge for the period, net exchange differences, other movements)
- The carrying amount of **internally-generated intangible assets**

The financial statements should also disclose the following.

- In the case of intangible assets that are assessed as having an indefinite useful life, the carrying amounts and the reasons supporting that assessment
- For intangible assets acquired by way of a **government grant** and initially recognised at fair value, the **fair value initially recognised**, the **carrying amount**, and the accounting treatment for subsequent remeasurements

- The carrying amount, nature and remaining amortisation period of any intangible asset that is **material to the financial statements of the entity as a whole**
- The existence (if any) and amounts of intangible assets whose **title is restricted** and of intangible assets that have been **pledged as security** for liabilities
- The amount of any **commitments for the future acquisition of intangible assets**

Where intangible assets are accounted for at revalued amounts, disclosure is required of the following.

- The **effective date of the revaluation** (by class of intangible assets)
- The **carrying amount** of revalued intangible assets
- The carrying amount that would have been shown (by class of assets) **if the cost model had been used**, and the amount of amortisation that would have been charged
- The amount of any **revaluation surplus** on intangible assets, as at the beginning and end of the period, and movements in the surplus during the year (and any restrictions on the distribution of the balance to shareholders)

The financial statements should also disclose the amount of research and development expenditure that has been charged as an expense of the period.

Section summary

- An intangible asset should be recognised if, and only if, it is probable that future economic benefits will flow to the entity and the cost of the asset can be measured reliably.
- An asset is initially recognised at cost and subsequently carried either at cost or revalued amount.
- Costs that do not meet the recognition criteria should be expensed as incurred.
- An intangible asset with a finite useful life should be amortised over its useful life. An intangible asset with an indefinite useful life should not be amortised.

2 Goodwill

Introduction

This section looks at both internally generated and purchased goodwill.

2.1 Internally generated goodwill

Goodwill is **created by good relationships** between a business and its customers.

(a) By building up a **reputation** (by word of mouth perhaps) for high quality products or high standards of service

(b) By **responding promptly and helpfully** to queries and complaints from customers

(c) Through the **personality of the staff** and their attitudes to customers

The value of goodwill to a business might be **extremely significant**. However, goodwill is not usually valued in the accounts of a business at all, and we should not normally expect to find an amount for goodwill in its statement of financial position. For example, the welcoming smile of the bar staff may contribute more to a bar's profits than the fact that a new electronic cash register has recently been acquired. Even so, whereas the cash register will be recorded in the accounts as a non-current asset, the value of staff would be ignored for accounting purposes.

On reflection, we might agree with this omission of goodwill from the accounts of a business.

(a) The goodwill is **inherent** in the business but it has not been paid for, and it does not have an 'objective' value. We can guess at what such goodwill is worth, but such guesswork would be a matter of individual opinion, and not based on hard facts.

(b) Goodwill **changes** from day to day. One act of bad customer relations might damage goodwill and one act of good relations might improve it. Staff with a favourable personality might retire or leave to find another job, to be replaced by staff who need time to find their feet in the job, etc. Since goodwill is continually changing in value, it cannot realistically be recorded in the accounts of the business.

2.2 Purchased goodwill

There is one exception to the general rule that goodwill has no objective valuation. This is **when a business is sold**. People wishing to set up in business have a choice of how to do it – they can either buy their own long-term assets and inventory and set up their business from scratch, or they can buy up an existing business from a proprietor willing to sell it. When a buyer purchases an existing business, he will have to purchase not only its long-term assets and inventory (and perhaps take over its accounts payable and receivable too) but also the goodwill of the business.

Purchased goodwill is shown in the statement of financial position because it has been paid for. It has no tangible substance, and so it is an **intangible non-current asset**.

2.3 How is the value of purchased goodwill decided?

When a business is sold, there is likely to be some purchased goodwill in the selling price. But **how is the amount of this purchased goodwill decided**?

This is not really a problem for accountants, who must simply record the goodwill in the accounts of the new business. The value of the goodwill is a **matter for the purchaser and seller to agree upon in fixing the purchase/sale price**. However, two methods of valuation are worth mentioning here.

(a) The seller and buyer agree on a price **without specifically quantifying the goodwill.** The purchased goodwill will then be the difference between the price agreed and the value of the tangible assets in the books of the new business.

(b) However, the calculation of goodwill often precedes the fixing of the purchase price and becomes a **central element of negotiation**. There are many ways of arriving at a value for goodwill and most of them are related to the profit record of the business in question.

No matter how goodwill is calculated within the total agreed purchase price, the goodwill shown by the purchaser in his accounts will be **the difference between the purchase consideration and his own valuation of the tangible net assets acquired**. If A values his tangible net assets at $40,000, goodwill is agreed at $21,000 and B agrees to pay $61,000 for the business but values the tangible net assets at only $38,000, then the goodwill in B's books will be $61,000 – $38,000 = $23,000.

2.4 IFRS 3 Business combinations

IFRS 3 covers the accounting treatment of goodwill acquired in a business combination.

KEY TERM

GOODWILL. An asset representing the future economic benefits arising from other assets acquired in a business combination that are not individually identified and separately recognised. *(IFRS 3)*

Goodwill acquired in a business combination is **recognised as an asset.**

After initial recognition goodwill acquired in a business combination is measured **at the original amount less any accumulated impairment losses**. It is **not amortised**. Instead it is tested for impairment at least annually, in accordance with IAS 36 *Impairment of assets*.

Section summary

If a business has **goodwill**, it means that the value of the business as a going concern is greater than the value of its separate tangible assets. The valuation of goodwill is extremely subjective and fluctuates constantly. For this reason non-purchased goodwill is **not** shown as an asset in the statement of financial position.

When someone **purchases a business** as a going concern the purchaser and vendor will fix an agreed price which includes an element in respect of goodwill.

The amount at which goodwill is calculated is not an accounting problem, but a matter of agreement between the two parties.

Purchased goodwill arising on a business contribution is retained in the statement of financial position as an intangible asset under the requirements of **IFRS 3**. It must then be reviewed for impairment annually.

3 Research and development costs

Introduction

In this final section we examine research and development costs. We will look at IAS 38 and concentrate on their recognition, amortisation, impairment and disclosure.

3.1 Deferred development costs

Deferred development costs are the other type of intangible non-current asset you need to know about. Large companies may spend significant amounts of money on research and development (R & D) activities. Obviously, any amounts so expended must be credited to cash and debited to an account for research and development expenditure. The accounting problem is **how to treat the debit balance on the R & D account** at the end of the reporting period.

There are two possibilities.

(a) The debit balance may be classified as an **expense** and transferred to profit or loss. This is referred to as 'writing off' the expenditure. The argument here is that it is an expense just like rent or wages and its accounting treatment should be the same.

(b) The debit balance may be classified as an **asset** and included in the statement of financial position. This is referred to as 'capitalising' or 'carrying forward' or 'deferring' the expenditure. This argument is based on the accrual assumption. If R & D activity eventually leads to new or improved products which generate revenue, the costs should be carried forward to be matched against that revenue in future accounting periods.

So the main question surrounding research and development (R & D) costs is whether they should be treated as an expense or capitalised as an asset. This question is dealt with in IAS 38 *Intangible assets.*

IAS 38 was originally published in September 1998 and replaced IAS 9 *Research and development costs*.

3.2 Definitions

The following definitions are given by the standard.

KEY TERMS

An INTANGIBLE ASSET is an identifiable non-monetary asset without physical substance.

RESEARCH is original and planned investigation undertaken with the prospect of gaining new scientific or technical knowledge and understanding.

DEVELOPMENT is the application of research findings or other knowledge to a plan or design for the production of new or substantially improved materials, devices, products, processes, systems or services prior to the commencement of commercial production or use.

AMORTISATION is the systematic allocation of the depreciable amount of an intangible asset over its useful life.

USEFUL LIFE is either:

- the period of time over which an asset is expected to be used by the entity; or
- the number of production or similar units expected to be obtained from the asset by the entity

(IAS 38)

Exam alert

These definitions are very important. You must learn them as they will form an integral part of any discussion of IAS 38.

Although these definitions are usually well-understood, **in practice** it may not be so easy to identify the activities encompassed by R & D and the dividing line between the categories may be indistinct. Identification often depends on the type of business involved, the projects it undertakes and how it is organised.

The standard gives examples of activities which might be included in either research or development, or which are neither but may be closely associated with both.

- **Research**
  - Activities aimed at obtaining new knowledge
  - The search for applications of research findings or other knowledge
  - The search for product or process alternatives
  - The formulation and design of possible new or improved product or process alternatives
- **Development**
  - The design, construction and testing of pre-production prototypes and models
  - The design of tools, jigs, moulds and dies involving new technology
  - The design, construction and operation of a pilot plant that is not of a scale economically feasible for commercial production
  - The design, construction and testing of a chosen alternative for new/improved materials

3.3 Components of research and development costs

Research and development costs will include all costs that are **directly attributable** to research and development activities, or that can be **allocated on a reasonable basis.**

The standard lists the costs which may be included in R & D, where applicable (note that **selling costs are excluded**).

- **Salaries, wages** and other employment related costs of personnel engaged in R & D activities
- Costs of **materials and services** consumed in R & D activities
- **Depreciation** of property, plant and equipment to the extent that these assets are used for R & D activities
- **Overhead costs**, other than general administrative costs, related to R & D activities; these costs are allocated on bases similar to those used in allocating overhead costs to inventories (see IAS 2 *Inventories*)

- **Other costs**, such as the amortisation of patents and licences, to the extent that these assets are used for R & D activities

3.4 Recognition of R & D costs

The relationship between the R & D costs and the **economic benefit** expected to derive from them will determine the allocation of those costs to different periods. Recognition of the costs as an asset will only occur where it is probable that the cost will produce future economic benefits for the enterprise and where the costs can be measured reliably.

(a) In the case of **research costs**, this will not be the case due to uncertainty about the resulting benefit from them; and so they should be expensed in the period in which they arose.

(b) **Development activities** tend to be much further advanced than the research stage and so it may be possible to determine the likelihood of future economic benefit. Where it is possible to do so, the development costs should be carried forward as an asset.

3.4.1 Research costs

Research costs should be recognised as an **expense in the period in which they are incurred**. They should not be recognised as an asset in a later period.

3.4.2 Development costs

Alternative treatments are given for development costs, the use of which depends on the situation. Most of the time, development costs will be recognised as an **expense in the period in which they are incurred** unless the criteria for asset recognition identified below are met. Development costs initially recognised as an expense should not be recognised as an asset in a later period.

Development expenditure should be recognised as an asset only when the business can demonstrate **all** of the following.

- The technical feasibility of **completing** the intangible asset so that it will be available for use or sale
- Its intention to complete the intangible asset and **use or sell** it
- Its **ability** to use or sell the intangible asset
- How the intangible asset will generate probable **future economic benefits**. Among other things, the entity should demonstrate the existence of a market for the output of the intangible asset itself or, if it is to be used internally, the usefulness of the intangible asset
- The availability of adequate technical, financial and other **resources** to complete the development and to use or sell the intangible asset
- Its ability to **measure reliably** the expenditure attributable to the intangible asset during its development

Exam alert

Memorise these requirements as they are often examined.

There is also an important point about the carrying amount of the asset and recoverability. The development costs of a project recognised as an asset should not exceed the amount that it is probable will be **recovered from related future economic benefits**, after deducting further development costs, related production costs, and selling and administrative costs directly incurred in marketing the product.

3.5 Amortisation of development costs

Once capitalised as an asset, development costs must be **amortised** and recognised as an expense to match the costs with the related revenue or cost savings. This must be done on a systematic basis, so as to reflect the pattern in which the related economic benefits are recognised.

It is unlikely to be possible to **match exactly** the economic benefits obtained with the costs which are held as an asset simply because of the nature of development activities. The enterprise should consider either:

(a) the revenue or other benefits from the sale/use of the product/process; *or*

(b) the period of time over which the product/process is expected to be sold/used.

KEY POINT

If the pattern cannot be determined reliably, the straight-line method should be used.

The amortisation will begin when the **asset is available for use**.

3.6 Impairment of development costs

As with all assets, impairment (fall in value of an asset) is a possibility, but perhaps even more so in cases such as this. The development costs should be **written down** to the extent that the unamortised balance (taken together with further development costs, related production costs, and selling and administrative costs directly incurred in marketing the product) is no longer probable of being recovered from the expected future economic benefit.

3.7 Disclosure

For **each class of intangible assets** (including development costs), IAS 38 requires the following disclosures.

- The **method of amortisation** used
- The **useful life** of the assets or the amortisation rate used
- The **gross carrying amount**, the **accumulated amortisation** and the **accumulated impairment losses** as at the beginning and the end of the period
- A **reconciliation of the carrying amount** as at the beginning and at the end of the period (additions, retirements/disposals, revaluations, impairment losses, impairment losses reversed, amortisation charge for the period, net exchange differences, other movements)
- The carrying amount of **internally-generated intangible assets**

Question 7.4 — Research and development

Learning outcome C2(a)

Y Co is a research company which specialises in developing new materials and manufacturing processes for the furniture industry. The company receives payments from a variety of manufacturers, which pay for the right to use the company's patented fabrics and processes.

Research and development costs for the year ended 30 September 20X5 can be analysed as follows.

	$
Expenditure on continuing research projects	1,420,000
Amortisation of development expenditure capitalised in earlier years	240,000
New projects started during the year:	

Project A	280,000
New flame-proof padding. Expected to cost a total of $800,000 to develop. Expected total revenue $2,000,000 once work completed - probably late 20X6	
Project B	150,000
New colour-fast dye. Expected to cost a total of $3,000,000 to complete. Future revenues are likely to exceed $5,000,000. The completion date is uncertain because external funding will have to be obtained before research work can be completed.	
Project C	110,000
Investigation of new adhesive recently developed in aerospace industry. If this proves effective then Y Co may well generate significant income because it will be used in place of existing adhesives.	
	2,200,000

The company has a policy of capitalising all development expenditure where permitted by IAS 38.

Explain how the three research projects A, B and C will be dealt with in Y Co's statement of comprehensive income and statement of financial position.

In each case, explain your proposed treatment in terms of IAS 38 *Intangible assets* and, where relevant, in terms of the fundamental accounting assumptions of going concern and accruals, and the prudence concept.

Question 7.5

Disclosure

Learning outcome C2(a)

Show how the research and development costs in the question above will be disclosed in the accounts of Y Co. Assume the cost of capitalised development expenditure brought forward is $1,480,000, and that accumulated amortisation of $240,000 has been charged at the beginning of the year.

Show extracts from:

(a) Income statement
(b) Statement of financial position
(c) Notes to the accounts

Section summary

If the criteria laid down by IAS 38 are satisfied, development costs may be capitalised. They are then amortised, beginning from the time when the development project is available for use.

Impairment rules follow **IAS 36**. There are substantial disclosure requirements.

Chapter Roundup

- ✓ An intangible asset should be recognised if, and only if, it is probable that future economic benefits will flow to the entity and the cost of the asset can be measured reliably.
- ✓ An asset is initially recognised at cost and subsequently carried either at cost or revalued amount.
- ✓ Costs that do not meet the recognition criteria should be expensed as incurred.
- ✓ An intangible asset with a finite useful life should be amortised over its useful life. An intangible asset with an indefinite useful life should not be amortised.
- ✓ If a business has **goodwill**, it means that the value of the business as a going concern is greater than the value of its separate tangible assets. The valuation of goodwill is extremely subjective and fluctuates constantly. For this reason, non-purchased goodwill is **not** shown as an asset in the statement of financial position.
- ✓ When someone **purchases a business** as a going concern the purchaser and vendor will fix an agreed price which includes an element in respect of goodwill. The amount at which goodwill is calculated is not an accounting problem, but a matter of agreement between the two parties.
- ✓ **Purchased goodwill** arising on a business combination is retained in the statement of financial position as an intangible asset under the requirements of **IFRS 3**. It must then be reviewed for impairment annually.
- ✓ If the criteria laid down by IAS 38 are satisfied, development costs may be capitalised. They are then amortised, beginning from the time when the development project is available for use.
- ✓ **Impairment** rules follow **IAS 36**. There are substantial disclosure requirements.

Quick Quiz

1 Intangible assets can only be recognised in a company's accounts if:

- It is probable that .... will flow to the entity
- The cost can be ....

2 What are the criteria which must be met before development expenditure can be deferred?

3 Start up costs must be expensed.

True ☐

False ☐

4 How is goodwill measured under IFRS 3?

5 The following statements relate to intangible assets.

1 An intangible asset should be amortised on a systematic basis over the asset's useful life.

2 Internally generated goodwill may be carried in the statement of financial position if the value can be determined with reasonable certainty.

3 Internally generated brands can never be recognised as intangible assets.

Which of the above statements are consistent with IAS 38 *Intangible Assets*?

A 1 and 2 only
B 1 and 3 only
C 2 only
D 3 only

Answers to Quick Quiz

1 Future economic benefits. Measured reliably.

2 See Para 3.4.2. Learn these six requirements.

3 True

4 The difference between the aggregate of the fair value of the consideration transferred at the acquisition date and the amount of non-controlling interest and the net of the acquisition date amounts of the identifiable assets acquired and the liabilities assumed.

5 C See IAS 38 Paragraph 57.

Answers to Questions

7.1 Intangible asset

At the end of 20X3, the production process is recognised as an intangib e asset at a cost of $10,000. This is the expenditure incurred since the date when the recognition criteria were met, that is 1 December 20X3. The $90,000 expenditure incurred before 1 December 20X3 is expensed, because the recognition criteria were not met. It will never form part of the cost of the production process recognised in the statement of financial position.

7.2 Revaluation

In this example, the downward valuation of $500 can first be set against the revaluation surplus of $400. The revaluation surplus will be reduced to 0 and a charge of $100 made as an expense in 20X4.

7.3 Useful life

Factors to consider would include the following.

(a) Legal protection of the brand name and the control of the entity cver the (illegal) use by others of the brand name (ie control over pirating)

(b) Age of the brand name

(c) Status or position of the brand in its particular market

(d) Ability of the management of the entity to manage the brand narre and to measure activities that support the brand name (eg advertising and PR activities)

(e) Stability and geographical spread of the market in which the branded products are sold

(f) Pattern of benefits that the brand name is expected to generate over time

(g) Intention of the entity to use and promote the brand name over time (as evidenced perhaps by a business plan in which there will be substantial expenditure to promote the brand name)

7.4 Research and development

Project A

This project meets the criteria in IAS 38 for development expenditure to be recognised as an asset. These are as follows.

(a) The product or process is clearly defined and the costs attributable to the product or process can be separately identified and measured reliably.

(b) The technical feasibility of the product or process can be demonstrated.

(c) The enterprise intends to produce and market, or use, the product or process and has the ability to do so.

(d) The existence of a market for the product or process or, if it is to be used internally rather than sold, its usefulness to the enterprise, can be demonstrated.

(e) Adequate resources exist, or their availability can be demonstrated, to complete the project and market or use the product or process.

The capitalisation of development costs in a company which is a going concern means that these are accrued in order that they can be matched against the income they are expected to generate.

Hence the costs of $280,000 incurred to date should be transferred from research and development costs to capitalised development expenditure and carried forward until revenues are generated; they should then be matched with those revenues.

Project B

Whilst this project meets most of the criteria discussed above which would enable the costs to be carried forward it fails on the requirement that 'adequate resources exist, or their availability can be demonstrated, to complete the project'.

Hence it would be prudent to write off these costs. Once funding is obtained the situation can then be reassessed and these and future costs may be capitalised. In this case the prudence concept overrides the accruals assumption.

Project C

This is a research project according to IAS 38, ie original and planned investigation undertaken with the prospect of gaining new scientific or technical knowledge or understanding.

There is no certainty as to its ultimate success or commercial viability and therefore it cannot be considered to be a development project. IAS 38 therefore requires that costs be written off as incurred. Once again, prudence overrides the accruals assumption.

7.5 Disclosure

(a) INCOME STATEMENT (EXTRACT)

	$
Research expenditure (Project C + 1,420,000)	1,530,000
Development costs (Project B)	150,000
Amortisation of capitalised development costs	240,000

(b) STATEMENT OF FINANCIAL POSITION (EXTRACT)

	$
Non-current assets	
Intangible assets	
Deferred development costs	1,280,000

(c) NOTE TO ACCOUNTS

Deferred development costs

	$
Cost	
Balance b/f	1,480,000
Additions during year (Project A)	280,000
Balance c/f	1,760,000
Amortisation	
Balance b/f	240,000
Charge during year	240,000
Balance c/f	480,000
Net book value at 30 September 20X5	1,280,000
Net book value at 30 September 20X4	1,240,000

Now try these questions from the Exam Question Bank

Number	Level	Marks	Time
Q18	Examination	5	9 mins

IAS 17 : LEASES

Leasing transactions are extremely common so this is an important practical subject. **Lease accounting is regulated by IAS 17**, which was introduced because of abuses in the use of lease accounting by companies. IAS 17 was revised in December 2003.

These companies effectively 'owned' an asset and 'owed' a debt for its purchase, but showed neither the asset nor the liability on the statement of financial position because they were not required to do so.

This is called **'off-balance sheet finance'**.

In this chapter we look at operating and finance leases and how to apportion these over the lease term.

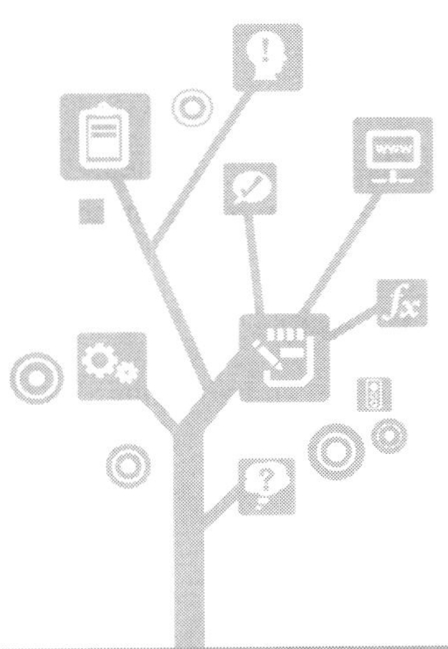

topic list	learning outcomes	syllabus references	ability required
1 Types of lease	C2(a)	C2(xi)	comprehension
2 Lessees	C2(a)	C2(xi)	application

1 Types of lease

Introduction

This section examines operating and finance leases and how to distinguish between them.

1.1 IAS 17

Where goods are acquired other than on immediate cash terms, arrangements have to be made in respect of the future payments on those goods. In the simplest case of **credit sales**, the purchaser is allowed a period of time (say one month) to settle the outstanding amount and the normal accounting procedure in respect of receivables/payables will be adopted. However, in recent years there has been considerable growth in leasing agreements (some types of lease are called **hire purchase agreements** in some countries).

IAS 17 *Leases* standardises the accounting treatment and disclosure of assets held under lease.

In a leasing transaction there is a **contract** between the lessor and the lessee for the hire of an asset. The lessor retains legal ownership but conveys to the lessee the right to use the asset for an agreed period of time in return for specified rentals. IAS 17 defines a lease and recognises two types.

KEY TERMS

LEASE. An agreement whereby the lessor conveys to the lessee in return for a payment or a series of payments the right to use an asset for an agreed period of time.

FINANCE LEASE. A lease that transfers substantially all the risks and rewards incident to ownership of an asset. Title may or may not eventually be transferred.

OPERATING LEASE. A lease other than a finance lease. *(IAS 17)*

To expand on the definition above, a finance lease should be presumed if at the inception of a lease the **present value of the minimum lease payments** is approximately equal to the **fair value of the leased asset**.

The present value should be calculated by using the **interest rate implicit in the lease**.

KEY TERMS

MINIMUM LEASE PAYMENTS. The payments over the lease term that the lessee is or can be required to make.

INTEREST RATE IMPLICIT IN THE LEASE

The discount rate that, at the inception of the lease, causes the aggregate present value of

(a) the minimum lease payments, and
(b) the unguaranteed residual value

to be equal to the sum of

(a) the fair value of the leased asset, and
(b) any initial direct costs of the lessor

LEASE TERM . The non-cancellable period for which the lessee has contracted to lease the asset together with any further terms for which the lessee has the option to continue to lease the asset, with or without further payment, when at the inception of the lease it is reasonably certain that the lessee will exercise the option.

ECONOMIC LIFE is either:

(a) the period over which an asset is expected to be economically usable by one or more users, or

(b) the number of production or similar units expected to be obtained from the asset by one or more users.

USEFUL LIFE is the estimated remaining period, from the beginning of the lease term, without limitation by the lease term, over which the economic benefits embodied in the asset are expected to be consumed by the entity.

1.2 Accounting for operating leases

Operating leases do not really pose an accounting problem. The lessee pays amounts periodically to the lessor and these are **charged to the income statement**. The lessor treats the leased asset as a non-current asset and depreciates it in the normal way. Rentals received from the lessee are credited to the income statement in the lessor's books.

Where the lessee is offered an incentive such as a **rent-free period** or **cashback incentive**, this is effectively a **discount**, which will be spread over the period of the operating lease in accordance with the accruals principle. For instance, if a company entered into a 4-year operating lease but was not required to make any payments until year 2, the total payments to be made over years 2-4 should be charged evenly over years 1-4.

Where a cashback incentive is received, the total amount payable over the lease term, less the cashback, should be charged evenly over the term of the lease. This can be done by crediting the cashback received to deferred income and releasing it to profit or loss over the lease term.

1.3 Accounting for finance leases

For assets held under **finance leases or hire purchase** this accounting treatment would not disclose the reality of the situation. If a **lessor** leases out an asset on a finance lease, the asset will probably never be seen on his premises or used in his business again. It would be inappropriate for a lessor to record such an asset as a non-current asset. In reality, what he owns is a **stream of cash flows receivable** from the lessee. **The asset is an amount receivable rather than a non-current asset.**

Similarly, a **lessee** may use a finance lease to fund the 'acquisition' of a major asset which he will then use in his business perhaps for many years. **The substance of the transaction is that he has acquired a non-current asset**, and this is reflected in the accounting treatment prescribed by IAS 17, even though in law the lessee never becomes the owner of the asset. The following diagram should help you decide whether a lease is an operating lease or a finance lease.

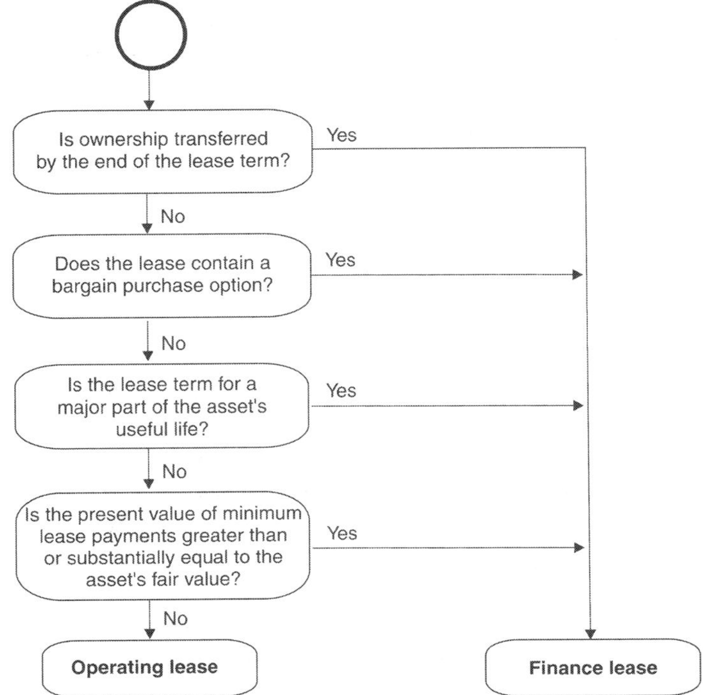

The standard also gives additional indicators of a lease that should be classified as a finance lease.

- the leased assets are of such a specialised nature that only the lessee can use them without major modifications
- if the lessee can cancel the lease, he must bear any losses suffered by the lessor associated with the cancellation
- the lessee has the ability to continue the lease for a secondary period at a rent that is substantially lower than market rent
- gains or losses due to fluctuation in the fair value of the residual value of the asset accrue to the lessee

The revised IAS 17 states that when classifying a lease of **land and buildings** the **land** element is normally classified as an **operating lease unless title passes to the lessee** at the end of the contract.

Exam skills

You **may** be required to decide whether a lease is an operating lease or a finance lease. The diagram above is worth learning..

Section summary

Under finance leases:

- Assets acquired should be capitalised
- The interest element of instalments should be charged against profit

Operating leases are rental agreements and all instalments are charged against profit.

2 Lessees

Introduction

This section explains the accounting treatment of a lease in the books of the lessee.

Exam skills

You are not required to know the accounting treatment of a finance lease in the books of the lessor.

2.1 Accounting treatment

IAS 17 requires that, when an asset changes hands under a **finance lease**, **lessor and lessee should account for the transaction as though it were a credit sale.** In the lessee's books therefore:

DEBIT	Asset account
CREDIT	Lessor (liability) account

The amount to be recorded in this way is the **lower of** the **fair value** and the **present value** of the **minimum lease payments**. This will generally be the purchase price of the asset.

IAS 17 states that it is not appropriate to show liabilities for leased assets as deductions from the leased assets. A distinction should be made between **current and non-current** lease liabilities, if the entity makes this distinction for other liabilities.

The asset should be **depreciated** (on the bases set out in IASs 16 and 38) over the shorter of:

- The lease term
- The asset's useful life

If there is reasonable certainty of eventual ownership of the asset, then it should be depreciated over its useful life.

2.2 Apportionment of rental payments

When the lessee makes a rental payment it will comprise two elements.

(a) An **interest charge** on the finance provided by the lessor. This proportion of each payment is interest payable and interest receivable in the statement of comprehensive income of the lessee and lessor respectively.

(b) A repayment of part of the **capital cost** of the asset. In the lessee's books this proportion of each rental payment must be debited to the lessor's account to reduce the outstanding liability. In the lessor's books, it must be credited to the lessee's account to reduce the amount owing (the debit of course is to cash).

The accounting problem is to decide what proportion of each instalment paid by the lessee represents interest, and what proportion represents a repayment of the capital advanced by the lessor. There are three apportionment methods you may encounter:

- The straight line method
- The actuarial method
- The sum-of-the-digits method

Exam skills

An examination question will always make it clear which method should be used. In theory, the aim is that the finance charge should reduce over the lease term in line with the outstanding liability. If you are given an interest rate, you will be expected to use the actuarial method. If not, use the sum-of-the-digits method.

The **straight-line method** is simple but does not provide a constant rate of interest. The interest amount is simply allocated equally over the lease periods. You are not likely to be asked to use this method in the exam, but you should know about it.

The **actuarial method** is the best and most scientific method. It derives from the common-sense assumption that the interest charged by a lessor company will equal the rate of return desired by the company, multiplied by the amount of capital it has invested.

(a) At the beginning of the lease the capital invested is equal to the fair value of the asset (less any initial deposit paid by the lessee).

(b) This amount reduces as each instalment is paid. It follows that the interest accruing is greatest in the early part of the lease term, and gradually reduces as capital is repaid. In this section, we will look at a simple example of the actuarial method.

The **sum-of-the-digits** method approximates to the actuarial method, splitting the total interest (without reference to a rate of interest) in such a way that the greater proportion falls in the earlier years. The procedure is as follows.

Assign a digit to each instalment. The digit 1 should be assigned to the final instalment, 2 to the penultimate instalment and so on.

Add the digits. A quick method of adding the digits is to use the formula $\frac{n(n+1)}{2}$ where n is the number of instalments. If there are twelve instalments, then the sum of the digits will be 78. For this reason, the sum of the digits method is sometimes called the **rule of 78**.

Calculate the interest charge included in each instalment. Do this by multiplying the total interest accruing over the lease term by the fraction:

$$\frac{\text{Digit applicable to the instalment}}{\text{Sum of the digits}}$$

Exam skills

Always pay attention to whether payments are made **in advance** or **in arrears**. Where payments are made in arrears there will be one more finance period than under an agreement where payments are made in advance.

Example: Apportionment methods

On 1 January 20X0 Bacchus Co, wine merchants, buys a small bottling and labelling machine from Silenus Co under a finance lease. The cash price of the machine was $7,710 while the amount to be paid was $10,000. The agreement required the immediate payment of a $2,000 deposit with the balance being settled in four equal annual instalments commencing on 31 December 20X0. The charge of $2,290 represents interest of 15% per annum, calculated on the remaining balance of the liability during each accounting period. Depreciation on the plant is to be provided for at the rate of 20% per annum on a straight line basis assuming a residual value of nil.

You are required to show the breakdown of each instalment between interest and capital, using in turn each of the apportionment methods described above.

Solution

In this example, enough detail is given to use either of the apportionment methods. In an examination question, you would normally be directed to use one method specifically.

(a) **Sum-of-the-digits method**

Each instalment is allocated a digit as follows.

Instalment	*Digit*
1st (20X0)	4
2nd (20X1)	3
3rd (20X2)	2
4th (20X3)	1
	10

Or using the formula, $\frac{4 \times 5}{2} = 10$.

The $2,290 interest charges can then be apportioned.

		$
1st instalment	$2,290 × 4/10	916
2nd instalment	$2,290 × 3/10	687
3rd instalment	$2,290 × 2/10	458
4th instalment	$2,290 × 1/10	229
		2,290

The breakdown is then as follows.

	1st instalment $	*2nd instalment* $	*3rd instalment* $	*4th instalment* $
Interest	916	687	458	229
Capital repayment (balance)	1,084	1,313	1,542	1,771
	2,000	2,000	2,000	2,000

(b) **Actuarial method**

Interest is calculated as 15% of the outstanding *capital* balance at the beginning of each year. The outstanding capital balance reduces each year by the capital element comprised in each instalment. The outstanding capital balance at 1 January 20X0 is $5,710 ($7,710 fair value less $2,000 deposit).

	Total $	*Capital* $	*Interest* $
Capital balance at 1 Jan 20X0		5,710	
1st instalment (interest = $5,710 × 15%)	2,000	1,144	856
Capital balance at 1 Jan 20X1		4,566	
2nd instalment (interest = $4,566 × 15%)	2,000	1,315	685
Capital balance at 1 Jan 20X2		3,251	
3rd instalment (interest = $3,251 × 15%)	2,000	1,512	488
Capital balance at 1 Jan 20X3		1,739	
4th instalment (interest = $1,739 × 15%)	2,000	1,739	261
	8,000		2,290
Capital balance at 1 Jan 20X4		–	

The journal entries at 1 January 20X0 will be:

(a)	DEBIT	Asset account	$7,710	
	CREDIT	Lessor payable: Silenus		$7,710
(b)	DEBIT	Lessor payable: Silenus	$2,000	
	CREDIT	Bank		$2,000

Entries at 31 December 20X0 will be:

(c)	DEBIT	Lessor payable: Silenus	$2,000	
	CREDIT	Bank		$2,000
(d)	DEBIT	Interest payable/finance charges	$856	
	CREDIT	Lessor payable: Silenus		$856

Entry (b) is the deposit. Entry (c) is the first instalment.

Entry (d) ensures that the interest element is recorded and is an annual adjustment. It is, of course, possible to make the full correct entry as each instalment is paid:

DEBIT	Interest payable/finance charges	$856	
	Lessor payable: Silenus	$1,144	
CREDIT	Bank		$2,000

However, in practice in many companies the interest/finance charge calculation is only made annually when preparing published accounts.

Thus, at the year end, whatever system is used during the year, the balance on the lessor payable will represent the outstanding capital liability. Future interest/finance charges are not a true liability as the capital could be paid off at any time, thus avoiding these charges.

Exam skills

If you are required to use the actuarial method in the exam, you will be given the interest rate.

Question 8.1 — Sum-of-the-digits method

Learning outcome C2(a)

Dundas Co purchased a machine under a finance lease on 1 January 20X6. The agreement provided for an immediate payment of $2,000, following by five equal instalments of $3,056, each instalment to be paid on 30 June and 31 December respectively. The cash price of the machine was $10,000. Dundas estimated that it would have a useful economic life of five years, and its residual value would then be $1,000. At the end of the lease, ownership will pass to Dundas Co.

In apportioning interest to respective accounting periods, the company uses the 'sum of digits' method.

Required

Show the following statement of financial position extracts relating to the machine as at 31 December 20X6, 20X7 and 20X8 respectively.

(a) Non-current assets: machine at net book value

(b) Current liabilities: obligation under finance lease

(c) Non-current liabilities: obligation under finance lease

Exam alert

When doing lease calculations, you must highlight the **answer** to the question. Many students can do the calculation correctly but struggle to select the correct answer to the question from their workings.

2.3 Disclosure requirements for lessees

IAS 17 (revised) requires the following disclosures by lessees in respect of **operating leases**.

- The total of future minimum lease payments under non-cancellable operating leases for each of the following periods:
  - Not later than one year;
  - Later than one year and not later than five years
  - Later than five years

This disclosure note is required because, although operating leases do not give rise to a creditor on the statement of financial position, they are non-cancellable and so they do entail a future financial commitment, which should be disclosed.

IAS 17 (revised) requires the following disclosures by lessees, in respect of **finance leases**.

- The **net carrying amount** at the end of the reporting period for each class of asset
- A **reconciliation** between the total of minimum lease payments at the end of the reporting period, and their present value. In addition, an entity should disclose the total of minimum lease payments at the end of the reporting period, and their present value, for each of the following periods:
  - Not later than one year
  - Later than one year and not later than five years
  - Later than five years
- **Contingent rents** recognised in income for the period
- Total of **future minimum sublease payments** expected to be received under non-cancellable subleases at the end of the reporting period
- A **general description** of the lessee's significant leasing arrangements including, but not limited to, the following:
  - The basis on which contingent rent payments are determined
  - The existence and terms of renewal or purchase options and escalation clauses
  - Restrictions imposed by lease arrangements, such as those concerning dividends, additional debt, and further leasing

IAS 17 encourages (but does not require) further disclosures, as appropriate.

Example: Lessee disclosures

These disclosure requirements will be illustrated for Bacchus Co (above example). Assume that Bacchus Co makes up its accounts to 31 December and uses the actuarial method to apportion finance charges.

Solution

The company's accounts for the first year of the lease, the year ended 31 December 20X0, would include the information given below.

STATEMENT OF FINANCIAL POSITION AS AT 31 DECEMBER 20X0 (EXTRACTS)

	$	$
Non-current assets		
Assets held under finance leases		
Plant and machinery at cost	7,710	
Less accumulated depreciation (20% × $7,710)	1,542	
		6,168
Current liabilities		
Obligations under finance leases		1,315
Non-current liabilities		
Obligations under finance leases $(1,512 + 1,739)		3,251

(Notice that only the outstanding **capital** element is disclosed under liabilities, ie the total of the minimum lease payments with future finance charges separately deducted.)

INCOME STATEMENT
FOR THE YEAR ENDED 31 DECEMBER 20X0

	$
Interest payable and similar charges	
Interest on finance leases	856

Section summary

- You must learn (through repeated practice) how to apply the actuarial and sum-of-the-digits methods of interest allocation.
- You must also learn the disclosure requirements of IAS 17.

Chapter Roundup

✓ Under finance leases:

  – Assets acquired should be capitalised
  – Interest element of instalments should be charged against profit.

✓ Operating leases are rental agreements and all instalments are charged against profit.

✓ You must learn (through repeated practice) how to apply the actuarial and sum-of-the-digits methods of interest allocation.

✓ You must also learn the disclosure requirements of IAS 17.

Quick Quiz

1 (a) .... leases transfer substantially all the risks and rewards of ownership.

  (b) .... leases are usually short-term rental agreements with the lessor being responsible for the repairs and maintenance of the asset.

2 A business acquires an asset under a finance lease. What is the double entry?

3 What is the formula to calculate each period's interest using sum of the digits?

4 List the disclosures required under IAS 17 for lessees.

5 A lorry has an expected useful life of six years. It is acquired under a four year finance lease and will probably be kept for its entire six year life. Over which period should it be depreciated?

6 A company leases a photocopier under an operating lease which expires in June 20X2. Its office is leased under an operating lease due to expire in January 20X3. How should past and future operating leases be disclosed in its 31 December 20X1 accounts?

Answers to Quick Quiz

1 (a) Finance leases
  (b) Operating leases

2 DEBIT Asset account
  CREDIT Lessor account

3 $$\frac{\text{Digit applicable to the instalment}}{\text{Sum of the digits}} \times \text{Total interest charge}$$

4 See Para 2.3.

5 As eventual ownership of the lorry is reasonably certain, it should be depreciated over its six year useful life.

6 The total operating lease rentals charged though the income statement should be disclosed. The payments committed to should be disclosed analysing them between those falling due in the next year and the second to fifth years.

Answers to Questions

8.1 Sum-of-the-digits method

	$
Cash price of machine	10,000
Initial payment 1 January 20X6	(2,000)
	8,000
Interest 20X6 (W)	4,368
Instalments paid 20X6 (3,056 × 2)	(6,112)
Balance 31 December 20X6	6,526
Interest 20X7 (W)	2,427
Instalments paid 20X7	(6,112)
Balance 31 December 20X7	2,571
Interest to 30 June 20X8	485
Instalment paid 30 June 20X8	(3,056)
	–

Working

	$
Sum of the digits = 5 + 4 + 3 + 2 + 1 = 15 (5 half year periods)	
Interest charge 20X6 = $\$7,280 \times \frac{5+4}{15}$	4,368
Interest charge 20X7 = $\$7,280 \times \frac{3+2}{15}$	2,427
Interest charge 20X8 = $\$7,280 \times \frac{1}{15}$	485
	7,280

(a) *Non-current assets: machines at net book value*

		$
At 31.12.X6	Machines at cost	10,000
	Accumulated depreciation	1,800
	Net book value	8,200
At 31.12.X7	Machines at cost	10,000
	Accumulated depreciation	3,600
	Net book value	6,400
At 31.12.X8	Machines at cost	10,000
	Accumulated depreciation	5,400
	Net book value	4,600

Working

	$
Depreciation: cost	10,000
residual value	1,000
	9,000

Economic life* = 5 years

Annual depreciation charge on a straight-line basis = $\frac{\$9,000}{5}$

= $1,800 per year

**Note.* Eventual ownership is certain – see para 2.1.

LEARNING MEDIA

(b) Current payables: obligation under finance lease

	$
At 31.12.X6 (6,256 – 2,571)	3,685
At 31.12.X7	2,571
At 31.12.X8	–

(c) *Non-current payables: obligation under finance lease*

	$
At 31.12.X6 (6,2,56 – 2,571)	2,571
At 31.12.X7	–
At 31.12.X8	–

Now try these questions from the Exam Question Bank

Number	Level	Marks	Time
Q14	Examination	5	9 mins

STATEMENTS OF CASH FLOWS

The importance of the distinction between cash and profit and the scant attention paid to this by the income statement has resulted in the development of statements of cash flows.

This chapter adopts a systematic approach to the preparation of statements of cash flows in examinations; you should learn this method and you will then be equipped for any problems in the exam itself.

The third section of the chapter looks at the information which is provided by statements of cash flows and how it should be analysed.

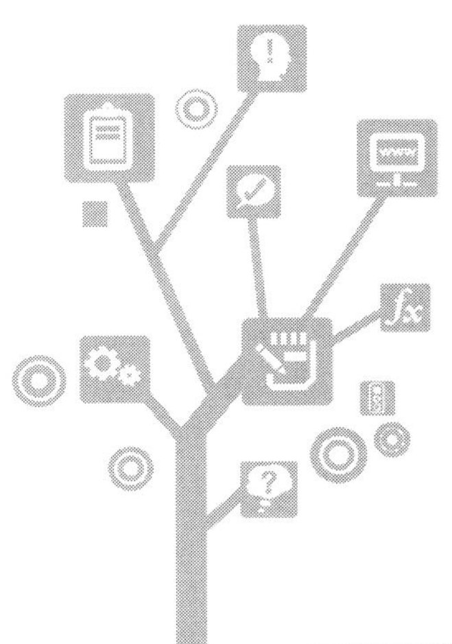

topic list	learning outcomes	syllabus references	ability required
1 IAS 7 *Statement of cash flows*	C1(a)	C1(ii)	application
2 Preparing a statement of cash flows	C1(a)	C1(ii)	application
3 Interpretation of statements of cash flows	C1(a)	C1(ii)	application

1 IAS 7 *Statement of cash flows*

Introduction

In this section we look at why statements of cash flows are useful. We also cover the required presentation of a statement of cash flows as per IAS 7.

1.1 Cash flow and profit

It has been argued that 'profit' does not always give a useful or meaningful picture of a company's operations. Readers of a company's financial statements might even be **misled by a reported profit figure**.

(a) Shareholders might believe that if a company makes a profit after tax, of say, $100,000 then this is the amount which it could afford to **pay as a dividend**. Unless the company has **sufficient cash** available to stay in business and also to pay a dividend, the shareholders' expectations would be wrong.

(b) Employees might believe that if a company makes profits, it can afford to **pay higher wages** next year. This opinion may not be correct: the ability to pay wages depends on the **availability of cash**.

(c) Survival of a business entity depends not so much on profits as on its **ability to pay its debts when they fall due**. Such payments might include 'revenue' items such as material purchases, wages, interest and taxation etc, but also capital payments for new non-current assets and the repayment of loan capital when this falls due (for example on the redemption of debentures).

From these examples, it may be apparent that a company's performance and prospects depend not so much on the 'profits' earned in a period, but more realistically on liquidity or **cash flows**.

1.2 Funds flow and cash flow

Some countries, either currently or in the past, have required the disclosure of additional statements based on **funds flow** rather than cash flow. However, the definition of 'funds' can be very vague and such statements often simply require a rearrangement of figures already provided in the statement of financial position and income statement. By contrast, a statement of cash flows is unambiguous and provides information which is additional to that provided in the rest of the accounts. It also lends itself to organisation by activity and not by classification in the statement of financial position.

Statements of cash flows are frequently given as an **additional statement**, supplementing the statement of financial position, statement of comprehensive income and related notes. The group aspects of statements of cash flows (and certain complex matters) have been excluded as they are beyond the scope of your syllabus.

1.3 Objective of IAS 7

The aim of IAS 7 is to provide information to users of financial statements about an entity's **ability to generate cash and cash equivalents**, as well as indicating the cash needs of the entity. The statement of cash flows provides *historical* information about cash and cash equivalents, classifying cash flows between operating, investing and financing activities.

1.4 Scope

A statement of cash flows should be presented as an **integral part** of an entity's financial statements. All types of entity can provide useful information about cash flows as the need for cash is universal, whatever the nature of their revenue-producing activities. Therefore **all entities are required by the standard to produce a statement of cash flows.**

1.5 Benefits of cash flow information

The use of statements of cash flows is very much **in conjunction** with the rest of the financial statements. Users can gain further appreciation of the change in net assets, of the entity's financial position (liquidity and solvency) and the entity's ability to adapt to changing circumstances by affecting the amount and timing of cash flows. Statements of cash flows **enhance comparability** as they are not affected by differing accounting policies used for the same type of transactions or events.

Cash flow information of a historical nature can be used as an indicator of the amount, timing and certainty of future cash flows. Past forecast cash flow information can be **checked for accuracy** as actual figures emerge. The relationship between profit and cash flows can be analysed as can changes in prices over time.

1.6 Definitions

The standard gives the following definitions, the most important of which are **cash** and **cash equivalents**.

KEY TERMS

CASH comprises cash on hand and demand deposits.

CASH EQUIVALENTS are short-term, highly liquid investments that are readily convertible to known amounts of cash and which are subject to an insignificant risk of changes in value.

CASH FLOWS are inflows and outflows of cash and cash equivalents.

OPERATING ACTIVITIES are the principal revenue-producing activities of the entity and other activities that are not investing or financing activities.

INVESTING ACTIVITIES are the acquisition and disposal of non-current assets and other investments not included in cash equivalents.

FINANCING ACTIVITIES are activities that result in changes in the size and composition of the contributed equity capital and borrowings of the entity. *(IAS 7)*

1.7 Cash and cash equivalents

The standard expands on the definition of cash equivalents: they are not held for investment or other long-term purposes, but rather to meet short-term cash commitments. To fulfil the above definition, an investment's **maturity date should normally be three months from its acquisition date**. It would usually be the case then that equity investments (ie shares in other companies) are *not* cash equivalents. An exception would be where preferred shares were acquired with a very close maturity date.

Loans and other borrowings from banks are classified as investing activities. In some countries, however, **bank overdrafts** are repayable on demand and are treated as part of an entity's total cash management system. In these circumstances an overdrawn balance will be included in cash and cash equivalents. Such banking arrangements are characterised by a balance which fluctuates between overdrawn and credit.

Movements between different types of cash and cash equivalent are not included in cash flows. The investment of surplus cash in cash equivalents is part of cash management, not part of operating, investing or financing activities.

1.8 Presentation of a statement of cash flows

IAS 7 requires statements of cash flows to report cash flows during the period classified by **operating, investing and financing activities.**

Example: Simple statement of cash flows

Flail Co commenced trading on 1 January 20X1 with a medium-term loan of $21,000 and a share issue which raised $35,000. The company purchased non-current assets for $21,000 cash, and during the year to 31 December 20X1 entered into the following transactions.

(a) Purchases from suppliers were $19,500, of which $2,550 was unpaid at the year end.
(b) Wages and salaries amounted to $10,500, of which $750 was unpaid at the year end.
(c) Interest on the loan of $2,100 was fully paid in the year and a repayment of $5,250 was made.
(d) Sales revenue was $29,400, including $900 receivables at the year end.
(e) Interest on cash deposits at the bank amounted to $75.
(f) A dividend of $4,000 was proposed as at 31 December 20X1.

You are required to prepare a statement of cash flows for the year ended 31 December 20X1.

Solution

FLAIL CO
STATEMENT OF CASH FLOWS
FOR THE YEAR ENDED 31 DECEMBER 20X1

	$	$
Cash flows from operating activities		
Cash received from customers ($29,400 – $900)	28,500	
Cash paid to suppliers ($19,500 – $2,550)	(16,950)	
Cash paid to and on behalf of employees ($10,500 – $750)	(9,750)	
Interest paid	(2,100)	
Interest received	75	
Net cash flow from operating activities		(225)
Investing activities		
Purchase of non-current assets		(21,000)
Financing activities		
Issue of shares	35,000	
Proceeds from medium-term loan	21,000	
Repayment of medium-term loan	(5,250)	
Net cash flow from financing activities		50,750
Net increase in cash and cash equivalents		29,525
Cash and cash equivalents at 1 January 20X1		–
Cash and cash equivalents at 31 December 20X1		29,525

Note that the dividend is only proposed and so there is no related cash flow in 20X1.

1.9 Presentation

The manner of presentation of cash flows from operating, investing and financing activities **depends on the nature of the entity**. By classifying cash flows between different activities in this way users can see the impact on cash and cash equivalents of each one, and their relationships with each other. We can look at each in more detail.

1.9.1 Operating activities

This is perhaps the key part of the statement of cash flows because it shows whether, and to what extent, companies can **generate cash from their operations**. It is these operating cash flows which must, in the end pay for all cash outflows relating to other activities, ie paying loan interest, dividends and so on.

Most of the components of cash flows from operating activities will be those items which **determine the net profit or loss of the entity**, ie they relate to the main revenue-producing activities of the entity. The standard gives the following as examples of cash flows from operating activities.

(a) Cash receipts from the sale of goods and the rendering of services
(b) Cash receipts from royalties, fees, commissions and other revenue
(c) Cash payments to suppliers for goods and services
(d) Cash payments to and on behalf of employees

Certain items may be included in the net profit or loss for the period which do *not* relate to operational cash flows, for example the profit or loss on the sale of a piece of plant will be included in net profit or loss, but the cash flows will be classed as **investing**.

1.9.2 Investing activities

The cash flows classified under this heading show the extent of new investment in **assets which will generate future profit and cash flows**. The standard gives the following examples of cash flows arising from investing activities.

(a) Cash payments to acquire property, plant and equipment, intangibles and other non-current assets, including those relating to capitalised development costs and self-constructed property, plant and equipment

(b) Cash receipts from sales of property, plant and equipment, intangibles and other non-current assets

(c) Cash payments to acquire shares or debentures of other entities

(d) Cash receipts from sales of shares or debentures of other entities

(e) Cash advances and loans made to other parties

(f) Cash receipts from the repayment of advances and loans made to other parties

1.9.3 Financing activities

This section of the statement of cash flows shows the share of cash which the entity's capital providers have claimed during the period. This is an indicator of **likely future interest and dividend payments**. The standard gives the following examples of cash flows which might arise under these headings.

(a) Cash proceeds from issuing shares

(b) Cash payments to owners to acquire or redeem the entity's shares

(c) Cash proceeds from issuing debentures, loans, notes, bonds, mortgages and other short or long-term borrowings

(d) Principal repayments of amounts borrowed under finance leases

Item (d) needs more explanation. Where the reporting entity owns an asset held under a finance lease, the amounts to go in the statement of cash flows under financing activities are repayments of the **principal (capital)** rather than the **interest**.

Example: Finance lease rental

The notes to the financial statements of Hayley Co show the following in respect of obligations under finance leases.

Year ended 30 June	*20X5*	*20X4*
	$'000	$'000
Amounts payable within one year	12	8
Within two to five years	110	66
	122	74
Less finance charges allocated to future periods	(14)	(8)
	108	66

Interest paid on finance leases in the year to 30 June 20X5 amounted to $6,000. Additions to property, plant and equipment acquired under finance leases were shown in the non-current asset note at $56,000.

Required

Calculate the capital repayment to be shown in the statement of cash flows of Hayley Co for the year to 30 June 20X5.

Solution

OBLIGATIONS UNDER FINANCE LEASES

	$'000		$'000
Capital repayment (bal fig)	14	Bal 1.7.X4	66
Bal 30.6.X5	108	Additions	56
	122		122

1.10 Reporting cash flows from operating activities

The standard offers a choice of method for this part of the statement of cash flows.

(a) **Direct method:** disclose major classes of gross cash receipts and gross cash payments

(b) **Indirect method**: net profit or loss is adjusted for the effects of transactions of a non-cash nature, any deferrals or accruals of past or future operating cash receipts or payments, and items of income or expense associated with investing or financing cash flows

Exam alert

You are required to know about the direct method but the indirect method is easier and more likely to be examined.

1.10.1 Using the direct method

There are different ways in which the **information about gross cash receipts and payments** can be obtained. The most obvious way is simply to extract the information from the accounting records. This may be a laborious task, however, and the indirect method below may be easier. The example and question above used the direct method.

1.10.2 Using the indirect method

This method is undoubtedly **easier** from the point of view of the preparer of the statement of cash flows. The net profit or loss for the period is adjusted for the following.

(a) Changes during the period in inventories, operating receivables and payables
(b) Non-cash items, eg depreciation, provisions, profits/losses on the sales of assets
(c) Other items, the cash flows from which should be classified under investing or financing activities.

A **proforma** of such a calculation, taken from the IAS, is as follows and this method may be more common in the exam. (The proforma has been amended to reflect changes to IFRS.)

	$
Cash flows from operating activities	
Net profit before taxation	X
Adjustments for:	
Depreciation	X
Profit (loss) on disposal of a non-current asset	X
Investment income	(X)
Interest expense	X
Operating profit before working capital changes	X
Increase in trade and other receivables	(X)
Decrease in inventories	X
Decrease in trade payables	(X)
Cash generated from operations	X
Interest paid	(X)
Income taxes paid	(X)
Net cash from operating activities	X

It is important to understand why **certain items are added and others subtracted**. Note the following points.

(a) Depreciation is not a cash expense, but is deducted in arriving at profit. It makes sense, therefore, to eliminate it by adding it back.

(b) By the same logic, a loss on a disposal of a non-current asset (arising through underprovision of depreciation) needs to be added back and a profit deducted.

(c) An increase in inventories means less cash – you have spent cash on buying inventory.

(d) An increase in receivables means the company's debtors have not paid as much, and therefore there is less cash.

(e) If we pay off payables, causing the figure to decrease, again we have less cash.

1.10.3 Indirect versus direct

The direct method is encouraged where the necessary information is not too costly to obtain, but IAS 7 does not require it. In practice, therefore, the direct method is rarely used. It is not obvious that businesses in practice are right in favouring the indirect method. It could be argued that companies ought to monitor their cash flows carefully enough on an ongoing basis to be able to use the direct method at minimal extra cost.

1.11 Interest and dividends

Cash flows from interest and dividends received and paid should each be **disclosed separately**. Each should be classified in a consistent manner from period to period as either operating, investing or financing activities.

Dividends paid by the entity can be classified in **one of two ways**.

(a) As a **financing cash flow**, showing the cost of obtaining financial resources.

(b) As a component of **cash flows from operating activities** so that users can assess the entity's ability to pay dividends out of operating cash flows.

1.12 Taxes on income

Cash flows arising from taxes on income should be **separately disclosed** and should be classified as cash flows from operating activities *unless* they can be specifically identified with financing and investing activities.

Taxation cash flows are often **difficult to match** to the originating underlying transaction, so most of the time all tax cash flows are classified as arising from operating activities.

Example of a statement of cash flows

In the next section we will look at the procedures for preparing a statement of cash flows. First, look at this **example**, adapted from the example given in the standard (which is based on a group and therefore beyond the scope of your syllabus).

Direct method

STATEMENT OF CASH FLOWS (DIRECT METHOD)
YEAR ENDED 31 DECEMBER 20X7

	$m	$m
Cash flows from operating activities		
Cash receipts from customers	30,330	
Cash paid to suppliers and employees	(27,600)	
Cash generated from operations	2,730	
Interest paid	(270)	
Income taxes paid	(900)	
Net cash from operating activities		1,560
Cash flows from investing activities		
Purchase of property, plant and equipment	(900)	
Proceeds from sale of equipment	20	
Interest received	200	
Dividends received	200	
Net cash used in investing activities		(480)
Cash flows from financing activities		
Proceeds from issuance of share capital	250	
Proceeds from long-term borrowings	250	
Dividends paid*	(1,290)	
Net cash used in financing activities		(790)
Net increase in cash and cash equivalents		290
Cash and cash equivalents at beginning of period		120
Cash and cash equivalents at end of period		410

* This could also be shown as an operating cash flow

Indirect method

STATEMENT OF CASH FLOWS (INDIRECT METHOD)
YEAR ENDED 31 DECEMBER 20X7

	$m	$m
Cash flows from operating activities		
Net profit before taxation	3,570	
Adjustments for:		
Depreciation	450	
Investment income	(500)	
Interest expense	400	
Operating profit before working capital changes	3,920	
Increase in trade and other receivables	(500)	
Decrease in inventories	1,050	
Decrease in trade payables	(1,740)	
Cash generated from operations	2,730	
Interest paid	(270)	
Income taxes paid	(900)	
Net cash from operating activities		1,560
Cash flows from investing activities		
Purchase of property, plant and equipment	(900)	
Proceeds from sale of equipment **	20	
Interest received	200	
Dividends received	200	
Net cash used in investing activities		(480)
Cash flows from financing activities		
Proceeds from issuance of share capital	250	
Proceeds from long-term borrowings	250	
Dividends paid*	(1,290)	
Net cash used in financing activities		(790)
Net increase in cash and cash equivalents		290
Cash and cash equivalents at beginning of period		120
Cash and cash equivalents at end of period		410

* This could also be shown as an operating cash flow

** The equipment was disposed of at its NBV, so no profit or loss arose.

Section summary

Statements of cash flows are a useful addition to the financial statements of companies because it is recognised that accounting profit is not the only indicator of a company's performance.

IAS 7 requires cash flows during the period to be classified by operating, investing and financing activities.

Cash flows from operating activities can be reported using the direct or indirect method.

2 Preparing a statement of cash flows

Introduction

This section will teach you how to prepare a statement of cash flows. This is an important skill for your exam.

2.1 Working capital adjustments

In essence, preparing a statement of cash flows is very straightforward. You should therefore simply learn the format and apply the steps noted in the example below. Note that the following items are treated in a way that might seem confusing, but the treatment is logical if you **think in terms of cash**.

(a) **Increase in inventory** is treated as **negative** (in brackets). This is because it represents a cash **outflow**; cash is being spent on inventory.

(b) An **increase in receivables** would be treated as **negative** for the same reasons; more receivables means less cash.

(c) By contrast an **increase in payables is positive** because cash is being retained and not used to settle accounts payable. There is therefore more of it.

Example: Preparation of a statement of cash flows

Kane Co's income statement for the year ended 31 December 20X2 and statements of financial position at 31 December 20X1 and 31 December 20X2 were as follows.

KANE CO
INCOME STATEMENT FOR THE YEAR ENDED 31 DECEMBER 20X2

	$'000	$'000
Sales		720
Raw materials consumed	70	
Staff costs	94	
Depreciation	118	
Loss on disposal of property, plant and equipment	18	
		300
Operating profit		420
Interest payable		28
Profit before tax		392
Taxation		124
Profit for the year		268

Note: Total dividends paid during the year were $66,000.

KANE CO
STATEMENT OF FINANCIAL POSITION AS AT 31 DECEMBER

	20X2		20X1	
	$'000	$'000	$'000	$'000
Assets				
Property, plant and equipment				
Cost	1,596		1,560	
Depreciation	318		224	
		1,278		1,336
Current assets				
Inventory	24		20	
Trade receivables	76		58	
Bank	48		56	
		148		134
Total assets		1,426		1,470
Equity and liabilities				
Share capital	360		340	
Share premium	36		24	
Retained earnings	716		514	
		1,112		878
Non-current liabilities				
Long-term loans		200		500
Current liabilities				
Trade payables	12		6	
Taxation	102		86	
		114		92
		1,426		1,470

During the year, the company paid $90,000 for a new piece of machinery.

Required

Prepare a statement of cash flows for Kane Co for the year ended 31 December 20X2 in accordance with the requirements of IAS 7, using the indirect method.

Solution

Set out the proforma statement of cash flows with the headings required by IAS 7. You should leave plenty of space. Ideally, use three or more sheets of paper, one for the main statement, one for the notes and one for your workings. It is essential to know the formats well.

Begin with the **cash flows from operating activities** as far as possible. When preparing the statement from statements of financial position, you will usually have to calculate such items as depreciation, loss on sale of non-current assets, profit for the year and tax paid. Note that you may not be given the tax charge in the income statement. You will then have to assume that the tax paid in the year is last year's year-end provision and calculate the charge as the balancing figure.

Calculate the cash flow figures for purchase or sale of non-current assets, issue of shares and repayment of loans if these are not already given to you (as they may be).

You will now be able to complete the statement by slotting in the figures given or calculated.

KANE CO
STATEMENT OF CASH FLOWS FOR THE YEAR ENDED 31 DECEMBER 20X2

	$'000	$'000
Net cash flow from operating activities		
Profit before tax	392	
Depreciation charges	118	
Interest expense	28	
Loss on sale of property, plant and equipment	18	
Increase in inventories	(4)	
Increase in receivables	(18)	
Increase in payables	6	
Cash generated from operations	540	
Interest paid	(28)	
Dividends paid	(66)	
Tax paid (86 + 124 – 102)	(108)	
Net cash flow from operating activities		338
Cash flows from investing activities		
Payments to acquire property, plant and equipment	(90)	
Receipts from sales of property, plant and equipment (W)	12	
Net cash flows from investing activities		(78)
Cash outflow from financing activities		
Issues of share capital (360 + 36 – 340 – 24)	32	
Long-term loans repaid (500 – 200)	(300)	
Net cash outflow from financing activities		(268)
Decrease in cash and cash equivalents		(8)
Cash and cash equivalents at 1.1.X2		56
Cash and cash equivalents at 31.12.X2		48

Working: property, plant and equipment

COST

	$'000		$'000
At 1.1.X2	1,560	At 31.12.X2	1,596
Purchases	90	Disposals (balance)	54
	1,650		1,650

ACCUMULATED DEPRECIATION

	$'000		$'000
At 31.1.X2	318	At 1.1.X2	224
Depreciation on disposals (balance)	24	Charge for year	118
	342		342

	$'000
Carrying value of disposals	30
Net loss reported	(18)
Proceeds of disposals	12

Question 9.1

Statement of cash flows

Learning outcome C1(a)

Set out below are the financial statements of Emma Co. You are the financial controller, faced with the task of implementing IAS 7 *Statement of cash flows*.

EMMA CO
INCOME STATEMENT FOR THE YEAR ENDED 31 DECEMBER 20X2

	$'000
Sales revenue	2,553
Cost of sales	1,814
Gross profit	739
Distribution costs	125
Administrative expenses	264
Operating profit	350
Interest received	25
Interest paid	75
Profit before taxation	300
Taxation	140
Profit for the year	160

EMMA CO
STATEMENTS OF FINANCIAL POSITION AS AT 31 DECEMBER

	20X2 $'000	20X1 $'000
Assets		
Non-current assets		
Property, plant and equipment	380	305
Intangible assets	250	200
Investments	–	25
Current assets		
Inventories	150	102
Receivables	390	315
Short-term investments (highly liquid)	50	–
Cash in hand	2	1
Total assets	1,222	948
Equity and liabilities		
Equity		
Share capital ($1 ordinary shares)	200	150
Share premium account	160	150
Revaluation surplus	100	91
Retained earnings	260	180
Non-current liabilities		
Long-term loan	170	50
Current liabilities		
Trade payables	127	119
Bank overdraft	85	98
Taxation	120	110
Total equity and liabilities	1,222	948

The following information is available.

(a) The proceeds of the sale of non-current asset investments amounted to $30,000.

(b) Fixtures and fittings, with an original cost of $85,000 and a net book value of $45,000, were sold for $32,000 during the year.

(c) The following information relates to property, plant and equipment.

	31 December	
	20X2	*20X1*
	$'000	$'000
Cost	720	595
Accumulated depreciation	340	290
Carrying value	380	305

(d) 50,000 $1 ordinary shares were issued during the year at a premium of 20c per share.

(e) Dividends totalling $80,000 were paid in 20X2.

Required

Prepare a statement of cash flows for the year to 31 December 20X2 using the format laid out in IAS 7.

Section summary

You need to be aware of the **format** of the statement of cash flows as laid out in **IAS 7**. Setting out the format is an essential first stage in preparing the statement, so this format must be learnt.

Exam skills

Remember that every item in the statement of financial position will have some impact on the statement of cash flows. It will either appear in the statement or be part of an adjustment. Check back through the statement of financial position and make sure everything is accounted for.

3 Interpretation of statements of cash flows

Introduction

Here we briefly cover how to analyse a statement of cash flows. We then look at some advantages of cash flows accounting.

3.1 Uses of the statement of cash flows

IAS 7 *Statement of cash flows* was introduced on the basis that it would provide better, more comprehensive and more useful information than what was already shown in the financial statements. So what kind of information does the statement of cash flows, along with its notes, provide?

Some of the main areas where IAS 7 should provide information not found elsewhere in the financial statements are as follows.

(a) The **relationships between profit and cash** can be seen clearly and analysed accordingly.
(b) **Cash equivalents** are highlighted, giving a better picture of the liquidity of the company.
(c) **Financing inflows and outflows must be shown, rather than simply passed through reserves**.

One of the most important things to realise at this point is that it is wrong to try to assess the health or predict the death of a reporting entity solely on the basis of a single indicator. When analysing cash flow data, the **comparison should not just be between cash flows and profit, but also between cash flows over a period of time** (say three to five years).

Cash is not synonymous with profit on an annual basis, but you should also remember that the 'behaviour' of profit and cash flows will be very different. **Profit is smoothed out** through accruals, prepayments, provisions and other accounting conventions. This does not apply to cash, so the **cash flow figures** are likely to be **'lumpy'** in comparison. You must distinguish between this 'lumpiness' and the trends which will appear over time.

The **relationship between profit and cash flows will vary constantly**. Note that healthy companies do not always have reported profits exceeding operating cash flows. Similarly, unhealthy companies can have operating cash flows well in excess of reported profit. The value of comparing them is in determining the extent to which earned profits are being converted into the necessary cash flows.

Profit is not as important as the extent to which a company can **convert its profits into cash on a continuing basis.** This process should be judged over a period longer than one year. The cash flows should be compared with profits over the same periods to decide how successfully the reporting entity has converted earnings into cash.

3.2 The advantages of cash flow accounting

The advantages of cash flow accounting are as follows.

(a) Survival in business depends on the **ability to generate** cash. Cash flow accounting directs attention towards this critical issue.

(b) Cash flow is **more comprehensive** than 'profit' which is dependent on accounting conventions and concepts.

(c) Suppliers and lenders are more interested in an entity's ability to repay them than in its profitability. Whereas 'profits' might indicate that cash is likely to be available, cash flow accounting is more direct with its message.

(d) Cash flow reporting provides a better means of **comparing the results** of different companies than traditional profit reporting.

(e) Cash flow reporting **satisfies the needs of all users** better.

  (i) For **management**, it provides the sort of information on which decisions should be taken: (in management accounting, 'relevant costs' to a decision are future cash flows); traditional profit accounting does not help with decision-making.

  (ii) For **shareholders and auditors**, cash flow accounting can provide a satisfactory basis for stewardship accounting.

  (iii) As described previously, the information needs of **creditors and employees** will be better served by cash flow accounting.

(f) Cash flow forecasts are **easier to prepare**, as well as more useful, than profit forecasts.

(g) They can in some respects be **audited more easily** than accounts based on the accruals concept.

(h) The accruals concept is confusing, and cash flows are **more easily understood**.

(i) Cash flow accounting should be both retrospective, and also include a forecast for the future. This is of **great information value** to all users of accounting information.

(j) **Forecasts** can subsequently be **monitored** by the publication of variance statements which compare actual cash flows against the forecast.

Section summary

Note that you may be expected to analyse or interpret a statement of cash flows.

Chapter Roundup

- ✓ **Statements of cash flows** are a useful addition to the financial statements of companies because it is recognised that accounting profit is not the only indicator of a company's performance.
- ✓ IAS 7 requires cash flows during the period to be classified by operating, investing and financing activities.
- ✓ Cash flows from operating activities can be reported using the direct or indirect method.
- ✓ You need to be aware of the **format** of the statement as laid out in **IAS 7**. Setting out the format is an essential first stage in preparing the statement, so this format must be learnt.
- ✓ Note that you may be expected to **analyse** or **interpret** a statement of cash flows.

Quick Quiz

1 What is the aim of a statement of cash flows?

2 The standard headings in IAS 7 *Statement of cash flows* are:

- O.................... a.....................
- I.................... a......................
- F.................... a......................
- Net...................... in C........................ and ....

3 Cash equivalents are current asset investments which will mature or can be redeemed within three months of the year end.

True ☐
False ☐

4 Why are you more likely to encounter the indirect method as opposed to the direct method?

5 List five advantages of cash flow accounting.

6 List the steps that should be followed to prepare a statement of cash flows.

Answers to Quick Quiz

1 To indicate an entity's ability to generate cash and cash equivalents.

2
- Operating activities
- Investing activities
- Financing activities
- Net increase (decrease) in cash and cash equivalents

3 False. See the definition in paragraph 1.6 if you are not sure about this.

4 The indirect method utilises figures which appear in the financial statements. The figures required for the direct method may not be readily available.

5 See paragraph 2.1.

6
- Set out the proforma statement of cash flows
- Complete the reconciliation of profit before tax to net cash from operating activities
- Calculate cash flow figures for purchase or sale of non-current assets, issue of shares and repayment of loans
- Insert figures given or calculated into statement of cash flows

Answers to Questions

9.1 Statement of cash flows

EMMA CO
STATEMENT OF CASH FLOWS FOR THE YEAR ENDED 31 DECEMBER 20X2

	$'000	$'000
Net cash flows from operating activities		
Profit before tax	300	
Depreciation charge (W1)	90	
Net interest charge	50	
Loss on sale of property, plant and equipment (45 – 32)	13	
Profit on sale of non-current asset investments (30 – 25)	(5)	
(Increase)/decrease in inventories	(48)	
(Increase)/decrease in receivables	(75)	
Increase/(decrease) in payables	8	
Cash generated from operating activities	333	
Interest received	25	
Interest paid	(75)	
Dividends paid	(80)	
Tax paid (110 + 140 – 120)	(130)	
Net cash flows from operating activities		73
Cash flows from investing activities		
Payments to acquire property, plant and equipment (W2)	(201)	
Payments to acquire intangible non-current assets	(50)	
Receipts from sales of property, plant and equipment	32	
Receipts from sale of non-current asset investments	30	
Net cash outflow from investing activities		(189)
Cash flows from financing activities		
Issue of share capital	60	
Long-term loan	120	
Net cash flows from financing		180
Increase in cash and cash equivalents		64
Net cash and cash equivalents at 1.1 X2		(97)
Cash and cash equivalents at 31.12.X2		(33)

Workings

1 Depreciation charge

	$'000	$'000
Depreciation at 31 December 20X2		340
Depreciation 31 December 20X1	290	
Depreciation on assets sold (85 – 45)	40	
		250
Charge for the year		90

2 Purchase of property, plant and equipment

PROPERTY, PLANT AND EQUIPMENT

	$'000		$'000
1.1.X2 Balance b/d	595	Disposals	85
Revaluation (100 – 91)	9		
Purchases (bal fig)	201	31.12.X2 Balance c/d	720
	805		805

Now try these questions from the Exam Question Bank

Number	Level	Marks	Time
Q20	Examination	30	54 mins
Q21	Examination	30	54 mins

MISCELLANEOUS STANDARDS

IAS 37 and IAS 10 are very important as they can affect many items in the accounts. Students sometimes get them confused with each other, so make sure you learn all the relevant definitions and understand the standard accounting treatment.

Related party disclosures are important to users of accounts. Make sure you understand why. You must also know what constitutes a related party.

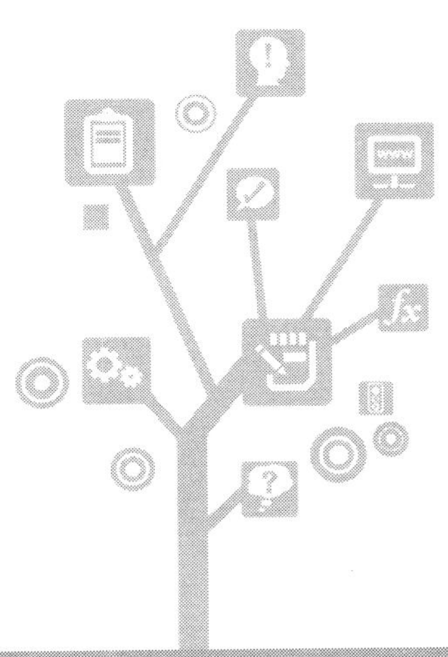

topic list	learning outcomes	syllabus references	ability required
1 IAS 37 *Provisions, contingent liabilities and contingent assets*	C2(a)	C2(x)	application
2 IAS 10 *Events after the reporting period*	C2(a)	C2(ix)	application
3 IAS 24 *Related party disclosures*	C2(a)	C2(vii)	application

1 IAS 37 *Provisions, contingent liabilities and contingent assets*

Introduction

This long section introduces provisions, contingent liabilities and contingent assets. You will need to be able to recognise these in a given scenario.

1.1 Dealing with uncertainty

As we have seen with regard to events after the reporting period, financial statements must include **all the information necessary for an understanding of the company's financial position**. Provisions, contingent liabilities and contingent assets are 'uncertainties' that must be accounted for consistently if we are to achieve this understanding.

1.2 Objective

IAS 37 *Provisions, contingent liabilities and contingent assets* aims to ensure that appropriate **recognition criteria** and **measurement bases** are applied to provisions, contingent liabilities and contingent assets and that **sufficient information** is disclosed in the **notes** to the financial statements to enable users to understand their nature, timing and amount.

1.3 Provisions

You will be familiar with provisions (allowances) for depreciation and doubtful debts from your earlier studies. The provisions addressed by IAS 37 are, however, rather different.

Before IAS 37, there was no accounting standard dealing with provisions. Companies wanting to show their results in the most favourable light used to make large 'one off' provisions in years where a high level of underlying profit was generated. These provisions, often known as 'big bath' provisions, were then available to shield expenditure in future years when perhaps the underlying profits were not as good.

In other words, provisions were used for profit smoothing. Profit smoothing is misleading.

KEY POINT

The key aim of IAS 37 is to ensure that provisions are made only where there are valid grounds for them.

IAS 37 views a provision as a liability.

KEY TERMS

A PROVISION is a liability of uncertain timing or amount.

A LIABILITY is an obligation of an entity to transfer economic benefits as a result of past transactions or events.

(IAS 37)

The IAS distinguishes provisions from other liabilities such as trade payables and accruals. This is on the basis that for a provision there is **uncertainty** about the timing or amount of the future expenditure. Whilst uncertainty is clearly present in the case of certain accruals the uncertainty is generally much less than for provisions.

1.4 Recognition

IAS 37 states that a provision should be **recognised** as a liability in the financial statements when:

- An entity has a **present obligation** (legal or constructive) as a result of a past event
- It is probable that a **transfer of economic benefits** will be required to settle the obligation
- A **reliable estimate** can be made of the obligation

1.5 Meaning of obligation

It is fairly clear what a legal obligation is. However, you may not know what a **constructive obligation** is.

KEY TERM

IAS 37 defines a CONSTRUCTIVE OBLIGATION as

'An obligation that derives from an entity's actions where:

- by an established pattern of past practice, published policies or a sufficiently specific current statement the entity has indicated to other parties that it will accept certain responsibilities; and
- as a result, the entity has created a valid expectation on the part of those other parties that it will discharge those responsibilities.

Question 10.1

Recognising a provision

Learning outcome C2(a)

In which of the following circumstances might a provision be recognised?

(a) On 13 December 20X9 the board of an entity decided to close down a division. The accounting date of the company is 31 December. Before 31 December 20X9 the decision was not communicated to any of those affected and no other steps were taken to implement the decision.

(b) The board agreed a detailed closure plan on 20 December 20X9 and details were given to customers and employees.

(c) A company obliged to incur clean up costs for environmental damage (that has already been caused).

(d) A company intends to carry out future expenditure to operate in a particular way in the future.

1.5.1 Probable transfer of economic benefits

For the purpose of the IAS, a transfer of economic benefits is regarded as '**probable**' if the event is **more likely than not** to occur. This appears to indicate a probability of more than 50%. However, the standard makes it clear that where there is a number of similar obligations the probability should be based on considering the population as a whole, rather than one single item.

Example: Transfer of economic benefits

If a company has entered into a warranty obligation then the probability of transfer of economic benefits may well be extremely small in respect of one specific item. However, when considering the population as a whole the probability of some transfer of economic benefits is quite likely to be much higher. If there is a **greater than 50% probability** of some transfer of economic benefits then a **provision** should be made for the **expected amount**.

1.6 Measurement of provisions

KEY POINT

The amount recognised as a provision should be the best estimate of the expenditure required to settle the present obligation at the end of the reporting period.

The estimates will be determined by the **judgement** of the entity's management supplemented by the experience of similar transactions.

Allowance is made for **uncertainty**. Where the provision being measured involves a large population of items, the obligation is estimated by weighting all possible outcomes by their discounted probabilities, ie **expected value**.

Question 10.2 — Expected value

Learning outcome C2(a)

Parker Co sells goods with a warranty under which customers are covered for the cost of repairs of any manufacturing defect that becomes apparent within the first six months of purchase. The company's past experience and future expectations indicate the following pattern of likely repairs.

% of goods sold	Defects	Cost of repairs $m
75	None	–
20	Minor	1.0
5	Major	4.0

What is the expected cost of repairs?

Where the effect of the **time value of money** is material, the amount of a provision should be the **present value** of the expenditure required to settle the obligation. An appropriate **discount** rate should be used.

The discount rate should be a **pre-tax rate** that reflects current market assessments of the time value of money. **The discount rate(s) should not reflect risks for which future cash flow estimates have been adjusted.**

1.7 Provisions: other issues

1.7.1 Future events

Future events which are reasonably expected to occur (eg new legislation, changes in technology) may affect the amount required to settle the enterprise's obligation and should be taken into account.

1.7.2 Expected disposal of assets

Gains from the expected disposal of assets should not be taken into account in measuring a provision.

1.7.3 Reimbursements

Some or all of the expenditure needed to settle a provision may be expected to be recovered from a third party. If so, the **reimbursement should be recognised only when it is virtually certain that reimbursement will be received if the entity settles the obligation**.

(a) The reimbursement should be treated as a separate asset, and the amount recognised should not be greater than the provision itself.

(b) The provision and the amount recognised for reimbursement may be netted off in profit or loss.

1.7.4 Changes in provisions

Provisions should be reviewed at the end of each reporting period and adjusted to reflect the current best estimate. If it is no longer probable that a transfer of economic benefits will be required to settle the obligation, the provision should be reversed.

1.7.5 Use of provisions

A provision should be used only for expenditures for which the provision was originally recognised. Setting expenditures against a provision that was originally recognised for another purpose would conceal the impact of two different events.

1.7.6 Future operating losses

Provisions should not be recognised for future operating losses. They do not meet the definition of a liability and the general recognition criteria set out in the standard.

1.7.7 Onerous contracts

If an entity has a contract that is onerous, the present obligation under the contract **should be recognised and measured** as a provision. An example might be vacant leasehold property.

KEY TERM

An ONEROUS CONTRACT is a contract entered into with another party under which the unavoidable costs of fulfilling the terms of the contract exceed any revenues expected to be received from the goods or services supplied or purchased directly or indirectly under the contract and where the entity would have to compensate the other party if it did not fulfil the terms of the contract.

1.8 Examples of possible provisions

It is easier to see what IAS 37 is driving at if you look at examples of those items which are possible provisions under this standard. Some of these we have already touched on.

(a) **Warranties**. These are argued to be genuine provisions as on past experience it is probable, ie more likely than not, that some claims will emerge. The provision must be estimated, however, on the basis of the class as a whole and not on individual claims. There is a clear legal obligation in this case.

(b) **Major repairs**. In the past it has been quite popular for companies to provide for expenditure on a major overhaul to be accrued gradually over the intervening years between overhauls. Under IAS 37 this is no longer be possible as IAS 37 holds that this is a mere intention to carry out repairs, not an obligation. The entity can always sell the asset in the meantime. The only solution is to treat major assets such as aircraft, ships, furnaces etc as a series of smaller assets where each part is depreciated over different lives. Thus any major overhaul may be argued to be replacement and therefore capital rather than revenue expenditure.

(c) **Self insurance**. A number of companies have created a provision for self insurance based on the expected cost of making good fire damage etc instead of paying premiums to an insurance company. Under IAS 37 this provision is no longer justifiable as the entity has no obligation until a fire or accident occurs. No obligation exists until that time.

(d) **Environmental contamination**. If the company has an environment policy such that other parties would expect the company to clean up any contamination or if the company has broken current environmental legislation then a provision for environmental damage must be made.

(e) **Decommissioning or abandonment costs**. When an oil company initially purchases an oilfield it is put under a legal obligation to decommission the site at the end of its life. Prior to IAS 37 most oil companies set up the provision gradually over the life of the field so that no one year would be unduly burdened with the cost.

    IAS 37, however, insists that a legal obligation exists on the initial expenditure on the field and therefore a liability exists immediately. This would appear to result in a large charge to profit and loss in the first year of operation of the field. However, the IAS takes the view that the cost of purchasing the field in the first place is not only the cost of the field itself but also the costs of putting it right again. Thus all the costs of abandonment may be capitalised.

(f) **Restructuring**. This is considered in detail below.

1.9 Provisions for restructuring

One of the main purposes of IAS 37 was to target abuses of provisions for restructuring. Accordingly, IAS 37 lays down **strict criteria** to determine when such a provision can be made.

IAS 37 defines a RESTRUCTURING as:

A programme that is planned and is controlled by management and materially changes either:

- the scope of a business undertaken by an entity; or
- the manner in which that business is conducted.

The IAS gives the following **examples** of events that may fall under the definition of restructuring.

- The **sale or termination** of a line of business
- The **closure of business locations** in a country or region or the **relocation** of business activities from one country region to another
- **Changes in management structure**, for example, the elimination of a layer of management
- **Fundamental reorganisations** that have a material effect on the **nature and focus** of the entity's operations

The question is whether or not an entity has an obligation - legal or constructive - at the end of the reporting period.

- An entity must have a **detailed formal plan** for the restructuring.
- It must have **raised a valid expectation** in those affected that it will carry out the restructuring by starting to implement that plan or announcing its main features to those affected by it

A mere management decision is not normally sufficient. Management decisions may sometimes trigger off recognition, but only if earlier events such as negotiations with employee representatives and other interested parties have been concluded subject only to management approval.

Where the restructuring involves the **sale of an operation** then IAS 37 states that no obligation arises until the entity has entered into a **binding sale agreement**. This is because until this has occurred the entity will be able to change its mind and withdraw from the sale even if its intentions have been announced publicly.

1.9.1 Costs to be included within a restructuring provision

The IAS states that a restructuring provision should include only the **direct expenditures** arising from the restructuring, which are those that are both:

- **Necessarily entailed** by the restructuring; and
- Not associated with the **ongoing activities** of the entity.

The following costs should specifically **not** be included within a restructuring provision.

- **Retraining** or relocating continuing staff
- **Marketing**
- **Investment in new systems** and distribution networks

1.9.2 Disclosure

Disclosures for provisions fall into two parts.

- Disclosure of details of the **change in carrying value** of a provision from the beginning to the end of the year
- Disclosure of the **background** to the making of the provision and the uncertainties affecting its outcome

1.10 Contingent liabilities

Now that you understand provisions it will be easier to understand contingent assets and liabilities.

IAS 37 defines a CONTINGENT LIABILITY as:

- A possible obligation that arises from past events and whose existence will be confirmed only by the occurrence or non-occurrence of one or more uncertain future events not wholly within the entity's control; or
- A present obligation that arises from past events but is not recognised because:
  - It is not probable that a transfer of economic benefits will be required to settle the obligation; or
  - The amount of the obligation cannot be measured with sufficient reliability.

As a rule of thumb, probable means **more than 50%** likely. **If an obligation is probable, it is not a contingent liability** - instead, a **provision is needed**.

1.10.1 Treatment of contingent liabilities

Contingent liabilities **should not be recognised in financial statements** but they **should be disclosed**. The required disclosures are:

- A brief description of the nature of the contingent liability
- An estimate of its financial effect
- An indication of the uncertainties that exist
- The possibility of any reimbursement

1.11 Contingent assets

IAS 37 defines a CONTINGENT ASSET as:

A possible asset that arises from past events and whose existence will be confirmed by the occurrence of one or more uncertain future events not wholly within the entity's control.

A contingent asset must not be recognised. Only when the realisation of the related economic benefits is **virtually certain** should recognition take place. At that point, **the asset is no longer a contingent asset**!

1.11.1 Disclosure: contingent liabilities

A **brief description** must be provided of all material contingent liabilities unless they are likely to be remote. In addition, provide

- An estimate of their **financial effect**
- Details of **any uncertainties**
- Details of any possible reimbursement

1.11.2 Disclosure: contingent assets

Contingent assets must only be disclosed in the notes if they are **probable**. In that case a brief description of the contingent asset should be provided along with an estimate of its likely financial effect.

1.11.3 'Let out'

IAS 37 permits reporting entities to avoid disclosure requirements relating to provisions, contingent liabilities and contingent assets if they would be expected to **seriously prejudice** the position of the entity in dispute with other parties. However, this should only be employed in **extremely rare** cases. Details of the general nature of the provision/contingencies must still be provided, together with an explanation of why it has not been disclosed.

You must practise the questions below to get the hang of IAS 37. But first, study the flow chart, taken from IAS 37, which is a good summary of its requirements.

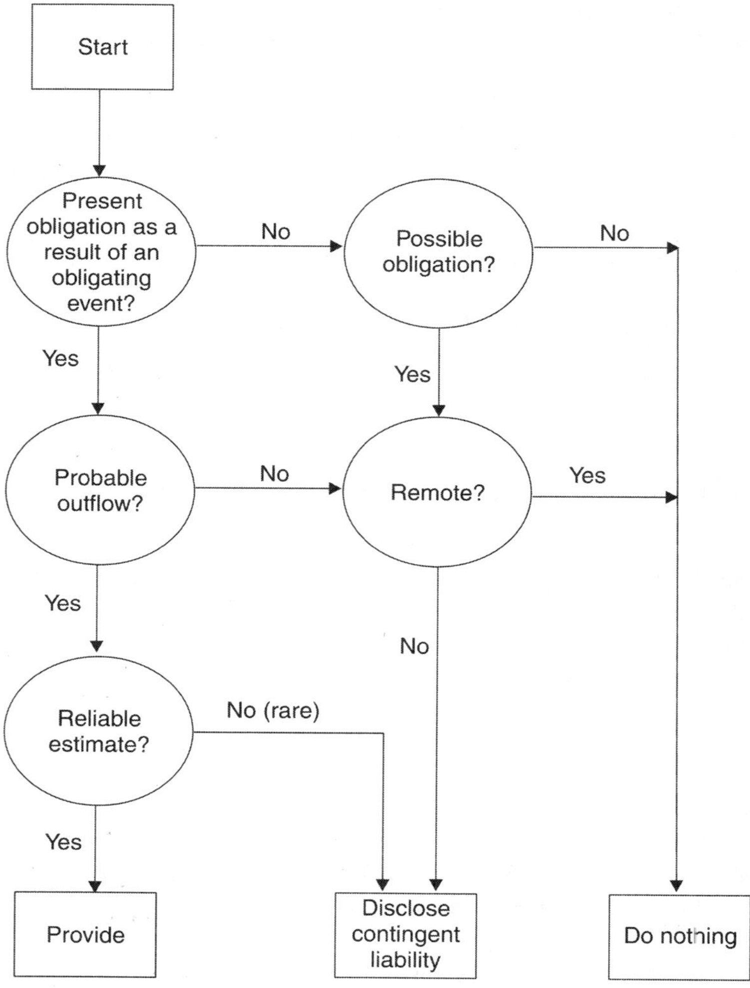

Exam skills

If you learn this flow chart you should be able to deal with most questions you are likely to meet in an exam.

Question 10.3 — Provide or not? (1)

Learning outcome C2(a)

During 20X0 Smack Co gives a guarantee of certain borrowings of Pony Co, whose financial condition at that time is sound. During 20X1, the financial condition of Pony Co deteriorates and at 30 June 20X1 Pony Co files for protection from its creditors.

What accounting treatment is required:

(a) At 31 December 20X0?
(b) At 31 December 20X1?

Question 10.4 Provide or not? (2)

Learning outcome C2(a)

Warren Co gives warranties at the time of sale to purchasers of its products. Under the terms of the warranty the manufacturer undertakes to make good, by repair or replacement, manufacturing defects that become apparent within a period of three years from the date of the sale. Should a provision be recognised?

Question 10.5 Provide or not? (3)

Learning outcome C2(a)

After a wedding in 20X0 ten people died, possibly as a result of food poisoning from products sold by Callow Co. Legal proceedings are started seeking damages from Callow but it disputes liability. Up to the date of approval of the financial statements for the year to 31 December 20X0, Callow's lawyers advise that it is probable that it will not be found liable. However, when Callow prepares the financial statements for the year to 31 December 20X1 its lawyers advise that, owing to developments in the case, it is probable that it will be found liable.

What is the required accounting treatment:

(a) At 31 December 20X0?
(b) At 31 December 20X1?

Section summary

- The objective of IAS 37 is to ensure that appropriate recognition criteria and measurement bases are applied to provisions and contingencies and that sufficient information is disclosed.
- The IAS seeks to ensure that provisions are **only recognised** when a **measurable obligation** exists. It includes detailed rules that can be used to ascertain when an obligation exists and how to measure the obligation.
- The standard attempts to **eliminate 'profit smoothing'**.

2 IAS 10 *Events after the reporting period*

Introduction

In this section we cover the reporting requirements where an event occurs after the end of the reporting period. In some instances, the financial statements will need to be amended for such an event.

2.1 Purpose of IAS 10

The financial statements are significant indicators of a company's success or failure. It is important, therefore, that they include all the information necessary for an understanding of the company's position.

IAS 10 (Revised) *Events after the reporting period* requires the provision of additional information in order to facilitate such an understanding. IAS 10 deals with events **after** the end of the reporting period which may affect the position at the end of the reporting period.

2.2 Definitions

The standard gives the following definition.

KEY TERM

EVENTS OCCURRING AFTER THE END OF THE REPORTING PERIOD are those events, both favourable and unfavourable, that occur between the end of the reporting period and the date on which the financial statements are authorised for issue. Two types of events can be identified.

- Those that provide evidence of conditions that existed at the end of the reporting period – *adjusting*
- Those that are indicative of conditions that arose after the end of the reporting period – *non-adjusting* *(IAS 10)*

2.3 Events occurring after the end of the reporting period

Between the end of the reporting period and the date the financial statements are authorised (ie for issue outside the organisation), events may occur which show that assets and liabilities at the end of the reporting period should be adjusted, or that disclosure of such events should be given.

2.4 Events requiring adjustment

The standard requires adjustment of assets and liabilities in certain circumstances.

An entity shall adjust the amounts recognised in its financial statements to reflect adjusting events after the end of the reporting period. An entity shall not adjust the amounts recognised in its financial statements to reflect non-adjusting events after the end of the reporting period. *(IAS 10)*

An **example** of additional evidence which becomes available after the end of the reporting period is where a **customer goes bankrupt, thus confirming that the trade account receivable balance at the year end is uncollectable.**

In relation to **going concern**, the standard states that, where operating results and the financial position have deteriorated after the end of the reporting period, it may be necessary to reconsider whether the going concern assumption is appropriate in the preparation of the financial statements.

Examples of **adjusting events** would be:

- evidence of a permanent diminution in property value prior to the year end
- sale of inventory after the end of the reporting period for less than its carrying value at the year end
- insolvency of a customer with a balance owing at the year end
- amounts received or paid in respect of legal or insurance claims which were in negotiation at the year end
- determination after the year end of the sale or purchase price of assets sold or purchased before the year end
- evidence of a permanent diminution in the value of a long-term investment prior to the year end
- discovery of error or fraud which shows that the financial statements were incorrect

2.5 Events not requiring adjustment

The standard then looks at events which do **not** require adjustment.

The standard gives the following examples of events which do **not** require adjustments:

- acquisition of, or disposal of, a subsidiary after the year end
- announcement of a plan to discontinue an operation
- major purchases and disposals of assets

- destruction of a production plant by fire after the end of the reporting period
- announcement or commencing implementation of a major restructuring
- share transactions after the end of the reporting period
- litigation commenced after the end of the reporting period

But note that, while they may be non-adjusting, some events after the end of the reporting period will require disclosure.

If non-adjusting events after the end of the reporting period are material, non-disclosure could influence the economic decisions of users taken on the basis of the financial statements. Accordingly, an entity shall disclose the following for each material category of non-adjusting event after the end of the reporting period:

(a) the nature of the event; and
(b) an estimate of its financial effect, or a statement that such an estimate cannot be made. *(IAS 10)*

The **example** given by the standard of such an event is where the **value of an investment falls between the end of the reporting period and the date the financial statements are authorised** for issue. The fall in value represents circumstances during the current period, not conditions existing at the previous end of the reporting period, so it is not appropriate to adjust the value of the investment in the financial statements. Disclosure is an aid to users, however, indicating 'unusual changes' in the state of assets and liabilities after the end of the reporting period.

The rule for **disclosure** of events occurring after the end of the reporting period which relate to conditions that arose after that date, is that disclosure should be made if non-disclosure would hinder the user's ability to make **proper evaluations** and decisions based on the financial statements. An example might be the acquisition of another business.

2.6 Dividends

Dividends on equity shares declared by the entity after the end of the reporting period should not be recognised as a liability at the end of the reporting period, but should be disclosed in the notes to the financial statements.

2.7 Disclosures

The following **disclosure requirements** are given **for events** which occur after the end of the reporting period which do not require adjustment. If disclosure of events occurring after the end of the reporting period is required, the following information should be provided.

(a) The nature of the event
(b) An estimate of the financial effect, or a statement that such an estimate cannot be made

Question 10.6 — Adjusting or not?

Learning outcome C2(a)

State whether the following events occurring after the end of the reporting period require an adjustment to the assets and liabilities of the financial statements.

(a) Purchase of an investment
(b) A change in the rate of corporate tax, applicable to the previous year
(c) An increase in pension benefits
(d) Losses due to fire
(e) A bad debt suddenly being paid
(f) The receipt of proceeds of sales or other evidence concerning the net realisable value of inventory
(g) A sudden decline in the value of property held as a long-term asset

Section summary

IAS 10 deals with **events occurring after the reporting period**. It distinguishes between adjusting and non-adjusting events and gives examples.

3 IAS 24 *Related party disclosures*

Introduction

This section introduces the area of related parties. We will look at what a related party is, what disclosures are required and why. We will meet related parties again when we cover groups in Chapter 13.

3.1 Why was a standard needed?

In the absence of information to the contrary, it is assumed that a reporting entity has **independent discretionary power** over its resources and transactions and pursues its activities independently of the interests of its individual owners, managers and others. Transactions are presumed to have been undertaken on an **arm's length basis**, ie on terms such as could have obtained in a transaction with an external party, in which each side bargained knowledgeably and freely, unaffected by any relationship between them.

These assumptions may not be justified when **related party relationships** exist, because the requisite conditions for competitive, free market dealings may not be present. Whilst the parties may endeavour to achieve arm's length bargaining the very nature of the relationship may preclude this occurring.

3.2 Objective

The objective of IAS 24 is to ensure that an entity's financial statements contain the disclosures necessary to draw attention to the possibility that its financial position and profit or loss may have been affected by the existence of related parties and by transactions and outstanding balances with such parties.

3.3 Scope

The standard applies in:

- Identifying related parties and related party transactions
- Identifying outstanding balances between related parties
- Identifying circumstances in which disclosure is required
- Determining the disclosures to be made

Note that the standard does not apply to the *measurement* of related party transactions. It is only concerned with disclosure.

Under the standard a party is a **related party** if:

(a) Directly or indirectly the party

  (i) Controls, is controlled by, or is under common control with, the entity (this includes parents, subsidiaries, fellow subsidiaries)

  (ii) Has an interest in the entity that gives it significant influence over the entity; or

  (iii) Has joint control over the entity

(b) The party is an associate of the entity

(c) The party is a joint venture in which the entity is a venturer

(d) The party is a member of the key management personnel of the entity or its parent

(e) The party is a close member of the family of any individual referred to in (a) or (d)

(f) The party is an entity that is controlled, jointly controlled or significantly influenced by, or a significant proportion of whose voting rights are held by, any individual referred to in (d) or (e)

(g) The party is a post-employment benefit plan for the benefit of employees of the entity, or of any entity that is a related party of the entity

The following are not necessarily related parties:

(a) Two entities simply because they have a director or other member of key management personnel in common

(b) Two venturers simply because they share control over a joint venture

(c) (i) Providers of finance
(ii) Trade unions
(iii) Public utilities; and
(iv) Government departments and agencies

(d) A customer, supplier, franchisor, distributor or general agent with whom the entity transacts a significant volume of business, merely by virtue of the resulting economic dependence. (In other words, this is not designated as *significant influence*.)

3.4 Definitions

The following important definitions are given in the standard:

KEY TERMS

RELATED PARTY TRANSACTION. A transfer of resources, services or obligations between related parties, regardless of whether a price is charged.

CONTROL. The power to govern the financial and operating policies of an entity so as to obtain benefits from its activities.

JOINT CONTROL. The contractually agreed sharing of control over an economic activity.

SIGNIFICANT INFLUENCE. The power to participate in the financial and operating policy decisions of an entity, but not control over those policies. Significant influence may be gained by share ownership, statute or agreement.

KEY MANAGEMENT PERSONNEL. Those persons having authority and responsibility for planning, directing and controlling the activities of the entity, directly or indirectly, including any director of that entity.

COMPENSATION. All employee benefits. This includes:

(a) short-term employee benefits such as wages, salaries and social security contributions, paid annual leave and paid sick leave, profit-sharing and bonuses

(b) post-employment benefits such as pensions, other retirement benefits, post-employment life insurance and post-employment medical care

(c) other long-term benefits, including long-service leave or sabbatical leave

(d) termination benefits; and

(e) share-based payment (IAS 24)

3.5 Disclosures

(a) **Relationships between parents and subsidiaries** are to be disclosed irrespective of whether any transactions have taken place.

(b) **Key management personnel compensation** is to be disclosed in total and for each of the categories (a) to (e) above.

(c) **Transactions between related parties** require disclosure of the relationship as well as details concerning the transaction, including the amount of the transaction(s), the amount of any outstanding balance(s) and any provisions or expenses in respect of doubtful debts due from related parties.

3.6 Transactions

The standard gives the following examples of transactions that are disclosed if they are with a related party:

(a) purchases or sales of goods
(b) purchases or sales of property and other assets
(c) rendering or receiving of services
(d) leases
(e) transfers of research and development
(f) transfers under licence agreement
(g) transfers under finance arrangements (such as loans)
(h) provisions of guarantees or collateral; and
(i) settlement of liabilities on behalf of the entity, or by the entity on behalf of another party

Exam alert

A question on IAS 24 may simply be on what constitutes a related party. Make sure you know this and are able to provide examples.

Section summary

IAS 24 is primarily a **disclosure statement**. It is concerned with improving the quality of information provided by published accounts.

Chapter Roundup

- ✓ The objective of IAS 37 is to ensure that appropriate recognition criteria and measurement bases are applied to provisions and contingencies and that sufficient information is disclosed.
- ✓ The IAS seeks to ensure that provisions are **only recognised** when a **measurable obligation** exists. It includes detailed rules that can be used to ascertain when an obligation exists and how to measure the obligation.
- ✓ The standard attempts to **eliminate 'profit smoothing'**.
- ✓ IAS 10 deals with **events occurring after the reporting period**. It distinguishes between adjusting and non-adjusting events and gives examples.
- ✓ **IAS 24** is primarily a **disclosure statement**. It is concerned with improving the quality of information provided by published accounts.

Quick Quiz

1 Define events occurring after the end of the reporting period.

2 A customer goes bankrupt after the end of the reporting period and his debt must be written off.

Adjusting event ☐

Non-adjusting event ☐

3 Inventory is lost in a fire after the end of the reporting period.

Adjusting event ☐

Non-adjusting event ☐

4 A provision is a .... of .... timing or amount.

5 A programme is undertaken by management which converts the previously wholly owned chain of restaurants they ran into franchises. Is this restructuring?

6 Define contingent asset and contingent liability.

7 Banks lending money to a company are deemed related parties by IAS 24.

True ☐

False ☐

Answers to Quick Quiz

1 Those events unfavourable and favourable, which occur between the end of the reporting period and the date on which the financial statements are authorised for issue.

2 Adjusting

3 Non-adjusting

4 Liability, uncertain

5 Yes. The manner in which the business is conducted has changed.

6 Refer to paragraphs 1.10 and 1.11

7 False (see Para 3.3).

Answers to Questions

10.1 Recognising a provision

(a) No provision would be recognised as the decision has not been implemented.

(b) A provision would be made in the 20X9 financial statements.

(c) A provision for such costs is appropriate.

(d) No present obligation exists and under IAS 37 no provision would be appropriate. This is because the entity could avoid the future expenditure by its future actions, maybe by changing its method of operation.

10.2 Expected value

The cost is found using 'expected values' (75% × $nil) + (20% × $1.0m) + (5% × $4.0m) = $400,000.

10.3 Provide or not? (1)

(a) **At 31 December 20X0**: There is a present obligation as a result of a past obligating event. The obligating event is the giving of the guarantee, which gives rise to a legal obligation. However, at 31 December 20X0 no transfer of economic benefits is probable in settlement of the obligation.

No provision is recognised. The guarantee is disclosed as a contingent liability unless the probability of any transfer is regarded as remote.

(b) **At 31 December 20X1**: As above, there is a present obligation as a result of a past obligating event, namely the giving of the guarantee. At 31 December 20X1 it is probable that a transfer of economic events will be required to settle the obligation. A provision is therefore recognised for the best estimate of the obligation.

10.4 Provide or not? (2)

Warren Co **cannot avoid** the cost of repairing or replacing all items of product that manifest manufacturing defects in respect of which warranties are given before the end of the reporting period, and a provision for the cost of this should therefore be made.

Warren Co is obliged to repair or replace items that fail within the entire warranty period. Therefore, in respect of **this year's sales**, the obligation provided for at the end of the reporting period, should be the cost of making good items for which defects have been notified but not yet processed, **plus** an estimate of costs in respect of the other items sold for which there is sufficient evidence that manufacturing defects **will** manifest themselves during their remaining periods of warranty cover.

10.5 Provide or not? (3)

(a) At 31 December 20X0

On the basis of the evidence available when the financial statements were approved, there is no obligation as a result of past events. No provision is recognised. The matter is disclosed as a contingent liability unless the probability of any transfer is regarded as remote.

(b) At 31 December 20X1

On the basis of the evidence available, there is a present obligation. A transfer of economic benefits in settlement is probable. A provision is recognised for the best estimate of the amount needed to settle the present obligation.

10.6 Adjusting or not?

(b), (e) and (f) require adjustment.

Now try these questions from the Exam Question Bank

Number	Level	Marks	Time
Q19	Examination	5	9 mins
Q22	Examination	5	9 mins

INVENTORIES AND CONSTRUCTION CONTRACTS

You have encountered inventory and its valuation in your earlier studies. Inventory and short-term work-in-progress valuation has a direct impact on a company's gross profit and it is usually a material item in any company's accounts. This is therefore an important subject area. If you have any doubts about accounting for inventories and methods of inventory valuation you would be advised to go back to your earlier study material and revise this topic.

Section 1 of this chapter goes over some of this ground again, concentrating on the effect of IAS 2. Section 2 goes on to discuss a new area, construction contracts, which are effectively long-term work in progress. You should find this topic fairly logical as long as you work through the examples and question carefully.

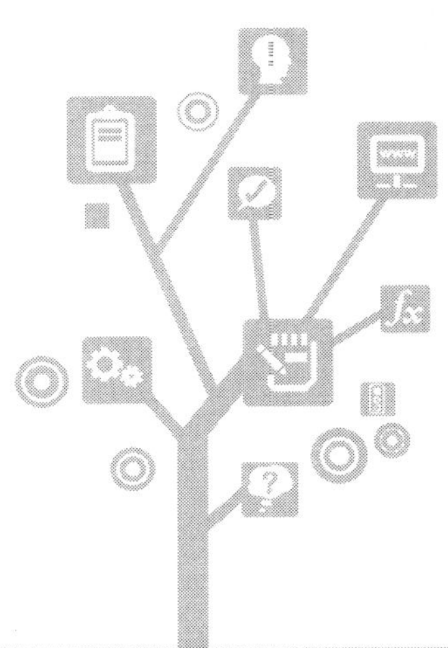

topic list	learning outcomes	syllabus references	ability required
1 Inventories and short-term WIP (IAS 2)	C2(a)	C2(vi)	application
2 IAS 11 *Construction contracts*	C2(a)	C2(viii)	application

1 Inventories and short-term WIP (IAS 2)

Introduction

In this section we develop the knowledge on inventories you have accumulated in previous papers. We will examine IAS 2 (revised) *Inventories,* specifically how the value of inventory should be measured and disclosed.

1.1 Valuing inventory

In most businesses the value put on inventory is an important factor in the determination of profit. Inventory valuation is, however, a highly subjective exercise and consequently there is a wide variety of different methods used in practice.

1.2 IAS 2 (revised) *Inventories*

IAS 2 lays out the required accounting treatment for inventories (sometimes called stocks) under the historical cost system. The major area of contention is the cost **value of inventory** to be recorded. This is recognised as an asset of the entity until the related revenues are recognised (ie the item is sold) at which point the inventory is recognised as an expense (ie cost of sales). Part or all of the cost of inventories may also be expensed if a write-down to **net realisable value** is necessary. The IAS also provides guidance on the cost formulas that are used to assign costs to inventories.

In other words, the fundamental accounting assumption of **accruals** requires costs to be matched with associated revenues. In order to achieve this, costs incurred for goods which remain unsold at the year end must be carried forward in the statement of financial position and matched against future revenues.

1.3 Scope

The following items are **excluded** from the scope of the standard.

- Work in progress under **construction contracts** (covered by IAS 11 *Construction contracts,* see Section 2)
- **Financial instruments** (ie shares, bonds)
- **Biological assets**

Certain inventories are exempt from the standard's **measurement rules**, ie those held by:

- Producers of **agricultural and forest products**
- **Commodity broker-traders**

1.4 Definitions

The standard gives the following important definitions.

INVENTORIES are assets:

- held for sale in the ordinary course of business;
- in the process of production for such sale; or
- in the form of materials or supplies to be consumed in the production process or in the rendering of services.

NET REALISABLE VALUE is the estimated selling price in the ordinary course of business less the estimated costs of completion and the estimated costs necessary to make the sale.

FAIR VALUE is the amount for which an asset could be exchanged or a liability settled between knowledgeable, willing parties in an arm's length transaction. *(IAS 2)*

Inventories can **include** any of the following.

- **Goods purchased and held for resale**, eg goods held for sale by a retailer, or land and buildings held for resale
- **Finished goods** produced
- **Work in progress** being produced
- Materials and supplies awaiting use in the production process (**raw materials**)

1.5 Measurement of inventories

KEY POINT

The standard states that '**Inventories should be measured at the lower of cost and net realisable value.**'.

1.6 Cost of inventories

The cost of inventories will consist of all costs of:

(a) **Purchase**
(b) **Costs of conversion**
(c) **Other costs** incurred in bringing the inventories to their present location and condition

1.6.1 Costs of purchase

The standard lists the following as comprising the costs of purchase of inventories:

(a) **Purchase price** *plus*

(b) **Import duties** and other taxes *plus*

(c) Transport, handling and any other costs **directly attributable** to the acquisition of finished goods, services and materials *less*

(d) **Trade discounts**, rebates and other similar amounts

1.6.2 Costs of conversion

Costs of conversion of inventories consist of two main parts.

(a) Costs **directly related** to the units of production, eg direct materials, direct labour

(b) Fixed and variable **production overheads** that are incurred in converting materials into finished goods, allocated on a systematic basis.

You may have come across the terms 'fixed production overheads' or 'variable production overheads' elsewhere in your studies. The standard defines them as follows.

KEY TERMS

FIXED PRODUCTION OVERHEADS are those indirect costs of production that remain relatively constant regardless of the volume of production, eg the cost of factory management and administration.

VARIABLE PRODUCTION OVERHEADS are those indirect costs of production that vary directly, or nearly directly, with the volume of production, eg indirect materials and labour. *(IAS 2)*

The standard emphasises that fixed production overheads must be allocated to items of inventory on the basis of the **normal capacity of the production facilities**. This is an important point.

(a) **Normal capacity** is the expected achievable production based on the average over several periods/seasons, under normal circumstances.

(b) The above figure should take account of the capacity lost through **planned maintenance**.

(c) If it approximates to the normal level of activity then the **actual level of production** can be used.

(d) **Low production** or **idle plant** will *not* result in a higher fixed overhead allocation to each unit.

(e) **Unallocated overheads** must be recognised as an expense in the period in which they were incurred.

(f) When production is **abnormally high**, the fixed production overhead allocated to each unit will be reduced, so avoiding inventories being stated at more than cost.

(g) The allocation of variable production overheads to each unit is based on the **actual use** of production facilities.

1.6.3 Other costs

Any other costs should only be recognised if they are incurred in bringing the inventories to their **present location and condition**.

The standard lists types of cost which **would not be included** in cost of inventories. Instead, they should be recognised as an **expense** in the period they are incurred.

- **Abnormal amounts** of wasted materials, labour or other production costs
- **Storage costs** (except costs which are necessary in the production process before a further production stage)
- **Administrative overheads** not incurred to bring inventories to their present location and condition
- **Selling costs**

1.7 Cost formulae

Cost of inventories should be assigned by **specific identification** of their individual costs for:

(a) Items that are not **ordinarily interchangeable**
(b) Goods or services produced and segregated for **specific projects**

Specific costs should be attributed to individual items of inventory when they are segregated for a specific project, but not where inventories consist of a large number of interchangeable (ie identical or very similar) items. In the latter case the rule is as specified below.

1.7.1 Accounting treatment

KEY POINT

The cost of inventories should be assigned by using the **first-in, first-out (FIFO)** or **weighted average** cost formula. (The LIFO formula (last in, first out) is **not permitted** by the revised IAS 2.)

Under the weighted average cost method, a recalculation can be made after each purchase, **or alternatively only at the period end**.

1.8 Net realisable value (NRV)

As a general rule assets should not be carried at amounts greater than those expected to be realised from their sale or use. In the case of inventories this amount could fall below cost when items are **damaged or become obsolete**, or where the **costs to completion have increased** in order to make the sale.

In fact we can identify the principal situations in which **NRV is likely to be less than cost**, ie where there has been:

(a) An **increase in costs** or a **fall in selling price**
(b) A **physical deterioration** in the condition of inventory
(c) **Obsolescence** of products
(d) A decision as part of the company's marketing strategy to manufacture and sell products at a **loss**
(e) **Errors in production or purchasing**

1.9 Disclosure

The financial statements should disclose the following.

(a) **Accounting policies** adopted in measuring inventories, including the cost formula used

(b) **Total carrying amount of inventories** and the carrying amount in classifications appropriate to the entity

(c) **Carrying amount** of inventories carried at fair value less costs to sell (NRV)

Question 11.1 — Inventory valuation

Learning outcomes C2(a)

You are the accountant at Water Pumps Co, and you have been asked to calculate the valuation of the company's inventory at cost at its year end of 30 April 20X5.

Water Pumps manufactures a range of pumps. The pumps are assembled from components bought by Water Pumps (the company does not manufacture any parts).

The company does not use a standard costing system, and work in progress and finished goods are valued as follows.

(a) Material costs are determined from the product specification, which lists the components required to make a pump.

(b) The company produces a range of pumps. Employees record the hours spent on assembling each type of pump, this information is input into the payroll system which prints the total hours spent each week assembling each type of pump. All employees assembling pumps are paid at the same rate and there is no overtime.

(c) Overheads are added to the inventory value in accordance with IAS 2 *Inventories.* The financial accounting records are used to determine the overhead cost, and this is applied as a percentage based on the direct labour cost.

For direct labour costs, you have agreed that the labour expended for a unit in work in progress is half that of a completed unit.

The draft accounts show the following materials and direct labour costs in inventory.

	Raw materials	*Work in progress*	*Finished goods*
Materials ($)	74,786	85,692	152,693
Direct labour ($)		13,072	46,584

The costs incurred in April, as recorded in the financial accounting records, were as follows.

	$
Direct labour	61,320
Selling costs	43,550
Depreciation and finance costs of production machines	4,490
Distribution costs	6,570
Factory manager's wage	2,560
Other production overheads	24,820
Purchasing and accounting costs relating to production	5,450
Other accounting costs	7,130
Other administration overheads	24,770

For your calculations assume that all work in progress and finished goods were produced in April 20X5 and that the company was operating at a normal level of activity.

Required

Calculate the value of overheads which should be added to work in progress and finished goods in accordance with IAS 2 *Inventories*.

Note. You should include details and a description of your workings and all figures should be calculated to the nearest $.

Section summary

IAS 2 *Inventories* requires that the statement of financial position should show **inventories** classified in a manner appropriate to the entity. Common **classifications** are:

- Merchandise
- Production supplies
- Materials
- Work-in-progress
- Finished goods

The use of **LIFO** is **prohibited** under IAS 2.

Full details of inventory carried at **NRV** as well as the reversal of any previous write down should be disclosed

2 IAS 11 *Construction contracts*

Introduction

In this section we introduce construction contracts. We will look at the required treatments and disclosures under IAS 11. Make sure that you work through and understand all the examples.

2.1 Income and expenditure

Imagine that you are the accountant at a construction company. Your company is building a large tower block that will house offices, under a contract with an investment company. It will take three years to build the block and over that time you will obviously have to pay for building materials, wages of workers on the building, architects' fees and so on. You will receive periodic payments from the investment company at various predetermined stages of the construction. How do you decide, in each of the three

years, **what to include as income and expenditure** for the contract in the statement of comprehensive income?

This is the problem tackled by IAS 11 *Construction contracts*.

Example: Construction contract

A numerical example might help to illustrate the problem. Suppose that a contract is started on 1 January 20X5, with an estimated completion date of 31 December 20X6. The final contract price is $1,500,000. In the first year, to 31 December 20X5:

(a) Costs incurred amounted to $600,000.

(b) Half the work on the contract was completed.

(c) Certificates of work completed have been issued, to the value of $750,000. (*Note*. It is usual, in a construction contract, for a qualified person such as an architect or engineer to inspect the work completed, and if it is satisfactory, to issue certificates. This will then be the notification to the customer that progress payments are now due to the contractor. Progress payments are commonly the amount of valuation on the work certificates issued, minus a precautionary retention of 10%).

(d) It is estimated with reasonable certainty that further costs to completion in 20X6 will be $600,000.

What is the contract profit in 20X5, and what entries would be made for the contract at 31 December 20X5 if:

(a) Profits are deferred until the completion of the contract?
(b) A proportion of the estimated revenue and profit is credited to the profit or loss in 20X5?

Solution

(a) If profits were deferred until the completion of the contract in 20X6, the revenue and profit recognised on the contract in 20X5 would be nil, and the value of work in progress on 31 December 20X5 would be $600,000. IAS 11 takes the view that this policy is unreasonable, because in 20X6, the total profit of $300,000 would be recorded. Since the contract revenues are earned throughout 20X5 and 20X6, a profit of nil in 20X5 and $300,000 in 20X6 would be contrary to the accruals concept of accounting.

(b) **It is fairer to recognise revenue and profit throughout the duration of the contract.**

As at 31 December 20X5 revenue of $750,000 should be matched with cost of sales of $600,000 in the statement of comprehensive income, leaving an attributable profit for 20X5 of $150,000.

The only entry in the statement of financial position as at 31 December 20X5 is a receivable of $750,000 recognising that the company is owed this amount for work done to date. No balance remains for work in progress, the whole $600,000 having been recognised in cost of sales.

2.2 What is a construction contract?

A contract which needs IAS 11 treatment does not have to last for a period of more than one year. The main point is that the contract activity **starts in one financial period and ends in another**, thus creating the problem: to which of two or more periods should contract income and costs be allocated? In fact the definition given in the IAS of a construction contract is very straightforward.

KEY TERMS

CONSTRUCTION CONTRACT. A contract specifically negotiated for the construction of an asset or a combination of assets that are closely interrelated or interdependent in terms of their design, technology and function or their ultimate purpose or use. *(IAS 11)*

The standard differentiates between fixed price contracts and cost plus contracts.

FIXED PRICE CONTRACT. A contract in which the contractor agrees to a fixed contract price, or a fixed rate per unit of output, which in some cases is subject to cost escalation clauses.

COST PLUS CONTRACT. A construction contract in which the contractor is reimbursed for allowable or otherwise defined costs, plus a percentage of these costs or a fixed fee.

Construction contracts may involve the building of one asset, eg a bridge, or a series of interrelated assets eg an oil refinery. They may also include **rendering of services** (eg architects) or restoring or demolishing an asset.

2.3 Combining and segmenting construction contracts

The standard lays out the factors which determine whether the construction of a **series of assets** under one contract should be treated as several contracts.

- **Separate proposals** are submitted for each asset
- **Separate negotiations** are undertaken for each asset; the customer can accept/reject each individually
- **Identifiable costs and revenues** can be separated for each asset

There are also circumstances where a **group of contracts** should be treated as **one single construction contract**.

- The group of contracts are negotiated as a **single package**
- Contracts are **closely interrelated**, with an overall profit margin
- The contracts are performed **concurrently** or **in a continuous sequence**

2.4 Contract revenue

Contract revenue will be the **amount specified in the contract**, subject to variations in the contract work, incentive payments and claims *if* these will probably give rise to revenue and *if* they can be reliably measured. The result is that contract revenue is measured at the **fair value** of received or receivable revenue.

The standard elaborates on the types of uncertainty, which depend on the outcome of future events, that affect the **measurement of contract revenue**.

- An **agreed variation** (increase/decrease)
- **Cost escalation clauses** in a fixed price contract (increase)
- **Penalties** imposed due to delays by the contractor (decrease)
- **Number of units** varies in a contract for fixed prices per unit (increase/decrease)

In the case of any variation, claim or incentive payment, two factors should be assessed to determine whether contract revenue should be recognised.

(a) Whether it is **probable** that the customer will accept the variation/claim, or that the contract is sufficiently advanced that the performance criteria will be met

(b) Whether the amount of the revenue can be **measured reliably**

2.5 Contract costs

Contract costs consist of:

- Costs relating **directly** to the contract
- Costs attributable to general contract activity which can be **allocated** to the contract, such as insurance, cost of design and technical assistance not directly related to a specific contract and construction overheads
- Any other costs which can be **charged to the customer** under the contract, which may include general administration costs and development costs

Costs that **relate directly** to a specific contract include the following.

- **Site labour costs**, including site supervision
- Costs of **materials** used in construction
- **Depreciation** of plant and equipment used on the contract
- Costs of **moving** plant, equipment and materials to and from the contract site
- Costs of **hiring** plant and equipment
- Costs of **design and technical assistance** that are directly related to the contract
- Estimated costs of **rectification and guarantee work**, including expected warranty costs
- **Claims from third parties**

General contract activity costs should be **allocated systematically and rationally**, and all costs with similar characteristics should be treated **consistently**. The allocation should be based on the **normal level** of construction activity.

Some costs **cannot be attributed** to contract activity and so the following should be **excluded** from construction contract costs.

- **General administration costs** (unless reimbursement is specified in contract)
- **Selling costs**
- **R&D** (unless reimbursement is specified in contract)
- **Depreciation** of idle plant and equipment not used on any particular contract

2.6 Recognition of contract revenue and expenses

Revenue and costs associated with a contract should be recognised according to the stage of completion of the contract at the end of the reporting period, but *only when* the **outcome of the activity can be estimated reliably**. If a loss is predicted on a contract, then it should be recognised immediately. This is often known as the **percentage of completion method**.

A reliable estimate of the outcome of a construction contract can only be made when **certain conditions** have been met, and these conditions will be different for fixed price and cost plus contracts.

- **Fixed price contracts**
  - Probable that economic benefits of the contract will flow to the entity
  - Total contract revenue can be reliably measured
  - Stage of completion at the period end and costs to complete the contract can be reliably measured
  - Costs attributable to the contract can be identified clearly and be reliably measured (actual costs can be compared to previous estimates)

- **Cost plus contracts**
  - Probable that economic benefits of the contract will flow to the entity
  - Costs attributable to the contract (whether or not reimbursable) can be identified clearly and be reliably measured

The **percentage of completion method** is an application of the accruals assumption. Contract revenue is matched to the contract costs incurred in reaching the stage of completion, so revenue, costs and profit are attributed to the proportion of work completed.

We can **summarise** the treatment as follows.

- Recognise **contract revenue** as revenue in the accounting periods in which the work is performed
- Recognise **contract costs** as an expense in the accounting period in which the work to which they relate is performed
- Any **expected excess** of total contract costs over total contract revenue should be recognised as an expense immediately
- Any costs incurred which relate to **future activity** should be recognised as an asset if it is probable that they will be recovered (often called contract work in progress, ie amounts due from the customer)
- Where amounts have been recognised as contract revenue, but their **collectability** from the customer becomes doubtful, such amounts should be recognised as an expense, not a deduction from revenue

2.7 When can reliable estimates be made?

IAS 11 only allows contract revenue and costs to be recognised when the outcome of the contract can be predicted, ie when it is probable that the economic benefits attached to the contract will flow to the entity. IAS 11 states that this can only be when a contract has been agreed which establishes the following.

- The **enforceable rights** of each party in respect of the asset to be constructed
- The **consideration** that is to be exchanged
- **Terms and manner of settlement**

In addition, the entity should have an **effective internal financial budgeting and reporting system**, in order to review and revise the estimates of contract revenue and costs as the contract progresses.

2.8 Determining the stage of completion

How should you decide on the stage of completion of any contract? The standard lists several methods.

- Proportion of contract costs incurred for work carried out to date
- Surveys of work carried out
- Physical proportion of the contract work completed

Example: Stage of completion

Centrepoint Co have a fixed price contract to build a tower block. The initial amount of revenue agreed is \$220m. At the beginning of the contract on 1 January 20X6 our initial estimate of the contract costs is \$200m. At the end of 20X6 our estimate of the total costs has risen to \$202m.

During 20X7 the customer agrees to a variation which increases expected revenue from the contract by \$5m and causes additional costs of \$3m. At the end of 20X7 there are materials stored on site for use during the following period which cost \$2.5m.

We have decided to determine the stage of completion of the contract by calculating the proportion that contract costs incurred for work to date bear to the latest estimated total contract costs. The contract costs incurred at the end of each year were 20X6: \$52.52m, 20X7: \$154.2m (including materials in store), 20X8 \$205m.

Required

Calculate the stage of completion for each year of the contract and show how revenues, costs and profits will be recognised in each year.

Solution

We can summarise the financial data for each year end during the construction period as follows.

	20X6	*20X7*	*20X8*
	\$'000	\$'000	\$'000
Initial amount of revenue agreed in the contract	220,000	220,000	220,000
Variation	–	5,000	5,000
Total contract revenue	220,000	225,000	225,000
Contract costs incurred to date	52,520	154,200	205,000
Contract costs to complete	149,480	50,800	–
Total estimated contract costs	202,000	205,000	205,000
Estimated profit	18,000	20,000	20,000
Stage of completion	26.0%	74.0%	100.0%

The stage of completion has been calculated using the formula:

$$\frac{\text{Contract costs incurred to date}}{\text{Total estimated contract costs}}$$

The stage of completion in 20X7 is calculated by deducting the \$2.5m of materials held for the following period from the costs incurred up to that year end, ie \$154.2m – \$2.5m = \$151.7m. \$151.7m/\$205m = 74%.

Revenue, expenses and profit will be recognised in profit or loss as follows.

	To date	*Recognised in prior years*	*Recognised in current year*
	\$'000	\$'000	\$'000
20X6 Revenue (\$220m × 26%)	57,200		
Costs (\$202m × 26%)	52,520		
	4,680		
20X7 Revenue (\$225m × 74%)	166,500	57,200	109,300
Costs (\$205m × 74%)	151,700	52,520	99,180
	14,800	4,680	10,120
20X8 Revenue (\$225m × 100%)	225,000	166,500	58,500
Costs (\$205m × 100%)	205,000	151,700	53,300
	20,000	14,800	5,200

You can see from the above example that, when the stage of completion is determined using the contract costs incurred to date, only contract costs reflecting the work to date should be included in costs incurred to date.

- Exclude costs relating to **future activity**, eg cost of materials delivered but not yet used
- Exclude payments made to subcontractors **in advance** of work performed

2.9 Outcome of the contract cannot be predicted reliably

When the contract's outcome cannot be predicted reliably the following treatment should be followed.

- Only recognise revenue to the extent of contract costs incurred which are expected to be **recoverable**
- Recognise contract costs as an **expense** in the period they are incurred

This **no profit/no loss approach** reflects the situation near the beginning of a contract, ie the outcome cannot be reliably estimated, but it is likely that costs will be recovered.

Contract costs which **cannot be recovered** should be recognised as an expense straight away. IAS 11 lists the following situations where this might occur.

- The contract is **not fully enforceable**, ie its validity is seriously questioned
- The completion of the contract is subject to the outcome of **pending litigation or legislation**
- The contract relates to properties which will probably be **expropriated or condemned**
- The customer is **unable to meet its obligations** under the contract
- The contractor **cannot complete** the contract or in any other way meet its obligations under the contract

Where these **uncertainties cease to exist,** contract revenue and costs should be recognised as normal, ie by reference to the stage of completion.

2.10 Recognition of expected losses

Any loss on a contract should be **recognised as soon as it is foreseen**. The loss will be the amount by which total expected contract revenue is exceeded by total expected contract costs. The loss amount is not affected by whether work has started on the contract, the stage of completion of the work or profits on other contracts (unless they are related contracts treated as a single contract).

Exam skills

The treatment of expected losses is very important and students often miss it. An exam question may give you a contract on which a loss is expected.

2.11 Changes in estimates

The effect of any change in the estimate of contract revenue or costs or the outcome of a contract should be accounted for as a **change in accounting estimate** under IAS 8 *Accounting policies, changes in accounting estimates and errors*.

Example: Changes in estimates

The example below shows the effect of a change in estimate of costs on the figures that appear in the statement of comprehensive income and statement of financial position.

Battersby Co enters into a three-year contract.

Estimated revenue = $20,000
Estimated total cost = $16,000.

However, during Year 2, management revises its estimate of total costs incurred and thus the outcome of the contract. As a result, during Year 2, a loss is recognised on the contract for the year, even though the contract will still be profitable overall.

	Year 1	*Year 2*	*Year 3*
	$	$	$
Estimated revenue	20,000	20,000	20,000
Estimated total cost	16,000	18,000	18,000
Estimated total profit	4,000	2,000	2,000
Cost incurred to date	$8,000	$13,500	$18,000
Percentage of completion	50%	75%	100%
Recognised profit/(loss) to date	$2,000	($500)	$500
Cumulative recognised profit	$2,000	$1,500	$2,000

Progress billings of $8,000, $8,000 and $4,000 are made on the last day of each year and are received in the first month of the following year. The asset at the end of each year is:

Gross amounts due to/from customers	*Year 1*	*Year 2*	*Year 3*
	$	$	$
Costs incurred	8,000	13,500	18,000
Recognised profits	2,000	2,000	2,500
(Recognised losses)	–	(500)	(500)
(Progress billings)	(8,000)	(16,000)	(20,000)
Amount recognised as an asset/(liability) (unbilled contract revenue)	2,000	(1,000)	0

In addition, at each year end, the entity recognises a trade receivable for the amount outstanding at the end of the year of $8,000, $8,000 and $4,000.

2.12 Disclosures

The following should be disclosed under IAS 11

- Contract revenue recognised as **revenue in the period**
- **Methods used** to determine the **contract revenue**
- **Methods used** to determine **stage of completion** of contracts which are in progress

For **contracts in progress** at the end of the reporting period, show the following.

- **Total costs incurred** and recognised profits (less recognised losses) to date
- **Advances** received
- **Retentions** (progress billings not paid until the satisfaction of certain conditions)

Amounts owed by customers and to sub-contractors for contract work must be **shown gross as an asset and a liability respectively**. These are determined by comparing the total costs incurred plus recognised profits to the sum of recognised losses and progress billings, as you will see in the question below.

Any **contingent gains or losses**, eg due to warranty costs, claims, penalties or possible losses, should be disclosed in accordance with IAS 37 *Provisions, contingent liabilities and contingent assets*.

Example: Disclosure

Suppose that Tract Ore Co finishes its first year of operations in which all contract costs were paid in cash and all progress billings and advances were received in cash. For contracts W, X and Z only:

(a) contract costs include costs of materials purchased for use in the contract which have not been used at the period end; and

(b) customers have advanced sums to the contractor for work not yet performed.

The relevant figures for all contracts at the end of Tract Ore's first year of trading are as follows.

	V	*W*	*X*	*Y*	*Z*	*Total*
	$m	$m	$m	$m	$m	$m
Contract revenue recognised	37.7	135.2	98.8	52.0	14.3	338.0
Contract expenses recognised	28.6	117.0	91.0	65.0	14.3	315.9
Expected losses recognised	–	–	–	10.4	7.8	18.2
Recognised profits less recognised losses	9.1	18.2	7.8	(23.4)	(7.8)	3.9
Contract costs incurred in the period	28.6	132.6	117.0	65.0	26.0	369.2
Contract expenses recognised	28.6	117.0	91.0	65.0	14.3	315.9
Contract expenses that relate to future activity recognised as an asset	–	15.6	26.0	–	11.7	53.3
Contract revenue	37.7	135.2	98.8	52.0	14.3	338.0
Progress billings	26.0	135.2	98.8	46.8	14.3	321.1
Unbilled contract revenue	11.7	–	–	5.2	–	16.9
Advances	–	20.8	5.2	–	6.5	32.5

Required

Show the figures that should be disclosed under IAS 11.

Solution

Following IAS 11, the required disclosures would be as follows.

	$m
Contract revenue recognised in the period	338.0
Contract costs incurred and recognised profits (less recognised losses) to date (W)	373.1
Advances received	32.5
Gross amount due from customers for contract work: asset (W)	57.2
Gross amount due to customers for contract work: liability (W)	(5.2)

Workings

These amounts are calculated as follows.

	V	*W*	*X*	*Y*	*Z*	*Total*
	$m	$m	$m	$m	$m	$m
Contract costs incurred	28.6	132.6	117.0	65.0	26.0	369.2
Recognised profits less recognised losses	9.1	18.2	7.8	(23.4)	(7.8)	3.9
	37.7	150.8	124.8	41.6	18.2	373.1
Progress billings	26.0	135.2	98.8	46.8	14.3	321.1
Due from customers	11.7	15.6	26.0		3.9	57.2
Due to customers				(5.2)		(5.2)

2.13 Summary of accounting treatment

The following summarises the accounting treatment for long-term contracts – **make sure that you understand it.**

2.13.1 Statement of comprehensive income

(a) **Revenue and costs**

(i) Sales revenue and associated costs should be recorded in the income statement section as the contract activity progresses.

(ii) Include an appropriate proportion of total contract value as sales revenue in the income statement.

(iii) The costs incurred in reaching that stage of completion are matched with this sales revenue, resulting in the reporting of results which can be attributed to the proportion of work completed.

(iv) Sales revenue is the value of work carried out to date.

(b) **Profit recognised in the contract**

(i) It must reflect the proportion of work carried out.
(ii) It should take into account any known inequalities in profitability in the various stages of a contract.

2.13.2 Statement of financial position

(a) **Asset**

	$
Costs incurred plus recognised profits	X
Progress billings plus recognised losses	(X)
Gross amount due from customers	X

(b) **Liability**

	$
Costs incurred plus recognised profits	X
Progress billings plus recognised losses	(X)
Gross amount due to customers	(X)

(c) Separate disclosure must also be made of:

(i) costs incurred and recognised profits (less recognised losses) to date
(ii) the amount of advances received
(iii) the amount of retentions

Question 11.2 Construction contracts

Learning outcomes C2(a)

The main business of Santolina Co is construction contracts. At the end of September 20X3 there is an uncompleted contract on the books, details of which are as follows.

Date commenced	1.4.X1
Expected completed date	23.12.X3
	$
Final contract price	290,000
Costs to 30.9.X3	210,450
Value of work certified to 30.9.X3	230,000
Progress billings to 30.9.X3	210,000
Cash received to 30.9.X3	194,000
Estimated costs to completion at 30.9.X3	20,600

Required

Prepare calculations showing the amounts to be included in the statement of financial position at 30 September 20X3 in respect of the above contract.

2.14 IAS 11 example

This example is given in the appendix to IAS 11. Work through it and make sure you understand it.

A construction contractor has a fixed price contract for 9,000 (presumably $'000) to build a bridge. The initial amount of revenue agreed in the contract is 9,000. The contractor's initial estimate of contract costs is 8,000. It will take three years to build the bridge. By the end of year 1, the contractor's estimate of contract costs has increased to 8,050.

In year 2, the customer approves a variation resulting in an increase in contract revenue of 200 and estimated additional contract costs of 150. At the end of year 2, costs incurred include 100 for standard materials stored on site to be used in year 3 to complete the project.

The contractor determines the stage of completion of the contract by calculating the proportion that contract costs incurred for work performed to date bear to the latest estimated total contract costs. A summary of the financial data during the construction period is as follows:

	Year 1	Year 2	Year 3
Initial amount of revenue agreed in contract	9,000	9,000	9,000
Variation	–	200	200
Total contract revenue	9,000	9,200	9,200
Contract costs incurred to date	2,093	6,168	8,200
Contract costs to complete	5,957	2,023	–
Total estimated contract costs	8,050	8,200	8,200
Estimated profit	950	1,000	1,000
Stage of completion	26%	74%	100%

The stage of completion for year 2 (74%) is determined by excluding from contract costs incurred for work performed to date the 100 of standard materials stored at the site for use in year 3.

The amounts of revenue, expenses and profit recognised in the statement of comprehensive income in the three years are as follows:

	To date	*Recognised in prior years*	*Recognised in current year*
Year 1			
Revenue (9,000 × 26%)	2,340	–	2,340
Expenses (8,050 × 26%)	2,093	–	2,093
Profit	247	–	247
Year 2			
Revenue (9,200 × 74%)	6,808	2,340	4,468
Expenses (8,200 × 74%)	6,068	2,093	3,975
Profit	740	247	493
Year 3			
Revenue (9,200 × 100%)	9,200	6,808	2,392
Expenses	8,200	6,068	2,132
Profit	1,000	740	260

Here is another example illustrating the disclosures required under IAS 11.

A contractor has five contracts in progress at the end of year 1 as follows:

	A	*B*	*C*	*D*	*E*	*Total*
Contract revenue recognised	145	520	380	200	55	1,300
Contract expenses recognised	110	450	350	250	55	1,215
Expected losses recognised	–	–	–	40	30	70
Recognised profits less recognised losses	35	70	30	(90)	(30)	15
Contract costs incurred in the period	110	510	450	250	100	1,420
Contract costs incurred recognised as expenses	110	450	350	250	55	1,215
Contract costs relating to future activity (WIP)	–	60	100	–	45	205
Contract revenue (as above)	145	520	380	200	55	1,300
Progress billings	100	520	380	180	55	1,235
Unbilled contract revenue	45	–	–	20	–	65
Advances	–	80	20	–	25	125

The amounts to be disclosed in accordance with IAS 11 are as follows:

Contract revenue recognised as revenue in the period	1,300
Contract costs incurred and recognised profits less recognised losses to date	1,435
Advances received	125
Gross amount due from customers for contract work (asset)	220
Gross amounts due to customers for contract work (liability)	(20)

These amounts are calculated as follows:

	A	*B*	*C*	*D*	*E*	*Total*
Contract costs incurred	110	510	450	250	100	1,420
Recognised profits less recognised losses	35	70	30	(90)	(30)	15
	145	580	480	160	70	1,435
Progress billings	100	520	380	180	55	1,235
Due from customers	45	60	100	–	15	220
Due to customers	–	–	–	(20)	–	(20)

Note that, where you are dealing with a single construction contract, there will be *either* a gross amount due to customers *or* a gross amount due from customers. Here we are dealing with more than one contract and, instead of showing a net balance of 200 due from customers, the standard requires the asset and the liability to be shown separately.

Exam skills

In the exam, **gross amounts due to customers** should be shown as a current liability.

Section summary

The rules for calculating accounting entries on **construction contracts** can be summarised as follows.

- When the outcome of a construction contract can be estimated reliably, contract revenue and contract costs ... shall be recognised as revenue and expenses respectively by reference to the stage of completion of the contract.
- When it is probable that total contract costs will exceed total contract revenue, the expected loss shall be recognised as an expense immediately.

Chapter Roundup

- ✓ IAS 2 *Inventories* requires that the statement of financial position should show **inventories** classified in a manner appropriate to the entity. Common **classifications** are:
  - Merchandise
  - Production supplies
  - Materials
  - Work-in-progress
  - Finished goods
- ✓ The use of **LIFO** is **prohibited** under the revised IAS 2.
- ✓ Full details of inventory carried at **NRV** as well as the reversal of any previous write down should be disclosed.
- ✓ The rules for calculating accounting entries on **construction contracts** can be summarised as follows.
  - When the outcome of a construction contract can be estimated reliably, contract revenue and contract costs... shall be recognised as revenue and expenses respectively by reference to the stage of completion of the contract.
  - When it is probable that total contract costs will exceed total contract revenue, the expected loss shall be recognised as an expense immediately.

Quick Quiz

1 Net realisable value = Selling price **less** .... **less** ....

2 Which inventory costing method is allowed under IAS 2?

(a) FIFO (b) LIFO

3 Any expected loss on a construction contract must be recognised, in full, in the year it was identified.

True ☐

False ☐

4 How is the value of a construction contract disclosed in the statement of financial position?

5 Which items in the statement of comprehensive income and statement of financial position are potentially affected by construction contracts?

Answers to Quick Quiz

1 Net realisable value = selling price **less** costs to completion **less** costs necessary to make the sale.

2 (a) FIFO. LIFO is not allowed.

3 True

4 See Paragraph 2.13

5 Statement of comprehensive income: revenue and cost of sales.

Statement of financial position: inventories, receivables, liabilities.

Answers to Questions

11.1 Inventory valuation

Calculation of overheads for inventory

Production overheads are as follows.

	$
Depreciation/finance costs	4,490
Factory manager's wage	2,560
Other production overheads	24,820
Accounting/purchase costs	5,450
	37,320

Direct labour = $61,320

$\therefore$ Production overhead rate = $\frac{37,320}{61,320}$ = 60.86%

Inventory valuation

	Raw materials	*WIP*	*Finished goods*	*Total*
	$	$	$	$
Materials	74,786	85,692	152,693	313,171
Direct labour	–	13,072	46,584	59,656
Production overhead (at 60.86% of labour)	–	7,956	28,351	36,307
	74,786	106,720	227,628	409,134

Variable overheads will be included in the cost of inventory.

11.2 Construction contracts

The estimated final profit is:

	$
Final contract price	290,000
Less: costs to date	(210,450)
estimated future costs	(20,600)
Estimated final profit	58,950

The attributable profit is found as follows.

$$\text{Estimated final profit} \times \frac{\text{Work certified}}{\text{Total contract work}}$$

$$\$58,950 \times \frac{230,000}{290,000}$$

Attributable profit = $46,753

	$
Costs incurred plus recognised profits (210,450 + 46,753)	257,203
Progress billings	(210,000)
Gross amount due from customers (asset)	47,203

Now try these questions from the Exam Question Bank

Number	Level	Marks	Time
Q12	Examination	10	18 mins
Q16	Examination	5	9 mins

CAPITAL TRANSACTIONS AND FINANCIAL INSTRUMENTS

The treatment of share issues is an important accounting topic and is covered in this chapter. Financial instruments are a complex area but you are only required to know the rules governing share capital transactions.

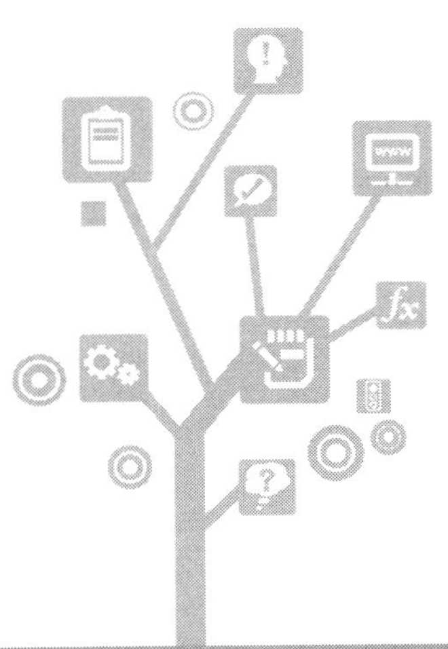

topic list	learning outcomes	syllabus references	ability required
1 The issue and forfeiture of shares	C2(b)	C2(xii)	comprehension
2 Purchase of own shares	C2(b)	C2(xii)	comprehension
3 Financial instruments	C2(b)	C2(xii)	comprehension

1 The issue and forfeiture of shares

Introduction

In this section we look at how shares are issued in the UK. We then cover the accounting treatment for the issue of shares. Work carefully through the examples at the end of this chapter.

1.1 Share issues

A company can increase its share capital by means of a **share issue**. Here we will look at the specific accounting entries necessary for such an issue, including where a share premium account is required (when the price of the share is greater than its nominal value).

KEY POINT

Local rules and procedures may vary – below the UK rules are given.

1.2 General rules and procedures

KEY TERM

As a general rule, if a company issues ordinary shares for cash it must first offer them to its existing ordinary shareholders in proportion to their shareholdings. This is called a RIGHTS ISSUE because members may obtain new shares in right of their existing holdings.

If they do not accept the shares within 21 days, the company may then offer the shares to non-members. A private company may, by the terms of its memorandum or articles, permanently exclude the members' right of pre-emption (as just described). A public company may authorise its directors (by special resolution) to allot ordinary shares for cash without first offering the shares to members.

When a company issues shares it must obtain consideration at least equal in value to the nominal value of the shares (to issue shares **at par value** means to obtain equal value): shares cannot be issued at a discount. The entire consideration does not have to be received at the time of allotment, and the holder of such **partly-paid shares** is liable to pay the balance. Usually the company may make a 'call' for the balance or any part of it under a procedure laid down in the articles whenever the directors decide to do so. When a call has been made the capital is 'called-up' to that extent, and when the shareholders pay the call it is 'paid-up' to that extent (including in each case previous amounts due or paid). If the company goes into liquidation the liquidator is entitled to call up any balance outstanding.

KEY TERMS

Although a company may not allot shares for a consideration of less value than the nominal value of the shares, it is free to obtain a consideration of greater value. The excess of the consideration over the nominal value of the shares is SHARE PREMIUM which must be credited to a statutory SHARE PREMIUM ACCOUNT as part of the fixed capital.

Except when a **rights issue** is made to existing members, it is generally considered to be the duty of directors to obtain the highest possible price for the shares, and so to maximise the premium (if any). A rights issue is an issue of shares to existing shareholders. The shares are offered for cash but at a discount to the current market price, and are offered to shareholders in proportion to their existing holdings. For instance a '1 for 4' issue means that a shareholder can buy one new share for each four that he currently holds.

The **share premium account** may be repaid to members (or otherwise eliminated) under a reduction of share capital authorised by the court, but it may not be distributed as dividend because it is a **non-distributable reserve**. It may, however, be applied in the following ways:

(a) Issuing fully paid bonus shares to the members (explained below).

(b) Writing off:

- Preliminary expenses of company formation
- Share or loan stock issue expenses (including commissions and discounts)

(c) In certain circumstances, paying any premium payable when the company redeems redeemable shares or debentures.

KEY TERM

In issuing shares a company, instead of requiring its members to provide new consideration, may capitalise available reserves in paying up the shares wholly or in part. This procedure, called making a BONUS ISSUE of shares, is only permitted to the extent that the articles provide for it (and the correct procedure must be observed).

Since reserves (which in some cases might be distributed as dividends) are part of the shareholders' funds, the effect is to convert them into permanent capital. The members pay for their additional shares by forgoing whatever rights they had to the reserves. Any reserve may be reclassified in this way, including a share premium account or other statutory reserve.

Examples of the treatment for both **bonus issues** and **rights issues** are given towards the end of this section.

1.3 Accounting for an issue of shares for cash

If subscription monies are payable in instalments, entries are made initially to **application and allotment accounts** and **call accounts**. Balances on these accounts are eventually transferred to share capital and share premium accounts. Issue costs will normally be debited to the share premium account.

Occasionally (though rarely nowadays) a shareholder may fail to pay amounts due on allotment or on a call. If the articles of association so allow, the company may (after due warning) confiscate the shares without refund of any amounts paid to date. The shares are not cancelled but their called up value is transferred from share capital account to a **forfeited shares account** (the share premium account, if any, is not affected) until they are reissued. Forfeited shares may be reissued at any price provided that the total amount received (from both applicants) is not less than the par value of the shares.

Example: Accounting for an issue of shares for cash

Ibex wished to issue 500,000 $1 ordinary shares, 60c (including 10c premium) per share payable on application, 20c on allotment and the final 30c on call, four months later. The prospectus was published and applications for 600,000 shares were received. The directors rejected 'small' applicants for a total of 100,000 shares and allotted the remainder. Show the journal entries involved in respect of the issue, assuming that all cheques were banked on receipt.

Solution

JOURNAL

(a)	DEBIT	Bank	$360,000	
	CREDIT	Application and allotment account		$360,000
		Being amounts received on application		
(b)	DEBIT	Application and allotment account	$60,000	
	CREDIT	Bank		$60,000
		Being return of application money to unsuccessful subscribers		
(c)	DEBIT	Application and allotment account	$400,000	
	CREDIT	Share capital account		$350,000
	CREDIT	Share premium account		$50,000
		Being allotment of shares		

(At this stage the total of the balances on the share capital account and share premium account shows the total amount receivable on application and allotment, while the debit balance on the application and allotment account records how much of that amount is still outstanding.)

(d)	DEBIT	Bank	$100,000	
	CREDIT	Application and allotment account		$100,000
	Being receipt of amounts due on allotment			

(This entry closes the application and allotment account.)

(e)	DEBIT	Call account	$150,000	
	CREDIT	Share capital account		$150,000
	Being the amount of the call on shares to make them fully paid			

(The share capital account is credited with the full amount due on the call, and the call account records the actual receipt of the money.)

(f)	DEBIT	Bank	$150,000	
	CREDIT	Call account		$150,000
	Being receipt of call money due			

If, in the example, shares had been allotted on a proportional basis, each subscriber would have received five-sixths of the number of shares applied for. There would therefore be no need for entry (b) above, and each subscriber's surplus application money would be applied to the amount due from him or her on allotment. Entry (c) above would remain the same, but entry (d) would be:

DEBIT	Bank	$40,000	
CREDIT	Application and allotment account		$40,000
Being receipt of amounts due on allotment			

After the call was made the money due on 10,000 of the shares was not received. The directors of Ibex (after due notice) forfeited the shares and subsequently reissued them at a price of 75c each. The journal entries (a) to (e) above would remain the same, but the subsequent entries would be:

(g)	DEBIT	Bank	$147,000	
	CREDIT	Call account		$147,000
	Being receipt of call money			

(If a statement of financial position were drawn up at this stage, the debit balance on call account, being the $3,000 still receivable, would be shown as called up share capital not paid.)

(h)	DEBIT	Investments: own shares *	$3,000	
	CREDIT	Call account		$3,000
	Being the forfeiture of the shares (The shares are now held by the company ready for re-issue.)			

When the shares are reissued the journal entries made are as follows.

(i)	DEBIT	Bank	$7,500	
	CREDIT	Investments: own shares *		$7,500
	Being proceeds of reissue of shares			
(j)	DEBIT	Investments: own shares	$4,500	
	CREDIT	Share premium account		$4,500
	Being transfer of the premium on the reissued shares to share premium account.			

(This is an additional premium obtained on the reissue of shares and is the excess of reissue price over the unpaid calls: 10,000 @ 45c.)

* OR a forfeiture account

The combined example may be worked in ledger account form.

BANK ACCOUNT

	$		$
Application & allotment a/c	360,000	Application & allotment a/c	60,000
Application & allotment a/c	100,000	Balance c/d	554,500
Call a/c	147,000		
Investments: own shares	7,500		
	614,500		614,500

APPLICATION AND ALLOTMENT ACCOUNT

	$		$
Bank (100,000 @ 60c)	60,000	Bank (600,000 @ 60c)	360,000
Ordinary share capital a/c:		Bank (500,000 @ 20c)	100,000
(500,000 @ 70c)	350,000		
Share premium a/c:			
(500,000 @ 10c)	50,000		
	460,000		460,000

SHARE CAPITAL ACCOUNT: $1 ORDINARY SHARES

	$		$
Balance c/d	500,000	Application & allotment a/c	350,000
		Call a/c	150,000
	500,000		500,000

SHARE PREMIUM ACCOUNT

	$		$
Balance	54,500	Application & allotment a/c	50,000
		Investments: own shares	4,500
	54,500		54,500

CALL ACCOUNT

	$		$
Ordinary share capital a/c		Bank (490,000 @ 30c)	147,000
(500,000 @ 30c)	150,000	Investments : own shares	3,000
	150,000		150,000

INVESTMENTS: OWN SHARES

	$		$
Call a/c	3,000	Bank (10,000 @ 75c)	7,500
Share premium account	4,500		
	7,500		7,500

Ibex statements of financial position would be as follows.

(a) **After the call (but before forfeiture)**

	$
Current assets	
Receivables: called up share capital not paid	3,000
Cash at bank	547,000
	550,000
Equity	
Called up share capital: 500,000 $1 ordinary shares	500,000
Share premium account	50,000
	550,000

(b) **After the forfeiture (but before reissue)**

	$
Current assets	
Investments: own shares	3,000
Cash at bank	547,000
	550,000
Equity	
Called up share capital: 500,000 $1 ord shares	500,000
Share premium account	50,000
	550,000

(c) **After the reissue**

	$
Current assets	
Cash at bank	554,500
Equity	
Called up share capital: 500,000 $1 ord shares fully paid	500,000
Share premium account	54,500
	554,500

Example: Bonus issues

BUBBLES CO
STATEMENT OF FINANCIAL POSITION (EXTRACT)

	$'000	$'000
Equity		
Share capital		
$1 ordinary shares (fully paid)		1,000
Share premium	500	
Retained earnings	2,000	
		2,500
		3,500

Bubbles decided to make a '3 for 2' bonus issue (ie 3 new shares for every 2 already held). The double entry is as follows.

		$'000	$'000
DEBIT	Share premium	500	
	Retained earnings	1,000	
CREDIT	Ordinary share capital		1,500

After the issue the statement of financial position is as follows.

	$'000
Equity	
Share capital	
$1 ordinary shares (fully paid)	2,500
Retained earnings	1,000
	3,500

1,500,000 new ('bonus') shares are issued to existing shareholders, so that if Mr X previously held 20,000 shares he will now hold 50,000. The total value of his holding should theoretically remain the same however, since the net assets of the company remain unchanged and his share of those net assets remains at 2% (50,000/2,500,000; previously 20,000/1,000,000).

Example: Rights issues

Bubbles (above) decides to make a rights issue, shortly after the bonus issue. The terms are '1 for 5 @ $1.20' (one new share for every five already held, at a price of $1.20). Assuming that all shareholders take up their rights (which they are not obliged to) the double entry is as follows.

		$'000	$'000
DEBIT	Cash	600	
CREDIT	Ordinary share capital		500
CREDIT	Share premium		100

Mr X who previously held 50,000 shares will now hold 60,000, and the value of his holding should increase (theoretically at least) because the net assets of the company will increase. The new statement of financial position will show:

	$'000	$'000
Equity		
Share capital		
$1 ordinary shares		3,000
Share premium	100	
Retained earnings	1,000	
		1,100
		4,100

The increase in funds of $600,000 represents the cash raised from the issue of 500,000 new shares at a price of $1.20 each.

1.4 Summary of procedure and accounting entries

The following procedure is followed for the issue and forfeiture of shares.

(a) **Application**: where potential shareholders apply for shares in the company and send cash to cover the amount applied for.

(b) **Allotment**: the company allocates shares to the successful applicants and returns cash to unsuccessful applicants.

(c) **Call**: where the purchase price is payable in instalments, the company will call for instalments on their due dates of payment.

(d) **Forfeiture**: if a shareholder fails to pay a call, his shares may be forfeited without the need to return the money he has paid. These forfeited shares may then be reissued to other shareholders.

The following summarises the relevant accounting entries.

(a) DEBIT Bank
CREDIT Application and allotment a/c
Application proceeds

(b) DEBIT Application and allotment a/c
CREDIT Bank
Money returned to over-subscribers

(c) DEBIT Bank
CREDIT Application and allotment a/c
Cash on allotment

(d) DEBIT Application and allotment a/c
CREDIT Share capital
CREDIT Share premium
Allotment of shares

(e) DEBIT Call a/c
CREDIT Share capital
Call of final instalment owed

(f) DEBIT Bank
CREDIT Call a/c
Cash receipts banked

(g) DEBIT Investment: own shares (or forfeit a/c)
CREDIT Call a/c
Forfeited shares

(h) DEBIT Bank
CREDIT Investment: own shares
Reissue forfeited shares

(i) DEBIT Investment: own shares
CREDIT Share premium a/c
Additional premium on reissue

Question 12.1 Issue of shares

Learning outcome C2(b)

Haggot Co issued 50,000 $1 shares at $1.20 per share. Monies due were as follows.

On application	50c including premium
On allotment	30c
Call	40c

Applications were received amounting to $30,000 (ie for 60,000 shares).

At the call, 1,000 shares were forfeited. These were subsequently reissued for $1.10 cash.

Required

Write up the relevant ledger accounts for the above issue.

Section summary

Shares may be issued to existing shareholders via a rights issue or a bonus issue. Alternately they can be issued to new shareholders.

2 Purchase of own shares

Introduction

In this section we look at how and why a company might purchase its own shares.

2.1 Reduction of capital

Limited liability companies may be permitted to cancel unissued shares and in that way reduce their **authorised** share capital. That change does not alter the financial position of any company.

If a limited liability company wishes to **reduce its issued share capital** (and incidentally its authorised capital of which the issued capital is part) it may do so provided that certain conditions are met (set by national legislation). For example:

(a) It must have the power to do so in its **articles** of association
(b) It must pass a **special resolution**
(c) It must obtain **confirmation** of the reduction **from the court**

Requirement (a) is usually a matter of procedure. Articles usually contain the necessary power. If not, the company in general meeting would first pass a special resolution to alter the articles appropriately and then proceed to pass a special resolution to reduce the capital.

There are various basic methods of reducing share capital. Three of the most common are discussed here.

(a) **Extinguish or reduce liability on partly paid shares**. A company may have issued $1 (par) shares 75c paid up. The outstanding liability of 25c per share may be eliminated altogether by reducing each share to 75c (par) fully paid or some intermediate figure, eg 80c (par) 75c paid. Nothing is returned to the shareholders but the company gives up a claim against them for money which it could call up whenever needed.

(b) **Cancel paid up share capital which has been lost or which is no longer represented by available assets.** Suppose that the issued shares are $1 (par) fully paid but the net assets now represent a value of only 50c per share. The difference is probably matched by a debit balance on the retained reserves. The company could reduce the par value of its $1 shares to 50c (or some intermediate figure) and apply the amount to write off the debit balance wholly or in part. It would then be able to resume payment of dividends out of future profits without being obliged to make good past losses. The resources of the company are not reduced by this procedure of part cancellation of nominal value of shares but it avoids having to rebuild lost capital by retaining profits.

(c) **Pay off part of the paid up share capital out of surplus assets.** The company might repay to shareholders, say, 30c in cash per $1 share by reducing the par value of the share to 70c. This reduces the assets of the company by 30c per share.

2.2 Role of court in reduction of capital

In many countries the sanction of the court (or equivalent) may be required for a redemption of shares or reduction in capital. The purpose here is **creditor protection**. The reduction in capital must not put at risk a company's ability to pay its debts. If it did so, then shareholders would be favoured over creditors for distributions from the company. Creditors may be allowed to petition the court against the proposed transaction, but the company may be able to override this by paying off its creditors. The details will vary from country to country.

2.3 Share premium account

Whenever a company obtains for its shares a consideration in excess of their par value, it must usually transfer the excess to a share premium account (capital in excess of par account). The general rule is that the **share premium account is subject to the same restrictions as share capital**. However, it may be possible to make a bonus issue using the share premium account (reducing share premium in order to increase issued share capital).

There may be an **exemption** from the general rules on setting up a share premium account, in certain circumstances where new shares are issued as consideration for the acquisition of shares in another company.

Examples of the **other likely permitted uses of share premium** are to pay:

(a) Capital expenses such as preliminary expenses of forming the company
(b) A discount on the issue of shares or debentures
(c) A premium (if any) paid on redemption of debentures

Some companies may also be able to use a share premium account in purchasing or redeeming their own shares out of capital. It must be emphasised that these rules will vary from country to country according to national legislation.

2.4 Purchase by a company of its own shares

In some countries, there is a **general prohibition** against any voluntary acquisition by a company of its own shares. In other countries, it is possible for a company to voluntarily acquire and keep its own shares, although there may be a limit on the time for which they can be held. For the rest of the chapter, however, we will assume that any of its own shares purchased by a company cannot be held and must be **cancelled immediately**.

One way to preserve reserves for creditor protection is to prevent companies from repurchasing shares except by transferring a sum equal to the par value of shares purchased from distributable profit reserves to a non-distributable reserve, which here we will call the '**capital redemption reserve**'. This reduction in distributable reserves is an example of the **capitalisation of profits**, where previously distributable profits become undistributable.

Such regulations prevent companies from reducing their share capital investment so as to put creditors of the company at risk. This excess of non-distributable over distributable reserves is often referred to as the "creditor's buffer."

Example: Capitalisation of profits

Suppose, for example, that Muffin Co decided to repurchase and cancel $100,000 of its ordinary share capital. A statement of financial position of the company is currently as follows.

	$	$
Assets		
Cash		100,000
Other assets		300,000
		400,000
Equity and liabilities		
Equity		
Ordinary shares	130,000	
Retained earnings	150,000	
		280,000
Liabilities		
Trade accounts payable		120,000
		400,000

Now if Muffin were able to repurchase the shares without making any transfer from retained earnings to a capital redemption reserve, the effect of the share redemption on the statement of financial position would be as follows.

		$
Assets		
Non-cash assets		300,000
Equity and liabilities		
Equity		
Ordinary shares	30,000	
Retained earnings	150,000	
		180,000
Trade accounts payable		120,000
		300,000

In this example, the company would still be able to pay dividends out of profits of up to $150,000. If it did, the creditors of the company would be highly vulnerable, financing $120,000 out of a total of $150,000 assets of the company.

The regulations prevent such extreme situations arising. On repurchase of the shares, Muffin would have been required to transfer $100,000 from its retained earnings to a non-distributable reserve, called here a capital redemption reserve. The effect of the repurchase of shares on the statement of financial position would have been:

	$	$
Assets		
Non-cash assets		300,000
Equity and liabilities		
Equity		
Ordinary shares	30,000	
Reserves		
Distributable (retained earnings)	50,000	
Non-distributable (capital redemption reserve)	100,000	
		180,000
Trade accounts payable		120,000
		300,000

The maximum distributable profits are now $50,000. If Muffin paid all these as a dividend, there would still be $250,000 of assets left in the company, just over half of which would be financed by non-distributable equity capital.

2.5 Treasury shares

Since 2003, entities have been allowed to repurchase their own shares and retain them in treasury, rather than cancelling them. These 'treasury shares' can then be re-issued in the future or issued as part of an employee share scheme.

An entity is allowed to hold up to 10% of its issued share capital as 'treasury shares'. They are shown in the statement of financial position as a deduction from equity.

For instance, a company has 500,000 $1 shares in issue and $200,000 in share premium. It reacquires 100,000 shares for $1.40.

The shares re-acquired are classified as treasury shares and presented as follows:

	$'000
Share capital: $1 shares fully paid	500
Share premium	200
	700
Treasury shares	(140)
	560

When a company repurchases its own shares, this should normally be financed:

(a) **Out of distributable profits**, OR
(b) **Out of the proceeds** of a new issue of shares.

In addition, if there is any premium on repurchase, it may be the rule that **the premium must be paid out of distributable profits**, except that if the shares were issued at a premium, then any premium payable on their repurchase may be paid out of the proceeds of a new share issue made for the purpose, up to an amount equal to the lesser of:

(a) The aggregate premiums received on issue of the shares; and
(b) The balance on the share premium account (including premium on issue of the new shares).

This may seem complicated, but it makes logical sense. A numerical example might help.

Example: Repurchase of shares

Suppose that Jingle Co intends to repurchase 10,000 shares of $1 each at a premium of 5 cents per share. The repurchase must be financed in one of the following ways.

(a) Jingle Co could purchase its own shares wholly out of distributable profits. It must then transfer to the capital redemption reserve an amount equal to the par value of the shares repurchased. The accounting entries would be as follows.

		$	$
DEBIT	Share capital account	10,000	
	Retained earnings (premium on repurchase)	500	
CREDIT	Cash		10,500
DEBIT	Retained earnings	10,000	
CREDIT	Capital redemption reserve		10,000

(b) Jingle Co could purchase its shares wholly or partly out of the proceeds of a new share issue. It must transfer to the capital redemption reserve an amount by which the par value of the shares repurchased exceeds the *aggregate* proceeds from the new issue (ie par value of new shares issued plus share premium). The premium of $500 must be paid out of distributable profits. The accounting entries would be as follows.

		$	$
DEBIT	Share capital account (repurchased shares)	10,000	
	Retained earnings (premium)	500	
CREDIT	Cash (repurchase of shares)		10,500
DEBIT	Cash (from new issue)	10,000	
CREDIT	Share capital account		10,000

No credit to the capital redemption reserve is necessary because there is no decrease in the creditors' buffer.

(c) Jingle Co may finance the repurchase out of a combination of a new share issue and distributable profits. Imagine the repurchase in the same example as in (b) were made by issuing 5,000 new $1 shares at par, and paying $5,500 out of distributable profits. The accounting entries would be as follows.

		$	$
DEBIT	Share capital account (repurchased shares)	10,000	
	Retained earnings (premium)	500	
CREDIT	Cash (repurchase of shares)		10,500
DEBIT	Cash (from new issue)	5,000	
CREDIT	Share capital account		5,000
DEBIT	Retained earnings	5,000	
CREDIT	Capital redemption reserve		5,000

(d) Jingle Co could purchase its shares out of the proceeds of a new share issue (as the shares to be repurchased were issues at a premium). Assuming a new issue of 10,000 $1 shares at a premium of 8c per share, the accounting entries would be as follows.

		$	$
DEBIT	Cash (from new issue)	10,800	
CREDIT	Share capital account		10,000
	Share premium account		800
DEBIT	Share capital account (repurchased shares)	10,000	
	Share premium account	300	
	Retained earnings	200	
CREDIT	Cash (repurchase of shares)		10,500

No capital redemption reserve is required, as in (b) above. The repurchase is financed entirely by a new issue of shares.

2.6 Commercial reasons for altering capital structure

These include the following.

- Greater **security of finance**
- Better **image** for third parties
- A **'neater' statement of financial position**
- **Borrowing repaid** sooner
- **Cost of borrowing** reduced

Question 12.2 Purchase of own shares

Learning outcome C2(b)

Set out below is the summarised statement of financial position of A Co at 30 June 20X5.

	A
	$'000
Net assets	520
Equity	
Called up share capital $1 ordinary shares	300
Share premium account	60
Retained earnings	160
	520

On 1 July 20X5 A Co purchased and cancelled 50,000 of its own ordinary shares as follows.

A Co purchased its own shares at 150c each. The shares were originally issued at a premium of 20c. The repurchase was partly financed by the issue at par of 5,000 new shares of $1 each.

Required

Prepare the summarised statement of financial position of A Co at 1 July 20X5 immediately after the above transactions have been effected.

2.7 Redeemable preference shares

We have been dealing up to now with the repurchase or redemption of **ordinary** shares. The rules and the necessary accounting for redemption of **redeemable preference shares** are quite different. IAS 32 classifies a redeemable preference share as a **liability**, not an equity instrument. This is explained in the next section on **financial instruments**.

Section summary

You must be able to carry out **simple calculations** showing the amounts to be transferred to the **capital redemption reserve** on purchase of own shares and how the amount of any **premium** on redemption would be treated.

3 Financial instruments

Naw FA7P Ch. 10 Section 5

Introduction

This section looks at financial instruments and the rules in IAS 32 and IAS 39.

3.1 IAS 32 and IAS 39

(a) IAS 32 *Financial instruments: Disclosure and presentation* deals with:

- (i) The classification of financial instruments between liabilities and equity
- (ii) Presentation of certain compound instruments
- (iii) The disclosure of information about financial instruments

(b) IAS 39 *Financial instruments: Recognition and measurement* deals with:

- (i) Recognition and derecognition
- (ii) The measurement of financial instruments

3.2 Definitions

The most important definitions are common to both standards.

KEY TERMS

FINANCIAL INSTRUMENT. Any contract that gives rise to both a financial asset of one entity and a financial liability or equity instrument of another entity.

FINANCIAL ASSET. Any asset that is:

(a) cash

(b) an equity instrument of another entity

(c) a contractual right to receive cash or another financial asset from another entity; or to exchange financial instruments with another entity under conditions that are potentially favourable to the entity

FINANCIAL LIABILITY. Any liability that is a contractual obligation:

(a) to deliver cash or another financial asset to another entity; or

(b) to exchange financial instruments with another entity under conditions that are potentially unfavourable *(IAS 32 and IAS 39)*

3.3 Assets and liabilities

Examples of **financial assets** include:

(a) Trade receivables
(b) Options
(c) Shares (when used as an investment)

Examples of **financial liabilities** include:

(a) Trade payables
(b) Loans payable
(c) Redeemable preference (non-equity) shares

Exam alert

IAS 32 and IAS 39 are long and complex. All you need to know about is the treatment of preference shares and the distinction between liabilities and equity.

3.4 Liabilities and equity

The main thrust of IAS 32 is that financial instruments should be presented according to their **substance, not merely their legal form**. In particular, entities which issue financial instruments should classify them (or their component parts) as **either financial liabilities, or equity**.

The classification of a financial instrument as a liability or as equity depends on the following.

- The **substance of the contractual arrangement** on initial recognition
- The definitions of a **financial liability** and an **equity instrument**

How should a **financial liability be distinguished from an equity instrument**? The critical feature of a **liability** is an **obligation** to transfer economic benefit. Therefore a financial instrument is a financial liability if there is a **contractual obligation** on the issuer either to deliver cash or another financial asset to the holder or to exchange another financial instrument with the holder under potentially unfavourable conditions to the issuer.

The financial liability exists **regardless of the way in which the contractual obligation will be settled**. The issuer's ability to satisfy an obligation may be restricted, eg by lack of access to foreign currency, but this is irrelevant as it does not remove the issuer's obligation or the holder's right under the instrument.

Where the above critical feature is *not* met, then the financial instrument is an **equity instrument**. IAS 32 explains that although the holder of an equity instrument may be entitled to a *pro rata* share of any distributions out of equity, the issuer does *not* have a contractual obligation to make such a distribution.

Although substance and legal form are often **consistent with each other**, this is not always the case. In particular, a financial instrument may have the legal form of equity, but in substance it is in fact a liability.

3.5 IAS 32 and redeemable (or cumulative) preference shares

Many entities issue **preference shares** which must be **redeemed** by the issuer for a fixed (or determinable) amount at a fixed (or determinable) future date. Alternatively, the holder may have the right to require the issuer to redeem the shares at or after a certain date for a fixed amount. In such cases, the issuer has an **obligation**. Therefore the instrument is a **financial liability** and should be classified as such. The issuer will also have an obligation to the holder of a preference share if the share is **cumulative**. In this case the issuer is obliged to pay the dividend each year, and the preference share will be classified as a liability. Preference shares which are non-cumulative and non-redeemable will be classified as equity.

The classification of the financial instrument is made when it is **first recognised** and this classification will continue until the financial instrument is removed from the entity's statement of financial position.

3.6 Measurement of financial instruments: IAS 39

Financial instruments are initially measured at the **fair value** of the consideration given or received (ie, **cost**) **plus** (in most cases) **transaction costs** that are **directly attributable** to the acquisition or issue of the financial instrument.

The **exception** to this rule is where a financial instrument is designated as **at fair value through profit or loss**. In this case, **transaction costs** are **not** added to fair value at initial recognition.

The fair value of the consideration is normally the transaction price or market price. If market prices are not reliable, the fair value may be **estimated** using a valuation technique (for example, by discounting cash flows).

3.7 IAS 39 and redeemable preference shares

An entity which issues redeemable preference shares must account for the transaction according to IAS 39. Redeemable preference shares are classified as a **financial liability**. Payment of **dividends** on redeemable preference shares is treated as if it were payment of the **finance charge on a redeemable loan**.

3.8 Accounting for finance charges

How is the finance charge on a financial instrument calculated? It can be measured as the difference between the amount paid or received for the instrument, including any transaction costs, and all amounts received or paid subsequent to that – interest or dividends, amount payable or receivable on maturity. This amount must then be allocated over the life of the instrument.

IAS 39 prescribes the **effective interest method** of allocating the finance charge (or the interest receivable, in the case of the purchaser) over the life of the liability.

KEY TERM

The EFFECTIVE INTEREST RATE is the rate that exactly discounts estimated future cash payments or receipts through the expected life of the financial instrument. (IAS 39)

Example: Allocation of interest receivable

On 1 January 20X1 Abacus Co purchases a debt instrument for its fair value of $1,000. The debt instrument is due to mature on 31 December 20X5. The instrument has a principal amount of $1,250 and carries fixed interest of 4.72% paid annually.

How should Abacus Co account for the debt instrument over its five year term?

Solution

The interest receivable will be calculated as follows.

	$
Interest:	
5 years × $59 (1,250 × 4.72%)	295
Amount at maturity	1,250
Purchase cost	(1,000)
Interest receivable	545

This interest receivable must be allocated over the five year term. Here the effective interest rate is 10%.

So the allocation would be as follows.

Year	*Financial asset at beginning of year*	*Interest income for year*	*Interest received during year*	*Financial asset at end of year*
	$	$	$	$
20X1	1,000	100	(59)	1,041
20X2	1,041	104	(59)	1,086
20X3	1,086	109	(59)	1,136
20X4	1,136	113	(59)	1,190
20X5	1,190	119	(59)	1,250

Each year the carrying amount of the financial asset is increased by the interest income for the year (DR Asset/CR Interest receivable) and reduced by the interest actually received during the year (DR Cash/CR Asset).

As Abacus was the **purchaser** of the financial instrument, we were dealing with **interest receivable**, rather than finance charge.

Now we will take the example of a finance charge.

Example: Allocation of finance charge

On 1 January 20X1 Abacus Co also issues 20 million $1 5% preference shares redeemable at par after 4 years. Issue costs are $2 million. The finance charge is calculated as follows.

	$m
Receipt from issue (20m – 2m)	18
Dividend payable over 4 years (20 × 5% ×4)	(4)
Payable on redemption	(20)
Finance charge	(6)

The effective interest rate is approximately 8% and the allocation is as follows.

Year	*Statement of financial position liability*	*Finance charge for year 8%*	*Dividends paid*	*Statement of financial position liability*
	$m	$m	$m	$m
20X1	18	1.44	(1)	18.44
20X2	18.44	1.48	(1)	18.92
20X3	18.92	1.52	(1)	19.44
20X4	19.44	1.55	(1)	19.99

So by the redemption date the carrying value of the liability has been increased from the amount originally received ($18m) to the amount needed to redeem the shares ($20m).

Exam skills

If you were required to calculate finance charges or interest receivable on a financial instrument in the exam, you would be told the effective interest rate.

3.9 IFRS 7

IFRS 7 *Financial Instruments: Disclosures* adds to, and replaces, the disclosure requirements of IAS 32. The two main categories of disclosure required by IFRS 7 are:

(a) Information about the significance of financial instruments
(b) Information about the nature and extent of risks arising from financial instruments.

IFRS 7 came into force in January 2007.

Section summary

- IAS 32 and IAS 39 deal with financial instruments. IAS 32 deals with presentation and disclosure. IAS 39 sets out principles for recognising and measuring financial assets and liabilities.
- Financial instruments must be classified as liabilities or equity.
- The substance of the financial instrument is more important than its legal form.
- The critical feature of a financial liability is the contractual obligation to deliver cash or another financial instrument.
- Redeemable preference shares are classified as a financial liability.

Chapter Roundup

- ✓ Shares may be issued to existing shareholders via a rights issue or a bonus issue. Alternatively they can be issued to new shareholders.
- ✓ You must be able to carry out **simple calculations** showing the amounts to be transferred to the **capital redemption reserve** on purchase of own shares, and how the amount of any **premium** on redemption would be treated.
- ✓ IAS 32 and IAS 39 deal with financial instruments. IAS 32 deals with presentation and disclosure. IAS 39 sets out principles for recognising and measuring financial assets and liabilities.
- ✓ Financial instruments must be classified as liabilities or equity.
- ✓ The substance of the financial instrument is more important than its legal form.
- ✓ The critical feature of a financial liability is the contractual obligation to deliver cash or another financial instrument.
- ✓ Redeemable preference shares are classified as a financial liability.

Quick Quiz

1 To which purposes can a share premium account be applied?

(i) Writing off share/debenture issue expenses
(ii) Paying a premium on redemption
(iii) Issuing fully paid bonus shares to members

Which is correct?

A (i) and (ii)
B (i) and (iii)
C (ii) and (iii)
D All the above

2 If a company has not got the power to reduce its issued share capital, per the original articles of association, then it can never do so.

True ☐

False ☐

3 A company can redeem shares out of which sources of funds?

(i) Distributable profits
(ii) Proceeds of new shares
(iii) The share premium account

A All three
B (i) and (ii)
C (ii) and (iii)
D (i) and (iii)

4 How are redeemable preference shares accounted for by the entity that issues them?

5 Define a financial instrument.

Answers to Quick Quiz

1 D

2 False, it can pass a special resolution to change the articles.

3 B

4 As a financial liability.

5 Any contract that gives rise to both a financial asset of one entity and a financial liability or equity instrument of another entity.

Answers to Questions

12.1 Issue of shares

APPLICATION AND ALLOTMENT A/C

	$		$
Bank	5,000	Bank	30,000
Share capital	30,000	Bank	15,000
Share premium	10,000		
	45,000		45,000

BANK

	$		$
App & allot a/c	30,000	App & allot a/c	5,000
App & allot a/c	15,000		
Call	19,600		
Forfeit	1,100	C/d	60,700
	65,700		65,700

SHARE CAPITAL

	$		$
		App & allot	30,000
C/d	50,000	Call	20,000
	50,000		50,000

SHARE PREMIUM

	$		$
		App & allot a/c	10,000
C/d	10,700	Investments : own shares	700
	10,700		10,700

CALL A/C

	$		$
Share capital	20,000	Bank	19,600
		Forfeit	400
	20,000		20,000

INVESTMENT IN OWN SHARES

	$		$
Call a/c	400	Bank	1,100
Share premium	700		
	1,100		1,100

12.2 Purchase of own shares

	$	$
Cost of redemption (repurchase) (50,000 × $1.50)		75,000
Premium on redemption (50,000 × 50c)		25,000
No premium arises on the new issue.		
Distributable profits		
Retained earnings before redemption		160,000
Premium on redemption (must come out of distributable profits, no premium on new issue)		(25,000)
		135,000
Remainder of redemption costs	50,000	
Proceeds of new issue 5,000 × $1	(5,000)	
Remainder out of distributable profits		(45,000)
Balance on retained earnings		90,000
Transfer to capital redemption reserve		
Par value of shares redeemed		50,000
Proceeds of new issue		(5,000)
Balance to CRR		45,000

STATEMENT OF FINANCIAL POSITION AS AT 1 JULY 20X5

	$'000
Total assets	450
Equity and liabilities	
Ordinary shares	255
Share premium	60
Capital redemption reserve	45
	360
Retained earnings	90
	450

Now try these questions from the Exam Question Bank

Number	Level	Marks	Time
Q15	Examinaticn	54	30 mins
Q23	Examinaticn	5	9 mins

GROUP FINANCIAL STATEMENTS

Part C

INTRODUCTION TO GROUP ACCOUNTING

Consolidation is an important area of your syllabus.

The key to consolidation questions in the examination is to adopt a logical approach and to practise as many questions as possible.

In this chapter we will look at the major definitions in consolidation. These matters are fundamental to your comprehension of group accounts, so make sure you can understand them and then **learn them**.

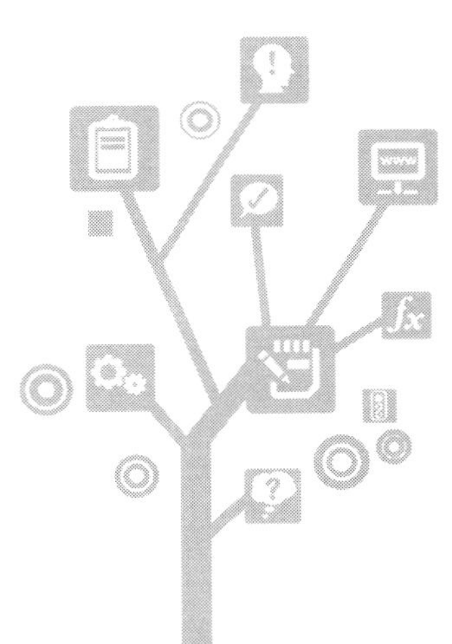

topic list	learning outcomes	syllabus references	ability required
1 Group accounts	C1(b)	C1(iii)	application
2 IAS 27 *Consolidated and separate financial statements*	C1(b)	C1(iii)	application
3 Content of group accounts	C1(b)	C1(iii)	application
4 Group accounts: the related parties issue	C1(b)	C1(iii)	application

1 Group accounts

Introduction

In traditional accounting terminology, a **group of companies** consists of a **parent company** and one or more **subsidiary companies** which are controlled by the parent company.

There are many reasons for businesses to operate as groups including for the goodwill associated with the names of the subsidiaries, for tax or legal purposes and so forth. In many countries, company law requires that the results of a group should be presented as a whole. Unfortunately, it is not possible simply to add all the results together and this chapter and those following will teach you how to **consolidate** all the results of companies within a group.

1.1 Accounting standards

We will be looking at three accounting standards in this and the next three chapters.

- IAS 27 *Consolidated and separate financial statements*
- IFRS 3 *Business combinations*
- IAS 28 *Investments in associates*

These standards are all concerned with different aspects of group accounts, but there is some overlap between them, particularly between IFRS 3 and IAS 27. These two standards have been recently revised.

In this and the next chapter we will concentrate on IAS 27, which covers the basic group definitions and consolidation procedures of a parent-subsidiary relationship. First of all, however, we will look at all the important definitions involved in group accounts, which **determine how to treat each particular type of investment** in group accounts.

1.2 Definitions

We will look at some of these definitions in more detail later, but they are useful here in that they give you an overview of all aspects of group accounts.

KEY TERMS

- CONTROL. The power to govern the financial and operating policies of an entity so as to obtain benefits from its activities. *(IFRS 3, IASs 27, 28)*
- SUBSIDIARY. An entity that is controlled by another entity (known as the parent). *(IASs 27, 28)*
- PARENT. An entity that has one or more subsidiaries. *(IAS 27)*
- GROUP. A parent and all its subsidiaries. *(IAS 27)*
- ASSOCIATE. An entity, including an unincorporated entity such as a partnership, in which an investor has significant influence and which is neither a subsidiary nor a joint venture of the investor. *(IAS 28)*
- SIGNIFICANT INFLUENCE is the power to participate in the financial and operating policy decisions of an investee or an economic activity but is not control or joint control over those policies.*(IAS 28)*

We can summarise the different types of investment *and* the required accounting for them as follows.

Investment	Criteria	Required treatment in group accounts
Subsidiary	Control	Full consolidation
Associate	Significant influence	Equity accounting (see Chapter 16)
Investment which is none of the above	Asset held for accretion of wealth	As per IAS 39

1.3 Investments in subsidiaries

The important point here is **control**. In nearly all questions in your examination, the holding company or parent will own all of the ordinary shares in the subsidiary and therefore have control. We will cover the situation where the holding company or parent holds less than 100% of the ordinary shares in the subsidiary but still has control in Chapter 14.

You will cover more complex group structures in the *Financial Management* paper.

1.3.1 Accounting treatment in group accounts

IAS 27 requires a parent to present consolidated financial statements, in which the accounts of the parent and subsidiary (or subsidiaries) are combined and presented **as a single entity**.

1.4 Investments in associates

This type of investment is something less than a subsidiary, but more than a simple investment. The key criterion here is **significant influence**. This is defined as the 'power to participate', but *not* to 'control' (which would make the investment a subsidiary).

Significant influence can be determined by the holding of voting rights (usually attached to shares) in the entity. IAS 28 states that if an investor holds **20% or more** of the voting power of the investee, it can be presumed that the investor has significant influence over the investee, *unless* it can be clearly shown that this is not the case.

Significant influence can be presumed *not* to exist if the investor holds **less than 20%** of the voting power of the investee, unless it can be demonstrated otherwise.

The **existence of significant influence** is evidenced in one or more of the following ways.

(a) Representation on the **board of directors** (or equivalent) of the investee
(b) Participation in the **policy making process**
(c) **Material transactions** between investor and investee
(d) Interchange of management personnel
(e) Provision of essential technical information

1.4.1 Accounting treatment in group accounts

IAS 28 requires the use of the **equity method** of accounting for investments in associates. This method will be explained in detail in Chapter 16.

Question 13.1 Treatments

Learning outcome C1(b)

The section summary after this question will give an augmented version of the table given in Paragraph 1.2 above. Before you look at it, see if you can write out the table yourself.

Section summary

Many large businesses consist of several companies controlled by one central or administrative company. Together these companies are called a **group**. The controlling company, called the parent or **holding company**, will own some or all of the shares in the other companies, called subsidiaries.

Investment	Criteria	Required treatment in group accounts
Subsidiary	Control	Full consolidation (IAS 27)
Associate	Significant influence (20%+ rule)	Equity accounting (IAS 28)
Investment which is none of the above	Asset held for accretion of wealth	As for single company accounts (IAS 39)

2 IAS 27 *Consolidated and separate financial statements*

Introduction

IAS 27 requires a parent to present **consolidated** financial statements. When a parent issues consolidated financial statements, it should consolidate **all subsidiaries**, both foreign and domestic. In this section we look at the basic rules in IAS 27.

KEY TERM

CONSOLIDATED FINANCIAL STATEMENTS. The financial statements of a group presented as those of a single economic entity. *(IAS 27)*

2.1 Exemption from preparing group accounts

A parent **need not present** consolidated financial statements if and only if all of the following hold:

(a) The parent is itself a **wholly-owned subsidiary** or it is a **partially owned subsidiary** of another entity and its other owners, including those not otherwise entitled to vote, have been informed about, and do not object to, the parent not presenting consolidated financial statements

(b) Its securities are **not publicly traded**

(c) It is **not in the process of issuing securities** in public securities markets; and

(d) The **ultimate or intermediate parent** publishes consolidated financial statements that comply with International Financial Reporting Standards

A parent that does not present consolidated financial statements must comply with the IAS 27 rules on separate financial statements (discussed later in this section).

2.2 Exclusion of a subsidiary from consolidation

The rules on exclusion of subsidiaries from consolidation are necessarily strict, because this is a common method used by entities to manipulate their results. If a subsidiary which carries a large amount of debt can be excluded, then the gearing of the group as a whole will be improved. In other words, this is a way of taking debt **out of the statement of financial position**.

IAS 27 did originally allow a subsidiary to be excluded from consolidation in certain circumstances. This exclusion was then removed by IFRS 5.

Subsidiaries held for sale are accounted for in accordance with IFRS 5 *Non-current assets held for sale and discontinued operations*.

It has been argued in the past that subsidiaries should be excluded from consolidation on the grounds of **dissimilar activities**, ie the activities of the subsidiary are so different to the activities of the other companies within the group that to include its results in the consolidation would be misleading. IAS 27 rejects this argument: exclusion on these grounds is not justified because better (relevant) information can be provided about such subsidiaries by consolidating their results and then giving additional information about the different business activities of the subsidiary.

2.3 Different reporting dates

In most cases, all group companies will prepare accounts to the same reporting date. One or more subsidiaries may, however, prepare accounts to a different reporting date from the parent and the bulk of other subsidiaries in the group.

In such cases the subsidiary may prepare additional statements to the reporting date of the rest of the group, for consolidation purposes. If this is not possible, the subsidiary's accounts may still be used for the consolidation, *provided that* the gap between the reporting dates is **three months or less**.

Where a subsidiary's accounts are drawn up to a different accounting date, **adjustments should be made** for the effects of significant transactions or other events that occur between that date and the parent's reporting date.

2.4 Uniform accounting policies

Consolidated financial statements should be prepared using **the same accounting policies** for like transactions and other events in similar circumstances.

Adjustments must be made where members of a group use different accounting policies, so that their financial statements are suitable for consolidation.

2.5 Date of inclusion/exclusion

The results of subsidiary undertakings are included in the consolidated financial statements from:

(a) the date of 'acquisition', ie the **date control passes to the parent**, to
(b) the date of 'disposal', ie the **date control passes from the parent**.

Once an investment is no longer a subsidiary, it should be treated as an associate under IAS 28 (if applicable) or as an investment under IAS 39.

Exam alert

All F1 examination questions will cover situations where the date of acquisition is the same as the start of the accounting period.

2.6 Accounting for subsidiaries and associates in the parent's separate financial statements

A parent company will usually produce its own single company financial statements. In these statements, investments in subsidiaries and associates included in the consolidated financial statements should be *either*:

(a) Accounted for at **cost**, *or*
(b) In accordance with **IAS 39**.

Where subsidiaries are **classified as held for sale** in accordance with IFRS 5 they should be accounted for in accordance with IFRS 5.

2.7 Disclosure

The disclosure requirements for **consolidated financial statements** are as follows.

(a) The reporting date of the financial statements of a subsidiary when such financial statements are used to prepare consolidated financial statements and are as of a reporting date or for a period that is different from that of the parent, and the **reason** for using a **different reporting date or different period**

(b) The nature and extent of any **restrictions** on the ability of subsidiaries to **transfer funds** to the parent in the form of cash dividends, repayment of loans or advances (ie borrowing arrangements, regulatory restraints etc)

When a parent prepares separate financial statements in addition to consolidated financial statements, the separate financial statements must disclose:

(a) The fact that the statements are separate financial statements and the reasons why they have been prepared if not required by law

(b) Information about investments and the method used to account for them, as above.

Section summary

IAS 27 covers the basic rules and definitions of the parent-subsidiary relationship.

3 Content of group accounts

New notes required.

Introduction

In this section we look at what is included in group accounts.

3.1 Content of group accounts

The information contained in the individual statements of a parent company and each of its subsidiaries does not give a picture of the group's total activities. A **separate set of group statements** can be prepared from the individual ones. Remember that a group has no separate (legal) existence, except for accounting purposes.

Consolidated accounts are one form of group accounts which combines the information contained in the separate accounts of a holding company and its subsidiaries as if they were the accounts of a single entity. 'Group accounts' and 'consolidated accounts' are terms often used synonymously.

In simple terms a set of consolidated accounts is prepared by **adding together** the assets and liabilities of the parent company and each subsidiary. The **whole** of the assets and liabilities of each company are included.

Most parent companies present their own individual accounts and their group accounts in a single **package**. The package typically comprises the following.

- **Parent company financial statements**, which will include 'investments in subsidiary undertakings' as an asset in the statement of financial position, and income from subsidiaries (dividends) in the statement of comprehensive income
- **Consolidated statement of financial position**
- **Consolidated statement of comprehensive income** (or separate income statement)
- **Consolidated statement of cash flows**

It may not be necessary to publish all of the parent company's financial statements, depending on local or national regulations.

Section summary

It is important to distinguish between the parent company individual accounts and the group accounts.

4 Group accounts: the related parties issue

Introduction

IAS 24 draws attention to the significance of related party relationships and transactions – that transactions between the parties may not be 'at arm's length' and that users of the accounts must be made aware of this, as it may affect their view of the financial statements. You first met the concept of a related party in Chapter 10.

4.1 Individual company accounts

The relationship between a parent and a subsidiary is the most obvious example of a related party relationship and it offers a number of opportunities for manipulating results. Some of these may be aimed at improving the parent's individual financial statements.

Any of the following could take place:

- The subsidiary sells goods to the parent company at an artificially low price. This increases parent company profit while reducing profit in the subsidiary, thus increasing profit available for distribution to parent company shareholders .
- The parent sells goods to the subsidiary at an artificially high price. This has the same result as above.
- The subsidiary makes a loan to the parent at an artificially low rate of interest or the parent makes a loan to the subsidiary at an artificially high rate of interest. The loans will be cancelled on consolidation but the interest payments will transfer profits from the subsidiary to the parent.
- The parent can sell an asset to the subsidiary at an amount in excess of its carrying amount. This again serves to transfer profit (and cash) to the parent.

The transactions above seek to improve the **individual** parent company accounts at the expense of the individual subsidiary accounts. Dividends are paid to shareholders on the basis of these individual company financial statements, not the consolidated financial statements. IAS 27 reduces the opportunities for improving the appearance of consolidated financial statements in this way.

4.2 Disposal of subsidiaries

While the situations above are all concerned with improving the appearance of the parent company or group financial statements at the expense of those of the subsidiary, there may be occasions where the **opposite** is the intention.

For instance, when a parent company has decided to dispose of its shares in a poorly-performing subsidiary, it may seek to enhance the results of that subsidiary for the purpose of selling at a profit. In this case, transactions such as those at 4.1 above may be undertaken in the other direction – to transfer profit from the **parent** to the **subsidiary**.

4.3 Effect on trading

Even where no related party transactions have taken place, the parent/subsidiary relationship can still affect how the parties do business. For instance if, prior to acquisition by the parent, the subsidiary had a major customer or supplier who was a competitor of the parent, that trading arrangement can be expected to cease. The subsidiary may itself have been a competitor of the parent, in which case it may now have had to withdraw from certain markets in favour of the parent.

Look out for any of these issues in a consolidated accounts question.

Section summary

Parent companies and subsidiaries are **related parties** as per IAS 24. This relationship can be exploited.

Chapter Roundup

- ✓ Many large businesses consist of several companies controlled by one central or administrative company. Together these companies are called a **group**. The controlling company, called the **parent** or **holding company** will own some or all of the shares in the other companies, called **subsidiaries**.

Investment	Criteria	Required treatment in group accounts
Subsidiary	Control (> 50% rule)	Full consolidation (IAS 27)
Associate	Significant influence (20% + rule)	Equity accounting (IAS 28)
Investment which is none of the above	Asset held for accretion of wealth	As for single company accounts (IAS 39)

- ✓ IAS 27 covers the basic rules and definitions of the parent-subsidiary relationship.
- ✓ It is important to distinguish between the parent company individual accounts and the group accounts.
- ✓ Parent companies and subsidiaries are **related parties** as per IAS 24. This relationship can be exploited.

Quick Quiz

1 Define a 'subsidiary'.

2 What accounting treatment does IAS 27 require of a parent company?

3 When is a parent exempted from preparing consolidated financial statements?

4 Under what circumstances should subsidiary undertakings be excluded from consolidation?

5 How should an investment in a subsidiary be accounted for in the separate financial statements of the parent?

Answers to Quick Quiz

1 An entity that is controlled by another entity.

2 The accounts of parent and subsidiary are combined and presented as a single entity.

3 When the parent is itself a wholly owned subsidiary, or a partially owned subsidiary and the non-controlling interests do not object.

4 Very rarely, if at all. See section 2.1.

5 (a) At cost, or
(b) In accordance with IAS 39.

CONSOLIDATED STATEMENT OF FINANCIAL POSITION

This chapter introduces the **basic procedures** required in consolidation and gives a formal step plan for carrying out a statement of financial position consolidation. This step procedure should be useful to you as a starting guide for answering any question, but remember that you cannot rely on it to answer the question for you.

Each question must be approached and **answered on its own merits**. Examiners often put small extra or different problems in because, as they are always reminding students, it is not possible to 'rote-learn' consolidation.

The **method of consolidation** shown here uses schedules for workings rather than the ledger accounts used in some other texts. This is because we believe that ledger accounts lead students to 'learn' the consolidation journals without thinking about what they are doing - always a dangerous practice in consolidation questions.

There are plenty of questions and examples in this chapter - work through *all* of them carefully.

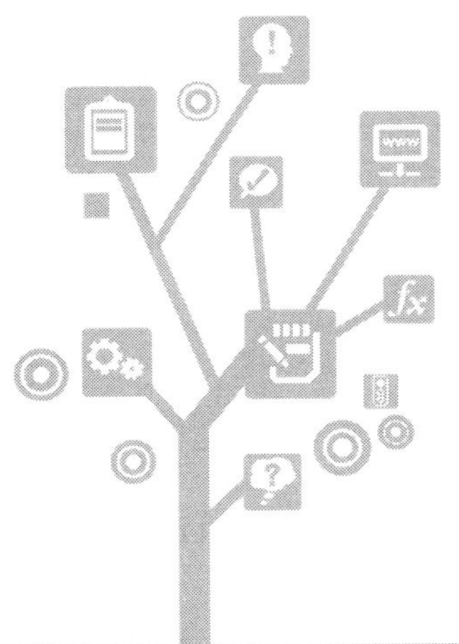

topic list	learning outcomes	syllabus references	ability required
1 IAS 27 Summary of consolidation procedures	C1(c)	C1(iii)	application
2 Dividends paid by a subsidiary	C1(c)	C1(iii)	application
3 Goodwill arising on consolidation	C1(c),(d)	C1(iii)	application
4 Intra-group trading	C1(c)	C1(iii)	application
5 Intra-group sales of non-current assets	C1(c)	C1(iii)	application
6 Dividends and pre-acquisition profits	C1(c)	C1(iii)	application
7 Fair values in acquisition accounting	C1(c),(d)	C1(iii)	application
8 Non-controlling interest	C1(c)	C1(iii)	application

1 IAS 27 Summary of consolidation procedures

FA Ch. 3 section 1

Introduction

How are consolidated financial statements prepared? IAS 27 lays out the basic procedures and we will consider these in the rest of this chapter.

1.1 Basic procedure

The financial statements of a parent and its subsidiaries are **combined on a line-by-line basis** by adding together like items of assets, liabilities, equity, income and expenses. The following steps are then taken, in order that the consolidated financial statements should **show financial information about the group as if it was a single entity**.

The carrying amount of the parent's **investment in each subsidiary** and the parent's **share of the equity** of each subsidiary are **eliminated or cancelled.**

Goodwill on consolidation should be dealt with according to IFRS 3.

Calculate retained earnings. **Dividends paid** by a subsidiary must be accounted for.

IAS 27 states that all intragroup balances and transactions, income and expenses shall be **eliminated in full. Unrealised losses** resulting from intragroup transactions should also be eliminated *unless* cost can be recovered. This will be explained later in this chapter.

1.2 Cancellation and part cancellation

The preparation of a consolidated statement of financial position, in a very simple form, consists of two procedures.

(a) Take the individual accounts of the parent company and each subsidiary and **cancel out items** which appear as an asset in one company and a liability in another.

(b) Add together all the uncancelled assets and liabilities throughout the group.

Items requiring cancellation may include the following.

(a) The asset **'shares in subsidiary companies'** which appears in the parent company's accounts will be matched with the liability 'share capital' in the subsidiaries' accounts.

(b) There may be **intra-group trading** within the group. For example, S Co may sell goods on credit to P Co. P Co would then be a receivable in the accounts of S Co, while S Co would be a payable in the accounts of P Co.

Example: cancellation

P Co regularly sells goods to its one subsidiary company, S Co, which it has owned since S Co's incorporation. The statement of financial position of the two companies on 31 December 20X6 are given here.

STATEMENT OF FINANCIAL POSITION AS AT 31 DECEMBER 20X6

	P Co	*S Co*
	$	$
Assets		
Non-current assets		
Property, plant and equipment	35,000	45,000
Investment in 40,000 $1 shares in S Co at cost	40,000	
	75,000	
Current assets		
Inventories	16,000	12,000
Receivables: S Co	2,000	
Other	6,000	9,000
Cash at bank	1,000	
Total assets	100,000	66,000
Equity and liabilities		
Equity		
40,000 $1 ordinary shares		40,000
70,000 $1 ordinary shares	70,000	
Retained earnings	16,000	19,000
	86,000	59,000
Current liabilities		
Bank overdraft		3,000
Payables: P Co		2,000
Payables: Other	14,000	2,000
Total equity and liabilities	100,000	66,000

Required

Prepare the consolidated statement of financial position of P Co at 31 December 20X6.

Solution

The cancelling items are:

(a) P Co's asset 'investment in shares of S Co' ($40,000) cancels with S Co's liability 'share capital' ($40,000);

(b) P Co's asset 'receivables: S Co' ($2,000) cancels with S Co's liability 'payables: P Co' ($2,000).

The remaining assets and liabilities are added together to produce the following consolidated statement of financial position.

P CO
CONSOLIDATED STATEMENT OF FINANCIAL POSITION AS AT 31 DECEMBER 20X6

	$	$
Assets		
Non-current assets		
Property, plant and equipment		80,000
Current assets		
Inventories	28,000	
Receivables	15,000	
Cash at bank	1,000	
		44,000
Total assets		124,000

LEARNING MEDIA

	$	$
Equity and liabilities		
Equity		
70,000 $1 ordinary shares	70,000	
Retained earnings	35,000	
	105,000	
Current liabilities		
Bank overdraft	3,000	
Payables	16,000	
		19,000
Total equity and liabilities		124,000

Note the following.

(a) P Co's bank balance is **not netted off** with S Co's bank overdraft. To offset one against the other would be less informative and would conflict with the principle that assets and liabilities should not be netted off.

(b) The share capital in the consolidated statement of financial position is the **share capital of the parent company alone**. This must *always* be the case, no matter how complex the consolidation, because the share capital of subsidiary companies must *always* be a wholly cancelling item.

1.3 Part cancellation

An item may appear in the statements of financial position of a parent company and its subsidiary, but not at the same amounts.

(a) The parent company may have acquired **shares in the subsidiary** at a price **greater or less than their par value**. The asset will appear in the parent company's accounts at cost, while the liability will appear in the subsidiary's accounts at par value. This raises the issue of **goodwill**, which is dealt with later in this chapter.

(b) The inter-company trading balances may be out of step because of **goods or cash in transit**.

(c) One company may have **issued loan stock** of which a **proportion only** is taken up by the other company.

The following question illustrates the techniques needed to deal with items (b) and (c) above. The procedure is to **cancel as far as possible**. The remaining uncancelled amounts will appear in the consolidated statement of financial position.

(a) **Uncancelled loan stock** will appear as a **liability of the group**.

(b) **Uncancelled balances on intra-group accounts** represent **goods or cash in transit**, which will appear in the consolidated statement of financial position.

Exam alert

A Section C question in the pilot paper asks candidates to produce a consolidated statement of financial position.

Question 14.1 — Cancellation

Learning outcome C1(c)

The statements of financial position of P Co and of its subsidiary S Co have been made up to 30 June. P Co has owned all the ordinary shares and 40% of the loan stock of S Co since its incorporation.

P CO
STATEMENT OF FINANCIAL POSITION AS AT 30 JUNE

	$	$
Assets		
Non-current assets		
Property, plant and equipment	120,000	
Investment in S Co, at cost		
80,000 ordinary shares of $1 each	80,000	
$20,000 of 12% loan stock in S Co	20,000	
		220,000
Current assets		
Inventories	50,000	
Receivables	40,000	
Current account with S Co	18,000	
Cash	4,000	
		112,000
Total assets		332,000
Equity and liabilities		
Equity		
Ordinary shares of $1 each, fully paid	100,000	
Retained earnings	95,000	
		195,000
Non-current liabilities		
10% loan stock		75,000
Current liabilities		
Payables	47,000	
Taxation	15,000	
		62,000
Total equity and liabilities		332,000

S CO
STATEMENT OF FINANCIAL POSITION AS AT 30 JUNE

	$	$
Assets		
Property, plant and equipment		100,000
Current assets		
Inventories	60,000	
Receivables	30,000	
Cash	6,000	
		96,000
Total assets		196,000
Equity and liabilities		
Equity		
80,000 ordinary shares of $1 each, fully paid	80,000	
Retained earnings	28,000	
		108,000
Non-current liabilities		
12% loan stock		50,000
Current liabilities		
Payables	16,000	
Taxation	10,000	
Current account with P Co	12,000	
		38,000
Total equity and liabilities		196,000

The difference on current account arises because of goods in transit.

Required

Prepare the consolidated statement of financial position of P Co.

Section summary

- The basic procedure of consolidation combines the financial statements of a parent and its subsidiaries on a line-by-line basis by adding together like items.
- Items which appear as an asset in one company and a liability in another are cancelled out.
- Items to be cancelled include intra-group trading, shares the parent owns in the subsidiary company or loan stock.
- If an item appears in the statements of financial position of a parent company and its subsidiary at different amounts, the procedure is to cancel as far as possible. The remaining uncancelled amounts will appear in the consolidated statement of financial position.

2 Dividends paid by a subsidiary

FA Ch.3 section 4

Introduction

This brief section covers how to treat dividends paid by a subsidiary company during the year.

When a subsidiary company pays a **dividend** during the year the accounting treatment is not difficult. Suppose S Co, a 100% subsidiary of P Co, pays a dividend of $1,000 on the last day of its accounting period. Its total reserves before paying the dividend stood at $5,000.

(a) The parent company receives $1,000 of the dividend, debiting cash and crediting profit or loss. This will be cancelled on consolidation.

(b) The remaining balance of retained earnings in S Co's statement of financial position ($4,000) will be consolidated in the normal way.

Section summary

Dividends paid from a subsidiary to a parent company are cancelled on consolidation.

3 Goodwill arising on consolidation

FA Ch.3 section 4.

Introduction

In the examples we have looked at so far the cost of shares acquired by the parent company has always been equal to the par value of those shares. This is seldom the case in practice and we must now consider some more complicated examples.

3.1 Accounting

To begin with, **we will examine the entries made by the parent company in its own statement of financial position when it acquires shares.**

When a company P Co wishes to **purchase shares** in a company S Co it must pay the previous owners of those shares. The most obvious form of payment would be in **cash**. Suppose P Co purchases all 40,000 $1 shares in S Co and pays $60,000 cash to the previous shareholders in consideration. The entries in P Co's books would be:

DEBIT	Investment in S Co at cost	$60,000	
CREDIT	Bank		$60,000

However, the previous shareholders might be prepared to accept some other form of consideration. For example, they might accept an agreed number of **shares** in P Co. P Co would then issue new shares in the agreed number and allot them to the former shareholders of S Co. This kind of deal might be attractive to P Co since it avoids the need for a heavy cash outlay. The former shareholders of S Co would retain an indirect interest in that company's profitability via their new holding in its parent company.

Continuing the example, suppose that instead of $60,000 cash the shareholders of S Co agreed to accept one $1 ordinary share in P Co for every two $1 ordinary shares in S Co. P Co would then need to issue and allot 20,000 new $1 shares. How would this transaction be recorded in the books of P Co?

The former shareholders of S Co have presumably agreed to accept 20,000 shares in P Co because they consider each of those shares to have a value of $3. This gives us the following method of recording the transaction in P Co's books.

DEBIT	Investment in S Co	$60,000	
CREDIT	Share capital		$20,000
	Share premium account		$40,000

The amount which P Co records in its books as the cost of its investment in S Co may be more or less than the book value of the assets it acquires. Suppose that S Co in the previous example has nil reserves and nil liabilities, so that its share capital of $40,000 is balanced by tangible assets with a book value of $40,000. For simplicity, assume that the book value of S Co's assets is the same as their market or fair value.

Now when the directors of P Co agree to pay $60,000 for a 100% investment in S Co they must believe that, in addition to its tangible assets of $40,000, S Co must also have intangible assets worth $20,000. This amount of $20,000 paid over and above the value of the tangible assets acquired is called **goodwill arising on consolidation** (sometimes **premium on acquisition**).

Following the normal cancellation procedure the $40,000 share capital in S Co's statement of financial position could be cancelled against $40,000 of the 'investment in S Co' in the statement of financial position of P Co. This would leave a $20,000 debit uncancelled in the parent company's accounts and this $20,000 would appear in the consolidated statement of financial position under the caption 'Intangible non-current assets: goodwill arising on consolidation'.

3.2 Goodwill and pre-acquisition profits

Up to now we have assumed that S Co had nil retained earnings when its shares were purchased by P Co. Assuming instead that S Co had earned profits of $8,000 in the period before acquisition, its statement of financial position just before the purchase would look as follows.

	$
Total assets	48,000
Share capital	40,000
Retained earnings	8,000
	48,000

If P Co now purchases all the shares in S Co it will acquire total assets worth $48,000 at a cost of $60,000. Clearly in this case S Co's intangible assets (goodwill) are being valued at $12,000. It should be apparent that any earnings retained by the subsidiary **prior to its acquisition** by the parent company must be **incorporated in the cancellation** process so as to arrive at a figure for goodwill arising on consolidation. In other words, not only S Co's share capital, but also its **pre-acquisition** retained earnings, must be cancelled against the asset 'investment in S Co' in the accounts of the parent company. The uncancelled balance of $12,000 appears in the consolidated statement of financial position.

The consequence of this is that **any pre-acquisition retained earnings of a subsidiary company are not aggregated with the parent company's retained earnings** in the consolidated statement of financial position. The figure of consolidated retained earnings comprises the retained earnings of the parent

company plus the **post-acquisition retained earnings only of subsidiary companies**. The post-acquisition retained earnings are simply retained earnings now *less* retained earnings at acquisition.

Example: goodwill and pre-acquisition profits

Sing Co acquired the ordinary shares of Wing Co on 31 March when the draft statements of financial position of each company were as follows.

SING CO
STATEMENT OF FINANCIAL POSITION AS AT 31 MARCH

	$
Assets	
Non-current assets	
Investment in 50,000 shares of Wing Co at cost	80,000
Current assets	40,000
Total assets	120,000
Equity and liabilities	
Equity	
Ordinary shares	75,000
Retained earnings	45,000
Total equity and liabilities	120,000

WING CO
STATEMENT OF FINANCIAL POSITION AS AT 31 MARCH

	$
Current assets	60,000
Equity	
50,000 ordinary shares of $1 each	50,000
Retained earnings	10,000
	60,000

Prepare the consolidated statement of financial position as at 31 March.

Solution

The technique to adopt here is to produce a new working: 'Goodwill'. A proforma working is set out below.

Goodwill

	$	$
Consideration transferred		X
Net assets acquired as represented by:		
Ordinary share capital	X	
Share premium	X	
Retained earnings on acquisition	X	
		(X)
Goodwill		X

Applying this to our example the working will look like this.

	$	$
Consideration transferred		80,000
Net assets acquired as represented by:		
Ordinary share capital	50,000	
Retained earnings on acquisition	10,000	
		(60,000)
Goodwill		20,000

SING CO
CONSOLIDATED STATEMENT OF FINANCIAL POSITION AS AT 31 MARCH

	$
Assets	
Non-current assets	
Goodwill arising on consolidation (W)	20,000
Current assets (40,000 + 60,000)	100,000
	120,000
Equity	
Ordinary shares	75,000
Retained earnings	45,000
	120,000

3.3 Impairment of goodwill

Goodwill arising on consolidation is subjected to an annual impairment review and impairment may be expressed as an amount or as a percentage. The double entry to write off the impairment is:
DEBIT Group retained earnings CREDIT Goodwill.

3.4 Gain on a bargain purchase

Goodwill arising on consolidation is one form of **purchased goodwill**, and is governed by IFRS 3. As explained in an earlier chapter, IFRS 3 requires that goodwill arising on consolidation should **be capitalised in the consolidated statement of financial position** and **reviewed for impairment every year**.

Goodwill arising on consolidation is the difference between the cost of an acquisition and the value of the subsidiary's net assets acquired. This difference can be **negative**: the aggregate of the fair values of the separable net assets acquired may **exceed** what the parent company paid for them. IFRS 3 refers to this as a 'bargain purchase'. In this situation:

(a) An entity should first **re-assess** the amounts at which it has measured both the cost of the combination and the acquiree's identifiable net assets. This exercise should **identify any errors**.

(b) Any **excess remaining** should be **recognised immediately** in profit or loss.

3.5 Forms of consideration

The consideration paid by the parent for the shares in the subsidiary can take different forms and this will affect the calculation of goodwill. Here are some examples:

3.5.1 Contingent consideration

The parent acquired 100% of the subsidiary's $100m share capital on 1 Jan 20X6 for a cash payment of $150m and a further payment of $50m on 31 March 20X7 if the subsidiary's post acquisition profits have exceeded an agreed figure by that date.

In the financial statements for the year to 31 December 20X6 $50m will be added to the cost of the combination, discounted as appropriate.

IFRS 3 requires the acquisition-date **fair value** of contingent consideration to be recognised as part of the consideration for the acquiree.

3.5.2 Deferred consideration

An agreement may be made that part of the consideration for the combination will be paid at a future date. This consideration will therefore be discounted to its present value using the acquiring entity's cost of capital.

The parent acquired 100% of the subsidiary's 80m $1 shares on 1 Jan 20X6. It paid $3.50 per share and agreed to pay a further $108m on 1 Jan 20X8.

The parent company's cost of capital is 8%.

In the financial statements for the year to 31 December 20X6 the cost of the combination will be as follows:

	$m
80m shares × $3.50	280
Deferred consideration:	
$108m × 1/1.08	100
Total consideration	380

At 31 December 20X7, the cost of the combination will be unchanged but $8 will be charged to finance costs, being the unwinding of the discount on the deferred consideration.

3.5.3 Share exchange

The parent has acquired 12,000 $1 shares in the subsidiary by issuing 5 of its own $1 shares for every 4 shares in the subsidiary. The market value of the parent company's shares is $6.

Cost of the combination:

	$
12,000 × 5/4 × $6	90,000

Note that this is credited to the share capital and share premium of the parent company as follows:

	DR	*CR*
Investment in subsidiary	90,000	
Share capital ($12,000 × 5/4)		15,000
Share premium ($12,000 × 5/4 × 5)		75,000

3.5.4 Expenses and issue costs

All expenses of the combination are written off as incurred. This includes finder's fees; advisory, legal, accounting, valuation and other professional or consulting fees and general administrative costs.

Section summary

- Consideration transferred when a parent acquires a subsidiary could be in the form of cash or shares. Consideration can be contingent, deferred or in the form of a share exchange.

- The amount that the parent pays over and above the value of tangible assets acquired in the subsidiary in called **goodwill**. Goodwill arising on consolidation is subject to an annual impairment review.
- Pre-acquisition retained earnings of a subsidiary company are not aggregated with the parent company's retained earnings on consolidation.

4 Intra-group trading

Introduction

We have already come across cases where one company in a group engages in trading with another group company. This section covers how to deal with this situation in a consolidation question.

4.1 Unrealised profit

Any receivable/payable balances outstanding between the companies are cancelled on consolidation. No further problem arises if all such intra-group transactions are **undertaken at cost**, without any mark-up for profit.

However, each company in a group is a separate trading entity and may wish to treat other group companies in the same way as any other customer. In this case, a company (say A Co) may buy goods at one price and sell them at a higher price to another group company (B Co). The accounts of A Co will quite properly include the profit earned on sales to B Co; and similarly B Co's statement of financial position will include inventories at their cost to B Co, ie at the amount at which they were purchased from A Co.

This gives rise to two problems.

(a) Although A Co makes a profit as soon as it sells goods to B Co, the group does not make a sale or achieve a profit until an outside customer buys the goods from B Co.

(b) Any purchases from A Co which remain unsold by B Co at the year end will be included in B Co's inventory. Their value in the statement of financial position will be their cost to B Co, which is not the same as their cost to the group.

The objective of consolidated accounts is to present the financial position of several connected companies as that of a single entity, the group. This means that **in a consolidated statement of financial position the only profits recognised should be those earned by the group** in providing goods or services to outsiders. Similarly, inventory in the consolidated statement of financial position should be valued at cost to the group.

Suppose that a holding company P Co buys goods for $1,600 and sells them to a wholly owned subsidiary S Co for $2,000. The goods are in S Co's inventory at the year end and appear in S Co's statement of financial position at $2,000. In this case, P Co will record a profit of $400 in its individual accounts, but from the group's point of view the figures are:

Cost	$1,600
External sales	nil
Closing inventory at cost	$1,600
Profit/loss	nil

If we add together the figures for retained earnings and inventory in the individual statements of financial position of P Co and S Co the resulting figures for consolidated retained earnings and consolidated inventory will each be overstated by $400. A **consolidation adjustment** is therefore necessary as follows.

DEBIT	Group retained earnings
CREDIT	Group inventory (statement of financial position)

with the amount of **profit unrealised** by the group.

Question 14.2

Unrealised profit

Learning outcome C1(c)

P Co acquired all the shares in S Co one year ago when the reserves of S Co stood at $10,000. Draft statements of financial position for each company are as follows.

	P Co		S Co	
	$	$	$	$
Assets				
Non-current assets				
Property, plant and equipment	80,000			40,000
Investment in S Co at cost	46,000			
		126,000		
Current assets		40,000		30,000
Total assets		166,000		70,000
Equity and liabilities				
Equity				
Ordinary shares of $1 each	100,000		30,000	
Retained earnings	45,000		22,000	
		145,000		52,000
Current liabilities		21,000		18,000
Total equity and liabilities		166,000		70,000

During the year S Co sold goods to P Co for $50,000, the profit to S Co being 20% of selling price. At the end of the reporting period, $15,000 of these goods remained unsold in the inventories of P Co. At the same date, P Co owed S Co $12,000 for goods bought and this debt is included in the trade payables of P Co and the receivables of S Co. The goodwill arising on consolidation has been impaired. The amount of the impairment is $1,500.

Required

Prepare a draft consolidated statement of financial position for P Co.

Section summary

- In a consolidated statement of financial position, the only profits recognised should be those earned by the group in providing goods or services to outsiders.
- Inventory in the consolidated statement of financial position should be valued at cost to the group.
- Consolidation adjustments are necessary to remove unrealised profits in the group

5 Intra-group sales of non-current assets

FA Ch.3 section 8

Introduction

As well as engaging in trading activities with each other, group companies may on occasion wish to **transfer non-current assets.** In this section we will look at how this affects the consolidation process.

5.1 Accounting treatment

In their individual accounts the companies concerned will treat the transfer just like a sale between unconnected parties: the selling company will record a profit or loss on sale, while the purchasing company will record the asset at the amount paid to acquire it, and will use that amount as the basis for calculating depreciation.

On consolidation, the usual **'group entity' principle applies**. The consolidated statement of financial position must show assets at their cost to the group, and any depreciation charged must be based on that cost. Two consolidation adjustments will usually be needed to achieve this.

(a) An adjustment to alter retained earnings and non-current assets cost so as to remove any element of unrealised profit or loss. This is similar to the adjustment required in respect of unrealised profit in inventory.

(b) An adjustment to alter retained earnings and accumulated depreciation is made so that consolidated depreciation is based on the asset's cost to the group.

In practice, these steps are combined so that the retained earnings of the entity making the unrealised profit are debited with the unrealised profit less the additional depreciation.

The double entry is as follows.

(a) Sale by parent

DEBIT Group retained earnings
CREDIT Non-current assets

with the profit on disposal, less the additional depreciation.

(b) Sale by subsidiary

DEBIT Group retained earnings
CREDIT Non-current assets
with the profit on disposal, less additional depreciation

Example: intra-group sales of non-current assets

P Co owns 100% of S Co and on 1 January 20X1 S Co sells plant costing $10,000 to P Co for $12,500. The companies make up accounts to 31 December 20X1 and the balances on their retained earnings at that date are:

P Co	after charging depreciation of 10% on plant	$27,000
S Co	including profit on sale of plant	$18,000

Required

Show the working for consolidated retained earnings.

Solution

Retained earnings

	P Co $	*S Co* $
Per question	27,000	18,000
Disposal of plant		
Profit		(2,500)
Depreciation: 10% × $2,500		250
	27,000	15,750
Share of S Co	15,750	
	42,750	

The asset is written down to cost and depreciation on the 'profit' element is removed. The group profit for the year is thus reduced by a net ($2,500 – $250) = $2,250.

Section summary

The consolidated statement of financial position must show non-current assets at their cost to the group and any depreciation charged must be based on that cost.

6 Dividends and pre-acquisition profits

Introduction

A further problem in consolidation occurs when a subsidiary pays out **a dividend soon after acquisition.**

6.1 Pre-acquisition profits

The parent company, as a member of the subsidiary, is entitled to its share of the dividends paid but it is necessary to decide whether or not these dividends come out of the pre-acquisition profits of the subsidiary.

If the dividends come from **post-acquisition** profits there is no problem. The holding company simply **credits** the relevant amount to its **own statement of comprehensive income**, as with any other dividend income. The dividend received by the parent and paid by the subsidiary are then cancelled upon consolidation. The double entry is quite different, however, if the dividend is paid from **pre-acquisition profits**, being as follows.

DEBIT	Cash
CREDIT	Investment in subsidiary

Where the dividend is paid from pre-acquisition profits, it **reduces** the cost of the parent company's investment.

6.2 Is the dividend paid from pre-acquisition profits?

We need next to consider how it is decided whether a dividend is paid from pre-acquisition profits. The simplest example is where a parent acquires a subsidiary on the first day of an accounting period and the dividend was in respect of the previous accounting period. Clearly, the dividend was paid from profits earned in the period before acquisition.

The position is less straightforward if shares are acquired **during the subsidiary's accounting period**. The usual method of dealing with this is by **time-apportionment.**

Example: Pre-acquisition profits

P acquires a 100% interest in S on 1 September 20X0. S's year end is 31 December. On 10 January 20X1 S pays a dividend of $6,000 in respect of 20X0. However, as it relates to the year of acquisition, $2,000 (6,000 × $^{4}/_{12}$ is treated as being from post-acquisition profits and $4,000 (6,000 × $^{8}/_{12}$) is treated as being from pre-acquisition profits.

Why do we make this distinction? If we consider the situation of a holding company deciding whether to invest in a subsidiary, we can see the significance of a dividend paid from pre-acquisition profits. If the prospective subsidiary's financial statements disclose that it proposes to pay a dividend in the near future, the prospective holding company knows that if it invests in the shares some of its investment will be returned to it very soon. Also, a dividend paid out of pre-acquisition cannot be regarded as a return on the company's investment because it relates to the period before the investment was made. So we treat it as what it effectively is – a reduction in the cost of the investment.

Solution

To continue the example of P and S above, P has paid $200,000 for its 100% shareholding in S. At the date of acquisition S had share capital of $100,000 and retained earnings of $70,000.

In 20X1 S pays a $6,000 dividend. $4,000 is deemed to be from pre-acquisition profits. The goodwill calculation at 31 December 20X1 is as follows:

	$	$
Consideration transferred		200,000
Less pre-acquisition dividend		(4,000)
		196,000
Net assets acquired:		
Share capital	100,000	
Retained earnings	70,000	
		(170,000)
Goodwill		26,000

Section summary

When a dividend is paid from pre-acquisition profits it reduces the cost of the parent company's investment.

7 Fair values in acquisition accounting

Introduction

In this section we look at what fair value is and the adjustments necessary for consolidation.

7.1 Goodwill

To understand the importance of fair values in the acquisition of a subsidiary consider again what we mean by goodwill.

KEY TERM

GOODWILL. An asset representing the future economic benefits arising from other assets acquired in a business combination that are not individually identified and separately recognised.

Goodwill is recognised at the acquisition date and measured as the difference between the following.

(a) The acquisition-date fair value of the consideration transferred; and

(b) The net of the acquisition-date amounts of the identifiable assets acquired and the liabilities assumed measured in accordance with IFRS 3.

7.2 What is fair value?

Fair value is defined as follows by IFRS 3 and various other standards – it is an important definition.

KEY TERM

FAIR VALUE. The amount for which an asset could be exchanged, or a liability settled, between knowledgeable, willing parties in an arm's length transaction.

7.3 Fair value adjustment calculations

Until now we have calculated goodwill as the difference between the consideration transferred and the **book value** of net assets acquired by the group. If this calculation is to comply with the definition above we must ensure that the book value of the subsidiary's net assets is the same as their **fair value**.

There are two possible ways of achieving this.

(a) The **subsidiary company** might **incorporate any necessary revaluations** in its own books of account. In this case, we can proceed directly to the consolidation, taking asset values and reserves figures straight from the subsidiary company's statement of financial position.

(b) The **revaluations** may be made as a **consolidation adjustment without being incorporated** in the subsidiary company's books. In this case, we must make the necessary adjustments to the subsidiary's statement of financial position as a working. Only then can we proceed to the consolidation.

Note. Remember that when depreciating assets are revalued there may be a corresponding alteration in the amount of depreciation charged and accumulated.

Example: fair value adjustments

P Co acquired 100% of the ordinary shares of S Co on 1 September 20X5. At that date the fair value of S Co's non-current assets was $23,000 greater than their net book value, and the balance of retained earnings was $21,000. The statements of financial position of both companies at 31 August 20X6 are given below. S Co has not incorporated any revaluation in its books of account.

P CO
STATEMENT OF FINANCIAL POSITION AS AT 31 AUGUST 20X6

	$	$
Assets		
Non-current assets		
Property, plant and equipment	63,000	
Investment in S Co at cost	67,000	
		130,000
Current assets		82,000
Total assets		212,000
Equity and liabilities		
Equity		
Ordinary shares of $1 each	80,000	
Retained earnings	112,000	
		192,000
Current liabilities		20,000
Total equity and liabilities		212,000

S CO
STATEMENT OF FINANCIAL POSITION AS AT 31 AUGUST 20X6

	$	$
Assets		
Property, plant and equipment		28,000
Current assets		43,000
Total assets		71,000
Equity and liabilities		
Equity		
Ordinary shares of $1 each	20,000	
Retained earnings	41,000	
		61,000
Current liabilities		10,000
Total equity and liabilities		71,000

If S Co had revalued its non-current assets at 1 September 20X5, an addition of $3,000 would have been made to the depreciation charged for 20X5/X6.

Required

Prepare P Co's consolidated statement of financial position as at 31 August 20X6.

Solution

P CO
CONSOLIDATED STATEMENT OF FINANCIAL POSITION AS AT 31 AUGUST 20X6

	$	$
Non-current assets		
Property, plant and equipment $(63,000 + 48,000)*	111,000	
Goodwill (W1)	3,000	
		114,000
Current assets (82,000 + 43,000)		125,000
		239,000
Equity and liabilities		
Equity		
Ordinary shares of $1 each	80,000	
Retained earnings (W2)	129,000	
		209,000
Current liabilities (20,000 + 10,000)		30,000
		239,000

* (28,000 + 23,000 – 3,000)

1 *Goodwill*

	$	$
Consideration transferred		67,000
Net assets acquired as represented by		
Ordinary share capital	20,000	
Retained earnings	21,000	
Fair value adjustment	23,000	
		(64,000)
Goodwill		3,000

2 *Retained earnings*

	P Co $	*S Co* $
Per question	112,000	41,000
Pre acquisition profits		(21,000)
Depreciation adjustment		(3,000)
Post acquisition S Co	17,000	17,000
Group retained earnings	129,000	

Question 14.3

Fair value

Learning outcome C1(d)

An asset is recorded in S Co's books at its historical cost of $4,000. On 1 January 20X5 P Co bought 100% of S Co's equity. Its directors attributed a fair value of $3,000 to the asset as at that date. It had been depreciated for two years out of an expected life of four years on the straight line basis. There was no expected residual value. On 30 June 20X5 the asset was sold for $2,600. What is the profit or loss on disposal of this asset to be recorded in S Co's accounts and in P Co's consolidated accounts for the year ended 31 December 20X5?

7.4 IFRS 3 Fair values

IFRS 3 sets out **general principles** for arriving at the fair values of a subsidiary's assets and liabilities. To qualify for recognition, the assets acquired and liabilities assumed must meet the definitions of assets and liabilities in the *Framework for the Preparation and Presentation of Financial Statements* at the acquisition date.

The acquiree's identifiable assets and liabilities might include assets and liabilities **not previously recognised** in the acquiree's financial statements. For example, a brand name that the acquiree did not recognise as an asset in its financial statements because it was developed internally.

Section summary

- Fair values are very important in calculating goodwill.
- **Goodwill** should be calculated **after revaluing** the subsidiary company's assets to fair value.
- If the subsidiary does not incorporate the revaluation in its own accounts, it should be done as a **consolidation adjustment**.
- The accounting requirements and disclosures of the **fair value exercise** are covered by **IFRS 3**.

8 Non-controlling interest

FA Ch.3 section 3

Introduction

So far we have only looked at subsidiaries that are completely owned by the parent. In this section we look at what to do if the subsidiary is not 100% owned.

8.1 Basic procedure

If a subsidiary is only partly owned, some of the assets and liabilities on the statement of financial position will be owned by outside investors. These **outside investors** are known as the **non-controlling interest**.

KEY TERM

NON-CONTROLLING INTEREST. The equity in a subsidiary not attributable, directly or indirectly, to a parent. *(IFRS 3, IAS 27)*

Non-controlling interest should be presented in the consolidated statement of financial position **within equity, separately from the parent shareholders' equity**.

Aggregate the assets and liabilities in the statement of financial position ie 100% P + 100% S irrespective of how much P actually owns. This shows the amount of net assets **controlled** by the group. Share capital is that of the parent only.

Calculate the non-controlling interest share of the subsidiary's net assets (share capital plus reserves).

Balance of subsidiary's reserves are consolidated (after cancelling any intra-group items).

Example: non-controlling interest

P Co has owned 75% of the share capital of S Co since the date of S Co's incorporation. Their latest statements of financial position are given below.

P CO
STATEMENT OF FINANCIAL POSITION

	$	$
Assets		
Non-current assets		
Property, plant and equipment	50,000	
30,000 $1 ordinary shares in S Co at cost	30,000	
		80,000
Current assets		45,000
Total assets		125,000
Equity and liabilities		
Equity		
80,000 $1 ordinary shares	80,000	
Retained earnings	25,000	
		105,000
Current liabilities		20,000
Total equity and liabilities		125,000

S CO
STATEMENT OF FINANCIAL POSITION

	$	$
Assets		
Property, plant and equipment		35,000
Current assets		35,000
Total assets		70,000
Equity and liabilities		
Equity		
40,000 $1 ordinary shares	40,000	
Retained earnings	10,000	
		50,000
Current liabilities		20,000
Total equity and liabilities		70,000

Required

Prepare the consolidated statement of financial position.

Solution

All of S Co's net assets are consolidated despite the fact that the company is only 75% owned. The amount of net assets attributable to non-controlling interests is calculated as follows.

	$
Non-controlling share of share capital (25% × $40,000)	10,000
Non-controlling share of retained earnings (25% × $10,000)	2,500
	12,500

Of S Co's share capital of $40,000, $10,000 is included in the figure for non-controlling interest, while $30,000 is cancelled with P Co's asset 'investment in S Co'.

The consolidated statement of financial position can now be prepared.

P GROUP
CONSOLIDATED STATEMENT OF FINANCIAL POSITION

	$	$
Assets		
Property, plant and equipment		85,000
Current assets		80,000
Total assets		165,000
Equity and liabilities		
Equity attributable to owners of the parent		
Share capital	80,000	
Retained earnings $(25,000 + (75% × $10,000))	32,500	
		112,500
Non-controlling interest		12,500
		125,000
Current liabilities		40,000
Total equity and liabilities		165,000

8.2 Goodwill and non-controlling interest

Not let us look at what would happen if Sing Co had obtained less than 100% of the shares of Wing Co in the example in Section 3.2.

If Sing Co had paid $80,000 for 40,000 shares in Wing P Co, the goodwill working would be as follows:

	$
Consideration transferred	80,000
Non-controlling interest (60,000 × 20%)	12,000
Net assets acquired	(60,000)
Goodwill	32,000

Sing Co has paid the same amount but acquired a smaller shareholding, so the goodwill is increased.

Note: Work out the net assets and **then** the non-controlling interest.

Section summary

- Non-controlling interest is the equity in a subsidiary not attributable, directly or indirectly, to a parent. It should be presented in the consolidated statement of financial position **within equity, separately from the parent shareholders' equity**.

Chapter Roundup

- ✓ The basic procedure of consolidation combines the financial statements of a parent and its subsidiaries on a line-by-line basis by adding together like items.
- ✓ Items which appear as an asset in one company and a liability in another are cancelled out.
- ✓ Items to be cancelled include intra-group trading, shares the parent owns in the subsidiary company or loan stock.
- ✓ If an item appears in the statements of financial position of a parent company and its subsidiary at different amounts, the procedure is to cancel as far as possible. The remaining uncancelled amounts will appear in the consolidated statement of financial position.
- ✓ Dividends paid from a subsidiary to a parent company are cancelled on consolidation.
- ✓ Consideration when a parent acquires a subsidiary could be in the form of cash or shares. Consideration can be contingent, deferred or in the form of a share exchange.
- ✓ The amount that the parent pays over and above the value of tangible assets acquired in the subsidiary is called goodwill. Goodwill is subject to an annual impairment review.
- ✓ Pre-acquisition retained earnings of a subsidiary company are not aggregated with the parent company's retained earnings on consolidation.
- ✓ In a consolidated statement of financial position, the only profits recognised should be those earned by the group in providing goods or services to outsiders.
- ✓ Inventory in the consolidated statement of financial position should be valued at cost to the group.
- ✓ Consolidation adjustments are necessary to remove unrealised profits in the group.
- ✓ The consolidated statement of financial position must show non-current assets at their cost to the group and any depreciation charged must be based on that cost.
- ✓ When a dividend is paid from pre-acquisition profits it reduces the cost of the parent company's investment.
- ✓ Fair values are very important in calculating goodwill.
- ✓ **Goodwill** should be calculated **after revaluing** the subsidiary company's assets to fair value.
- ✓ If the subsidiary does not incorporate the revaluation in its own accounts, it should be done as a **consolidation adjustment**.
- ✓ The accounting requirements and disclosures of the **fair value exercise** are covered by **IFRS 3**.
- ✓ Non-controlling interest is the equity in a subsidiary not attributable, directly or indirectly, to a parent. It interest should be presented in the consolidated statement of financial position **within equity, separately from the parent shareholders' equity**

Quick Quiz

1 Chicken Co owns 100% of Egg Co. Egg Co sells goods to Chicken Co at cost plus 50%. The total invoiced sales to Chicken Co by Egg Co in the year ended 31 December 20X9 were $900,000 and, of these sales, goods which had been invoiced at $60,000 were held in inventory by Chicken Co at 31 December 20X9. What is the reduction in aggregate group gross profit?

2 Major Co, which makes up its accounts to 31 December, has a 100% owned subsidiary Minor Co. Minor Co sells goods to Major Co at a mark-up on cost of 33.33%. At 31 December 20X8, Major had $12,000 of such goods in its inventory and at 31 December 20X9 had $15,000 of such goods in its inventory.

What is the amount by which the consolidated profit attributable to Major Co's shareholders should be adjusted in respect of the above?

Ignore taxation

A $1,000 Debit
B $800 Credit
C $750 Credit
D $750 Debit

3 Goodwill is always positive. True or false?

4 What entries are made in the workings to record the pre-acquisition profits of a subsidiary?

5 What entries are made in the parent company's accounts to record a dividend received from a subsidiary's pre-acquisition profits?

6 What guidelines are given by IFRS 3 in relation to valuing land and buildings fairly?

Answers to Quick Quiz

1 $\$60{,}000 \times \frac{50}{150} = \$20{,}000$

2 D $(15{,}000 - 12{,}000) \times \frac{33.3}{133.3}$

3 False. Goodwill can be negative if the purchaser has 'got a bargain'.

4 See Para 3.2

5 DEBIT Cash
CREDIT Investment in subsidiary

6 Market value is the best guideline.

Answers to Questions

14.1 Cancellation

P CO: CONSOLIDATED STATEMENT OF FINANCIAL POSITION AS AT 30 JUNE

	$	$
Assets		
Non-current assets		
Property, plant and equipment (120,000 + 100,000)		220,000
Current assets		
Inventories (50,000 + 60,000)	110,000	
Goods in transit (18,000 – 12,000)	6,000	
Receivables (40,000 + 30,000)	70,000	
Cash (4,000 + 6,000)	10,000	
		196,000
Total assets		416,000
Equity and liabilities		
Equity		
Ordinary shares of $1 each, fully paid (parent)	100,000	
Retained earnings (95,000 + 28,000)	123,000	
		223,000
Non-current liabilities		
10% loan stock	75,000	
12% loan stock (50,000 × 60%)	30,000	
		105,000
Current liabilities		
Payables (47,000 + 16,000)	63,000	
Taxation (15,000 + 10,000)	25,000	
		88,000
Total equity and liabilities		416,000

Note especially how:

(a) The uncancelled loan stock in S Co becomes a liability of the group

(b) The goods in transit is the difference between the current accounts ($18,000 – $12,000)

(c) The investment in S Co's shares is cancelled against S Co's share capital

14.2 Unrealised profit

Prepare the proforma statement of financial position and transfer figures from P Co and S Co before calculating workings and making any necessary adjustments.

P CO: CONSOLIDATED STATEMENT OF FINANCIAL POSITION

	$	$
Assets		
Non-current assets		
Property, plant and equipment (80,000 + 40,000)	120,000	
Goodwill (6,000 – 1,500)	4,500	
		124,500
Current assets (W3)		55,000
Total assets		179,500
Equity and liabilities		
Equity		
Ordinary shares of $1 each	100,000	
Retained earnings (W2)	52,500	
		152,500
Current liabilities (W4)		27,000
Total equity and liabilities		179,500

Workings

1 *Goodwill*

	$	$
Consideration transferred		46,000
Net assets acquired as represented by		
Share capital	30,000	
Retained earnings	10,000	
		(40,000)
Goodwill		6,000

2 *Retained earnings*

	P Co	*S Co*
	$	$
Retained earnings per question	45,000	22,000
Unrealised profit: 20% × $15,000		(3,000)
Pre-acquisition		(10,000)
		9,000
Share of S Co	9,000	
Goodwill impairment loss	(1,500)	
	52,500	

3 *Current assets*

	$	$
In P Co's statement of financial position		40,000
In S Co's statement of financial position	30,000	
Less S Co's current account with P Co cancelled	(12,000)	
		18,000
		58,000
Less unrealised profit excluded from inventory valuation		(3,000)
		55,000

4 *Current liabilities*

	$
In P Co's statement of financial position	21,000
Less P Co's current account with S Co cancelled	(12,000)
	9,000
In S Co's statement of financial position	18,000
	27,000

14.3 Fair value

S Co: NBV at disposal (at historical cost) = $4,000 × 1½/4 = $1,500

∴ Profit on disposal = $1,100 (depreciation charge for the year = $500)

P Co: NBV at disposal (at fair value) = $3,000 × 1½/2 = $2,250

∴ Profit on disposal for consolidation = $350 (depreciation for the year = $750).

Now try these questions from the Exam Question Bank

Number	Level	Marks	Time
Q25	Examination	20	36 mins

CONSOLIDATED STATEMENT OF COMPREHENSIVE INCOME

This chapter deals with the consolidated income statement and the consolidated statement of comprehensive income.

Most of the consolidation adjustments will involve the **income statement**, so that is the focus of this chapter.

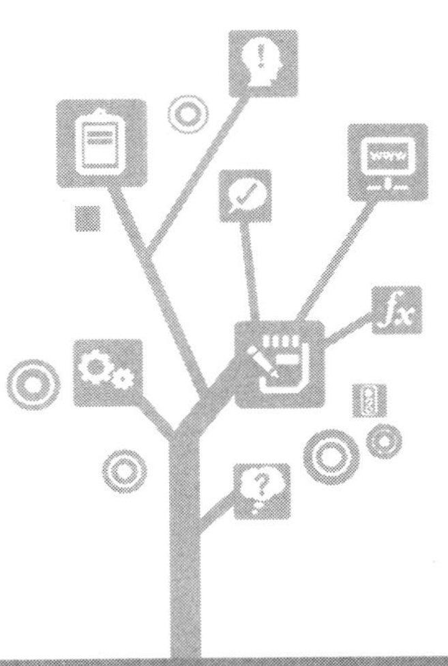

topic list	learning outcomes	syllabus references	ability required
1 The consolidated income statement	C1(c)	C1(iii)	application
2 The consolidated statement of comprehensive income	C1(c)	C1(iii)	application

1 The consolidated income statement

Introduction

In the previous chapter you studied how to prepare the consolidated statement of financial position. Now you will learn how to apply those techniques to prepare a consolidated income statement.

1.1 Consolidation procedure

It is customary to prepare a working paper (or **consolidation schedule**) on which the individual income statements are set out side by side and totalled to form the basis of the consolidated income statement.

Exam skills

In an examination it is very much quicker not to do this. Use workings to show the calculation of complex figures and show the derivation of others on the face of the income statement, as shown in our examples.

Example: consolidated income statement

P Co acquired 100% of the ordinary shares of S Co on that company's incorporation in 20X3. The summarised income statements and movement on retained earnings of the two companies for the year ending 31 December 20X6 are set out below.

	P Co	*S Co*
	$	$
Sales revenue	75,000	38,000
Cost of sales	(30,000)	(20,000)
Gross profit	45,000	18,000
Administrative expenses	(14,000)	(8,000)
Profit before tax	31,000	10,000
Income tax expense	(10,000)	(2,000)
Profit for the year	21,000	8,000

Note: Movement on retained earnings

Retained earnings brought forward	87,000	17,000
Profit for the year	21,000	8,000
Retained earnings carried forward	108,000	25,000

Required

Prepare the consolidated income statement and extract from the statement of changes in equity showing retained earnings.

Solution

P CO
CONSOLIDATED INCOME STATEMENT
FOR THE YEAR ENDED 31 DECEMBER 20X6

	$
Sales revenue (75 + 38)	113,000
Cost of sales (30 + 20)	(50,000)
Gross profit	63,000
Administrative expenses (14 + 8)	(22,000)
Profit before tax	41,000
Income tax expense	(12,000)
Profit for the year	29,000

STATEMENT OF CHANGES IN EQUITY (EXTRACT)

	Retained Earnings $
Balance at 1 January 20X6	104,000
Total comprehensive income for the year	29,000
Balance at 31 December 20X6	133,000

We will now look at the complications introduced by **inter-company trading, inter-company dividends** and **non-controlling interests** in the subsidiary.

1.2 Intra-group trading

Like the consolidated statement of financial position, the consolidated income statement should deal with the results of the group as those of a single entity. When one company in a group sells goods to another an identical amount is added to the sales revenue of the first company and to the cost of sales of the second. Yet as far as the entity's dealings with outsiders are concerned no sale has taken place.

The consolidated figures for sales revenue and cost of sales should represent **sales to**, and **purchases from, outsiders**. An adjustment is therefore necessary to reduce the sales revenue and cost of sales figures by the value of intra-group sales during the year.

We have also seen in an earlier chapter that any unrealised profits on intra-group trading should be excluded from the figure for group profits. This will occur whenever goods sold at a profit within the group remain in the inventory of the purchasing company at the year end. The best way to deal with this is to **calculate the unrealised profit on unsold inventories at the year end and reduce consolidated gross profit by this amount**. Cost of sales will be the balancing figure.

Example: Intra-group trading

Suppose in our earlier example that S Co had recorded sales of $5,000 to P Co during 20X6. S Co had purchased these goods from outside suppliers at a cost of $3,000. One half of the goods remained in P Co's inventory at 31 December 20X6. Prepare the revised consolidated income statement.

Solution

The consolidated income statement for the year ended 31 December 20X6 would now be as follows.

	$
Sales revenue (75 + 38 – 5)	108,000
Cost of sales (30 + 20 – 5 + 1*)	(46,000)
Gross profit (45 + 18 – 1*)	62,000
Administrative expenses	(22,000)
Profit before taxation	40,000
Income tax expense	(12,000)
Profit for the year	28,000

Statement of changes in equity

	Retained earnings
Balance at 1 January 20X6	104,000
Total comprehensive income for the year	28,000
Balance at 31 December 20X6	132,000

*Unrealised profit: ½ × ($5,000 – $3,000)

An adjustment will be made for the unrealised profit against the inventory figure in the consolidated statement of financial position.

1.3 Intra-group dividends

In our example so far we have assumed that S Co retains all of its after-tax profit. It may be, however, that S Co distributes some of its profits as dividends. Group retained earnings are only adjusted for dividends paid to the parent company shareholders. Dividends paid by the subsidiary to the parent are cancelled on consolidation.

1.4 Non-controlling interests

In the consolidated income statement non-controlling interest is brought in as a one-line adjustment at the end of the income statement.

(a) Down to the line **'profit for the year'** the **whole** of the subsidiary's results is included without reference to group share or non-controlling share. A **one-line adjustment** is then inserted to deduct the non-controlling share of the subsidiary's profit.

(b) The non-controlling share of the subsidiary's retained earnings brought forward is **excluded** from group retained earnings. This means that the carried forward figure is the figure which would appear in the statement of financial position for group retained earnings

Example: Non-controlling interests

Carrying on with our previous example, show the effect on the income statement if S Co was a 75% owned subsidiary.

Solution

The consolidated income statement for the year ended 31 December 20X6 would now be as follows.

	$
Sales revenue	108,000
Cost of sales	(46,000)
Gross profit	62,000
Administrative expenses	(22,000)
Profit before taxation	40,000
Income tax expense	(12,000)
Profit for the year	28,000
Profit attributable to:	
Owners of the parent	26,250
Non-controlling interest ((8,000 – 1,000) × 25%)	1,750
	28,000

Section summary

The table below summarises the main points about the consolidated income statement.

Purpose	To show the results of the group for an accounting period as if it were a single entity.
Sales revenue to profit for year	100% P + 100% S (excluding adjustments for inter-company transactions).
Reason	To show the results of the group which were controlled by the parent company.
Intra-group sales	Strip out inter-company activity from both sales revenue and cost of sales.
Unrealised profit on intra-group sales	(a) Goods sold by P. Increase cost of sales by unrealised profit. (b) Goods sold by S. Increase cost of sales by full amount of unrealised profit
Depreciation	If the value of S's non-current assets have been subjected to a fair value uplift then any additional depreciation must be charged in the consolidated income statement.
Transfer of non-current assets	Expenses must be increased by any profit on the transfer and reduced by any additional depreciation arising from the increased carrying value of the asset.
Non-controlling interest	Brought in as a one-line adjustment at the end of the income statement.

2 The consolidated statement of comprehensive income

Introduction

A consolidated statement of comprehensive income will be easy to produce once you have done the income statement. In this section, we take the last question and add an item of comprehensive income to illustrate this.

Example: consolidated statement of comprehensive income

Using the answer to the previous example, show the consolidated statement of comprehensive income if S Co made a $20,000 revaluation gain on one of its properties during the year.

Solution

	$
Sales revenue	108,000
Cost of sales	(46,000)
Gross profit	62,000
Administrative expenses	(22,000)
Profit before taxation	40,000
Income tax expense	(12,000)
Profit for the year	28,000
Other comprehensive income:	
Gain on property revaluation	20,000
Total comprehensive income for the year	48,000
Total comprehensive income attributable to:	
Owners of the parent	41,250
Non-controlling interest (27,000 x 25%)	6,750
	48,000

If we were using the two-statement format (as explained in Chapter 4) we would produce a separate income statement and statement of comprehensive income. The separable consolidated statement of comprehensive income would be as follows.

CONSOLIDATED STATEMENT OF COMPREHENSIVE INCOME

Profit for the year	28,000
Other comprehensive income:	
Gain on property revaluation	20,000
Total comprehensive income for the year	48,000
Total comprehensive income attributable to:	
Owners of the parent	41,250
Non-controlling interest	6,750
	48,000

These amounts would appear in the consolidated statement of changes in equity as follows:

	Retained earnings $'000	*Revaluation surplus* $'000	*Non-controlling interest* $'000	*Total* $'000
Total comprehensive income for the year	26,250	15,000	6,750	48,000

Section summary

The consolidated statement of comprehensive income is produced using the consolidated income statement as a basis.

Chapter Roundup

✓ The table below summarises the main points about the consolidated income statement.

Purpose	To show the results of the group for an accounting period as if it were a single entity.
Sales revenue to profit for year	100% P + 100% S (excluding adjustments for inter-company transactions).
Reason	To show the results of the group which were controlled by the parent company.
Intra-group sales	Strip out inter-company activity from both sales revenue and cost of sales.
Unrealised profit on intra-group sales	(a) Goods sold by P. Increase cost of sales by unrealised profit. (b) Goods sold by S. Increase cost of sales by full amount of unrealised profit.
Depreciation	If the value of S's non-current assets have been subjected to a fair value uplift then any additional depreciation must be charged in the consolidated income statement.
Non-controlling interest	Brought in as a one-line adjustment at the end of the income statement.

✓ The consolidated statement of comprehensive income is produced using the consolidated income statement as a basis.

Quick Quiz

1 Where does unrealised profit on intra-group trading appear in the income statement?

2 At the beginning of the year a 100% subsidiary transfers a non-current asset to the parent for $500,000. It's carrying value was $400,000 and it has 4 years of useful life left. How is this accounted for at the end of the year in the consolidated income statement?

3 Whales owns 100% of Porpoise. The gross profit for each company for the year ended 31 March 20X7 is calculated as follows:

	Whales $	Porpoise $
Revenue	120,000	70,000
Cost of sales	(80,000)	(50,000)
Gross profit	40,000	20,000

During the year Porpoise made sales to Whales amounting to $30,000. $15,000 of these sales were in inventories at the year end. Profit made on the year end inventories items amounted to $2,000.

Required

Calculate group revenue, cost of sales and gross profit..

4 Barley has owned 100% of the issued share capital of Oats for many years. Barley sells goods to Oats at cost plus 20%. The following information is available for the year.

	Revenue $
Barley	460,000
Oats	120,000

During the year Barley sold goods to Oats for $60,000, of which $18,000 were still held in inventory by Oats at the year end.

At what amount should total revenue appear in the consolidated income statement?

A $520,000
B $530,000
C $538,000
D $562,000

5 Ufton is the sole subsidiary of Walcot. The cost of sales figures for 20X1 for Walcot and Ufton were $11 million and $10 million respectively. During 20X1 Walcot sold goods which had cost $2 million to Ufton for $3 million. Ufton has not yet sold any of these goods.

What is the consolidated cost of sales figure for 20X1?
A $16 million
B $18 million
C $19 million
D $20 million

Answers to Quick Quiz

1 It is added to cost of sales and so deducted from gross profit.

2

	$
Unrealised profit	100,000
Additional depreciation (100 ÷ 4)	(25,000)
Net charge to income statement	75,000

3

	Whales $	Porpoise $	Adj $	Consol $
Revenue	120,000	70,000	(30,000)	160,000
C of S – per Q	(80,000)	(50,000)	30,000	
– Provision for unrealised profit		(2,000)		(102,000)
GP	40,000	18,000	–	58,000

The intra-group sale is eliminated in the **adjustments column**. It has no effect on the overall profit. The unrealised profit is eliminated by increasing the cost of sales of the selling company.

4 A Revenue = 460,000 + 120,000 – 60,000

= $520,000

5 C

	Walcct $m	*Ufton* $m	*Adj* $m	*Consol* $m
Cost of sales	(11)	(10)	3	(19)
Provision for unrealised profit	(1)			

Now try these questions from the Exam Question Bank

Number	Level	Marks	Time
Q25	Examination	20	36 mins
Q26	Examination	20	36 mins

ASSOCIATES

In this chapter we deal with the treatment of associates in the consolidated financial statements. As the group's share of profit in the associate appears in the income statement section, we have concentrated on the separate income statement.

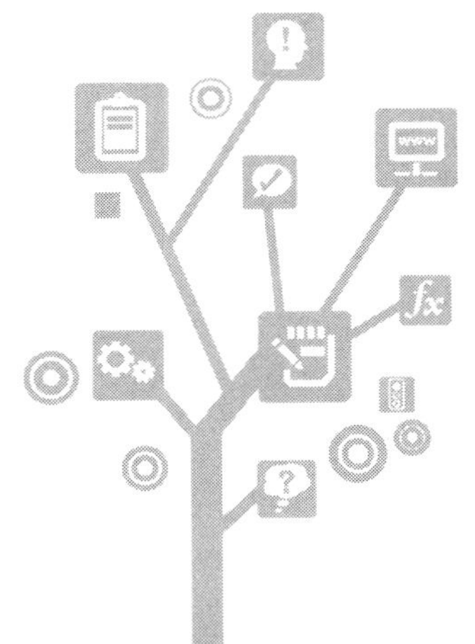

topic list	learning outcomes	syllabus references	ability required
1 Accounting for associates	C1(c)	C1(iii)	application
2 The equity method	C1(c)	C1(iii)	application
3 Income statement and statement of financial position	C1(c)	C1(iii)	application

1 Accounting for associates

Introduction

Accounting for associates is covered by IAS 28 *Investments in associates*. The investing company does not have control, as it does with a subsidiary, but it does have **significant influence**.

1.1 Definitions

We looked at some of the important definitions in Chapter 13. These are repeated here with some additional important terms.

KEY TERMS

- ASSOCIATE. An entity, including an unincorporated entity such as a partnership, over which an investor has significant influence and which is neither a subsidiary nor an interest in a joint venture.
- SIGNIFICANT INFLUENCE is the power to participate in the financial and operating policy decisions of the investee but is not control or joint control over those policies.
- EQUITY METHOD. A method of accounting whereby the investment is initially recorded at cost and adjusted thereafter for the post-acquisition change in the investor's share of net assets of the investee. The profit or loss of the investor includes the investor's share of the profit or loss of the investee.

We have already looked at how the **status** of an investment in an associate should be determined. Go back to Section 1 of Chapter 13 to revise it. (Note that any **potential voting rights** should be taken into account in assessing whether the investor has **significant influence** over the investee.)

IAS 28 requires all investments in associates to be accounted for in the consolidated accounts using the equity method, *unless* the investment is classified as 'held for sale' in accordance with IFRS 5 in which case it should be accounted for under IFRS 5 (see Chapter 5), or the exemption in the paragraph below applies.

An investor is exempt from applying the equity method if:

(a) It is a parent exempt from preparing consolidated financial statements under IAS 27, or

(b) All of the following apply:

(i) The investor is a **wholly-owned subsidiary** or it is a **partially owned subsidiary** of another entity and its other owners, including those not otherwise entitled to vote, have been informed about, and do not object to, the investor not applying the equity method;

(ii) The investor's securities are **not publicly traded**

(iii) It is **not in the process of issuing securities** in public securities markets; and

(iv) The **ultimate or intermediate parent** publishes consolidated financial statements that comply with International Financial Reporting Standards.

The use of the equity method should be **discontinued** from the date that the investor **ceases to have significant influence.**

From that date, the investor shall account for the investment in accordance with IAS 39 *Financial instruments: recognition and measurement*.

The following points are also relevant and are similar to a parent-subsidiary consolidation situation.

(a) Use financial statements drawn up to the **same reporting date.**

(b) If this is impracticable, adjust the financial statements for **significant transactions/ events** in the intervening period. The difference between the reporting date of the associate and that of the investor must be no more than three months.

(c) Use **uniform accounting policies** for like transactions and events in similar circumstances, adjusting the associate's statements to reflect group policies if necessary.

1.2 Separate financial statements of the investor

If an investor **issues consolidated financial statements** (because it has subsidiaries), an investment in an associate should be *either*:

(a) Accounted for at **cost**, or
(b) In accordance with **IAS 39** (at fair value)

In its separate financial statements.

If an investor that does ***not*** **issue consolidated financial statements** (ie it has no subsidiaries) but has an investment in an associate this should similarly be included in the financial statements of the investor either at cost, or in accordance with IAS 39.

Section summary

IAS 28 requires that, in consolidated accounts, **associates** should be accounted for using **equity accounting principles.**

2 The equity method

Introduction

In this section we look at how to apply the equity method using a simple example. More complex situations will be covered later in this chapter.

2.1 Application of the equity method: consolidated accounts

Exam alert

A Section B exam question could ask you to explain the equity method.

Many of the procedures required to apply the equity method are the same as are required for full consolidation. In particular, **intra-group unrealised profits** must be excluded.

2.1.1 Consolidated income statement

The basic principle is that the investing company (X Co) should take account of its **share of the earnings** of the associate, Y Co, whether or not Y Co distributes the earnings as dividends. X Co achieves this by adding to consolidated profit the group's share of Y Co's profit after tax.

Notice the difference between this treatment and the **consolidation** of a subsidiary company's results. If Y Co were a 100% owned subsidiary, X Co would take credit for the whole of its sales revenue, cost of sales etc.

Under equity accounting, the associate's sales revenue, cost of sales and so on are ***not* amalgamated** with those of the group. Instead the group share only of the associate's profit after tax is added to the group profit.

2.1.2 Consolidated statement of financial position

A figure for **investment in associates** is shown which at the time of the acquisition must be stated at cost. This amount will increase (decrease) each year by the amount of the group's share of the associated company's profit (loss) for the year.

Example: associate

P Co, acquires 25,000 of the 100,000 $1 ordinary shares in A Co for $60,000 on 1 January 20X8. In the year to 31 December 20X8, A Co earns profits after tax of $24,000, from which it pays a dividend of $6,000.

How will A Co's results be accounted for in the individual and consolidated accounts of P Co for the year ended 31 December 20X8?

Solution

In the **individual accounts** of P Co, the investment will be recorded on 1 January 20X8 at cost. Unless there is an impairment in the value of the investment (see below), this amount will remain in the individual statement of financial position of P Co permanently. The only entry in P Co's individual income statement will be to record dividends received. For the year ended 31 December 20X8, P Co will:

DEBIT	Cash	$1,500	
CREDIT	Share of profit of associates		$1,500

In the **consolidated accounts** of P Co equity accounting principles will be used to account for the investment in A Co. Consolidated profit after tax will include the group's share of A Co's profit after tax (25% × $24,000 = $6,000). To the extent that this has been distributed as dividend, it is already included in P Co's individual accounts and will automatically be brought into the consolidated results. That part of the group's share of profit in the associate which has not been distributed as dividend ($4,500) will be brought into consolidation by the following adjustment.

DEBIT	Investment in associates	$4,500	
CREDIT	Share of profit of associates		$4,500

The asset 'Investment in associates' is then stated at $64,500, being cost plus the group share of post-acquisition retained profits.

Section summary

- Under the equity method, the investing company should take account of its share of earnings of the associate by adding to consolidated profit the group's share of the associate's profit after tax.
- A figure for investments in associates is shown on the statement of financial position.

3 Income statement and statement of financial position

Introduction

A **consolidation schedule** may be used to prepare the consolidated income statement.

3.1 Consolidated income statement illustration

The following **consolidation schedule** relates to the P Co group, consisting of the parent company, an 100% owned subsidiary (S Co) and an associate (A Co) in which the group has a 30% interest.

	Group $'000	P Co $'000	S Co $'000	A Co $'000
Sales revenue	1,400	600	800	300
Cost of sales	770	370	400	120
Gross profit	630	230	400	180
Administrative expenses	290	110	180	80
	340	120	220	100
Interest receivable	30	30	–	–
	370	150	220	100
Interest payable	(20)	–	(20)	–
Share of profit of associate ((100 – 43) × 30%)	17	–	–	
Profit before taxation	367	150	200	100
Income tax expense				
Group	(145)	(55)	(90)	
Associate		–	–	(43)
Profit for the year	222	95	110	57

Note the following

(a) Group sales revenue, group gross profit and costs such as depreciation etc exclude the sales revenue, gross profit and costs etc of associated companies.

(b) The group share of the associated company profits is credited to the group income statement. If the associated company has been acquired during the year, it would be necessary to deduct the pre-acquisition profits (remembering to allow for tax on current year profits).

3.2 Pro-forma consolidated income statement

The following is a **suggested layout** (using the figures given in the illustration above) for the consolidated income statement for a company having subsidiaries as well as associated companies.

	$'000
Sales revenue	1,400
Cost of sales	770
Gross profit	630
Administrative expenses	290
	340
Other income: interest receivable	30
	370
Finance costs	(20)
	350
Share of profit of associate (30 – 13)	17
Profit before taxation	367
Income tax expense	(145)
Profit for the year	222

3.3 Consolidated statement of financial position

In the consolidated statement of financial position the investment in associates should be shown as:

- Cost of the investment in the associate; plus
- Group share of post acquisition profits; less
- Any amounts paid out as dividends; less
- Any amount written off the investment

As explained earlier, the consolidated statement of financial position will contain an **asset 'Investment in associates'**. The amount at which this asset is stated will be its original cost plus the group's share of any **profits earned since acquisition** which have not been distributed as dividends.

Example: consolidated statement of financial position

On 1 January 20X6 the net assets of A Co amount to $220,000, financed by 100,000 $1 ordinary shares and revenue reserves of $120,000. P Co, acquires 30,000 of the shares in A Co for $75,000. During the year ended 31 December 20X6 A Co's profit after tax is $30,000, from which dividends of $12,000 are paid.

Required

Show how P Co's investment in A Co would appear in the consolidated statement of financial position at 31 December 20X6.

Solution

CONSOLIDATED STATEMENT OF FINANCIAL POSITION
AS AT 31 DECEMBER 20X6 (EXTRACT)

	$
Non-current assets	
Investment in associated company	
Cost	75,000
Group share of post-acquisition retained profits	
(30% × $18,000)	5,400
	80,400

Exam alert

Exam questions could require the preparation of consolidated financial statements using the equity method where an associate is to be included.

Question 16.1 Associate I

Learning outcome C1(a)

These are the draft accounts of Parent Co and its subsidiaries and of Associate Co. Parent Co acquired 40% of the equity capital of Associate Co three years ago when the latter's reserves stood at $40,000.

SUMMARISED STATEMENTS OF FINANCIAL POSITION

	Parent Co	*Associate Co*
	$'000	$'000
Non-current assets	220	170
Investment in Associate at cost	60	–
Loan to Associate Co	20	–
Current assets	100	50
Loan from Parent Co	–	(20)
	400	200
Share capital ($1 shares)	250	100
Retained earnings	150	100
	400	200

SUMMARISED INCOME STATEMENTS

	Parent Co	*Associate Co*
	$'000	$'000
Profit before tax	95	80
Taxation expense	35	30
Net profit for the year	60	50

Required

Prepare the summarised consolidated accounts of Parent Co.

Question 16.2

Associate II

Learning outcome C1(c)

Alfred Co bought a 25% shareholding on 31 December 20X8 in Grimbald Co at a cost of $38,000.

During the year to 31 December 20X9 Grimbald Co made a profit before tax of $82,000 and the taxation charge on the year's profits was $32,000. A dividend of $20,000 was paid on 31 December out of these profits.

Required

Calculate the entries for the associate which would appear in the consolidated accounts of the Alfred group, in accordance with the requirements of IAS 28.

3.4 'Upstream' and 'downstream' transactions

'Upstream' transactions are, for example, sales of assets from an associate to the investor. 'Downstream' transactions are, for example, sales of assets from the investor to an associate.

Profits and losses resulting from 'upstream' and 'downstream' transactions between an investor and an associate are eliminated to the extent of the investor's interest in the associate. This is very similar to the procedure for eliminating intra-group transactions between a parent and a subsidiary. The important thing to remember is that **only the group's share is eliminated**.

Example: downstream transaction

A Co holds 25% of the equity shares in B Co. During the year, A Co makes sales of $1,000,000 to B Co at cost plus a 25% mark-up. At the year-end, B Co has all these goods still in inventories.

Solution

A Co has made an unrealised profit of $200,000 (1,000,000 × 25/125) on its sales to the associate. The group's share (25%) of this must be eliminated:

DEBIT	Cost of sales (consolidated income statement)	$50,000	
CREDIT	Investment in associate (consolidated statement of financial position)		$50,000

Because the sale was made to the associate, the group's share of the unsold inventory forms part of the investment in the associate at the year-end. If the associate had made the sale to the parent, the adjustment would have been:

DEBIT	Cost of sales (consolidated income statement)	$50,000	
CREDIT	Inventories (consolidated statement of financial position)		$50,000

3.5 Associate's losses

When the equity method is being used and the investor's share of losses of the associate equals or exceeds its interest in the associate, the investor should **discontinue** including its share of further losses. The investment is reported at nil value. The interest in the associate is normally the carrying amount of the investment in the associate, but it also includes any other long-term interests, for example, long term receivables or loans.

After the investor's interest is reduced to nil, **additional losses** should only be recognised where the investor has incurred obligations or made payments on behalf of the associate (for example, if it has guaranteed amounts owed to third parties by the associate).

Section summary

In the **consolidated income statement** the investing group takes credit for its **share of the after-tax profits** of associates, whether or not they are distributed as dividends.

- In the **consolidated statement of financial position**, the investment in associates should be shown as:
  - **Cost of the investment in the associate**; plus
  - Group share of post-acquisition profits; less
  - Any amounts paid out as dividends and any amounts written off.

Chapter Roundup

- ✓ IAS 28 requires that, in consolidated accounts, **associates** should be accounted for using **equity accounting principles**.
- ✓ Under the equity method, the investing company should take account of its share of earnings of the associate by adding to consolidated profit the group's share of the associate's profit after tax.
- ✓ A figure for investments in associates is shown on the statement of financial position.
- ✓ In the **consolidated income statement** the investing group takes credit for its **share of the after-tax profits** of associates, whether or not they are distributed as dividends.
- ✓ In the consolidated **statement of financial position**, the investment in associates should be shown as:
  - **Cost of the investment in the associate**; plus
  - Group share of post-acquisition profits; less
  - Any amounts paid out as dividends and any amounts written off.

Quick Quiz

1. Define an associate.
2. How should associates be accounted for in the separate financial statements of the investor?
3. What is the effect of the equity method on the consolidated income statement and statement of financial position?

Answers to Quick Quiz

1. An entity in which an investor has a significant influence, but which is not a subsidiary or a joint venture of the investor.
2. Either at cost or in accordance with IAS 39.
3. *Income statement.* Investing company includes its share of the earnings of the associate, by adding its share of profit after tax.

   Statement of financial position. Investment in associates is initially included in assets at cost. This will increase or decrease each year according to whether the associated company makes a profit or loss.

Answers to Questions

16.1 Associate I

PARENT CO
CONSOLIDATED INCOME STATEMENT

	$'000
Net profit	95
Share of profits of associated company (50 × 40%)	20
Profit before tax	115
Taxation	(35)
Profit attributable to the members of Parent Co	80

PARENT CO
CONSOLIDATED STATEMENT OF FINANCIAL POSITION

	$'000
Assets	
Non-current assets	220
Investment in associate (see note)	104
Current assets	100
Total assets	424
Equity and liabilities	
Share capital	250
Retained earnings (W)	174
Total equity and liabilities	424

Note

	$'000
Investment in associate	
Cost of investment	60
Share of post-acquisition retained earnings (W)	24
Loan to associate	20
	104

Working

Retained earnings	*Parent & Subsidiaries*	*Associate*
	$'000	$'000
Per question	150	100
Pre-acquisition		40
Post-acquisition		60
Group share in associate ($60 × 40%)	24	
Group retained earnings	174	

16.2 Associate II

CONSOLIDATED INCOME STATEMENT

	$
Group share of profit of associate (82,000 × 25%)	20,500
Less taxation (32,000 × 25%)	(8,000)
Share of profit of associate	12,500

CONSOLIDATED STATEMENT OF FINANCIAL POSITION

	$
Investment in associate	45,500

Working

	$
Cost of investment	38,000
Share of post-acquisition retained earnings ((82,000 – 32,000 – 20,000) × 25%)	7,500
	45,500

Now try these questions from the Exam Question Bank

Number	Level	Marks	Time
Q25	Examination	20	36 mins

PRINCIPLES OF BUSINESS TAXATION

Part D

GENERAL PRINCIPLES OF TAXATION

All businesses have to pay tax in some form. This chapter forms a general introduction to the subject.

In Section 1, we look at the general principles of taxation.

As taxat on is so important to the business, Section 2 looks at how it is administered. Finally, in Section 3, we look at the collection of tax and powers of enforcement.

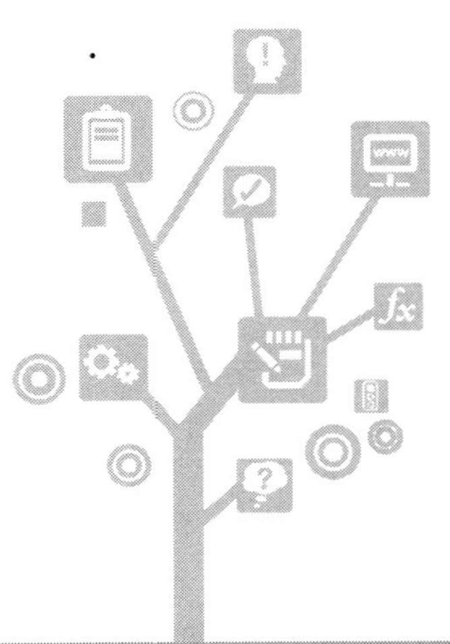

topic list	learning outcomes	syllabus references	ability required
1 Principles of taxation	A1(a),(b),(e), A3(a)	A1(i),(ii),(iii), A3(i)	comprehension
2 Administration of tax	A1(c)	A1(vi),(vii)	comprehension
3 Collection and enforcement	A1(c),(d)	A1(viii)	comprehension

1 Principles of taxation FATP Ch.1

Introduction

In this section we introduce some general tax concepts. We will then look at the calculation of some direct taxes.

1.1 Types of taxation

Direct taxation is charged directly on the person, or enterprise, who is intended to pay the tax. Examples include personal income taxes, company income tax, tax on capital gains.

Indirect taxation is charged indirectly on the final consumer of the goods or services. An example of a sales tax (eg VAT in the UK; TVA in France).

The person liable to pay tax is called a **taxable person**. This includes an individual, an estate of a deceased person, a trust fund, a partnership, a limited company and any other body set up to carry out a trade for profit (eg the bar at a golf club).

A taxable person normally only pays tax in the country where he or she is resident. We will look at this in detail in Chapter 18. The tax authority able to charge tax is called the **competent jurisdiction**.

Question 17.1 Indirect tax

Learning outcome A1(c)

Which of the following is an indirect tax?

A Tax on capital gains
B Personal income tax
C Sales tax
D Company income tax

1.2 Sources of tax rules

1.2.1 Domestic tax legislation and court rulings

The main source of tax rules arises from the domestic tax legislation of the country, eg in the UK, the annual Finance Act. Although the legislators try to think of all possible situations, business is always changing and so the law may have to be interpreted by the courts. This gives rise to court rulings that have the force of law.

1.2.2 Domestic tax authority practice

Every tax authority develops its own practice on how the law is applied. For example, UK tax law states that employees should be taxed on all 'benefits' supplied by the employer. However, in practice, certain benefits are exempted from the rules because it would be too time consuming to account for them and they yield little in the way of tax.

1.2.3 Supranational bodies

Supranational bodies, such as the European Union (EU), can affect tax rules. The EU has a number of rules on value added or sales tax, which have to be applied by all members of the EU.

1.2.4 International tax treaties

Some businesses trade in many different countries of the world, so called 'multi-national' companies. This means that their profits will be subject to tax in the local countries they trade in, as well as the country where the company has its headquarters. This could mean that the company pays tax on certain profits twice. In order to avoid this 'double tax', countries enter into tax treaties which set out which country gets to tax the profits and to allow relief for local taxes paid, for example withholding taxes. We will look at this in more detail in Chapter 18.

1.3 Direct taxes

We will look at direct taxes on company profits in detail in Chapter 19, when we consider IAS 12 *Income taxes*. However it is worth looking at the general rules.

1.3.1 Taxable profit

KEY TERM

TAXABLE PROFIT is the accounting profit adjusted according to the tax rules and is the amount on which tax is actually paid.

1.3.2 Adjustments to accounting profit

The following statement shows the kind of adjustments needed to arrive at taxable profit.

		$'000	$'000
Accounting profit			5,000
Add: disallowable expenditure:	entertaining	50	
	formation and acquisition costs	100	
	book depreciation	250	
			400
			5,400
Less: non-taxable income		10	
tax allowable depreciation		140	
			(150)
Taxable profit			5,250

Here the accounting profit is $5m, but the tax will be paid on the taxable profit of $5.25m. If the tax rate is 30%, the tax due is $1,575,000 (30% × $5,250,000). Lay people usually expect the tax to be 30% of accounting profit ($1,500,000).

Note: 'Book depreciation' will have been deducted in the statement of comprehensive income but is not allowable for tax. 'Tax allowable depreciation' is based upon the rules laid down by the tax authority. In the UK this allowable deduction is referred to as 'capital allowance'.

Capital allowances are sometimes used to encourage businesses to invest. For instance, on some assets there may be 100% first year allowance. Over the life of an asset, capital allowances must account for the purchase price of the asset less any amount realised on disposal. When disposal takes place, there is often a 'balancing charge'; or 'balancing allowance'.

For instance:

	$
Purchase price of asset	50,000
Capital allowances received	(40,000)
Remaining value for tax purposes	10,000
Realised on disposal	(15,000)
Balancing charge – tax due on	(5,000)

If the asset had realised $7,000 on disposal, the company would have received a balancing allowance of $3,000 – this is deducted from the taxable profit.

1.3.3 Plant and machinery

In the UK, capital expenditure on plant and machinery qualifies for capital allowances if the plant or machinery is used for a qualifying activity, such as a trade. 'Plant' is not defined by the legislation, although some specific exclusions and inclusions are given. The word 'machinery' may be taken to have its normal everyday meaning. The statutory exclusions are as follows.

- Expenditure on a **building** and on any asset which is incorporated in a building or is of a kind normally incorporated into buildings does not qualify as expenditure on plant.
- Expenditure on **structures** and on works involving the alteration of land does not qualify as expenditure on plant. A 'structure' is a fixed structure of any kind, other than a building.
- **Land** or an interest in land does not qualify as plant and machinery. For this purpose 'land' excludes buildings, structures and assets which are installed or fixed to land in such a way as to become part of the land for general legal purposes.
- Capital expenditure on **computer software** (both programs and data) normally qualifies as expenditure on plant and machinery.

1.3.4 Pooling expenditure

Most expenditure on plant and machinery is put into a pool of expenditure (the main pool) on which capital allowances may be claimed. An addition increases the pool whilst a disposal decreases it.

Businesses can claim an **Annual Investment Allowance (AIA)** on a set amount spent on plant or machinery. Expenditure in excess of this set amount is pooled in the same accounting period.

1.3.5 Writing down allowances

KEY TERM

A WRITING DOWN ALLOWANCE (WDA) is given on pooled expenditure **at the rate of 20% a year** (on a reducing balance basis). The WDA is calculated on the tax written down value (TWDV) of pooled plant, after adding the current period's additions and taking out the current period's disposals.

When plant is sold, proceeds (but **limited to a maximum of the original cost**) are taken out of the pool. Provided that the trade is still being carried on, the pool balance remaining is written down in the future by WDAs, even if there are no assets left.

Question 17.2 Capital allowances

Learning outcomes A1(e), A3(a)

Talbot is a company making up accounts to 5 April each year. At 5 April 20X8, the tax written down value on the main pool is $20,000.

In the year to 5 April 20X9, Talbot bought the following assets:

1 June 20X8	Machine	$40,000
12 November 20X8	Van	$17,500

Plant was disposed of on 15 December 20X8 for $12,000 (original cost $16,000).

Calculate the maximum capital allowances claim that Talbot can make for the year ended 5 April 20X9. Assume the AIA is $50,000.

1.3.6 First year allowances

Sometimes a 100% first year allowance (FYA) is available on purchased assets. For example, in the UK expenditure incurred on low emission motor cars registered between 17 April 2002 and 31 March 2013 qualifies for a 100% first year allowance. A first year allowance, as its name suggests, is given in the year the expenditure is incurred.

1.3.7 The disposal value of assets

The most common disposal value at which assets are entered in a capital allowances computation is the sale proceeds. There is an overriding rule that the capital allowances disposal value cannot exceed the original purchase price.

Balancing charges occur when the disposal value deducted exceeds the balance remaining in the pool. The charge equals the excess and is effectively a negative capital allowance, increasing profits.

1.3.8 Special rate pool

Some assets are not dealt with in the main pool but in a special rate pool with a lower writing down allowance of 10%. In the UK, this includes expenditure on thermal insulation, long life assets and features integral to a building.

Long life assets are assets with an expected working life of 25 years or more. Plant and machinery in dwelling houses, retail shops, showrooms, hotels and offices and motor cars are not treated as long life assets.

Features which are integral to a building include electrical and lighting systems, cold water systems, space or water heating systems, powered systems of ventilation, cooling or air conditioning, lifts and escalators.

The Annual Investment Allowance can apply to expenditure on such assets. The taxpayer can decide how to allocate the AIA and it will be more tax efficient to set the allowance against special rate pool expenditure in priority to main pool expenditure.

Question 17.3 Capital allowances 2

Learning outcomes A1(e), A3(a)

Winton has been trading for many years, making up accounts to 5 April each year. The tax written down value of the main pool at 5 April 20X8 was $120,000. Assume the AIA is $50,000.

In the year to 5 April 20X9, Winton had the following expenditure:

10 June 20X8	General plant costing $45,000
12 December 20X8	Lighting system in shop $40,000
26 January 20X9	Delivery van $15,000
4 March 20X9	Lifts $20,000

Calculate the maximum capital allowances claim that Winton can make for the tax year ended 5 April 20X9.

Exam alert

Items which are allowed or disallowed for tax purposes vary according to the tax regime. For instance, business entertaining is generally disallowed in the UK. In an exam question you will be told which expenses are allowed or disallowed.

1.3.9 Types of adjustment

The adjustments are of two types:

- absolute
- timing

Absolute adjustments are **permanently disallowed** for tax purposes, such as entertaining expenses and formation and acquisition costs in the example above. These types of expenses are never allowable. Some income may not be taxable at all, eg government grants.

Timing adjustments mean that the expenditure will eventually be **allowed in full**, but there are **timing differences** between the accounting 'book depreciation' and 'tax allowable depreciation'. In our example above the book depreciation is $250,000 but the tax allowable depreciation is only $140,000. There is a timing difference of $110,000. We will look at this again in Chapter 19, when we deal with deferred tax.

1.3.10 Recharacterisation rules

An otherwise profitable company may have high interest payments, leading to a low taxable income. This has an adverse effect on government tax revenue. In some countries, such as the US, interest payments above a certain level can be **recharacterised** as dividend payments, which are not an allowable expense. This is likely to be applied where the loans in question are between group companies. This has consequences because **advanced taxes** or **withholding taxes** may be payable.

Advanced taxes may be charged on dividends. This is a proportion of the dividend which is paid to the tax authorities as an advanced payment on account of the final tax liability. If the advanced tax rate is 20%, then the dividend is considered to be 80% and the advanced tax due is 20/80 or 1/4 of the dividend.

Withholding taxes arise when dividends are paid by a company in one tax jurisdiction to a company in a different tax jurisdiction. They are similar to advanced taxes, but can be reduced as a result of a double taxation treaty (see Chapter 18).

1.3.11 Schedular system and loss relief

Some countries, such as the UK, tax different types of income according to different rules. This is known as a **schedular system**. A business may receive income from a number of different sources, such as:

- trading profit
- capital gains
- loan interest
- royalties
- rent received.

Some governments want to tax income from different source at different rates.

For instance, in the UK, rental income may be taxed according to Schedule A rules but company profits are taxed according to a different set of rules under Schedule D1.

When losses arise, tax relief will be given according to the schedule rules. So losses on Schedule A rents are usually carried forward to be relieved against future profits on the same property. Company losses under Schedule D1 may also be carried forward to be relieved against future profits from the same trade. However, the company may also use losses in other ways, eg set against capital gains or carried back and set against profit of a previous year.

The position regarding **relief for trading losses** can best be summarised as follows. When an enterprise sustains a trading loss in its financial year, it cannot claim a refund of tax for that year. However, there are a number of other possible ways of relieving the loss.

- Carry it forward against future trading profits

- Offset it against other income or capital gains of the same period
- Carry it back against profits of previous periods
- Offset it against the profits of another group company (see section 1.3.12)

Some countries do not allow **capital gains/losses** to be offset against **trading gains/losses** and vice versa.

Some countries do not allow losses to be carried back and some restrict the number of years for which they can be carried forward. When a business ceases trading, there may be provision for **terminal losses**. In the UK, a business calculates the losses for the last twelve months ending on the day trade ceases. If necessary, **time apportionment** is used. These terminal losses can then be carried back and offset against the final year of assessment and the three previous tax years.

1.3.12 Group relief

Tax rules are also necessary to deal with tax losses in groups which you covered in Part C of this text. In the UK, losses of one group subsidiary may be set against the profits of another group subsidiary. When assets are transferred between group companies, capital gains tax is deferred until the asset is sold outside the group. In effect, UK group relief rules treat the group as one entity for tax purposes.

This UK treatment is an example of **tax consolidation.** In general, if a group of enterprises are recognised as a **tax group**, it is possible for them to gain relief for trading losses by offsetting the losses of one group member against the profits of another group member. The rules for group relief will vary from country to country, as will the rules for recognition of a tax group (which may differ from the rules under which groups are recognised for financial reporting purposes).

Some countries also have their own regulations for recognising **tax groups for capital gains purposes**. It is not usually possible to offset capital losses and gains between the group members. However, there are usually provisions that allow the transfer of assets between group members without recognising a capital gain or loss. The calculation of the gain and the payment of the tax are usually **deferred** until the asset is sold outside the tax group. Good tax planning is needed to ensure that all asset sales to third parties take place through just one group member. These provisions can then be used to accumulate all the group's capital gains and losses in that member, thereby effectively obtaining offset.

Exam alert

In any exam question you will be told what rules apply.

1.3.13 Basis of assessment

The rules for calculating a tax liability are known as the **basis of assessment**. This basis depends on the type of income and the taxable person. In the UK, the bases of assessment for the different types of income are embodied in the schedular system, discussed above. The basis of assessment also governs how the tax liability of a particular person or organisation is computed. The examples below are from the UK tax system.

- An employee is taxed on the income actually earned during the tax year.
- A self-employed person is taxed on the profits of his or her financial year.
- A limited liability company is taxed on the profits of its financial year.

In the UK, a tax year runs from 6 April in one year to 5 April in the following year. So the 2008/09 tax year runs from 6 April 2008 to 5 April 2009. An employee will be taxed on his or her earnings for the tax year.

However a self-employed person will prepare financial statements for his or her financial year and it is highly unlikely that this will be the same as the tax year. For example, the financial statements may cover the year from 1 January to 31 December 2008. Under the rules for Schedule D1, the whole of the profit will be taxed in the tax year 2008/09 ie the tax year in which the financial year ends.

In contrast, the profit for a limited liability company is taxed according to tax financial years. A tax financial year ends on 31 March. In calculating the tax due, the profit is split between tax financial years and taxed according. So if a company makes a taxable profit of $12,000 for the year ended 31 December 2009, $3,000 will be taxed on the rates for the year ended 31 March 2008 and $9,000 will be taxed on the rates for the year ended 31 March 2009.

If the tax rate on companies is 30% in the year ended 31 March 2008 and 25% in the year ended 31 March 2009. What is the total tax due on the profits for the year ended 31 December 2008?

The answer is $3,150 ($3,000 @ 30% + $9,000 @ 25%).

Exam alert

The above examples from the UK tax regime are **for illustration purposes only**. You do not need to learn these. If you are set a question on this in the exam, you will be given full details of the basis of assessment to be used.

1.4 Classification and characteristics of taxation – the tax base

Although the details of taxes differ between countries, there are certain classes and characteristics of taxation that are common to most tax regimes.

Taxes can be classified according to their **tax base** (what is being taxed). They can be based on any or all of the following items.

- Income or profits (personal income tax and company income tax)
- Assets (tax on capital gains, wealth and inheritance taxes)
- Consumption (taxes on alcohol, cigarettes or fuel and sales taxes)

Note that the OECD has a more detailed classification of taxes which can be reviewed at http://www.oecd.org/dataoecd/20/39/35589632.pdf

We have considered tax on income or profits in section 1.3 above. In the rest of this section we will consider tax on assets and consumption.

1.4.1 Capital gains

When an asset is disposed of for more than its original cost, a 'capital gain' arises. Governments are naturally very anxious to tax this. Different tax jurisdictions have different rules concerning the taxation of capital gains.

In the UK, the largest capital gains are probably made on the sales of residential property, but these are exempt from taxation as long as the property constitutes a 'main residence'. Other items are also excluded, such as cars, boats and caravans, and the UK government probably makes most of its capital gains tax revenue from gains made on transfers of shares in companies listed on the Stock Exchange.

Some countries allow the original cost of the asset to be adjusted up to current prices by the use of an index, such as the Retail Price Index, before calculating the capital gain. This prevents the taxpayer from having to pay tax on a paper gain, which is simply the result of inflation. In addition, there may be an annual exemption from capital gains tax. In this case, each individual is allowed to make capital gains up to an annual limit each year. Any gains in excess of this amount are charged to tax.

An entity may sell an asset and realise a chargeable gain. However, it may then need to replace the asset. If the entity pays tax on the capital gain, this will reduce the proceeds available for reinvestment. Therefore, some countries allow the tax charge on the disposal of a business asset to be **deferred** until the replacement asset is disposed of. If this is a type of asset that will have to be continuously replaced (such as manufacturing machinery), then this deferral could go on indefinitely. In some tax jurisdictions, this is known as **rollover relief**.

1.4.2 Capital losses

Capital losses are generally accounted for in the same way as capital gains. Most countries allow capital losses to be offset against current or future capital gains. Note that where annual exemptions are available, these may be given after losses have been offset (as in the UK). In this case, the loss relief may effectively be lost.

Example: Capital gains and losses

Assume that an individual makes capital gains of $15,000 and capital losses of $4,000 in the same year. The tax regime requires losses to be offset against gains, before using the annual exemption of $7,500. How much is chargeable to tax?

Chargeable gain = $15,000 – $4,000 – $7,500
= $3,500

However if the losses were $10,000, the chargeable gain would be calculated as follows.

Chargeable gain = $15,000 – $10,000 – $5,000
= $NIL

The taxpayer has effectively lost tax relief of $2,500, unless he makes other gains during the year to use up the balance of the annual exemption ($7,500 – $5,000).

1.4.3 Wealth taxes

A number of countries levy wealth taxes, either on individuals or on entities or on both. This will involve measurement and valuation of assets each year. The tax is usually a straight percentage, for example 2%, of total net worth (total assets less total liabilities).

1.4.4 Inheritance tax

Inheritance taxes are usually levied on a deceased person's estate. As most people do not like the idea of inherited wealth, governments usually find that inheritance taxes are a popular option. Therefore, a number of countries do have inheritance taxes. However, the threat of this tax may make people give away their wealth before they die. Therefore some tax regimes also tax lifetime gifts.

The level where the tax starts to operate must not be set too low or too many people will find that they are liable to the tax. Therefore, there is likely to be an exemption of a considerable amount before the tax comes into force. There may also be exemptions for legacies to the surviving spouse, to charities and for certain lifetime gifts.

In the UK, there are a number of exemptions on lifetime gifts, these include:

- Gifts out of normal income
- Marriage gifts to close relatives
- Gifts to spouse
- Gifts to charities
- Potentially exempt transfers (no tax if the donor survives seven years after making the gift)

There are usually exemptions for business assets as well. This allows a family business to be passed on to the next generation without being taxed out of existence.

Tax authorities usually find that inheritance taxes are expensive to administer and that the tax yield is quite low. However, governments persist in using these taxes as they are popularly seen as being a redistribution of wealth from the 'privileged'.

1.4.5 Property taxes

Some countries operate systems under which people are taxed on their property – usually land and buildings, but sometimes including other assets. The UK has a system whereby individuals and businesses are taxed at a local level on the basis of the value of their property.

1.4.6 Consumption taxes

Consumption taxes are added to the purchase price of goods. They include excise duties and sales tax. They are often levied most heavily on those items not considered necessary to maintain life.

The UK has a long and proud tradition of taxing alcohol and cigarettes. The government is also very enthusiastic about taxing the motorist. It is hampered in its efforts only by the fact that increased duty on motor fuel increases distribution costs, which increases the cost of the foodstuffs trundled daily up and down the motorways. Foodstuffs are unfortunately necessary to life.

The other major consumption tax in the EU is currently tax on added value (TVA or VAT). This is levied on all goods and services except those specifically excluded (such as food and education). It is very cheap to collect and yields enormous revenues.

A consumption tax is an example of an indirect tax and we will be looking at indirect taxes in detail in Chapter 18.

1.4.7 Characteristics of taxation

The economist, Adam Smith, wrote about the **canons of taxation.** His original characteristics of a 'good tax' were **equity, certainty, convenience and efficiency.** In the US, these characteristics are included among the 10 principles that form the CPA Institute's 'Guiding Principles of Good Tax Policy'.

The three **major** principles recognised today are:

(a) **Equity**: the tax burden should be fairly distributed

(b) **Efficiency**: tax should be easy and cheap to collect.

(c) **Economic effects**: the government must consider the effect of taxation policy on various sectors of the economy.

Efficiency is best achieved by the use of 'unpaid tax collectors', such as businesses which have to charge and account for sales tax; and employers who have to collect and account for payroll taxes.

Economic effects are sometimes overlooked, with disastrous consequences. For instance, the increase in employers' tax in the UK had a serious effect on many government departments that carry huge payrolls. The government had neglected to take into account that it was, in fact, taxing itself.

1.5 Tax framework

When considering the tax framework, there are a number of general principles that you need to understand.

1.5.1 Tax rate structure

A government will structure its tax rates according to where it wishes the burden of taxation to fall. There is a general agreement that people on higher incomes should pay more tax, but governments have learned that punitive rates at the top lead to higher levels of avoidance and evasion.

In the UK, Harold Wilson's Labour government in the 1960s sought to 'soak the rich' with a top rate of 98%. This led to an exodus from the country of film stars and pop singers, who thereafter paid no UK tax at all.

There are four possible structures.

- A **proportional** tax rate structure taxes all income at the same rate, so the same proportion of all income is taken in tax.
- A **progressive** tax rate structure takes a higher proportion in tax as income rises.
- A **regressive** structure would take a decreasing proportion as income rises.
- A **stepped** tax rate structure increases the tax burden in stages.

Most Western countries use a progressive tax rate structure.

1.5.2 Tax gap

This is the gap between the tax theoretically collectable and the amount actually collected. The tax authorities work unceasingly to minimise this gap.

1.5.3 Hypothecation

The government can choose to ring-fence certain types of tax revenue as being for the purposes of certain types of expenditure. This prevents the money being spent on anything else and is known as **hypothecation**.

An example, in the UK, is the revenue from the 'congestion charge' levied on London motorists. This can only be spent on transport in the capital.

Section summary

- Taxation can be one of two forms: direct or indirect
- Tax rules arise from a number of sources. There are four main ones.
  - Domestic tax legislation and court rulings
  - Domestic tax authority practice
  - Supranational bodies
  - International tax treaties
- The financial statements show the **accounting profit** for the accounting period. However the local tax rules will normally require certain adjustments in order to arrive at the **taxable profit**.

2 Administration of tax

Introduction

In this section on administration of tax we cover record keeping, returns and deadlines.

2.1 Record keeping and retention

Obviously a business needs to keep records of the tax it pays. It makes no difference if the tax is a cost to the business (eg tax on business profits) or whether the business acts merely as a tax collector (eg employee tax).

However, tax records usually need to be kept in more detail than is strictly necessary for pure accounting purposes. For example, records of employee taxation will need to be kept in great detail for every employee. This is so that the business can satisfy the tax authority that is has complied with the law.

Most tax authorities have the power to inspect business records to ensure compliance. If mistakes are made, the tax authority may be able to re-open earlier years and collect back taxes owed. In the UK, the Inland Revenue have the power to go back six tax years if errors are found. Therefore tax records may need to be kept longer than normal, eg payroll records are usually kept for at least six years in the UK.

Notice also that tax years may not be the same as accounting years. In the UK, the tax year runs from 6 April in one year to 5 April in the following year. Very few companies have a 5 April accounting year end.

Question 17.4 Retention periods

Learning outcome A1(c)

Blam is incorporated in the UK. Its company year end is 31 December. How long should it keep the records of employee taxation of the year ended 31 December 20X0?

2.2 Returns

Businesses need to make **returns** of the different taxes that they have deducted on behalf of the government. They also make returns of their taxable profits, so that they pay the correct income tax and/or capital gains tax.

2.3 Deadlines

There are deadlines for reporting to the tax authorities. These deadlines apply both to the reporting of the taxable profit of the business and also for returns of taxes collected on behalf of the tax authorities.

For instance, in the UK, company income tax for small and medium enterprises has to be paid within 9 months of the end of the accounting period. The company tax return has to be submitted within 12 months of the end of the period. At this point, any adjustment will be made to the amount originally paid. This allows the government to collect tax before the company's tax liability is finalised.

In the UK, a business has to file a return on employee taxes deducted within 6 weeks of the end of the tax year. For the tax year ended 5 April 2009, returns of employee taxes must be made by 19 May 2009.

Similarly, there are deadlines for the submission of records of VAT (sales tax) and other excise duties. The business may be fined for submitting returns late.

Tax due to, or collected on behalf of, the tax authorities must also be paid within a time limit. In the UK, employee taxes must be paid to the Inland Revenue on a monthly basis. The tax deducted for the tax month ended 5 January 2009 needs to be paid by 19 January 2009. Interest is charged for late payment and there may also be penalties charged for persistent late payment.

Deadlines allow the tax authority to forecast their cash receipts and give them a framework within which interest or penalties for late payment can be imposed.

Section summary

Tax records may need to be kept for **different periods** and retained for **longer intervals** than normal accounting records.

3 Collection and enforcement

Introduction

This section covers the collection and enforcement of tax in the UK. We then move on to look at the difference between tax avoidance and tax evasion.

3.1 Collection

The tax authorities in the UK have a specialised branch for collecting taxes due to the Government. The tax authorities review the returns received from taxpayers (whether individuals or businesses) and calculate the tax due. This figure is notified to the collector who then issues a demand to the taxpayer. If the tax is not paid on time, it is the collector who charges interest.

3.2 Enforcement

Tax authorities have the power to enforce compliance with the tax rules. These powers include the following.

(a) Power to review and query filed returns.
(b) Power to request special reports or returns.
(c) Power to examine records (generally extending back some years).
(d) Powers of entry and search.
(e) Exchange of information with tax authorities in other jurisdictions.

We have looked at (a) in Section 3.1. With regard to (b), the special report may take the form of asking for details of pay and tax deducted from an individual employee, where there are indications that the tax rules have been broken. There have been instances of casual employees having a number of jobs but using a number of false names, so that the tax authority has been defrauded.

(c) is generally carried out by appointment. However, where the tax authority believes fraud has occurred, it can obtain warrants to enter a business's premises and seize the records (d).

Point (e) has become very important as a counter-terrorism measure in recent years. One tax authority may become aware of funds being moved to another country in suspicious circumstances. It will then warn the tax authority in that other jurisdiction. Exchange of information is also useful in dealing with drug smuggling and money laundering. Tax authorities will only exchange information where a tax treaty exists with the other country.

3.3 Tax avoidance and tax evasion

Avoidance and evasion tend to be most common where the following situations apply:

- High tax rates, making it more worthwhile to avoid tax and to spend money on tax advice
- Imprecise wording of the tax laws, leaving loopholes to be exploited
- Insufficient penalties for tax evasion
- Perceived inequity in the tax laws, which makes evasion/avoidance seem more justified

When a tax authority becomes aware that so many businesses are avoiding tax by using a perceived loophole in the law, it may bring in **anti-avoidance legislation** to close the loophole. However this takes time and so modern laws usually include general anti-avoidance clauses in new tax bills to cover any loopholes. In other tax regimes, the tax authority may have to take the case to court to obtain a legal ruling as to whether a scheme is against the spirit of the law.

In countries such as the UK, case law is important in dealing with avoidance and evasion. The revenue authorities regularly bring cases against avoidance schemes and, where the court decides that

transactions have been undertaken solely for the purpose of avoiding tax, it will rule that these transactions should be disregarded. This creates a precedent for future cases and in this way loopholes are closed.

However, in the long term, if it wishes to minimise avoidance and evasion, a tax authority has to concentrate on the following:

(a) reducing opportunity by deducting tax at source whenever possible and keeping the tax system as simple as possible

(b) increasing the risk of detection by having an efficient system of checking tax returns and good communications with other tax authorities

(c) maximising penalties for evasion and making sure that this is well publicised

(d) making sure that the tax system is perceived as equitable and that the tax administration deals fairly and courteously with taxpayers

Section summary

- **Tax avoidance** is a way of arranging your affairs to take advantage of the tax rules to pay as little tax as possible. It is perfectly legal.
- **Tax evasion** is a way of paying less tax by **illegal methods**, eg not declaring the income or money laundering.

Chapter Roundup

- ✓ Taxation can be one of two forms: **direct** or **indirect**.
- ✓ Tax rules arise from a number of sources. There are four main ones.
  - Domestic tax legislation and court rulings
  - Domestic tax authority practice
  - Supranational bodies
  - International tax treaties
- ✓ The financial statements show the **accounting profit** for the accounting period. However the local tax rules will normally require certain adjustments in order to arrive at the **taxable profit**.
- ✓ Tax records may need to be kept for **different periods** and retained for **longer intervals** than normal accounting records.
- ✓ **Tax avoidance** is a way of arranging your affairs to take advantage of the tax rules to pay as little tax as possible. It is perfectly legal.
- ✓ **Tax evasion** is a way of paying less tax by **illegal methods**, eg not declaring the income, money laundering.

Quick Quiz

1 Taxable profit is the .... adjusted according to the tax rules and is the amount on which .... is actually paid. Complete the gaps.

2 Value added tax is an example of which kind of tax?

A Indirect tax
B Capital gains tax
C Direct tax
D Income tax

3 Adam Smith's characteristics of a 'good' tax were:.......................................
....

4 Tax evasion is illegal. True or false?

5 A system of taxation in which a higher proportion is paid in tax as income rises is known as....................................... ....

6 The tax year should always be the same as the accounting year. True or false?

Answers to Quick Quiz

1 Accounting profit; tax

2 A

3 Equity, certainty, convenience and efficiency

4 True

5 A **progressive** tax rate structure

6 False

Answers to Questions

17.1 Indirect tax

The answer is C, a sales tax. The others are all direct taxes.

17.2 Capital allowances

	AIA $	*Main pool* $	*Allowances* $
y/e 5 April 20X9			
TWDV b/f		20,000	
Additions qualifying for AIA			
1.6.X8 Machine	40,000		
12.11.X8 Van	17,500		
	57,500		
AIA	(50,000)		50,000
Transfer to main pool	7,500	7,500	
Disposal			
15.12.X8 Plant		(12,000)	
		15,500	
WDA @ 20%		(3,100)	3,100
TWDV c/f		12,400	
Maximum capital allowances			53,100

17.3 Capital allowances 2

The maximum capital allowances claim that Winton can make for the year to 5 April 20X9 is:

		AIA $	*Main pool* $	*Special rate pool* $	*Allowances* $
y/e 5 April 20X9					
TWDV b/f			120,000		
Additions qualifying for AIA					
12.12.X8	Lighting	40,000			
4.3.X9	Lifts	20,000			
		60,000			
AIA		(50,000)			50,000
Transfer balance to pool		10,000		10,000	
Other additions					
10.6.X8	Plant		45,000		
26.1.X9	Van		15,000		
			180,000		
WDA @ 20%			(36,000)		36,000
WDA @ 10%				(1,000)	1,000
TWDVs c/f			144,000	9,000	
Allowances					87,000

Note that the expenditure on the plant and van qualifies for the AIA, but it is more tax-efficient to set the allowance against special rate pool expenditure.

17.4 Retention periods

The year ended 31 December 20X0 is part of the year 20X1. Therefore the records need to be kept until at least 5 April 20X7.

TYPES OF TAXATION

In this chapter we look at three types of taxation – indirect taxes, employee taxes and international taxation.

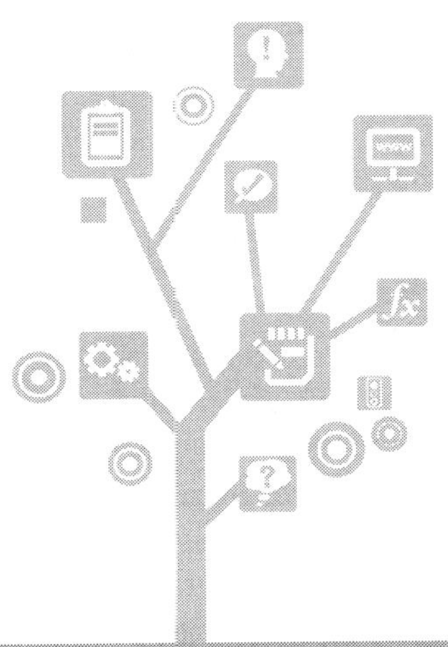

topic list	learning outcomes	syllabus references	ability required
1 Indirect taxes	A1(a),(e)	A1(iv)	comprehension
2 Value added tax	A1(e)	A1(iv)	comprehension
3 Employee tax	A1(e)	A1(v)	comprehension
4 International taxation	A2(a),(b)	A2(i)	comprehension
5 Double taxation treaties	A2(a),(b)	A2(i), A3(i)	comprehension

1 Indirect taxes

Introduction

This section looks at the different types of indirect taxes.

1.1 Types of indirect taxes

1.1.1 Unit taxes

Unit taxes are based on the number or weight of items, eg excise duties on cigarettes or tobacco.

1.1.2 Ad valorem taxes

Ad valorem taxes are based on the value, eg a sales tax or value added tax.

1.1.3 Import duty

Another form of indirect tax is the import duty. Import duties are often levied less to raise revenue than to protect domestic producers.

The US has traditionally had high import tariffs to protect its industries, but is now changing its position. For instance, a decade ago foreign cars were rarely seen in the US, now they are becoming very popular. The EU has of course removed most import tariffs between member states.

1.2 Excise duties

Excise duties are a 'unit' tax – they are levied on the **amount** of the commodity.

Governments apply excise duty to goods that have large sales volumes and are easy to **control**, ie there are a few large producers and products covered by the duty are easily defined.

Excise duty tends to be levied on four major commodities – alcohol, tobacco, oil products and motor vehicles. The tax is collected earlier in the supply chain than sales taxes. By the time the product reaches the final consumer the price will already include excise duty. For instance, each brewery will have an excise officer assigned to it, who will know exactly what quantities are being produced. Because they are collected early in the supply chain from a limited number of products, excise duties yield large amounts of revenue for low collection cost and are therefore popular with governments. They may seek to justify excise duty on the basis that increasing the cost of drinking, smoking and motoring is a means of curbing the consumer's enthusiasm for damaging his own health and that of the environment.

1.3 Wealth and property taxes

Some countries tax individuals and companies on the value of land and buildings or other valuable property or on 'total wealth' – for a company this would be its asset value.

Section summary

Indirect taxes are not actually paid by the company. Instead the company acts as a **tax collector** on behalf of the government. There are two types of indirect taxes: unit taxes and ad valorem taxes.

2 Value Added Tax

Introduction

In this section we examine VAT and its administration.

A sales tax can be single-stage (such as the retail sales tax applied in the US) or multi-stage (chargeable and deductible at different points in the supply chain) such as VAT. As value is added the tax increases cumulatively. However the business deducts the VAT it pays and pays over the balance to the government. The incidence of the tax is therefore on the final consumer of the goods or services.

Example

		Price net of VAT	*VAT @ 17.5%*	*Total price*
		$	$	$
(a)	Manufacturer buys raw materials	40	7	47
	Manufacturer makes and sells television to wholesaler	200	35	235
	Manufacturer pays VAT		28	
(b)	Wholesaler buys television	200	35	235
	Wholesaler sells television to retailer	320	56	376
	Wholesaler pays VAT		21	
(c)	Retailer buys television	320	56	376
	Retailer sells television	480	84	564
	Retailer pays VAT		28	
(d)	Customer buys television	480	84	564

The total tax of $84 is paid by the customer (the end user). The tax amounts paid by the manufacturer, the wholesaler and the retailer will all have been reclaimed.

	$
Supplier of raw materials	7
Manufacturer	28
Wholesaler	21
Retailer	28
Total VAT paid	84

Question 18.1

Sales tax

Learning outcome A1(e)

In the example above, the amount of value added tax paid in total is:

A $7
B $21
C $28
D $84

Exam skills

If you are given a figure including VAT of 17.5%, multiply this by 17.5/117.5 = 7/47 to get the VAT amount.

2.1 Business liability

VAT on sales is called **output tax**, while VAT on purchases is called **input tax**. Basically the business owes the tax authority the output tax it collects but deducts from this liability the input tax it pays.

Output tax	–	Input tax	=	Amount paid to tax authority

Some activities may be **exempt from VAT**, eg banking services. Traders who carry on exempt activities cannot reclaim VAT on inputs relating to those activities. Organisations who carry out only exempt activities (such as banks) are not allowed to register for VAT.

In our example, we used a tax rate of 17.5%. However different outputs may be taxed at different rates. In the UK, there are three rates of VAT.

(a) Standard rate of 17.5%*
(b) Reduced rate of 5%
(c) Zero rate (0%)

* Note that at time of going to print the standard rate in the UK was 17.5% for 2010.

2.2 VAT registration

The example in Section 2.1 above assumes that the supplier, manufacturer, wholesaler and retailer are all VAT-registered traders.

A VAT-registered trader must carry out the following tasks.

(a) Charge VAT on the goods and services sold at the rate prescribed by the government.

(b) Pay VAT on goods and services purchased from other businesses.

(c) Pay to Customs and Excise the difference between the VAT collected on sales and the VAT paid to suppliers for purchases. Payments are made at quarterly intervals.

However, if the input VAT paid exceeds the output tax, then the trader can claim a refund from Customs and Excise.

2.3 Irrecoverable VAT

There are some circumstances in which traders are not allowed to reclaim VAT paid on their inputs. In these cases the trader must bear the cost of VAT and account for it accordingly. Three such cases need to be considered.

- Non-registered persons
- Registered persons carrying on exempt activities
- Non-deductible inputs

Non-registered persons are traders whose sales (outputs) are below a certain minimum level and so need not register for VAT. Non-registered persons will pay VAT on their inputs and, because they are not registered, they cannot reclaim it. The VAT paid will effectively increase their costs. Non-registered persons do not charge VAT on their outputs.

Registered persons may be carrying on exempt activities. All outputs of registered traders are either taxable or exempt. Taxable outputs are charged to VAT at zero per cent (zero-rated items) or at 17.5% (standard-rated items). Some items are charged at the lower rate of 5% (eg domestic fuel), but this has limited application in business accounts.

Traders carrying on only exempt activities (such as banks) cannot be registered for VAT. Some traders and companies carry on a mixture of taxable and exempt activities. Such traders need to apportion the VAT paid on inputs. Only VAT relating to taxable outputs may be reclaimed (see Section 2.4 below).

There are a few special cases where the input tax is not deductible even for a taxable person with taxable outputs. These are as follows.

- VAT on cars is never reclaimable unless a car is acquired new for resale, ie by a car dealer.
- VAT on business entertaining is not deductible other than VAT on entertaining staff.
- VAT on expenses incurred on domestic accommodation for directors.
- VAT on non-business items passed through the business accounts with limited relief where the goods are used partly in the business.
- VAT unrelated to the making of supplies in the course of a business.

2.4 Partial exemption

Where an entity has wholly exempt outputs (such as a bank or financial institution), it cannot reclaim any input tax and is not allowed to register for VAT. (Contrast this with traders who have totally zero-rated outputs, such as farmers, who are allowed to register and obtain a refund of all of their input tax).

However, where a registered trader makes both taxable and exempt supplies, partial exemption applies. A number of schemes exist under which the input tax can be apportioned.

The simplest method is that any input tax wholly attributable to exempt outputs is not deductible, any input tax wholly attributable to taxable supplies is deductible in full and any remaining input tax is apportioned according to the percentage of exempt outputs.

For instance, if 30% of outputs were exempt, the trader would be able to deduct 70% (100% - 30%) of unallocated input tax.

Example: A has total sales of $700,000 before VAT. Purchases total $450,000 excluding VAT. The sales tax rate is 15% and 10% of the sales are exempt. How much VAT does A have to pay?

	$
Output tax (700,000 × 15%) × 90%	94,500
Input tax (450,000 × 15 %) × 90%	(60,750)
Amount payable	33,750

Example: B has total sales of $700,000 before VAT. Purchases total $450,000 excluding VAT. The VAT rate is 15%, 10% of the sales are exempt and 20% of inputs are directly related to these exempt supplies. How much VAT does B have to pay?

	$
Output tax (700,000 × 15%) × 90%	94,500
Input tax (450,000 × 15%) × 80% × 90%*	(48,600)
Amount payable	45,900

*The proportion related to exempt supplies (20%) is deducted and the remaining input tax is apportioned between taxable and exempt supplies.

2.5 Single-stage sales tax

TVA or VAT is a multi-level sales tax ie it is applied at each stage of the sales process, from manufacturer to wholesaler to retailer to customer.

It is also possible to have a single-stage sales tax. In the US there is a state sales tax levied at the point of sale. This tax is not payable until the goods are actually purchased, so it does not appear on any price tags. Tourists are understandably unimpressed when they get to the till and find that they have to pay the amount on the price tag plus x%.

2.6 Incidence/effective incidence

It is important to distinguish between formal and effective incidence. The **incidence** of a tax is on the person or organisation that pays it.

However, while the **formal incidence** of a sales tax is on the registered trader who has to pay it to the government, the **effective incidence** is on the customer who eventually bears the tax burden.

Section summary

- VAT is a multi-stage sales tax. It is chargeable and deductible at different points in the supply chain.
- VAT on sales is output tax. VAT on purchases is input tax.
- In the UK, there are three rates of VAT. These are standard rate, reduced rate and the zero rate.

3 Employee taxation

Introduction

Employees are liable to personal taxation and are responsible for dealing with their own tax liabilities. In the UK employees are taxed under the personal tax regime.

However, many tax regimes require the employer to operate a withholding tax (PAYE in the UK). This means that tax is deducted from the employee's pay and paid over to the government. The employer then reports total pay and tax deducted to the tax authority at the end of the tax year. This system ensures that all employees comply with the tax rules.

If the employee feels that he or she has paid too much tax, it is up to the individual to deal with the tax authority and obtain a refund. The employer merely acts as a tax collector.

3.1 Taxable income

In the UK, an employee is taxed on all income earned from the employment. This includes 'non cash' items (called **benefits in kind**). A list of examples follows.

- Basic pay
- Overtime
- Bonus and allowances
- Commission
- Statutory pay (eg statutory sick pay, statutory maternity pay, statutory paternity pay, statutory adoption pay)
- Redundancy pay
- Holiday pay
- Occupational pensions

3.2 Deductible expenses

Sometimes an employee can claim that expenses were incurred **wholly, exclusively and necessarily**, in the course of his or her employment. These expenses are then deductible for tax purposes, eg professional subscriptions, business travel, charitable donations and contributions to pension plans.

3.3 Tax codes

In order to make sure that benefits are taxed or expenses are claimed correctly, in the UK the tax authorities issue a tax code. This shows the amount of tax-free pay an employee can earn before paying tax. The employer is given the code and deducts tax accordingly. The employee is sent a detailed notice of how the tax code is calculated. If the employee feels that the code is wrong, it is up to the employee to contact the tax authorities and sort it out. The employer is purely a tax collector.

While placing a burden on employers, this system has major advantages for the government:

- It allows the tax to be collected earlier than would be the case if it were assessed on the employee's earnings at the end of the year.
- The costs of administering the system are borne by employers, rather than by the government.
- It greatly reduces the risks of default or late payment, helping government to minimise the tax gap.

It also makes tax payment easier for individuals, who do not have to deal with a large bill once or twice a year.

3.4 Social security contributions

Some taxes are called **social security** contributions because, in theory, they are used to pay for social security items such as pensions. In fact, the money raised is used as part of the general tax revenue. However, it is politically more acceptable to raise social security contributions than to raise taxes. For example, the UK government added a 1% social security levy to pay for hospitals and their needs. In the UK the social security contribution is National Insurance. It is paid by both the employee and the employer.

Section summary

Employee taxation is personal tax; the employer acts as a tax collector.

4 International taxation

Introduction

This section introduces some key concepts in international taxation. Business is now conducted on a far more global basis than it was twenty or even just ten years ago. Advances in technology, and in particular the growth of internet trading has meant that company residence is no longer just a concern for large conglomerates.

4.1 Corporate residence

As an example, consider the case of a company incorporated in Jersey in the British Channel Islands. Jersey has its independent tax authority and is a 'tax haven' because of its low tax rates. Usually the UK authorities will accept that the company is resident in Jersey, provided its **place of management** is also in Jersey. However if the company is run from offices in London, all board meetings take place in London and, in general, its place of management is in London, then the UK tax authorities will consider the company resident in the UK, not Jersey.

4.2 Taxable presence

A company does not need to be resident in a country in order to establish a **taxable presence** there. It may set up an **overseas subsidiary** or it may trade through a **branch**. However because the subsidiary or branch are resident in the foreign country, their profits will be taxable in that country. This may mean the company is taxed twice on its income, once in the overseas branch and once when profits are transferred to the parent.

A business trading abroad will have to decide whether it should do so through a subsidiary or a foreign branch. This decision will not be made principally on the basis of tax considerations, but the following tax issues apply:

- the holding company is liable to tax on foreign dividends received, while money transferred from a branch will not be treated as a dividend
- losses made by a non-resident subsidiary are not available for group relief
- the entity will be subject to capital gains tax on any capital gains made by a branch. This will not normally apply to capital gains made by a subsidiary
- the tax authorities will look carefully at transfer pricing arrangements between parent and foreign subsidiary, as this could be used to transfer profits abroad

4.3 Withholding taxes

4.3.1 Payments affected

If a company makes payments to an individual or another company resident in a different tax jurisdiction, it may have to pay **withholding tax** to the tax authority of its own jurisdiction.

The reason for this is to stop companies paying all their earnings abroad and then stopping trading without paying any tax to the tax authorities of the country where they are resident. Therefore the local tax authority will take a payment on account of the final tax liability by deducing at source a withholding tax from all payments sent abroad. The withholding tax can be as low as 5% or as high as 40%.

Payments affected are usually the following.

- Interest payments
- Dividends
- Royalties
- Capital gains accruing to non-residents

4.3.2 Underlying tax

When an entity receives a dividend from a foreign entity, the dividend has been paid out of taxed profits. Under some tax systems, the entity can obtain relief for the tax levied in the foreign country on the amount out of which their dividend was paid. This is referred to as the **underlying tax**.

Section summary

A company is resident in one country, even though it may trade in many countries. Usually a company is resident in the **place of incorporation**. However some tax authorities go on the basis of the **place of management**.

5 Double taxation treaties

Introduction

In order to establish more clearly which tax authority has jurisdiction, countries enter into **double taxation treaties**. These treaties seek to avoid a business having to pay tax twice on its income simply because it deals with two tax authorities. In this chapter we look at these treaties and how they work.

5.1 Double taxation treaties

A double taxation treaty (eg that between the UK and the USA) sets out which tax authority has jurisdiction. So a company incorporated in the UK which trades with the USA will be taxed primarily in the UK. The treaty defines a **permanent establishment** and directs that the business will be taxed in the country where it has its permanent establishment.

Where a double taxation treaty exists, provisions are usually made to reduce withholding taxes, or even to avoid paying withholding tax at all.

Another feature of a double taxation treaty is that where a company pays tax in Country A, but is resident in Country B, the tax authorities of Country B will give relief for the tax paid in Country A.

Example: double taxation relief

Manifold pays tax of $5,000 on profits of $50,000 in Country A. Manifold is resident in Country B and will normally have to pay tax of $10,000 on the same profits. Countries A and B have a double taxation treaty whereby Country B will allow full credit for taxes paid in Country A. Therefore Manifold's tax bill in Country B is reduced by the $5,000 paid in Country A. The result is that Manifold still pays $10,000 tax in total, however it is divided between two different countries.

	$	$
Country A – tax paid	5,000	5,000
Country B – tax due	10,000	
– double taxation relief	(5,000)	
– tax paid	5,000	5,000
		10,000

5.2 Methods of giving relief

The above example shows the method of giving full **deduction** for foreign taxes. This is not the only way of giving double taxation relief.

Relief may be given by **exemption**. In this case, if income is taxed in Country A, then it will not be taxed in Country B.

Another way of giving relief is by **credit**. This usually occurs where the tax rate in Country A is higher than that in Country B. Instead of deducting the full amount of tax paid in Country A, Country B credits the amount it would have paid in Country B, as follows.

	$
Income taxable	10,000
Tax paid in Country A (20%)	2,000
Tax due in Country B (15%)	1,500
Double taxation relief (restricted to 15%)	(1,500)
Tax payable in Country B	NIL

5.3 Branch

An entity may choose to trade in another country by setting up a subsidiary or by trading through a branch. Unlike a subsidiary, a branch is considered to be an overseas operation of the entity.

Therefore, the entity will be taxed on the profits of the branch in the country where the entity is resident. There may also be foreign tax levied on the profits of the branch (in the country where the branch is resident) and these will usually attract double taxation relief.

5.4 OECD Model treaty

The Organisation for Economic Co-operation and Development has published a model tax convention. This can be used as a basis for double taxation treaties between countries.

Under the OECD model, an entity is considered to have residence in the country in which it has a **permanent establishment**.

A permanent establishment includes:

- A place of management (Section 4.1)
- A branch (Section 4.2)
- An office
- A factory
- A workshop
- A mine, well or quarry

Note that this means that residence is determined on the basis of the country where the business is carried on, rather than the country of incorporation, which could be different.

Students do not need to know the OECD model tax convention in detail. However, it does make good background reading and students may like to access the document by using the following link: **http://www.oecd.org/dataoecd/52/34/1914467.pdf**

5.5 Double residence

An entity will be liable for corporate income tax in the country in which it is resident. It can deemed to be resident either by having its place of management and control in the country or by having been incorporated in the country.

An entity incorporated in one country and managed and controlled in another, can thus face the problem of double residence. It is taxable in two countries. This is resolved under the provisions of double tax treaties, based on the OECD model.

5.6 Other OECD projects

The OECD **Forum on Tax Administration** encourages discussion between tax administrations. By promoting the sharing of experiences, the forum aims to identify good tax administration practices.

Together the OECD, the IMF and the World Bank have created the **International Tax Dialogue** (ITD). The ITD has stated its main objectives as follows.

- Promote effective international dialogue between participating organisations and governments on taxation, giving all countries a real input into the discussion of tax administration and policy issues
- Identify and share good practices in taxation
- Provide a clearer focus for technical assistance on tax matters
- Avoid duplication of effort in respect of existing activities on tax matters

Section summary

- Double taxation treaties avoid the situation where a company pays tax on income twice because it deals with two different tax authorities.
- Relief may be given by deduction, exemption or credit.

Chapter Roundup

✓ Indirect taxes are not actually paid by the company. Instead the company acts as a **tax collector** on behalf of the government.

✓ There are two types of indirect taxes: **unit taxes** and **ad valorem taxes**.

✓ VAT is a multi-stage sales tax. It is chargeable and deductible at different points in the supply chain.

✓ VAT or sales is output tax. VAT on purchases is input tax.

✓ In the UK, there are three rates of VAT. These are standard rate, reduced rate and the zero rate.

✓ Employee taxation is personal tax; the employer acts as a tax collector.

✓ A company is resident in one country, even though it may trade in many countries. Usually a company is resident in the **place of incorporation**. However some tax authorities go on the basis of **place of management**.

✓ Double taxation treaties avoid the situation where a company pays tax on income twice because it deals with two different tax authorities.

✓ Relief may be given by deduction, exemption or credit.

Quick Quiz

1 Value added tax is an example of which kind of tax?

A Unit tax
B Ad valorem tax
C Direct tax
D Income tax

2 Peter is a VAT registered trader. In the quarter to 31 March 20X5 Peter sold goods for $40,000 (excluding VAT) and bought stock to sell for $17,900 (including VAT). Show the VAT figures for his VAT return for this quarter.

3 A withholding tax is:

A tax withheld from the tax authorities ☐

A tax deducted at source before payment of a dividend ☐

4 Name three advantages to government of employee income tax deducted at source by employers.

5 Under the OECD model treaty an entity is considered to have residence in the country in which it has a ………………… …………………

Answers to Quick Quiz

1 B

2

	$
Output tax ($40,000 × 17.5%)	7,000
Input tax ($17,900 × 7/47)*	(2,666)
Net VAT payable	4,334

*17.5/117.5 = 7/47

3 A tax deducted at source before payment of a dividend.

4
- It allows the tax to be collected earlier than would be the case if it were assessed on the employee's earnings at the end of the year.
- The costs of administering the system are borne by employers, rather than by the government.
- It greatly reduces the risks of default or late payment, helping government to minimise the tax gap.

5 Permanent establishment

Answers to Questions

18.1 Sales tax

D

Now try these questions from the Exam Question Bank

Number	Level	Marks	Time
Q1	Examination	5	9 mins
Q4	Examination	5	9 mins

IAS 12: INCOME TAXES

In almost all countries companies are taxed on the basis of their trading income. In some countries this may be called corporation or corporate tax, but we will follow the terminology of IAS 12 *Income taxes* and call it income tax.

In Section 1 we will look briefly at the two main systems for taxing corporate income: the **classical system** and the **imputation system**. Of course, each country will be different in its tax legislation and its method of accounting for taxation may reflect this.

There are two aspects of income tax which must be accounted for: **current tax** and **deferred tax**. These will be discussed in Sections 2 and 3 respectively.

Sections 4 to 7 cover the details of the standard, IAS 12.

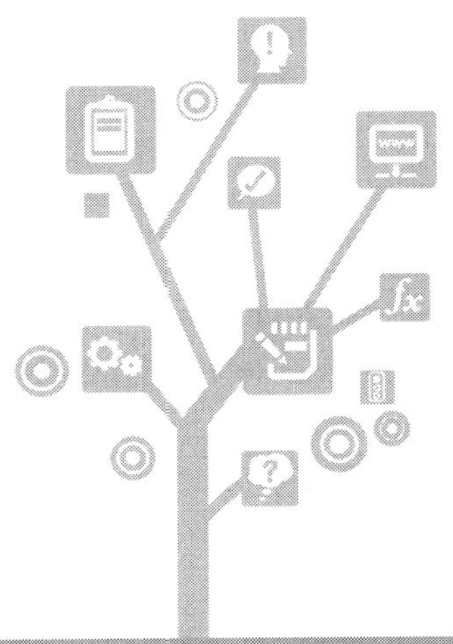

topic list	learning outcomes	syllabus references	ability required
1 Systems of taxing corporate income	A3(a)	A3(i)	application
2 Current tax	A4(a)	A4(i)	application
3 Deferred tax	A4(a)	A4(i)	application
4 Taxable temporary differences	A4(a)	A4(i)	application
5 Deductible temporary differences	A4(a)	A4(i)	application
6 Measurement and recognition of deferred tax	A4(a)	A4(i)	application
7 Presentation and disclosure of taxation	A4(a)	A4(i)	application

1 Systems of taxing corporate income

Introduction

In the rest of this chapter we will be looking at the question of how income tax is allocated between accounting periods. First of all, we will look at two different taxing methods, which are more to do with the **timing of payment** of tax, rather than with what the tax liability will be in the accounts.

1.1 Definitions

The **taxable profits** of an enterprise essentially comprise its net profit before dividends, adjusted for certain items where the tax treatment differs from the accounting treatment.

The amount of tax to which a company is assessed on its profit for an accounting period is called its **tax liability** for that period. In general, an enterprise must pay its tax liability a certain amount of time after the period end (although in some countries, enterprises may have to make monthly or quarterly 'payments on account').

1.2 Classical system

Under the classical system of taxation, company income tax is charged on all of the profits of the enterprise, distributed or not. Dividends are paid out of taxed profits and are then chargeable to personal income tax in the hands of the shareholder. This system is simple to administer but gives rise to double taxation of dividends. Where the shareholder is a **company**, the dividend is not liable to UK corporation tax. If this were not the case, the dividend could end up being taxed three times, as it will be included in income by the receiving company and may then be distributed to its own individual shareholders, who will now pay tax on it.

1.3 Imputation system

Under the imputation system, the company income tax that has already been paid is **imputed** to the shareholder as a tax credit. He pays income tax on the dividend but deducts the tax credit. This avoids the problem of double taxation.

The shareholder receives the net dividend. He is taxed on the gross dividend (amount received plus tax credit) and the tax credit is then deducted from his liability.

1.3.1 Partial imputation system

It is also possible to have a system of **partial imputation**, where the taxpayer receives a tax credit of only part of the underlying company income tax.

Some tax jurisdictions operate a **split rate system** in which distributed profits are taxable at a lower rate than retained profits. This can function under the classical, imputation or partial imputation system.

1.3.2 Split rate systems

Split rate systems charge a lower rate of income tax on distributed profits than on retained profits. This avoids double taxation of dividends.

Example: classical vs imputation system

Cadis Co supplies the following information.

	$
Year to 30 June 20X8	
Taxable profits	100,000
Dividend paid for the year (net)	24,500

The corporate income tax rate is 30% and shareholders pay income tax at 40% on dividends received.

Required

Calculate the total tax payable by Cadis Co and its shareholders as at 30 June 20X8 under:

(a) the classical system,
(b) the imputation system; and
(c) a partial imputation system where a tax credit of 25% is allowed.

Solution

(a) **Classical system**

	$
Corporate income tax paid by Cadis Co (100,000 × 30%)	30,000
Tax on dividends paid by shareholders (24,500 × 40%)	9,800
Total tax paid	39,800

(b) **Imputation system**

	$	$
Corporate income tax paid by Cadis Co		30,000
Shareholder:		
Net dividend received	24,500	
Tax credit (24,500 × 30/70)	10,500	
Gross dividend	35,000	
Tax at 40%	14,000	
Less tax credit	(10,500)	
		3,500
Total tax paid		33,500

(c) **Partial imputation system**

	$	$
Corporate income tax paid by Cadis Co		30,000
Shareholder:		
Net dividend received	24,500	
Tax credit (25%) (24,500 × 25/75)	8,167	
	32,667	
Tax at 40%	13,067	
Less tax credit	(8,167)	
		4,900
Total tax paid		34,900

Note that under the full imputation system (b), if company tax and income tax on individuals had been at the same rate, the shareholder's tax liability would have been nil. The payment due from shareholders in (b) is 10% of the gross dividend. This represents the difference between the company rate (30%) and the rate payable by individual shareholders (40%).

You can see that the classical system does not encourage the payment of dividends.

Exam alert

In the **exam**, the examiner will lay out in detail what type of tax system is in operation.

Section summary

- There are two main systems of taxing corporate income: **classical** and **imputation**.
- The classical system is much **simpler** but most countries do not use it.
- Obviously, rates of tax and tax rules **vary from country to country**.

2 Current tax

Introduction

Taxation consists of two components: current tax and deferred tax. In this section we will look at current tax. We will look at deferred tax in Section 3.

2.1 Accounting entries

You may have assumed until now that accounting for income tax was a very simple matter for companies. You would calculate the amount of tax due to be paid on the company's taxable profits and you would:

DEBIT	Tax charge (statement of comprehensive income)
CREDIT	Tax liability (statement of financial position)

with this amount.

However, it may take some time to finalise the company's accounts and therefore its tax liability.

Example: The company's tax charge for 20X5 is estimated at $55,000. The following entry is made in the financial statements:

DEBIT	Statement of comprehensive income (tax expense)	$55,000
CREDIT	Statement of financial position (tax payable)	$55,000

When the final tax liability is agreed with the tax authority, the amount payable is $58,000, and this amount is paid and posted as:

DEBIT	Statement of financial position (tax payable)	$58,000
CREDIT	Cash	$58,000

The account on the statement of financial position now has a DR balance of $3,000. This represents an **underprovision** of tax for 20X5. This tax has been paid but not charged to the statement of comprehensive income.

In the accounts for 20X6, this underprovision will be accounted for. If the estimated liability for 20X6 is $60,000, the following entries will be made:

DEBIT	Statement of comprehensive income	$60,000	Being current tax
		$3,000	Being prior year underprovision
CREDIT	Statement of financial position	$63,000	

The statement of financial position will now have a balance of $60,000, being the amount payable for the current year.

Complexities also arise when we consider the future tax consequences of what is going on in the accounts now. This is an aspect of tax called **deferred tax**, which we will look at in the next section.

2.2 IAS 12 Income taxes

The parts relating to current tax are fairly brief, because this is the simple and uncontroversial area of tax.

2.2.1 Definitions

These are some of the definitions given in IAS 12. We will look at the rest later.

KEY TERMS

ACCOUNTING PROFIT. Net profit or loss for a period before deducting tax expense.

TAXABLE PROFIT (TAX LOSS). The profit (loss) for a period, determined in accordance with the rules established by the taxation authorities, upon which income taxes are payable (recoverable).

TAX EXPENSE (TAX INCOME). The aggregate amount included in the determination of net profit or loss for the period in respect of current tax and deferred tax.

CURRENT TAX. The amount of income taxes payable (recoverable) in respect of the taxable profit (tax loss) for a period. *(IAS 12)*

Before we go any further, let us be clear about the difference between current and deferred tax.

(a) **Current tax** is the amount *actually payable* to the tax authorities in relation to the trading activities of the enterprise during the period.

(b) **Deferred tax** is an *accounting measure*, used to match the tax effects of transactions with their accounting impact and thereby produce less distorted results.

You should understand this a little better after working through Section 3.

2.2.2 Recognition of current tax liabilities and assets

IAS 12 requires any **unpaid tax** in respect of the current or prior periods to be recognised as a **liability**.

Conversely, any **excess tax** paid in respect of current or prior periods over what is due should be recognised as an asset.

Question 19.1 Tax charge and tax payable

Learning outcome A4(a)

In 20X8 Darton Co had taxable profits of $120,000. In the previous year (20X7) income tax on 20X7 profits had been estimated as $30,000. Tax is payable at 30%.

Required

Calculate tax payable and the charge for 20X8 if the tax due on 20X7 profits was subsequently agreed with the tax authorities as:

(a) $35,000; or
(b) $25,000.

Any under or over payments are not settled until the following year's tax payment is due.

Taking this a stage further, IAS 12 also requires recognition as an asset of the benefit relating to any tax loss that can be **carried back** to recover current tax of a previous period. This is acceptable because it is probable that the benefit will flow to the entity *and* it can be reliably measured.

Example: tax losses carried back

In 20X7 Eramu Co paid $50,000 in tax on its profits. In 20X8 the company made tax losses of $24,000. The local tax authority rules allow losses to be carried back to offset against current tax of prior years.

Required

Show the tax charge and tax liability for 20X8.

Solution

Tax repayment due on tax losses = 30% × $24,000 = $7,200.

The double entry will be:

DEBIT	Tax receivable (statement of financial position)	$7,200
CREDIT	Tax repayment (statement of comprehensive income)	$7,200

The tax receivable will be shown as an asset until the repayment is received from the tax authorities.

2.2.3 Measurement

Measurement of current tax liabilities (assets) for the current and prior periods is very simple. They are measured at the **amount expected to be paid to (recovered from) the tax authorities**. The tax rates (and tax laws) used should be those enacted (or substantively enacted) by the end of the reporting period.

2.2.4 Recognition of current tax

Normally, current tax is recognised as income or expense and included in the net profit or loss for the year, except in two cases.

(a) Tax arising from a **business combination** which is an acquisition is treated differently (not relevant for this syllabus).

(b) Tax arising from a transaction or event which is recognised **directly in equity** (in the same or a different period).

The rule in (b) is logical. If a transaction or event is charged or credited directly to equity, rather than to the statement of comprehensive income, then the related tax should be also. An example of such a situation is where, under IAS 8, an adjustment is made to the **opening balance of retained earnings** due to either a change in accounting policy that is applied retrospectively, or to the correction of a material error.

2.2.5 Presentation

In the statement of financial position, **tax assets and liabilities** should be shown separately from other assets and liabilities.

Current tax assets and liabilities can be **offset**, but this should happen only when certain conditions apply.

(a) The entity has a **legally enforceable right** to set off the recognised amounts.

(b) The entity intends to settle the amounts on a **net basis**, or to realise the asset and settle the liability at the same time.

The **tax expense (income)** related to the profit or loss should be shown in the statement of comprehensive income.

The **disclosure requirements** of IAS 12 are extensive and we will look at these later in the chapter.

Section summary

- Taxation consists of two components: current and deferred tax.
- IAS 12 covers both current and deferred tax.
- Current tax is the amount actually payable to the tax authorities in relation to the trading activities of the entity during the period.

3 Deferred tax

Introduction

Deferred tax is an accounting measure used to match the tax effects of transactions with their accounting impact. It is quite complex so read this section carefully working through all the examples.

Exam alert

Students invariably find deferred tax very confusing. You are unlikely to be asked any very complicated questions on deferred tax in this paper, so concentrate on understanding and being able to explain the purpose of deferred tax and to carry out basic calculations.

3.1 What is deferred tax?

When a company recognises an asset or liability, it expects to **recover or settle the carrying amount** of that asset or liability. In other words, it expects to sell or use up assets, and to pay off liabilities. What happens if that recovery or settlement is likely to make future tax payments larger (or smaller) than they would otherwise have been if the recovery or settlement had no tax consequences? In these circumstances, IAS 12 requires companies to recognise a **deferred tax liability** (or **deferred tax asset**).

3.2 Definitions

Don't worry too much if you don't understand the concept of deferred tax yet; things should become clearer as you work through this section. First of all, here are the definitions relating to deferred tax given in IAS 12.

KEY TERMS

DEFERRED TAX LIABILITIES are the amounts of income taxes payable in future periods in respect of taxable temporary differences.

DEFERRED TAX ASSETS are the amounts of income taxes recoverable in future periods in respect of:

- Deductible temporary differences
- The carry forward of unused tax losses
- The carry forward of unused tax credits

TEMPORARY DIFFERENCES are differences between the carrying amount of an asset or liability in the statement of financial position and its tax base. Temporary differences may be either:

- TAXABLE TEMPORARY DIFFERENCES, which are temporary differences that will result in taxable amounts in determining taxable profit (tax loss) of future periods when the carrying amount of the asset or liability is recovered or settled

- DEDUCTIBLE TEMPORARY DIFFERENCES, which are temporary differences that will result in amounts that are deductible in determining taxable profit (tax loss) of future periods when the carrying amount of the asset or liability is recovered or settled

The TAX BASE of an asset or liability is the amount attributed to that asset or liability for tax purposes.

(IAS 12)

We need to look at some of these definitions in more detail.

3.3 Tax base

We can expand on the definition given above by stating that the **tax base of an asset** is the amount that will be deductible for tax purposes against any taxable economic benefits that will flow to the entity when it recovers the carrying value of the asset. Where those economic benefits are not taxable, the tax base of the asset is the same as its carrying amount.

Question 19.2 — Tax base (1)

Learning outcome A4(a)

State the tax base of each of the following assets.

(a) A machine cost $10,000. For tax purposes, depreciation of $3,000 has already been deducted in the current and prior periods and the remaining cost will be deductible in future periods, either as depreciation or through a deduction on disposal. Revenue generated by using the machine is taxable, any gain on disposal of the machine will be taxable and any loss on disposal will be deductible for tax purposes.

(b) Interest receivable has a carrying amount of $1,000. The related interest revenue will be taxed on a cash basis.

(c) Trade receivables have a carrying amount of $10,000. The related revenue has already been included in taxable profit (tax loss).

(d) A loan receivable has a carrying amount of $1m. The repayment of the loan will have no tax consequences.

In the case of a **liability**, the tax base will be its carrying amount, less any amount that will be deducted for tax purposes in relation to the liability in future periods. For revenue received in advance, the tax base of the resulting liability is its carrying amount, less any amount of the revenue that will *not* be taxable in future periods.

Question 19.3 — Tax base (2)

Learning outcome A4(a)

State the tax base of each of the following liabilities.

(a) Current liabilities include accrued expenses with a carrying amount of $1,000. The related expense will be deducted for tax purposes on a cash basis.

(b) Current liabilities include interest revenue received in advance, with a carrying amount of $10,000. The related interest revenue was taxed on a cash basis.

(c) Current liabilities include accrued expenses with a carrying amount of $2,000. The related expense has already been deducted for tax purposes.

(d) Current liabilities include accrued fines and penalties with a carrying amount of $100. Fines and penalties are not deductible for tax purposes.

(e) A loan payable has a carrying amount of $1m. The repayment of the loan will have no tax consequences.

IAS 12 gives the following examples of circumstances in which the carrying amount of an asset or liability will be **equal to its tax base**.

- **Accrued expenses** which have already been deducted in determining an enterprise's current tax liability for the current or earlier periods.
- A **loan payable** is measured at the amount originally received and this amount is the same as the amount repayable on final maturity of the loan.
- **Accrued expenses** which will never be deductible for tax purposes.
- **Accrued income** will never be taxable.

3.4 Temporary differences

You may have found the definition of temporary differences somewhat confusing. Remember that accounting profits form the basis for computing **taxable profits**, on which the tax liability for the year is calculated; however, accounting profits and taxable profits are different. There are two reasons for the differences.

(a) **Permanent differences**. These occur when certain items of revenue or expense are excluded from the computation of taxable profits (for example, entertainment expenses may not be allowable for tax purposes).

(b) **Temporary differences**. These occur when items of revenue or expense are included in both accounting profits and taxable profits, but not for the same accounting period. For example, an expense which is allowable as a deduction in arriving at taxable profits for 20X7 might not be included in the financial accounts until 20X8 or later. In the long run, the total taxable profits and total accounting profits will be the same (except for permanent differences) so that timing differences originate in one period and are capable of reversal in one or more subsequent periods. Deferred tax is the tax attributable to **temporary differences.**

The distinction made in the definition between **taxable temporary differences** and **deductible temporary differences** can be made clearer by looking at the explanations and examples given in the standard and its appendices.

Exam skills

You should understand the difference between **permanent and temporary differences**.

Section summary

- Deferred tax is an **accounting device**. It does *not* represent tax payable to the tax authorities.
- The **tax base** of an asset or liability is the value of that asset or liability for tax purposes.
- Deferred tax is the tax attributable to **temporary differences**.

4 Taxable temporary differences

Introduction

In this section we will see how deferred tax assets and liabilities arise from taxable and deductible temporary differences.

KEY POINT

The rule to remember is that:

'All taxable temporary differences give rise to a deferred tax liability.'

4.1 Examples

The following are examples of circumstances that give rise to taxable temporary differences.

(a) **Interest revenue** received in arrears and included in accounting profit on the basis of time apportionment. It is included in taxable profit, however, on a cash basis.

(b) **Depreciation** of an asset is accelerated for tax purposes. When new assets are purchased, allowances may be available against taxable profits which exceed the amount of depreciation chargeable on the assets in the financial accounts for the year of purchase.

(c) **Development costs** which have been capitalised will be amortised in the statement of comprehensive income, but they were deducted in full from taxable profit in the period in which they were incurred.

Try to **understand the reasoning** behind the recognition of deferred tax liabilities on taxable temporary differences.

(a) When an **asset is recognised**, it is expected that its carrying amount will be recovered in the form of economic benefits that flow to the entity in future periods.

(b) If the carrying amount of the asset is **greater than** its tax base, then taxable economic benefits will also be greater than the amount that will be allowed as a deduction for tax purposes.

(c) The difference is therefore a **taxable temporary difference** and the obligation to pay the resulting income taxes in future periods is a **deferred tax liability**.

(d) As the entity recovers the carrying amount of the asset, the taxable temporary difference will **reverse** and the entity will have taxable profit.

(e) It is then probable that economic benefits will flow from the entity in the form of **tax payments**, and so the recognition of all deferred tax liabilities (except those excluded above) is required by IAS 12.

Example: taxable temporary differences

A company purchased an asset costing $1,500. At the end of 20X8 the carrying amount is $1,000. The cumulative depreciation for tax purposes is $900 and the current tax rate is 25%.

Required

Calculate the deferred tax liability for the asset.

Solution

Firstly, what is the tax base of the asset? It is $1,500 – $900 = $600.

In order to recover the carrying value of $1,000, the entity must earn taxable income of $1,000, but it will only be able to deduct $600 as a taxable expense. The entity must therefore pay income tax of $400 × 25% = $100 when the carrying value of the asset is recovered.

The entity must therefore recognise a deferred tax liability of $400 × 25% = $100, recognising the difference between the carrying amount of $1,000 and the tax base of $600 as a taxable temporary difference.

4.2 Timing differences

Some temporary differences are often called **timing differences**, when income or expense is included in accounting profit in one period, but is included in taxable profit in a different period. The main types of taxable temporary differences which are timing differences and which result in deferred tax liabilities are included in the examples given above.

- **Interest received** which is accounted for on an accruals basis, but which for tax purposes is included on a cash basis.
- **Accelerated depreciation** for tax purposes.
- Capitalised and amortised **development costs**.

Question 19.4 — Current and deferred tax

Learning outcome A4(a)

Jonquil Co buys equipment for $50,000 and depreciates it on a straight line basis over its expected useful life of five years. For tax purposes, the equipment is depreciated at 25% per annum on a straight line basis. Tax losses may be carried back against taxable profit of the previous five years. In year 20X0, the entity's taxable profit was $25,000. The tax rate is 40%.

Required

Assuming nil profits/losses after depreciation in years 20X1 to 20X5 show the current and deferred tax impact in years 20X1 to 20X5 of the acquisition of the equipment.

Exam alert

Questions on deferred tax in your exam will not be complex and will probably just be on depreciation/tax depreciation. So make sure you understand the question above.

Section summary

- With one or two exceptions, all taxable temporary differences give rise to a **deferred tax liability**.
- Many taxable temporary differences are **timing differences**.
- Timing differences arise when income or an expense is included in accounting profit in one period, but in taxable profit in a **different period**.

5 Deductible temporary differences

Introduction

In this section we look at what deductible temporary differences are, and how they give rise to a deferred tax asset.

5.1 Definition

Referring again to the key point given in Section 4 above.

'All deductible temporary differences give rise to a deferred tax asset.'

There is a proviso, however. The deferred tax asset must also satisfy the **recognition criteria** given in IAS 12. This is that a deferred tax asset should be recognised for all deductible temporary differences to the extent that it is **probable that taxable profit will be available** against which it can be utilised. This is an application of prudence. Before we look at this issue in more detail, let us consider some examples of deductible temporary differences.

5.2 Deductible temporary differences

(a) **Retirement benefit costs** (pension costs) are deducted from accounting profit as service is provided by the employee. They are not deducted in determining taxable profit until the entity pays either retirement benefits or contributions to a fund. (This may also apply to similar expenses.)

(b) **Accumulated depreciation** of an asset in the financial statements is greater than the accumulated depreciation allowed for tax purposes up to the balance sheet date.

(c) **Research costs** (or organisation/other start-up costs) are recognised as an expense for accounting purposes but are not deductible against taxable profits until a later period.

(d) Income is **deferred** in the statement of financial position, but has already been included in taxable profit in current/prior periods.

Example: deductible temporary differences

Pargatha Co recognises a liability of $10,000 for accrued product warranty costs on 31 December 20X7. These product warranty costs will not be deductible for tax purposes until the entity pays claims. The tax rate is 25%.

Required

State the deferred tax implications of this situation.

Solution

What is the tax base of the liability? It is nil (carrying amount of $10,000 less the amount that will be deductible for tax purposes in respect of the liability in future periods).

When the liability is settled for its carrying amount, the entity's future taxable profit will be reduced by $10,000 and so its future tax payments by $10,000 × 25% = $2,500.

The difference of $10,000 between the carrying amount ($10,000) and the tax base (nil) is a deductible temporary difference. The entity should therefore recognise a deferred tax asset of $10,000 × 25% = $2,500 **provided that** it is probable that the entity will earn sufficient taxable profits in future periods to benefit from a reduction in tax payments.

Section summary

- Deductible temporary differences give rise to a **deferred tax asset**.
- **Prudence** dictates that deferred tax assets can only be recognised when **sufficient future taxable profits** exist against which they can be utilised.

6 Measurement and recognition of deferred tax

Introduction

This short section examines the measurement and recognition of deferred tax.

6.1 Changes in tax rates

IAS 12 requires deferred tax assets and liabilities to be measured at the tax rates expected to apply in the period **when the asset is realised or liability settled**, based on tax rates and laws enacted (or substantively enacted) at the end of the reporting period. This is referred to as the **liability method**.

Example: tax rates

Suppose that Girdo Co begins trading on 1 January 20X7. In its first year it makes profits of $5m, the depreciation charge is $1m and the tax allowances on those assets is $1.5m. The rate of income tax is 30%.

Solution

The tax liability is $1.35m, but the debit in the statement of comprehensive income is increased by the deferred tax liability of 30% × $0.5m = $150,000. The total charge to the statement of comprehensive income is therefore $1.5m which is an effective tax rate of 30% on accounting profits (ie 30% × $5.0m).

6.2 Why do we recognise deferred tax?

(a) Adjustments for deferred tax are made in accordance with the **accruals concept** and in accordance with the definition of a **liability** in the Framework, ie a past event has given rise to an obligation in the form of increased taxation which will be payable in the future. The amount can be reliably estimated. A deferred tax asset similarly meets the definition of an **asset**.

(b) If the future tax consequences of transactions are not recognised, profit can be overstated, leading to overpayment of dividends and distortion of share price and EPS.

Section summary

- The liability method is where deferred assets and liabilities are measured at the tax rates expected to apply in the period when the asset is realised or liability settled.

7 Presentation and disclosure of taxation

Introduction

IAS 12 contains rules for comprehensive presentation and disclosure of taxation items. In this section we look at the key ones.

7.1 Presentation of tax assets and liabilities

These should be **presented separately** from other assets and liabilities in the statement of financial position. Deferred tax assets and liabilities should be distinguished from current tax assets and liabilities.

In addition, deferred tax assets/liabilities should *not* be classified as current assets/ liabilities, where an entity makes such as distinction.

7.2 Presentation of tax expense

The tax expense or income related to the profit or loss from ordinary activities should be presented in the statement of comprehensive income.

7.3 Disclosure

As you would expect, the major components of tax expense or income should be disclosed separately.

These will generally include the following.

(a) **Current tax expense** (income)

(b) Any adjustments recognised in the period for **current tax of prior periods** (ie for over/under statement in prior years)

(c) Amount of **deferred tax expense (income)** relating to the origination and reversal of **temporary differences**

(d) Tax expense relating to discontinued operations

Example of tax presentation

Alpha has a balance brought forward on current tax of $5,000,000. Tax paid during the period was $4,900,000 and the provision for the period is $3,000,000.

Alpha also has a balance brought forward on deferred tax of $2,600,000. The charge to the statement of comprehensive income for the period is $400,000.

Draw up the current and deferred tax accounts for the accounting period and show the disclosure in the statement of comprehensive income and statement of financial position.

Solution

CURRENT TAX

	$		$
Bank account	4,900,000	Bal b/f	5,000,000
Bal c/f	3,000,000	Statement of comprehensive income	2,900,000
	7,900,000		7,900,000
		Bal c/f	3,000,000

DEFERRED TAX

	$		$
Bal c/f	3,000,000	Bal b/f	2,600,000
		Statement of comprehensive income	400,000
	3,000,000		3,000,000
		Bal c/f	3,000,000

STATEMENT OF COMPREHENSIVE INCOME (EXTRACT)

Tax (Note 1)	3,300,000

STATEMENT OF FINANCIAL POSITION (EXTRACT)

Current liabilities	
Tax payable	3,000,000
Non current liabilities	
Deferred tax (Note 2)	3,000,000

Notes to the accounts

1 *Tax expense*

	$
Bal b/f	(5,000,000)
Tax paid	4,900,000
Tax for current period	3,000,000
Increase in deferred tax	400,000
Statement of comprehensive income	3,300,000

2 *Deferred tax*

	$
Bal b/f	2,600,000
Increase in period	400,000
	3,000,000

Section summary

- Deferred tax assets and liabilities must be presented separately from other assets and liabilities in the statement of financial position.

Chapter Roundup

- ✓ There are two main systems of taxing corporate income: the classical system and the imputation system.
- ✓ The classical systems is much **simpler** but most countries do not use it.
- ✓ Obviously, rates of tax and tax rules **vary from country to country**.
- ✓ Taxation consists of **two components**: current tax and deferred tax.
- ✓ **IAS 12** covers both current and deferred tax.
- ✓ Current tax is the amount actually payable to the tax authorities in relation to the trading activities of the enterprise during the period.
- ✓ Deferred tax is an **accounting device**. It does *not* represent tax payable to the tax authorities.
- ✓ The tax base of an asset or liability is the value of that asset or liability for tax purposes.
- ✓ Deferred tax is the attributable to **temporary differences**.
- ✓ With one or two expectations, all taxable temporary differences give rise to a **deferred tax liability**.
- ✓ Many taxable temporary differences are **timing differences**.
- ✓ Timing differences arise when income or an expense is included in accounting profit in one period, but in taxable profit in a **different period**.
- ✓ Deductible temporary differences give rise to a **deferred tax asset**.
- ✓ **Prudence** dictates that deferred tax assets can only be recognised when sufficient future taxable profits exist against which they can be utilised.
- ✓ The liability method is where deferred tax assets and liabilities are measured at the tax rates expected to apply in the period when the asset is realised or liability settled.
- ✓ Deferred tax assets and liabilities must be presented separately from other assets and liabilities in the statement of financial position.

Quick Quiz

1 What is the difference between the classical and imputation system of income tax?

2 The tax expense related to the profit from ordinary activities should be shown in the statement of comprehensive income.

True ☐

False ☐

3 Deferred tax liabilities are the amounts of income taxes payable in future periods in respect of ....

4 Give three examples of taxable temporary differences.

5 Current tax is the amount of income tax payable in respect of the .... for a period.

6 Deductible temporary differences give rise to a:

A Deferred tax asset
B Deferred tax liability

Answers to Quick Quiz

1 See Sections 1.2 and 1.3

2 True

3 Taxable temporary differences

4 Examples are:

- Interest revenue
- Depreciation
- Development costs
- Prepayments
- Sale of goods revenue

5 Taxable profit

6 A

Answers to Questions

19.1 Tax charge and tax payable

(a)

	$
Tax due on 20X8 profits ($120,000 × 30%)	36,000
Underpayment for 20X7	5,000
Tax charge and liability	41,000

(b)

	$
Tax due on 20X8 profits (as above)	36,000
Overpayment for 20X7	(5,000)
Tax charge and liability	31,000

Alternatively, the rebate due could be shown separately as income in the statement of comprehensive income and as an asset in the statement of financial position. An offset approach like this is, however, most likely.

19.2 Tax base (1)

(a) The tax base of the machine is $7,000.
(b) The tax base of the interest receivable is nil.
(c) The tax base of the trade receivables is $10,000.
(d) The tax base of the loan is $1m.

19.3 Tax base (2)

(a) The tax base of the accrued expenses is nil.
(b) The tax base of the interest received in advance is nil.
(c) The tax base of the accrued expenses is $2,000.
(d) The tax base of the accrued fines and penalties is $100.
(e) The tax base of the loan is $1m.

19.4 Current and deferred tax

Jonquil Co will recover the carrying amount of the equipment by using it to manufacture goods for resale. Therefore, the entity's current tax computation is as follows.

	20X1	*20X2*	*Year 20X3*	*20X4*	*20X5*
	$	$	$	$	$
Taxable income*	10,000	10,000	10,000	10,000	10,000
Depreciation for tax purposes	12,500	12,500	12,500	12,500	0
Taxable profit (tax loss)	(2,500)	(2,500)	(2,500)	(2,500)	10,000
Current tax expense (income) at 40%	(1,000)	(1,000)	(1,000)	(1,000)	4,000

* ie nil profit plus $50,000 ÷ 5 depreciation add-back.

The entity recognises a current tax asset at the end of years 20X1 to 20X4 because it recovers the benefit of the tax loss against the taxable profit of year 20X0.

The temporary differences associated with the equipment and the resulting deferred tax asset and liability and deferred tax expense and income are as follows.

	20X1	*20X2*	*Year 20X3*	*20X4*	*20X5*
	$	$	$	$	$
Carrying amount	40,000	30,000	20,000	10,000	0
Tax base	37,500	25,000	12,500	0	0
Taxable temporary difference	2,500	5,000	7,500	10,000	0
Opening deferred tax liability	0	1,000	2,000	3,000	4,000
Deferred tax expense (income): bal fig	1,000	1,000	1,000	1,000	(4,000)
Closing deferred tax liability @ 40%	1,000	2,000	3,000	4,000	0

The entity recognises the deferred tax liability in years 20X1 to 20X4 because the reversal of the taxable temporary difference will create taxable income in subsequent years. The entity's income statement is as follows.

	20X1	*20X2*	*Year 20X3*	*20X4*	*20X5*
	$	$	$	$	$
Income	10,000	10,000	10,000	10,000	10,000
Depreciation	10,000	10,000	10,000	10,000	10,000
Profit before tax	0	0	0	0	0
Current tax expense (income)	(1,000)	(1,000)	(1,000)	(1,000)	4,000
Deferred tax expense (income)	1,000	1,000	1,000	1,000	(4,000)
Total tax expense (income)	0	0	0	0	0
Net profit for the period	0	0	0	0	0

Now try these questions from the Exam Question Bank

Number	Level	Marks	Time
Q2	Examination	5	9 mins
Q3	Examination	5	9 mins
Q5	Examination	5	9 mins
Q21	Examination	30	54 mins
Q24	Examination	10	18 mins

OBJECTIVE TEST QUESTION AND ANSWER BANK

1 A company makes an accounting profit of $300,000 during the year. This includes non-taxable income of $50,000 and book depreciation of $30,000. In addition, expenses of $25,000 are disallowable for tax purposes. If the tax allowable depreciation totals $24,000, what is the taxable profit?

A $279,000
B $281,000
C $319,000
D $321,000

2 A company has sales of $200,000, excluding sales tax, in a period. Its purchases, excluding sales tax, total $150,000. It has no zero-rated sales but 20% of its purchases are zero-rated. Sales tax is 17.5%. What is the sales tax payable for the period?

A $7,447
B $8,750
C $14,000
D $29,750

3 Define the accruals basis of accounting in no more than 35 words.

4 When carrying out an audit an external auditor must satisfy himself of a number of matters. Identify which one of the following is not one of those matters?

A The accounts have been prepared by a qualified accountant
B Adequate accounting records have been kept
C The accounts have been prepared in accordance with the legislation
D The accounts are in agreement with accounting records

5 According to the IASB *Framework* the qualitative characteristics of financial statements are

A Understandability, consistency, reliability and going concern
B Understandability, prudence, reliability and relevance
C Understandability, relevance, reliability and comparability
D Prudence, consistency, relevance and accruals

6 T purchases production machinery costing $200,000 and having an estimated useful life of 20 years with a residual value of $4,000. After being in use for 6 years the remaining useful life of the machinery is revised and estimated to be 25 years, with an unchanged residual value. The annual depreciation charge after these events is $....................

7 Fill in the two series of missing words.

An asset is a resource controlled by an entity as a result of .... and from which .... are expected to flow to the entity.

8 IAS 37 *Provisions, contingent liabilities and contingent assets* requires that material contingencies, other than those where the probability of the outcome is remote, existing at the end of the reporting period should be treated as follows.

A Contingent assets and contingent liabilities must always be either accrued or disclosed in the financial statements

B Contingent liabilities must always be accrued and contingent assets must always be disclosed in the financial statements

C Contingent liabilities must always be either accrued or disclosed and contingent assets must always be disclosed in the financial statements

D Neither contingent assets nor contingent liabilities can be accrued in the financial statements

9 A company purchases a new machine and the costs involved in this are given below.

	$
Purchase price	680,000
Delivery costs	30,000
Installation costs	80,000
Cleaning costs after first production run	4,000

At what figure would the machine initially be included in the statement of financial position?
$......................

10 Which of the following is a source of tax rules?

A International accounting standards
B Local company legislation
C Local tax legislation
D Domestic accounting practice

11 H has prepared its financial statements for the year ending 30 June 20X8. On 15 July a major fraud was uncovered by the auditors which had taken place during the year to 30 June. On 31 July the company made a large loan stock issue which has significantly increased the company's gearing level.

In accordance with IAS 10 *Events after the reporting period*, how should the two events be treated in the financial statements?

	Fraud	*Loan stock issue*
A	Accrued in accounts	Disclosed in notes
B	Accrued in accounts	Accrued in accounts
C	Disclosed in notes	Disclosed in notes
D	Disclosed in notes	Accrued in accounts

12 F. Co. estimates its tax due for the year ended 30 June 20X8 to be $520,000. Tax for the year ended 30 June 20X7 was estimated at $475,000 and eventually settled at $503,000. A taxable temporary difference of $76,000 has arisen during the year due to accelerated tax allowances. The tax rate is 30%.

What is the tax charge in the statement of comprehensive income for the year ended 30 June 20X8?

A $520,000
B $542,800
C $548,000
D $570,800

13 According to IAS 36 *Impairment of assets* what is the recoverable amount of a non-current asset?

A Net selling price
B Value in use
C The higher of net selling price and value in use
D The lower of net selling price and value in use

14 Which of the following types of research and development expenditure must be written off in the year it is incurred?

A Market research costs confirming the ultimate commercial viability of a product
B Legal costs in connection with registration of a patent
C Costs of searching for possible alternative products
D Costs of research work which are to be reimbursed by a customer

15 If an auditor believes an item in the financial statements is materially misstated and he considers that the effect on the financial statements is *material,* but not *pervasive*, what type of audit report would be issued?

A Unqualified report
B Qualified report
C Disclaimer of opinion
D Adverse opinion

16 Which of the following statements are true with regards to an ethical code.

1 A code based on a set of principles rather than rules is more flexible in a rapidly changing environment

2 The CIMA *Code of ethics for professional accountants* is principles based

3 A code based on a set of rules requires accountants to evaluate and address threats to independence

A 2 only
B 1 and 2 only
C 2 and 3 only
D 1, 2 and 3

17 A provision for the cost of removing pollution arising from a company's operations should be recognised if?

A The accounts would reveal an understated net profit figure without the provision

B The directors recognise that there is a legal or constructive obligation to remove the pollution by spending money in the future

C Other companies in the same industry have recognised similar provisions

D The company auditors instruct the directors to set up a provision.

18 According to IAS 36 *Impairment of assets*, how often should assets be tested for impairment?

A Every year
B Every 3 years
C Every time non-current assets are revalued
D When there is an indication that impairment may have occurred

19 G has revalued one of its buildings to $1,200,000 at 31 December 20X8. The building was purchased 8 years ago at a cost of $840,000 and is being depreciated over a period of 40 years.

The depreciation charge for the year ending 31 December 20X9 will be $.......................

20 Given below are details of one of S's construction contracts.

	$
Costs incurred to date	240,000
Estimated costs to completion	280,000
Progress payments invoiced	280,000
Total contract price	680,000

The contract is estimated to be 45% complete.

What figure would appear on the statement of financial position for the gross amount due from customers? $ ....

21 According to IAS 24 Related party disclosures, which of the following would not be a related party of Chen Co?

A An associated undertaking of Chen Co
B The managing director of Chen Co's parent company
C A company in which Chen Co holds a 10% investment
D Chen Co's pension fund for its employees

22 State the definition of a non-adjusting event in no more than twenty-five words.

23 Define a provision in no more than ten words.

24 Which of the following does not accurately describe '*true and fair view*'?

A It is a dynamic concept that evolves in response to changes in accounting and business practice

B Even reasonable business people and accountants may not share a consensus as to the degree of accuracy and completeness required

C Courts are likely to examine the meanings of the word 'true' and the word 'fair' in interpreting the meaning of 'true and fair'

D Courts are likely to look to the ordinary practices of professional accountants

25 A company is resident in Country Z. It has a branch in Country Y. The branch has taxable profits of $100,000, on which tax of $5,000 is paid. The tax rate in Country Z is 20% and there is a double taxation treaty between Countries Y and Z that allows tax relief on the full deduction basis. If the company has total taxable profits including those of the branch of $200,000, how much tax will it pay in Country Z?

A $20,000
B $25,000
C $35,000
D $40,000

26 Where is employee tax recorded in a set of financial statements?

A Charged to employee costs in the statement of comprehensive income
B Not included in the financial statements at all
C Included as a payable in the statement of financial position
D Included as a receivable in the statement of financial position

27 A company has sales of $800,000, excluding sales tax, in a period. Its purchases, including sales tax, total $550,000. The rate of sales tax is 10%. If 25% of all sales are zero rated, what is the sales tax payable for the period?

A $10,000
B $20,000
C $22,500
D $30,000

28 A professional accountant in business has an immediate manager who is a very forceful, domineering individual. The manager has stated work in progress has increased by 200% during the current reporting period and instructed the professional accountant to report this level in the financial statements. Evidence is available which indicates that the work in progress has not increased by anywhere near the rate advised by the manager. What kind of threat to compliance with the fundamental principles for accountants in business is this?

29 A company has an accounting profit of $200,000 for the year. This includes depreciation of $25,000 and disallowable expenses of $10,000. If the tax allowable depreciation totals $30,000 and the tax rate is 30%, what is the tax payable?

A $55,500
B $58,500
C $60,000
D $61,500

30 Which of the following must be presented in the income statement according to IAS 1 (revised) *Presentation of Financial Statements*?

1 Tax expense
2 Revenue
3 Finance costs
4 Depreciation expense

A 1, 2, 3 and 4
B 1, 2 and 3 only
C 1, 3 and 4 only
D 2 and 4 only

31 When considering IFRS 5 *Non-current Assets Held for Sale and Discontinued Operations*, which of the following statements is true?

1 A discontinued operation must have been disposed of by the end of the reporting period.

2 A discontinued operation must be a separate major line of business or geographical area of operation.

3 A discontinued operation must be clearly distinguished operationally and for financial reporting purposes.

A 1, 2 and 3
B 1 and 2 only
C 2 and 3 only
D 1 and 3 only

32 Classify the following situations as finance or operating leases.

Situation	Lease type
A company leases machine tools. Legal title is transferred after three years.	
A company leases a photocopier. The present value of minimum lease payments is $2,000 but the fair value of the asset is $10,000.	
A company leases a car for a sales representative for a five-year period, after which the car will have come to the end of its useful economic life.	
A company acquires some equipment made bespoke to its specifications. To sell the equipment to a third party would require substantial modification.	

33 Information from the statement of cash flows and related notes of Gresham Co for the year ended 31 December 20X9 can be found in the table below.

	$
Depreciation	30,000
Profit on sale of non-current assets	5,000
Proceeds from sale of non-current assets	20,000
Purchase of non-current assets	25,000

If the carrying amount of property, plant and equipment was $110,000 on 31 December 20X8, what was it on 31 December 20X9?

A $85,000
B $90,000
C $70,000
D $80,000

34 A company has $500,000 4% redeemable preference shares in issue. According to IAS 32 *Financial Instruments: Presentation*, where will the dividend charge for the year be shown in the income statement?

A Dividends received
B Interest received
C Dividends paid
D Finance costs

35 Define a subsidiary in no more than 15 words.

36 Vaynor Co acquired 100% of the ordinary shares in Weeton Co and Yarlet Co some years ago. Extracts from the statements of financial position of the three companies as on 30 September 20X7 were as follows.

	Vaynor Co	*Weeton Co*	*Yarlet Co*
	$'000	$'000	$'000
Retained earnings	90	40	70

At acquisition Weeton Co had retained losses of $10,000 and Yarlet Co had retained earnings of $30,000.

The consolidated retained earnings of Vaynor Co on 30 September 20X7 were:

A $160,000
B $180,000
C 200,000
D $220,000

37 Milton Co owns all the share capital of Keynes Co. The following information is extracted from the individual company statements of financial position as on 31 December 20X1.

	Milton Co	Keynes Co
	$	$
Current assets	500,000	200,000
Current liabilities	220,000	90,000

Included in Milton Co's purchase ledger is a balance in respect of Keynes Co of $20,000. The balance on Milton Co's account in the sales ledger of Keynes Co is $22,000. The difference between those figures is accounted for by cash in transit.

If there are no other intra-group balances, what is the amount of current assets less current liabilities in the consolidated statement of financial position of Milton Co and its subsidiary?

A $368,000
B $370,000
C $388,000
D $390,000

38 Oxford Co owns 100% of the issued share capital of Cambridge Co, and sells goods to its subsidiary at a profit margin of 20%. At the year end their statements of financial position showed inventories of:

Oxford Co	$290,000
Cambridge Co	$160,000

The inventory of Cambridge Co included $40,000 of goods supplied by Oxford Co and there was inventory in transit from Oxford to Cambridge amounting to a further $20,000. At what amount should inventory be carried in the consolidated statement of financial position?

A $438,000
B $442,000
C $458,000
D $462,000

Using the following information answer questions 39 and 40

Patience Co has a wholly owned subsidiary, Bunthorne Co. During 20X1 Bunthorne Co sold goods to Patience Co for $40,000 which was cost plus 25%. At 31 December 20X1 $20,000 of these goods remained unsold.

39 In the consolidated income statement for the year ended 31 December 20X1 the revenue will be reduced by

A $20,000
B $30,000
C $32,000
D $40,000

40 In the consolidated income statement for the year ended 31 December 20X1 the profit will be reduced by

A $4,000
B $6,000
C $8,000
D $10,000

41 The following figures related to Sanderstead Co and its 100% subsidiary Croydon Co for the year ended 31 December 20X9.

	Sanderstead Co	*Croydon Co*
	$	$
Revenue	600,000	300,000
Cost of sales	(400,000)	(200,000)
Gross profit	200,000	100,000

During the year Sanderstead Co sold goods to Croydon Co for $20,000, making a profit of $5,000.

These goods were all sold by Croydon Co before the year end.

What are the amounts for total revenue and gross profit in the consolidated income statement of Sanderstead Co for the year ended 31 December 20X9?

	Revenue	*Gross profit*
A	$900,000	$300,000
B	$900,000	$295,000
C	$880,000	$300,000
D	$880,000	$295,000

42 Extracts from the income statements of Pik Co and its subsidiaries and Wik Co, its associate, for the year ended 31 March 20X6 are as follows.

	Pik Co (inc subsidiaries)	*Wik Co*
	$'000	$'000
Gross profit	2,900	1,600
Administrative expenses	(750)	(170)
Distribution costs	(140)	(190)
Dividends from Wik Co	20	–
Profit before tax	2,030	1,240
Income tax expense	(810)	(440)
Profit for the year	1,220	800

Pik Co acquired 25% of the ordinary shares in Wik Co on 1 April 20X3 when the retained earnings of Wik Co were $80,000.

At what amount should the profit before tax be shown in the consolidated income statement of Pik Co for the year ended 31 March 20X6?

A $2,010,000
B $2,210,000
C $2,340,000
D $3,270,000

43 Austen Co has owned 100% of Kipling Co and 30% of Dickens Co, an associate, for many years. At 31 December 20X5 the trade receivables and trade payables shown in the individual company statements of financial position were as follows.

	Austen Co	*Kipling Co*	*Dickens Co*
	$'000	$'000	$'000
Trade receivables	50	30	40
Trade payables	30	15	20
Trade payables included amounts owing to			
Austen Co	–	–	–
Kipling Co	2	–	4
Dickens Co	7	–	–
Other suppliers	21	15	16
	30	15	20

The inter-company accounts agreed after taking into account the following.

(1) An invoice for $3,000 posted by Kipling Co on 31 December 20X5 was not received by Austen Co until 2 January 20X6.

(2) A cheque for $6,000 posted by Austen Co on 30 December 20X5 was not received by Dickens Co until 4 January 20X6.

What amount should be shown as trade receivables in the consolidated statement of financial position of Austen Co?

A $75,000
B $79,000
C $87,000
D $115,000

1 B

	$	$
Accounting profit		300,000
Add: depreciation	30,000	
disallowed expenses	25,000	
		55,000
		355,000
Less: non-taxable income	50,000	
tax allowable depreciation	24,000	
		74,000
Taxable profit		281,000

2 C

	$
Output tax (200,000 x 17.5%)	35,000
Input tax ((150,000 x 80%) x 17.5%)	21,000
Payable	14,000

3 The accruals basis of accounting requires that the effects of transactions and other events are recognised when they occur, and they are recorded in the accounting records and reported in the financial statements of the periods to which they relate.

4 A In order to state that the financial statements show a true and fair view the auditor must satisfy himself that the other three matters are valid.

5 C

6 $5,488

	$
Cost	200,000
Depreciation $6 \times \left(\frac{200{,}000 - 4{,}000}{20}\right)$	58,800
NBV end year 6	141,200
Depreciation year 7 $\frac{141{,}200 - 4{,}000}{25}$	$5,488

7 An asset is a resource controlled by an entity as a result of **past transactions or events** and from which **future economic benefits** are expected to flow to the entity.

8 D Probable liabilities should be accrued

Possible liabilities should be disclosed

Contingent assets are only disclosed if they are probable

9 $790,000. The cost to appear initially in the statement of financial position is the cost of getting the machine ready for production. This will include the delivery and installation costs but not the cleaning costs after the first production run.

10 C Local tax legislation forms the basis of local taxation and so is a source of tax rules. The other options are all sources of accounting rules.

11 A The fraud is an adjusting event as it took place during the year to 30 June although it was not discovered until after the year end. The loan stock issue is a non-adjusting event but due to its materiality should be disclosed in the notes.

12 D

	$'000
Estimated charge 20X8	520,000
Underprovision 20X7	28,000
Transfer to deferred tax (76,000 × 30%)	22,800
	570,800

13 C The higher of net selling price and value in use.

14 C Items A and B are costs incurred in the *development* of a product. Note that while market research costs are not normally development costs, they *may be* treated as such when confirming ultimate commercial viability.

C is research and therefore must be written off.

D is work in progress (inventory) which you are being paid to do.

15 B Qualified report. See ISA 705 Modifications to the opinion in the independent auditor's report.

16 B A rules based system tends to remove the need to evaluate, as accountants can just check whether certain rules are being met or not, rather than applying the principles to given situations.

17 B It is the existence of an obligation which creates the need for a provision.

18 D

19 Depreciation charge $= \frac{\$1,200,000}{32 \text{ years}} = \$37,500$

20 $32,000

	$
Costs to date	240,000
Attributable profit (45% × (680 – 240 – 280))	72,000
Progress billings	(280,000)
Gross amount due from customers	32,000

21 C IAS 24 states that two or more parties are related if:

- One party has control of the other
- The parties are subject to common control
- One party has significant influence over the financial and operating policies of the other party
- One party has joint control over the other

A 10% investment in another company does not fall into any of these categories.

22 Non-adjusting events **arise after the end of the reporting period** and concern **conditions** which did **not exist** at that time.

23 A provision is a liability of uncertain timing or amount.

Note. Although the amount is uncertain, it should be susceptible to **measurement** with **sufficient reliability**. Where no reliable estimate can be made, a liability exists which cannot be recognised. Such a liability should be disclosed as a contingent liability.

24 C Courts are **not likely** to examine the individual meanings of the word 'true' and the word 'fair' in interpreting the meaning of 'true and fair'. The courts are likely to use an approach that applies the **concepts implied** by the **expression** '*true and fair*'.

25 C Total tax due is $40,000 ($200,000 x 20%) less double taxation relief for $5,000, leaves $35,000 to pay.

26 C The company acts as a tax collector on behalf of the tax authority. Therefore any tax deducted is put in a payable account until the money is actually paid to the tax authority. The balance on the payable account represents the amount collected but not yet paid over.

27 A

	$
Output tax (800,000 x 75% x 10%)	60,000
Input tax (550,000/110 x 10)	50,000
Payable	10,000

The important point to remember is that zero rated sales are still taxable supplies; they just pay tax at 0%. Therefore input tax does not need to be restricted.

28 Intimidation. The professional accountant is being intimidated by a dominant personality.

29 D

	$	$
Accounting profit		200,000
Add: depreciation	25,000	
disallowed expenses	10,000	
		35,000
		235,000
Less: tax allowable depreciation		30,000
Taxable profit		205,000

Tax payable = $205,000 x 30% = $61,500.

30 B All these items should be shown in the income statement except depreciation which may be disclosed in a note as per IAS 1 (revised)

31 C In order to be classified as discontinued, a component must either have been disposed of or be held for sale (provided that it is highly probable that it will be sold within 12 months of classification.

32

Situation	Lease type
A company leases machine tools. Legal title is transferred after three years.	Finance lease, because title is transferred and the company enjoys the risks and rewards of ownership before-hand.
A company leases a photocopier. The present value of minimum lease payments is $2,000 but the fair value of the asset is $10,000.	Operating lease, as the fair value of the asset is a lot more than the minimum lease payments.
A company leases a car for a sales representative for a five-year period, after which the car will have come to the end of its useful economic life.	Finance lease
A company acquires some equipment made bespoke to its specifications. To sell the equipment to a third party would require substantial modification.	Finance lease

33 B $90,000

NON-CURRENT ASSETS (CARRYING VALUE)

	$		$
Balance b/d	110,000	Depreciation	30,000
Additions	25,000	Disposals (Carrying value)	15,000
		Balance c/d	90,000
	135,000		135,000

34 D Payment of dividends on redeemable preference shares is treated as if it were payment of the finance charge on a redeemable loan.

35 A subsidiary is an entity that is controlled by another entity (known as the parent).

36 B

	$'000
Vaynor Co	90
Weeton Co (40+10)	50
Yarlet Co (70-30)	40
	180

37 D

	Milton Co $'000	*Keynes Co* $'000	*Adjustment* $'000	*Consolidated* $'000
Current assets	500	200	-22+2	680
Current liabilities	(220)	(90)	20	(290)
	280	110		390

38 C

	$'000
Oxford Co	290
Cambridge Co	160
In transit to Cambridge Co	20
Less: PURP ((40+20)x20%)	(12)
	458

39 D Reduce revenue by intra-group sales of $40,000.

40 A Reduce consolidated profit by provision for unrealised profit.

$$20,000 \times \frac{25}{125} = \$4,000$$

41 C

	Sanderstead Co $	*Croydon Co* $	*Adj* $	*Consol* $
Revenue	600,000	300,000	(20,000)	880,000
Cost of sales	(400,000)	(200,000)	20,000	(580,000)
Gross profit				300,000

42 B

	$'000
Pik Co (incl subsidiaries)	
Gross profit	2,900
Less Administrative expenses	(750)
Distribution costs	(140)
Share of profit of associates (25% × 800)	200
	2,210

43 A

	$'000	$'000
Austen Co		50
Kipling Co	30	
Less Intra group (2 + 3)	(5)	
		25
		75

EXAM QUESTION AND ANSWER BANK

What the examiner means

The very important table below has been prepared by CIMA to help you interpret exam questions.

Learning objectives	Verbs used	Definition
1 Knowledge What are you expected to know	• List • State • Define	• Make a list of • Express, fully or clearly, the details of/facts of • Give the exact meaning of
2 Comprehension What you are expected to understand	• Describe • Distinguish • Explain • Identify • Illustrate	• Communicate the key features of • Highlight the differences between • Make clear or intelligible/state the meaning of • Recognise, establish or select after consideration • Use an example to describe or explain something
3 Application How you are expected to apply your knowledge	• Apply • Calculate/compute • Demonstrate • Prepare • Reconcile • Solve • Tabulate	• Put to practical use • Ascertain or reckon mathematically • Prove with certainty or to exhibit by practical means • Make or get ready for use • Make or prove consistent/compatible • Find an answer to • Arrange in a table
4 Analysis How you are expected to analyse the detail of what you have learned	• Analyse • Categorise • Compare and contrast • Construct • Discuss • Interpret • Prioritise • Produce	• Examine in detail the structure of • Place into a defined class or division • Show the similarities and/or differences between • Build up or compile • Examine in detail by argument • Translate into intelligible or familiar terms • Place in order of priority or sequence for action • Create or bring into existence
5 Evaluation How you are expected to use your learning to evaluate, make decisions or recommendations	• Advise • Evaluate • Recommend	• Counsel, inform or notify • Appraise or assess the value of • Propose a course of action

Guidance in our Practice and Revision Kit focuses on how the verbs are used in questions.

1 Convex — 9 mins

Learning outcome A2(b)

Convex is a limited liability company incorporated in Switzerland. However its board are all English and board meetings are held regularly in London. Head office is in Switzerland but the main accountancy offices are in London and the chairman and the chief executive are based in London.

Required

(a) Where is the place of management of Convex? **(2 marks)**

(b) Would your answer to part (a) change if the following were the case?

(i) The Board are all Swiss nationals?

(ii) Board meetings are held in Switzerland with the main accounts offices in London and the chairman and chief Executive based in Switzerland? **(3 marks)**

(Total = 5 marks)

2 AB — 9 mins

Learning outcomes A4(a), C1(a)

AB has an allotted capital of $350,000 in fully paid 50c ordinary shares. At 31 December 20X6 the following balances were included in the company's statement of financial position.

	$
Estimated income tax liability on 20X6 profits	5,000
Deferred taxation account	29,400
Retained earnings b/f (credit)	43,000

The following information relates to the year ended 31 December 20X7.

(a) Income tax liability for 20X6 was agreed at $3,800 (December), paid January 20X8.

(b) Net profit for 20X7 (before tax) was calculated at $100,000.

(c) Income tax based on the 20X7 profits was estimated at $36,000.

(d) A transfer to the deferred taxation account of $7,000 for 20X7 is to be made in respect of capital allowances in excess of depreciation charges (the entire balance on the deferred tax account being of a similar nature).

Required

Complete the statement of comprehensive income for 20X7 starting with profit before tax and show how the final balances would be included in the statement of financial position at 31 December 20X7. Show the details given in the notes to the accounts.

Assume income tax at 25%. **(5 marks)**

3 Tax and dividends — 9 mins

Learning outcome A3(a)

(a) Company A has an accounting profit of $750,000. This total is after charging book depreciation of $300,000, formation expenses of $15,000 and entertaining expenses of $75,000. The figure also includes government grants received of $25,000.

The tax rate is 25%. Under A's tax regime, government grants are tax-free and formation and entertaining expenses are disallowable. If the tax allowable depreciation is $350,000, calculate the tax due for the current period. **(2 marks)**

(b) Company A has paid a dividend during the accounting period of $1,500,000. It operates in a country where a full imputation system applies. Personal income tax is 30%.

How much tax will be paid by its shareholders? **(3 marks)**

(Total = 5 marks)

4 VAT — 9 mins

Learning outcome A1(e)

A company has sales of $570,000 including VAT. Its purchases for the same period were $300,000 excluding VAT. The sales tax rate is 17.5%. Calculate the tax payable to the tax authorities if 20% of sales are zero-rated but only 15% of its purchases are zero-rated. **(5 marks)**

5 Company tax — 9 mins

Learning outcome A4(a)

J is a retail entity. Its tax rate is 25%. It has current tax payable brought forward from the year ended 30 June 20X4 of $765,000 and deferred tax payable of $200,000.

On 30 June 20X5, the estimated tax charge for the year ended 30 June 20X5 was $976,000. The actual tax charge for the year ended 30 June 20X4 was agreed with the tax authority and settled with a payment of $794,000. The deferred tax payable needs to be increased to $300,000 as at 30 June 20X5.

Required

Prepare the notes in respect of current and deferred tax as they would appear in the statement of comprehensive income and statement of financial position of J for the year ended 30 April 20X5.

(5 marks)

6 Regulatory influences — 9 mins

Learning outcome B1(a)

State three different regulatory influences on the preparation of the published accounts of quoted companies and briefly explain the role of each one. Comment briefly on the effectiveness of this regulatory system.

(5 marks)

7 Accounting standards 9 mins

Learning outcome B1(a)

There are those who suggest that any standard setting body is redundant because accounting standards are unnecessary. Other people feel that such standards should be produced, but by the government, so they are legislated.

Required

Discuss the statement that accounting standards are unnecessary for the purpose of regulating financial statements. **(5 marks)**

8 IASB 9 mins

Learning outcome B1(c)

Consider to what extent the IASB has succeeded in its aims and what problems it still faces.

(5 marks)

9 External auditors 9 mins

Learning outcome B1(g)

Describe the external auditors' responsibilities with respect to the financial statements.

(5 marks)

10 Audit report 9 mins

Learning outcome B1(g)

Explain what is meant by a 'qualified' audit report and describe the differences between a 'qualified' and an 'unqualified' report.

(5 marks)

11 New project 9 mins

Learning outcome B2(c)

A professional accountant in business has recently been put in charge of a new project by the finance director. However, the accountant does not have the required level of expertise for this project. The accountant is uncomfortable carrying out the work and is uncertain about what to say to the finance director.

Required

Identify the ethical issues in this situation and describe the action the accountant should take.

(5 marks)

12 C — 18 mins

Learning outcome C2(a)

C is a civil engineering company. It started work on two construction projects during the year ended 31 December 20X0. The following figures relate to those projects at the end of the reporting period.

	Maryhill bypass	*Rottenrow Centre*
	$'000	$'000
Contract price	9,000	8,000
Costs incurred to date	1,400	2,900
Estimated costs to completion	5,600	5,200
Value of work certified to date	2,800	3,000
Cash received from customer	2,600	3,400

C recognises revenues and profits on construction contracts on the basis of work certified to date.

Required

Calculate the figures which would appear in C's financial statements in respect of these two projects.

(5 marks each)

(Total = 10 marks)

13 IFRS 5 — 9 mins

Learning outcome C2(a)

At 30 November a manufacturing company decided to sell one of its processing plants and steps were taken to locate a buyer. After consultation with a property agent, who advised that prices in the area were expected to rise sharply over the next twelve months, senior management decided to raise the price of the building in anticipation of this. The buyers who were interested have now withdrawn due to the price rise but the directors are confident that in the new year, when property prices rise, they will obtain the price required. In the meantime, the processing plant is continuing to operate and handle customers orders.

At 31 December, will this plant be classified as 'held for sale' under IFRS 5? Explain your answer.

(5 marks)

14 Leases — 9 mins

Learning outcome C2(a)

The following definitions have been taken from the International Accounting Standards Board's *Framework for the Preparation and Presentation of Financial Statements*.

- 'An asset is a resource controlled by the entity as a result of past events and from which future economic benefits are expected to flow to the entity.'
- 'A liability is a present obligation of the entity arising from past events, the settlement of which is expected to result in an outflow from the entity of resources embodying economic benefits.'

IAS 17 *Leases* requires lessees to capitalise finance leases in their financial statements.

Required

Explain how IAS 17's treatment of finance leases applies the definitions of assets and liabilities.

(5 marks)

15 T

54 mins

Learning outcome C1(a)

T is a quoted company which owns a large number of hotels throughout the UK. The company's latest trial balance at 31 December 20X1 is as follows.

	$'000	$'000
Administrative expenses	3,000	
Bank	300	
Payables		1,700
Distribution costs	4,000	
Food purchases	2,100	
Heating and lighting (to be included in cost of sales)	3,000	
Hotel buildings: cost	490,000	
depreciation to date		46,200
Hotel fixtures and fittings: cost	18,000	
depreciation to date		9,400
Loan interest	4,950	
Interim dividend paid	1,000	
Loans, repayable 20X9		110,000
Retained earnings		86,000
Sales of accommodation and food		68,500
Share capital: $1 shares, fully paid		220,000
Inventory as at 31 December 20X0	400	
Taxation	50	
Wages: administrative staff	6,000	
housekeeping and restaurant staff	9,000	
	541,800	541,800

Additional information

(a) During the year the company spent a total of $12m on a new hotel and purchased new fixtures for $7m. These acquisitions have been included in the relevant trial balance totals.

(b) Hotels are to be depreciated by 2 per cent of cost, and fixtures and fittings by 25 per cent of the reducing balance, with a full year's depreciation to be charged in the year of acquisition. Depreciation is charged to cost of sales.

(c) Closing inventories of foodstuffs and other consumables were valued at $470,000 on 31 December 20X1.

(d) The balance on the taxation account is an underprovision remaining after the payment of the estimated income tax liability for the year ended 31 December 20X0. The directors have estimated the income tax liability for the year ended 31 December 20X1 at $10.2m.

(e) T took out a contract on 1 July 20X1 to lease a fleet of refrigerated vans. The lease agreement provided for 6 6-monthly payments in arrears of $60,000. The cash price of the vans would have been $300,000. The payment made in 20X1 has been charged to administrative expenses. T has now been advised that this is a finance lease and that the applicable interest rate is 10%. The vehicles should be depreciated by 20% per annum reducing balance.

(f) During 20X1 T issued 50m new shares at $1.20. The proceeds have all been credited to share capital.

Required

Prepare T's statement of comprehensive income for the year ended 31 December 20X1 and its statement of financial position at that date.

Notes to the accounts are not required.

(30 marks)

16 CEC 9 mins

Learning outcome C2(a)

After its end of year physical inventory count and valuation, the accounts staff of CEC have reached a valuation of $153,699 at cost for total inventories held at the year end.

However, on checking the figures, the chief bookkeeper has come across the following additional facts.

(a) The count includes damaged goods which originally cost $2,885. These could be repaired at a cost of $921 and sold for $3,600.

(b) The count excludes 300 units of item 730052 which were sold to a customer SC on a sale or return basis, at a price of $8 each. The original cost of the units was $5 each. SC has not yet indicated to CEC whether these goods have been accepted, or whether they will eventually be returned.

(c) The count includes 648 units of item 702422. These cost $7.30 each originally but because of dumping on the market by overseas suppliers, a price war has flared up and the unit cost price of the item has fallen to $6.50. The price reduction is expected to be temporary, lasting less than a year or so, although some observers of the market predict that the change might be permanent. CEC has already decided that if the price reduction lasts longer than six months, it will reduce its resale price of the item from $10.90 to about $10.

Required

Calculate the closing inventory figure for inclusion in the annual accounts of CEC, making whatever adjustments you consider necessary in view of items (a) to (c). Explain your treatment of each item.

(5 marks)

17 Plant and equipment 9 mins

Learning outcome C2(a)

A business's plant and equipment account and depreciation account at 31 December 20X8 show the following:

Year of purchase	*Cost*	*Accumulated depreciation*
	$	$
20X5	100,000	80,000
20X6	70,000	42,000
20X7	50,000	20,000
20X8	30,000	6,000
	250,000	148,000

Depreciation is calculated at 20% on a straight line basis with a full year's charge in the year of acquisition and none in the year of disposal.

During 20X9 the following transactions took place:

(a) Purchases of plant and equipment amounted to $150,000
(b) Plant that had been bought in 20X5 for $40,000 was sold for $5,000
(c) Plant that had been bought in 20X7 for $10,000 was damaged and had to be scrapped.

Required

Prepare the following ledger accounts as at 31 December 20X9:

Plant and equipment – cost
– accumulated depreciation
– disposals

(5 marks)

18 IT 9 mins

Learning outcome C2(a)

The accounts of IT at 1 January 20X6 include capitalised development costs of $26,500. During the year ended 31 December 20X6 IT purchased a new business. The consideration paid to the proprietor included $4,800 in respect of goodwill. The company also spent $7,900 in research and $3,500 on development activities.

The directors of IT intend to write off $1,200 in respect of impairment of goodwill. They believe that $22,600 of development costs should be carried forward at 31 December 20X6, in accordance with IAS 38.

Show the ledger accounts for goodwill and research and development in the books of IT.

(5 marks)

19 F 9 mins

Learning outcome C2(a)

F, an engineering company, makes up its financial statements to 31 March in each year. The financial statements for the year ended 31 March 20X1 showed revenue of $3m and trading profit of $400,000.

Before approval of the financial statements by the board of directors on 30 June 20X1 the following events took place.

(a) The financial statements of P for the year ended 28 February 20X1 were received which indicated a permanent decline in that company's financial position. F had bought shares in P some years ago and this purchase was included in unquoted investments at its cost of $100,000. The financial statements received indicated that this investment was now worth only $50,000.

(b) There was a fire at the company's warehouse on 30 April 20X1 when inventory to the value of $500,000 was destroyed. It transpired that the inventory in the warehouse was under-insured by some 50%.

(c) It was announced on 1 June 20X1 that the company's design for tank cleaning equipment had been approved by the major oil companies and this could result in an increase in the annual revenue of some $1m with a relative effect on profits.

Required

You are required to explain how, if at all, items (a) to (c) above should be reflected in the accounts of F for the year ended 31 March 20X1.

(5 marks)

20 B **54 mins**

Learning outcome C1(a)

The draft financial statements for B, a limited liability company, are set out below.

STATEMENT OF COMPREHENSIVE INCOME FOR THE YEAR ENDED 30 SEPTEMBER 20X1

	$'000
Revenue	600
Cost of sales	(410)
Gross profit	190
Profit on sale of non-current asset	10
	200
Depreciation	(30)
Other expenses	(70)
Interest expense	(15)
Profit for the year	85

STATEMENT OF FINANCIAL POSITION AS AT 30 SEPTEMBER

	20X1		*20X0*	
	$'000	$'000	$'000	$'000
Non-current assets (see note)		450		520
Current assets				
Inventory	65		50	
Receivables	80		30	
Bank and cash	30		15	
		175		95
Total assets		625		615
Equity and liabilities				
Share capital		400		400
Retained earnings		145		95
Non-current liability				
Loan		20		100
Current liabilities				
Payables		60		20
		625		615

Notes

The company purchased non-current assets for $40,000 during the year ended 30 September 20X1.

Dividends of $35,000 were paid during the year.

Ignore taxation.

Required

(a) Prepare a statement of cash flows for B for the year ended 30 September 20X1. **(15 marks)**

(b) In the year to 30 September 20X2 B had the following results:

	$'000
Revenue	640
Cost of sales	(400)
Gross profit	240
Depreciation	(30)
Other expenses	(35)
Interest expense	(15)
Profit for the year	160

Notes

1 Interest was paid up to date and the remaining loan paid off

2 There were no purchases or sales of non-current assets

3 $615,000 was received from customers and $390,000 paid to suppliers.

4 Cost of sales was:

	$'000
Opening inventory	65
Purchases	410
Closing inventory	(75)
	400

Required

Prepare the statement of financial position as at 30 September 20X2 **(15 marks)**

(Total = 30 marks)

21 Cat 54 mins

Learning outcome C1(a)

Set out below are the statements of financial position of Cat Co as at 30 June 20X1 and 20X2.

CAT CO
STATEMENT OF FINANCIAL POSITION AS AT 30 JUNE

	20X1		20X2	
	$	$	$	$
Assets				
Non-current assets				
Cost	85,000		119,000	
Depreciation	26,000		37,000	
		59,000		82,000
Current assets				
Inventories	34,000		40,000	
Receivables (trade)	26,000		24,000	
Cash at bank	10,000		13,500	
		70,000		77,500
Total assets		129,000		159,500
Equity and liabilities				
Equity				
Ordinary $1 shares	26,000		28,000	
Share premium	12,000		13,000	
Retained earnings	44,000		70,500	
		82,000		111,500
Non-current liabilities				
10% loan stock		20,000		10,000
Current liabilities				
Payables (trade)	15,000		23,000	
Taxation	12,000		15,000	
		27,000		38,000
Total equity and liabilities		129,000		159,500

Notes

1 No non-current assets were disposed of during the year.
2 Of the 10% loan stock, $10,000 was redeemed at par on 31 December 20X1.
3 Dividends of $13,000 were paid during the year.

Required

(a) Prepare a statement of cash flows for the year to 30 June 20X2, using the format specified in IAS 7. **(18 marks)**

(b) The 20X2 statement of financial position was drafted without taking account of the following adjustments:

(i) Capital allowances were received during 20X2 which exceeded depreciation by $15,000. The tax rate is 30%.

(ii) Inventory valued at $9,000 has been damaged. It can be sold for $6,000 following $2,000 remedial work.

(iii) A provision of $8,000 was made for possible costs following a legal case. This was incorrectly included in trade payables. The case has now been decided and only $3,000 is payable.

Required

Redraft the 20X2 statement of financial position to take account of these adjustments.

Note. This does **not** affect your answer to (a) **(12 marks)**

(Total = 30 marks)

22 ABA 9 mins

Learning outcome C2(a)

The directors of ABA, a limited liability company, are reviewing the draft accounts for the year ended 30 June 20X9. The net profit before tax currently stands at $923,000. The auditors have drawn their attention to the following matters:

(a) An announcement was made on 4 July that one of their customers, IMX, had gone into liquidation. The liquidator is estimating that suppliers will receive 30c in the $. The receivable in ABA's accounts regarding IMX stands at $325,000 at 30 June.

(b) A line of inventory valued at cost of $150,000 has become obsolete. It can only be disposed of for $200,000 via an agent who will require 20% of selling price. Other disposal costs will amount to $25,000.

(c) An outstanding claim for damages by an ex-employee who was injured in the warehouse is likely to amount to $50,000. No provision has been made for this as it was expected to be covered by insurance. However the insurance company are now claiming that certain safety procedures were not in place, rendering the cover invalid.

Required

Explain how each of these issues should be dealt with and show the effect on the net profit before tax. **(5 marks)**

23 L — 9 mins

Learning outcome C2(b)

L, a limited liability company, has the following capital structure:

	$'000
Share capital	
50c ordinary shares (fully paid)	15,000
Share premium	3,000
Retained earnings	27,000
	45,000

The following share issues are made:

(a) A '3 for 2' bonus issue, and then

(b) A '1 for 2' rights issue at 80c.

Show the capital structure following these issues, assuming all rights are taken up. **(5 marks)**

24 International tax — 9 mins

Learning outcome A2(a)

J has an overseas branch L, which made a profit adjusted for tax purposes of $8 million for the year ended 30 June 20X6. This figure is included in the financial statements to 30 June 20X6. Taxable profits of the overseas branch have suffered local tax at a rate of 15%. J calculates that its tax liability for the year to 30 June 20X6 will be $1.5m. Overseas tax has not been taken into account in computing this tax liability. The liability for the year ended 30 June 20X5 has been agreed at $970,000. The deferred tax payable needs to be reduced by $290,000 at 30 June 20X6. J has the following balances brought forward: Current tax: $976,000; Deferred tax: $300,000.

Required

Prepare the notes in respect of current and deferred tax as they would appear in the financial statements of J for the year ended 30 April 20X6.

(5 marks)

25 Andress Co — 36 mins

Learning outcome C1(c)

The income statements and statements of financial position for the year 20X0 for Andress Co, Bacall Co and Christie Co are given below.

INCOME STATEMENTS FOR THE YEAR ENDED 31 DECEMBER 20X0

	Andress Co	*Bacall Co*	*Christie Co*
	$	$	$
Revenue	10,000	7,000	9,000
Cost of sales	(6,000)	(2,000)	(4,500)
Gross profit	4,000	5,000	4,500
Expenses	(2,200)	(1,200)	(1,900)
Profit before taxation	1,800	3,800	2,600
Taxation	(800)	(800)	(600)
Profit for the year	1,000	3,000	2,000

STATEMENTS OF FINANCIAL POSITION AT 31 DECEMBER 20X0

	Andress Co $	Bacall Co $	Christie Co
Assets			
Non-current assets			
Property, plant and equipment	25,300	9,000	10,000
Investment in Bacall Co at cost	4,000	–	–
Investment in Christie Co at cost	1,000	–	–
	30,300	9,000	10,000
Current assets	21,500	7,000	4,000
Total assets	51,800	16,000	14,000
Equity and liabilities			
Equity			
Ordinary share capital	10,000	4,000	3,000
Share premium account	4,000	–	–
Retained earnings	2,800	7,000	4,000
Total equity	16,800	11,000	7,000
Non-current liabilities	10,000	2,000	3,000
Current liabilities	25,000	3,000	4,000
Total equity and liabilities	51,800	16,000	14,000

Additional information

(a) Andress Co has owned 100% of Bacall Co since incorporation.

(b) Andress Co purchased 25% of the shares in Christie Co for $1,000 on 1 January 20X0. Pre-acquisition retained earnings were $2,000.

(c) During the year, Andress Co sold goods to Christie Co for $1,500 at cost plus a 20% mark-up. These goods were still in the inventories of Christie Co at year-end.

Required

Prepare, for Andress Co, the consolidated income statement for the year ended 31 December 20X0 and the consolidated statement of financial position at that date.

(20 marks)

26 Fallowfield and Rusholme 36 mins

Learning outcome C1(c)

Fallowfield acquired a 100% holding in Rusholme three years ago when Rusholme's retained earnings balance stood at $16,000. Both businesses have been very successful since the acquisition and their respective income statements for the year ended 30 June 20X8 are as follows:

	Fallowfield $	Rusholme $
Revenue	403,400	193,000
Cost of sales	(207,400)	(92,600)
Gross profit	196,000	100,400
Other income	6,000	–
Distribution costs	(16,000)	(14,600)
Administrative expenses	(24,250)	(17,800)
Dividends from Rusholme	25,000	–
Profit before tax	186,750	68,000
Income tax expense	(61,750)	(22,000)
Profit for the year	125,000	46,000

STATEMENT OF CHANGES IN EQUITY (EXTRACTS)

	Fallowfield Retained earnings	*Rusholme Retained earnings*
	$	$
Balance at 1 July 20X7	163,000	61,000
Dividends	(40,000)	(25,000)
Total comprehensive income for the year	125,000	46,000
Balance at 30 June 20X8	248,000	82,000

(a) During the year Rusholme sold some goods to Fallowfield for $40,000, including 25% mark up. Half of these items were still in inventories at the year-end.

(b) Fallowfield sold plant costing $22,000 to Rushholme during the year. The profit on the sale has been shown as other income. Depreciation on plant is charged at 25%.

Required

Produce the consolidated income statement of Fallowfield Co and its subsidiary for the year ended 30 June 20X8, and an extract from the statement of changes in equity, showing retained earnings. Goodwill is to be ignored. **(20 marks)**

1 Convex

(a) Although the head office is in Switzerland, board meetings are held in London and the chairman and chief executive are based in London. **Therefore the place of management is London.**

(b) (i) The nationality of the Board Members is irrelevant to the place of management. Therefore the place of management is London.

(ii) As board meetings are held in Switzerland and the chairman and chief executive are based in Switzerland, **the place of management is Switzerland**. Although the accounting offices are in London, this does not affect the place where management decisions are made.

2 AB

> **Top tips.** This question is easier than it looks and similar to what you may see in the exam. Make sure you understand the answer.

STATEMENT OF COMPREHENSIVE INCOME FOR THE YEAR ENDED 31 DECEMBER 20X7 (EXTRACT)

	Note	$
Profit before tax		100,000
Income tax expense	3	(41,800)
Profit for the year		58,200

STATEMENT OF FINANCIAL POSITION AT 31 DECEMBER 20X7 (EXTRACT)

	$	*Note*
Equity and liabilities		
Issued capital of 700,000 50c ordinary shares fully paid	350,000	
Retained earnings	101,200	4
Non-current liabilities		
Deferred tax	36,400	2
Current liabilities		
Current tax	39,800	1

Notes to the statement of financial position and statement of financial position

1 *Current tax comprises*

	$
Income tax (3,800 + 36,000)	39,800

2 *Deferred tax*

	$
Balance at 1.1.20X7	29,400
Deferred tax expense	7,000
Balance at 31.12.20X7	36,400

3 *Tax on profit for the year*

	$
Income tax (at 25% on taxable profits of 20X7)	36,000
less overprovision on profits of 20X6	(1,200)
Transfer to deferred tax	7,000
	41,800

4 *Retained earnings*

	$
Profit for the year	58,200
Retained brought forward	43,000
Retained carried forward	101,200

3 Tax and dividends

> **Top tips.** Remember that the dividend is a **net** amount.

(a)

		$'000	$'000
Accounting profit			750
Add: disallowable expenditure:	entertaining	75	
	formation expenses	15	
	book depreciation	300	
			390
			1,140
Less: non-taxable income		25	
tax allowable depreciation		350	
			(375)
Taxable profit			765

The tax rate is 25%, so the tax due is $191,250 (25% × $765,000).

(b)

	$'000
Net dividend paid	1,500
Tax credit ($^{25}/_{75}$)	500
Gross dividend	2,000
Tax due at 30%	600
Less tax credit	(500)
Payable by shareholders	100

Note that this represents 5% of the gross dividend ie. the difference between the corporate and individual tax rates. If the individual tax rate is the same as the corporate rate, the shareholders have no additional tax to pay under the full imputation system.

4 VAT

	$
Output tax (see note)	70,000
Input tax (300,000 x 85%) x 17.5%	44,625
Tax payable	25,375

Note

Assume sales excluding VAT are Y.

Then zero-rated sales are 20% x Y and standard rated gross sales are Y x 80% x 1.175%.

So:

(20% x Y) + (Y x 80% x 1.175%) = 570,000

0.2Y + 0.94Y = 570,000

1.14Y = 570,000

Y = 500,000

Check: Net sales are $500,000, so VAT due is $500,000 x 80% x 17.5% ($70,000). This gives sales including VAT of $570,000.

5 Company tax

Top tips. Writing out T accounts will probably help here.

Tax on profit on ordinary activities – note to statement of comprehensive income

	$'000
Current tax	
Tax on profit for the year	976
Underprovision for previous period ($794,000 – $765,000)	29
Deferred tax	
Increase in provision ($300,000 - $200,000)	100
Total tax charge	1,105

Statement of financial position

	$'000
Non-current liabilities	
Deferred tax	300
Current liabilities	
Current tax	976

6 Regulatory influences

Top tips. Do not omit the requirement to **explain**. It is best to use **headings** to divide your answer.

Stock Exchange

A quoted company is a company whose shares are bought and sold on a stock exchange. This involves the signing of an agreement which requires compliance with the rules of that stock exchange. This would normally contain amongst other things the stock exchange's detailed rules on the information to be disclosed in listed companies' accounts. This, then, is one regulatory influence on a listed company's accounts. The stock exchange may enforce compliance by monitoring accounts and reserving the right to withdraw a company's shares from the stock exchange: ie the company's shares would no longer be traded through the stock exchange. In many countries there is, however, no statutory requirement to obey these rules.

Local legislation

In most countries, companies have to comply with the local companies legislation, which lays down detailed requirements on the preparation of accounts. Company law is often quite detailed, partly because of external influences such as EU Directives. Another reason to increase statutory regulation is that listed companies are under great pressure to show profit growth and an obvious way to achieve this is to manipulate accounting policies. If this involves breaking the law, as opposed to ignoring professional guidance, company directors may think twice before bending the rules - or, at least, this is often a government's hope.

Standard-setters

Professional guidance is given by the national and international standard-setters. Prescriptive guidance is given in accounting standards which must be applied in all accounts intended to show a 'true and fair view' or 'present fairly in all material respects'. IFRSs and national standards are issued after extensive consultation and are revised as required to reflect economic or legal changes. In some countries, legislation requires details of non-compliance to be disclosed in the accounts. 'Defective' accounts can be revised under court order if necessary and directors signing such accounts can be prosecuted and fined (or even imprisoned).

The potential for the IASB's influence in this area is substantial.

7 Accounting standards

The users of financial information – shareholders, suppliers, management, employees, business contacts, financial specialists, government and the general public - are entitled to this information about a business entity to a greater or lesser degree. However, the needs and expectations of these groups will vary.

The preparers of the financial information often find themselves in the position of having to reconcile the interests of different groups in the best way for the business entity. For example whilst shareholders are looking for increased profits to support higher dividends, employees will expect higher wage increases; and yet higher profits without corresponding higher tax allowances (increased capital allowances for example) will result in a larger tax bill.

Without accounting standards to prescribe how certain transactions should be treated, preparers **would be tempted to produce financial information which meets the expectations of the favoured user group**. For example creative accounting methods, such as off balance sheet finance, could be used to enhance a company's statement of financial position to make it more attractive to investors/lenders.

The aim of accounting standards is that they should regulate financial information in order that it shows the following characteristics, amongst others.

(a) Objectivity
(b) Comparability
(c) Completeness
(d) Consistency

8 IASB

The main aims of the IASB are:

(a) To develop, in the public interest, a **single** set of understandable and enforceable accounting standards

(b) To promote the **use** and rigorous **application** of those standards

(c) To bring about the **convergence** of national accounting standards and International Financial Reporting Standards.

The tendency of the IASB has been to concentrate on the first very specific aim, and to leave the second and third slightly more vague aims to follow behind.

The IASB's recent target has been to produce a set of 'core standards' which the worldwide body representing stock exchanges, IOSCO, can accept for all cross-border listings. In theory, this would mean that, say, a German company that prepares its accounts using IASs would be accepted for a listing on the Tokyo Stock Exchange.

IOSCO has given the core standards qualified endorsement and with the new standards and improvements to existing standards issued in 2003 and 2004, the IASB claims to have now established a 'stable platform' of standards.

However, individual stock exchanges may still make life difficult for foreign companies by insisting on substantial additional disclosures. The IASB is facing an uphill struggle, but there have been substantial successes, notably the EC decision that the consolidated accounts of listed companies must comply with IFRS from 2005.

In recent years the IASB has also been pursuing an additional objective – convergence of International Financial Reporting Standards and standards produced in the US by the FASB. There is now a timetable for convergence between IFRS and US GAAP. When this is achieved it will greatly increase the influence of the IASB.

9 External auditors

The external auditors' responsibilities with respect to the financial statements are concerned with deciding whether the accounts show a **true and fair view** of the affairs of the company for the year. The auditors must express an **opinion** on the financial statements to this effect.

The auditors conduct an audit which examines the figures in the financial statements and agrees them back to the underlying accounting information. They are required to satisfy themselves that the directors have prepared the accounts correctly and that there is no materially misleading information within them. To this end the auditors have a statutory right to all information and explanations deemed necessary to perform the audit.

The external auditors report to the members of the company and their responsibility is limited to the expression of this opinion.

They are not responsible for the accounting systems, or for the detection of all fraud and error. While auditors will report on whether or not the accounting system is satisfactory, and will design their tests in order to have **a good chance of detecting any material fraud or error**, these issues are the responsibility of the directors.

10 Audit report

If the auditors' work leads them to conclude that the financial statements are free from material error or misstatement and that they give a true and fair view of the financial affairs of the company then they will issue an **unqualified opinion**. This opinion covers the statement of comprehensive income, the statement of financial position and the notes to the accounts. By convention the opinion usually covers the statement of cash flows as well. They also review the directors report to ensure that this does not contain information which is materially misleading or which conflicts with elements of the financial statements. The auditors' report is the statement of their opinion on these elements of the financial statements. They state explicitly that the statement of financial position reflects the state of the company's affairs at the year end and that the statement of comprehensive income gives the company's profit or loss for the year. The report also covers a number of other elements, such as the fact that adequate accounting records were kept, by exception.

A qualified report contains a qualified opinion because the auditors are concerned that the financial statements do not or may not give a true and fair view. This may occur due to **an inability to obtain sufficient appropriate audit evidence** or a material misstatement of the financial statements.

The extent of the qualification is determined by whether the misstatement or inability to obtain sufficient appropriate audit evidence is merely **material** or is **pervasive**.

When the auditors issue a qualified report it must contain a full explanation of the reasons for the qualification and, where possible, a quantification of the effects on the financial statements. This means that a qualified report will contain at least one more paragraph than an unqualified report.

The qualified report should leave the reader in no doubt as to its meaning and the implications it has on an understanding of the financial statements.

11 New project

Ethical issues

The accountant has been asked to manage a project for which he or she does not have sufficient expertise. This is a threat to the fundamental principle of **professional competence and due care**. The CIMA *code of ethics for professional accountants* specifically requires accountants to only undertake tasks for which they have sufficient experience.

The finance director may be unaware that the accountant does not possess the requisite knowledge for the project in question. It may be tempting for the accountant to ignore the issue, especially if he or she is concerned that their reputation is discredited or they are hoping for a promotion within the business. This is a threat to the fundamental principle of **professional behaviour**. Under the CIMA Code, accountants in business should not intentionally mislead employers as to their level of expertise.

Action to take

Initially, the accountant should inform the finance director of his or her concerns and discuss an appropriate course of action. The problem may be alleviated by the accountant attending further training or if there are only specific areas where he or she lacks expertise, consulting with others on these areas. If none of these safeguards are appropriate then the management of the project should be reassigned to a member of staff with the correct experience.

If the finance director insists the accountant manages the project after being made aware of his or her lack of expertise, the accountant should raise the matter with the next level of management, if this exists.

The accountant should only contact external parties if a satisfactory response cannot be obtained internally. It may be appropriate to contact CIMA or an independent professional advisor. As confidentiality rules apply, legal advice should be sought before contacting an external party.

The accountant should only refuse to manage the new project as a last resort.

12 C

> **Top tips.** Begin by working out the profit/loss on each contract. The loss is recognised in full. Cost of sales is a balancing figure.

	Maryhill bypass $'000	*Rottenrow Centre* $'000
Statement of comprehensive income		
Revenue	2,800	3,000
Cost of sales	(2,178)	(3,100)
Profit/(loss)	622	(100)
Statement of financial position		
Costs to date plus recognised profits (1,400 + 622/2,900)	2,022	2,900
Progress billings plus recognised losses (2,600/3,400 + 100)	(2,600)	(3,500)
Gross amount due to customers for contract work (liability)	(578)	(600)

Working: Profit/loss on contract

Maryhill: $[9{,}000 - (1{,}400 + 5{,}600)] \times \frac{2{,}800}{9{,}000} = 622$

Rottenrow: $8{,}000 - (2{,}900 + 5{,}200) = (100)$

13 IFRS 5

Top tips. Read this question carefully. The definition of 'held for sale' is quite specific.

The plant will not be classified as 'held for sale'.

For this to be the case, the asset must be available for immediate sale and its sale must be **highly probable**. For the sale to be highly probable, the asset must be actively marketed for sale at a price that is reasonable in relation to its current fair value.

This property is being marketed at a price which is **above** its current fair value. It is improbable that it will be sold at that price until property prices rise. This delay has been imposed by the seller, so it cannot be said that his intention is to sell the plant immediately. Therefore it cannot be classified as 'held for sale'.

14 Leases

Top tips. The principle of 'substance over form' is important here. Consider what the position would be if lessees were not required to capitalise finance leases.

IAS 17 is an example of substance triumphing over form. In legal terms **the lessor may be the owner of the asset, but the lessee enjoys all the risks and rewards which ownership of the asset would convey**. This is the key element to IAS 17. The lessee is deemed to have an asset as they must maintain and run the asset through its useful life.

The lessee enjoys the future economic benefits of the asset as a result of entering into the lease. There is a corresponding liability which is the obligation to pay the instalments on the lease until it expires. Assets and liabilities cannot be netted off. If finance leases were treated in a similar manner to the existing treatment of operating leases then no asset would be recognised and lease payments would be recognised in profit or loss as they were incurred. This is off balance sheet finance. The company has assets in use and liabilities to lessors which are not recorded in the financial statements. This would be misleading to the users of the accounts and make it appear as though the assets which were recorded were more efficient in producing returns than was actually the case.

15 T

Top tips. This is similar to Section C questions in the exam. Make all your workings very clear, so you can see what you are doing.

T: STATEMENT OF COMPREHENSIVE INCOME
FOR THE YEAR ENDED 31 DECEMBER 20X1

	$'000
Revenue	68,500
Cost of sales (W2)	(26,010)
Gross profit	42,490
Distribution costs	(4,000)
Administrative expenses (W3)	(8,940)
	29,550
Financial costs (W9)	(4,965)
Profit before tax	24,585
Taxation (10,200 + 50) (W5)	(10,250)
Profit for the year	14,335

STATEMENT OF FINANCIAL POSITION AT 31 DECEMBER 20X1

	$'000	$'000
Non-current assets		
Property, plant and equipment		440,720
Current assets		
Inventory	470	
Cash at bank	300	
		770
Total assets		441,490
Equity and liabilities		
Equity		
Share capital (W8)		210,000
Share premium		10,000
Retained earnings (W6)		99,335
Non-current liabilities		
Loans		110,000
Amount due under finance lease		158
Current liabilities		
Trade payables	1,700	
Taxation	10,200	
Amount due under finance lease	97	
		11,997
Total equity and liabilities		441,490

Workings

1 *Depreciation*

	$'000
Hotels 490,000 @ 2%	9,800
Fixtures and fittings (18,000 – 9,400) @ 25%	2,150
Vans (300,000 × 20% × 6/12)	30
	11,980

2 *Cost of sales*

	$'000
Food purchases	2,100
Heating and lighting	3,000
Housekeeping and restaurant staff	9,000
Opening inventory	400
Closing inventory	(470)
Depreciation	11,980
	26,010

3 *Administrative expenses*

	$'000
Administration	3,000
Staff wages	6,000
Lease payment	(60)
	8,940

4 *Property, plant and equipment*

	Hotels $'000	Fixtures and fittings $'000	Vehicles $'000	Total $'000
Cost or valuation				
As at 1 January 20X1	478,000	11,000	–	489,000
Additions	12,000	7,000	300	19,300
As at 31 December 20X1	490,000	18,000	300	508,300
Depreciation				
As at 1 January 20X1	46,200	9,400	–	55,600
Charge for the year	9,800	2,150	30	11,980
As at 31 December 20X1	56,000	11,550	30	67,580
Net book value as at 31 December 20X1	434,000	6,450	270	440,720
Net book value as at 1 January 20X1	431,800	1,600	–	433,400

5 *Taxation*

	$'000
Taxation charge for the year	10,200
Underprovision from the previous year	50
	10,250

6 *Retained earnings*

	$'000
Profit for the year	14,335
Dividend paid	(1,000)
Retained for the period	13,335
Retained earnings b/f	86,000
Retained earnings c/f	99,335

7 *Finance lease*

	$'000
Cash price	300
Interest 10% × 6/12	15
Instalment 31/12/X1	(60)
Balance 31/12/X1	255
Interest 10% × 6/12	13
Instalment 30/6/X2	(60)
	208
Interest 10% × 6/12	10
Instalment 31/12/X2	(60)
Balance 31/12/X2	158
Balance 31/12/X1	255
Due within 1 year (120 – 13 – 10)	97
Due after 1 year	158
	255

8 *Share capital*

	$'000
Balance per trial balance	220,000
Transfer to share premium ($50m x 0.20)	(10,000)
	210,000

9 *Finance costs*

	$'000
Loan interest	4,950
Finance lease interest (W7)	15
	4,965

16 CEC

Top tips. This is a fairly easy question. Remember to **explain** each item.

Item	*Explanation*	*Adjustment* *Add to inventory value* $	*Subtract from inventory value* $
(a)	Cost $2,885. Net realisable value $(3,600 – 921) = $2,679. The inventory should be valued at the lower of cost and NRV. Since NRV is lower, the original valuation of inventories (at cost) will be reduced by $(2,885 – 2,679)		206
(b)	Inventory issued on sale or return and not yet accepted by the customer should be included in the valuation and valued at the lower of cost and NRV, here at $5 each (cost)	1,500	
(c)	The cost ($7.30) is below the current and foreseeable selling price ($10 or more) which is assumed to be the NRV of the item. Since the current valuation is at the lower of cost and NRV, no change in valuation is necessary	-	-
		1,500	206

	$	$
Original valuation of inventories, at cost		153,699
Adjustments and corrections:		
To increase valuation	1,500	
To decrease valuation	(206)	
		1294
Valuation of inventories for the annual accounts		154,993

17 Plant and equipment

Top tips. Do not forget the annual depreciation charge.

PLANT AND EQUIPMENT – COST

	DR $		*CR* $
Balance b/f	250,000	Plant 20X5 disposal	40,000
Purchases	150,000	Plant 20X7 disposal	10,000
		Balance c/d	350,000
	400,000		400,000
Balance b/d	350,000		

PLANT AND EQUIPMENT – ACCUMULATED DEPRECIATION

	DR $		*CR* $
Plant 20X5 disp	32,000	B/f	148,000
Plant 20X7 disp	4,000	Current year chg – 350,000 x 20%	70,000
Balance c/d	182,000		
	218,000		218,000
		Balance b/d	182,000

PLANT AND EQUIPMENT – DISPOSALS

	DR		CR
	$		$
Plant 20X5	40,000	Plant 20X5 depn	32,000
Plant 20X7	10,000	Plant 20X7 depn	4,000
		Plant 20X5 proceeds	5,000
		Losses on disposals	9,000
	50,000		50,000

18 IT

Top tips. The important point is to distinguish between the amounts actually spent during the year and the amounts taken to profit or loss.

PURCHASED GOODWILL

	$		$
Cash	4,800	Income statement: impairment loss	1,200
		Balance c/d	3,600
	4,800		4,800
Balance b/d	3,600		

RESEARCH AND DEVELOPMENT EXPENDITURE

	$		$
Balance b/f	26,500	∴ Income statement (7,900 +	
Cash: research	7,900	(26,500 + 3,500 – 22,600))	15,300
development	3,500	Development costs c/d	22,600
	37,900		37,900
Balance b/d	22,600		

19 F

Top tips. Remember that some events after the end of the reporting period, while not adjusting events, may still require disclosure.

The treatment of the events arising in the case of F would be as follows.

(a) The fall in value of the investment in P has arisen over the previous year and that company's financial accounts for the year to 28 February 20X1 provide additional evidence of conditions that existed at the end of the reporting period. The loss of $50,000 is material in terms of the trading profit figure and it should therefore be reflected in the financial statements of F. Due to the size and nature of the loss, it should be disclosed separately either in profit or loss or in the notes, according to IAS 1.

(b) The destruction of inventory by fire on 30 April (one month after the end of the reporting period) must be considered as a new condition which did not exist at the end of the reporting period. Since the loss is material, being $250,000, it should be disclosed separately, by way of a note describing the nature of the event and giving an estimate of its financial effect.

(c) The approval on 1 June of the company's design for tank cleaning equipment creates a new condition which did not exist at the end of the reporting period. This is, therefore, an event which does not require adjustment under IAS 10.

20 B

Top tips. This is very likely to be examined. Make sure you know the format. Do not neglect part (b).

(a) STATEMENT OF CASH FLOWS FOR THE YEAR ENDED 30 SEPTEMBER 20X1

	$'000	$'000
Profit before tax (85 + 15)		100
Adjustment for non-cash-flow items		
Profit on sale of non-current asset		(10)
Depreciation		30
Adjustment for working capital		120
Inventory		(15)
Receivables		(50)
Payables		40
Cash generated from operations		95
Interest paid		(15)
Net cash from operating activities		80
Cash flows from investing activities		
Sale of non-current asset (W2)	90	
Purchase of non-current assets	(40)	
Net cash from investing activities		50
Cash flows from financing activities		
Dividends paid	(35)	
Loan repaid	(80)	
Net cash used in financing activities		(115)
Net increase in cash and cash equivalents		15
Cash and cash equivalents at beginning of period		15
Cash and cash equivalents at end of period		30

Working

Sale of non-current assets

	$'000
Net book value (520 + 40 – 30 – 450)	80
Profit from sale	10
Proceeds on sale	90

(b) STATEMENT OF FINANCIAL POSITION AS AT 30 SEPTEMBER 20X2

	$'000	$'000
Non-current assets (450 – 30)		420
Current assets		
Inventory	75	
Receivables (80 + 640 – 615)	105	
Bank and cash (W)	220	400
Total assets		820
Equity and liabilities		
Share capital		400
Retained earnings (145 + 160)		305
Current liabilities (60 + 410 + 35 – 390)		115
		820

Working

Bank and cash

	$'000
Balance at 30 September 20X1	30
Received from customers	615
Paid to suppliers	(390)
Interest paid	(15)
Loan paid off	(20)
	220

21 Cat

Top tips. This question is easier than it looks. Work through it methodically.

(a) CAT CO
STATEMENT OF CASH FLOWS FOR THE YEAR ENDED 30 JUNE 20X2

	$	$
Cash flows from operating activities		
Profit before tax (W1)	54,500	
Interest expense	1,500	
Depreciation (37,000 – 26,000)	11,000	
Increase in inventories	(6,000)	
Decrease in receivables	2,000	
Increase in payables	8,000	
Interest paid	(1,500)	
Dividends paid	(13,000)	
Income tax paid (W2)	(12,000)	
Net cash from operating activities		44,500
Cash flows from investing activities		
Payments to acquire non-current assets (W3)		(34,000)
Net cash used in investing activities		10,500
Cash flows from financing activities		
Issue of ordinary share capital	3,000	
Redemption of loan stock	(10,000)	
Net cash used in financing activities		(7,000)
Net increase in cash and cash equivalents		3,500
Cash and cash equivalents at beginning of year		10,000
Cash and cash equivalents at end of year		13,500

Workings

1 *Profit before tax*

RETAINED EARNINGS

	$		$
Taxation	15,000	Balance b/f 1.7.X1	44,000
Dividends	13,000	Profit before tax (bal fig)	54,500
Balance c/f 30.6.X2	70,500		
	98,500		98,500

Profit for the year is after charging loan interest of 10% × 10,000 for 12 months and 10% × 10,000 for 6 months.

2 *Tax paid*

TAXATION

	$		$
Tax paid*	12,000	Balance b/f 1.7.X1	12,000
Balance c/f 30.6.X2	15,000	Tax charge	15,000
	27,000		27,000

*Note. The tax paid will be last year's year-end provision

3 *Non-current assets*

NON-CURRENT ASSETS

	$		$
Balance b/f 1.7.X1	85,000		
Purchases (bal fig)	34,000	Balance c/f 30.6.X2	119,000
	119,000		119,000

(b) STATEMENT OF FINANCIAL POSITION AS AT 30 JUNE 20X2

	$	$
Assets		
Non-current assets		
Cost	119,000	
Depreciation	(37,000)	
		82,000
Current assets		
Inventories (40,000 – 3,000 – 2,000)	35,000	
Receivables	24,000	
Cash	13,500	
		72,500
Total assets		154,500
Equity and liabilities		
Equity		
Ordinary $1 shares	28,000	
Share premium	13,000	
Retained earnings (W)	66,000	
		107,000
Non-current liabilities		
10% loan stock	10,000	
Deferred tax	4,500	
		14,500
Current liabilities		
Provision for legal costs	3,000	
Trade payables (23,000 – 8,000)	15,000	
Taxation	15,000	
		33,000
Total equity and liabilities		154,500

Working: Retained earnings

	$'000
As per draft statement of financial position	70,500
Transfer to deferred tax (15,000 x 30%)	(4,500)
Inventory adjustment	(5,000)
Reduction in provision	5,000
	66,000

22 ABA

Top tips. Do not forget to show effect of these adjustments on the net profit before tax.

(a) The value of the IMX receivable will have to be written down. If, as appears likely, something can be recovered, then the debt will not need to be written off entirely. It can be written down to 30c in the $. The write-down needed will be $227,500.

(b) NRV of this inventory is now:

	$
Sales proceeds	200,000
Less agents commission 20%	(40,000)
Less disposal costs	(25,000)
	135,000

As this is less than cost, the inventory should be written down by $15,000.

(c) It currently looks probable that this liability will not be met by the insurance company, so it should be provided for in full in accordance with IAS 37.

Effect on net profit before tax

	$
Draft net profit	923,000
IMX write-down	(227,500)
Inventory write-down	(15,000)
Provision for damages	(50,000)
Adjusted net profit	630,500

23 L

(a) '3 for 2' bonus issue

This involves the issue of 45m new 50c shares, financed from the share premium account and the retained earnings. The capital structure following this issue will be:

	$'000
Share capital (15,000 + 22,500)	37,500
Share premium	–
Retained earnings (27,000 – 19,500)	7,500
	45,000

(b) '1 for 2' rights issue at 80c

37.5m shares are now issued at 80c.

	$'000
Share capital (37,500 + 18,750)	56,250
Share premium (37.5m × 30c)	11,250
Retained earnings	7,500
	75,000

24 International tax

Top tips. This question covers a number of issues. Deal with each one separately.

Tax on profit on ordinary activities – note to statement of comprehensive income

	$'000
Current tax	
Tax on profit for the year	1,500
Overseas tax paid (note)	(1,200)
Overprovision for previous period ($976,000 - $970,000)	(6)
Deferred tax	
Decrease in provision ($300,000 - $290,000)	(10)
Total tax charge	284

Note: Tax paid by overseas branch = $8m x 15% = $1.2m.

STATEMENT OF FINANCIAL POSITION

	$m
Non-current liabilities	
Deferred tax	290
Current liabilities	
Current tax	300

25 Andress

Top tips. Write out your proforma statements before working methodically down the given information in this question.

ANDRESS
CONSOLIDATED INCOME STATEMENT FOR THE YEAR ENDED 31 DECEMBER 20X0

	$
Revenue (10,000 + 7,000)	17,000
Cost of sales (6,000 + 2,000 + 63 (W1))	(8,063)
Gross profit	8,937
Expenses (2,200 + 1,200)	(3,400)
Share of profit of associate (2,000 × 25%)	500
Profit before taxation	6,037
Taxation (800 + 800)	(1,600)
Profit for the year	(4,437)

ANDRESS
CONSOLIDATED STATEMENT OF FINANCIAL POSITION AT 31 DECEMBER 20X0

	$
Assets	
Non-current assets	
Property, plant and equipment (25,300 + 9,000)	34,300
Investment in associate (W2)	1,437
Current assets (21,500 + 7,000)	28,500
Total assets	64,237
Equity and liabilities	
Ordinary share capital	10,000
Share premium account	4,000
Retained earnings (2,800 + 7,000 + 500 – 63 (W2))	10,237
Total equity	24,237
Non-current liabilities (10,000 + 2,000)	12,000
Current liabilities (25,000 + 3,000)	28,000
Total equity and liabilities	64,237

Points to note

1 Andress has owned the shares in Bacall since incorporation and the shares were acquired at nominal value (4,000 shares for $4,000). There is therefore no difference between the value of the consideration transferred by Andress and the value of the assets it acquired.

Workings

1 *Unrealised profit*

$1,500 \times {}^{20}\!/_{120} \times 25\% = 63$

2 *Investment in associate*

	$
Cost of investment	1,000
Share of post-acquisition retained earnings ((4,000 – 2,000) × 25%)	500
Unrealised profit (W1)	(63)
	1,437

26 Fallowfield and Rusholme

CONSOLIDATED INCOME STATEMENT FOR THE YEAR ENDED 30 JUNE 20X8

	$
Revenue (403,400 + 193,000 – 40,000)	556,400
Cost of sales (207,400 + 92,600 – 40,000 + 4,000)	(264,000)
Gross profit	292,400
Distribution costs (16,000 + 14,600)	(30,600)
Administrative expenses (24,250 + 17,800 – (6,000 × 25%))	(40,550)
Profit before tax	221,250
Income tax expense (61,750 + 22,000)	(83,750)
Profit for the year	137,500

STATEMENT OF CHANGES IN EQUITY (EXTRACT)

	Retained earnings
	$
Balance at 1 July 20X7 (W1)	208,000
Dividends	(40,000)
Total comprehensive income for the year	137,500
Balance at 30 June 20X8 (W2)	305,500

Workings

1 *Retained earnings brought forward*

	Fallowfield	Rusholme
	$	$
Per question	163,000	61,000
Pre-acquisition retained earnings	–	(16,000)
	163,000	45,000
Share of Rusholme	45,000	
	208,000	

2 *Retained earnings carried forward*

	Fallowfield	Rusholme
	$	$
Per question	248,000	82,000
PUP	–	(4,000)
Pre-acquisition retained earnings		(16,000)
Disposal of plant		
Profit	(6,000)	
Depreciation (6,000 x 25%)	1,500	
	243,500	62,000
Share of Rusholme post-acquisition earnings	62,000	
	305,500	

INDEX

Note: Key terms and their references are given in **bold**

Absolute adjustments, 302
Accelerated depreciation, 335
Accounting device, 333
Accounting policies, 102
Accounting profit, 329
Accounting standards and choice, 11
Accruals basis, 16
Accrued expenses, 333
Accrued income, 333
Accumulated depreciation, 336
Actual and threatened litigation, 67
Actuarial method, 159
Ad valorem taxes, 314
Adoption of an IAS, 104
Advanced taxes, 302
Advantages of cash flow accounting, 181
Advantages of global harmonisation, 28
Adverse opinion, 42
Advocacy threat, 66
Allotment, 227
Amortisation of development costs, 149
Amortisation, 147
Amount expected to be paid to (recovered from) the tax authorities, 330
Analysis of cash flow statements, 180
Annual Investment Allowance (AIA), 300
Anti-avoidance legislation, 309
Application and allotment accounts, 223
Asset is realised, 337
Asset is recognised, 334
Asset, 18
Assets held for sale, 98
Associate, 244, 286
Audit committee, 67
Audit, 32
Auditors' report, 37

Barriers to harmonisation, 29
Benefits of cash flow information, 169
Bonus issue, 223
Borrowing costs, 132
Branch, 320
Bribery, 72
Business combination, 330

Call accounts, 223, 227
Capital, 21
Capital redemption reserve, 230
Carrying amount, 119
Cash, 169
Cash and cash equivalents, 169
Cash equivalents, 169
Cash flows, 169
Cash generating unit, 129
Change in accounting estimate, 102
Classical system, 326, 327
Close business relationships, 60
Code of ethics for professional accountants, 55
Comparability, 17
Compensation, 197
Competent jurisdiction, 298
Component of an entity, 100
Computer software, 300
Conceptual framework, **12**, 14
Confidentiality, 56
Conflict of interest, 68
Consolidated financial statements, 246
Construction contract, 208
Constructive obligation, 187
Contingent asset, 191
Contingent fees, 62
Contingent liability, 191
Contract revenue, 208
Control, 197, 244
Core standards, 6
Corporate finance, 65
Cost formulae, 204
Cost plus contract, 208
Cost, 118
Costs of conversion, 203
Costs of purchase, 203
Costs to sell, 99
Credit, 321
Current asset, 82
Current IASs, 8
Current liability, 82
Current tax expense, 338
Current tax of prior periods, 338
Current tax, 328, **329**

Deductible temporary differences, 332, 333, 336
Deduction, 321
Deferred tax assets, 331, 337
Deferred tax expense (income), 338
Deferred tax liabilities, 331, 334, 335
Deferred tax, 329
Depreciable amount, 114
Depreciation methods, 115
Depreciation, **114**, 115, 123, 334
Development costs, 334, 335
Development, 147
Direct method, 172
Direct taxation, 298
Directly in equity, 330
Disclaimer of opinion, 42
Discontinued operation, 100
Disposal group, 98
Dividends and pre-acquisition profits, 266
Dividends, 23, 195
Double taxation treaties, 321
Due care, 57
Due process, 7
Duties, 36

Economic life, 156
Effective interest rate, 236
Emphasis of matter, 45
Employment with assurance client, 61
Entity specific value, 118
Equal to its tax base, 333
Equity method, 286
Equity, 19
Ethics, 52
Events occurring after the reporting period, 194
Excess tax, 329
Exchanges of assets, 120
Exempt from VAT, 316
Exemption from preparing group accounts, 246
Exemption, 321
Expectation gap, 33
Expenses, 19
External audit, 32
Extortion, 72

Face of the income statement, 338
Fair presentation, 18
Fair value, 23, 99, 118, 203
Familiarity threat, 66
Family and personal relationships, 61
Finance lease, 156
Financial Accounting Standards Board (FASB), 12
Financial asset, 234
Financial instrument, 234
Financial interests, **60**
Financial liability, 234
Financing activities, 169, 171
First-in, first-out (FIFO), 204
Fixed price contract, 208
Fixed production overheads, 203
Forfeited shares, 223
Forfeiture, 227
Framework, 23
Fundamental principles, 55

Generally Accepted Accounting Principles (GAAP), 13
Gifts, 62, 72
Going concern, 16, 194
Goodwill and pre-acquisition profits, 259
Goodwill, 144, **145**, 267
Grease money, 72
Group, 244

Held for sale, 98, 110
High percentage of fees, 62
Hospitality, 62

IAS 2 Inventories, 202
IAS 8 Accounting policies, changes in accounting estimates and errors, 212, 330
IAS 12 Income taxes, 329
IAS 16 Property plant and equipment, 118
IAS 17 Accounting for leases, 156
IAS 18 Revenue, 23
IAS 23 Borrowing costs, 132
IAS 27 Consolidated and separate financial statements, 244, 254
IAS 28 Investments in associates, 286
IAS 36 Impairment of assets, 126
IAS 37 Provisions, contingent liabilities and contingent assets, 186, 213
IAS 38 Intangible assets, 146
IASB (International Accounting Standards Board), 4, 6; objectives, 4; structure, 4
IFRS 3 Business combinations, 138, 145, 267, 270
IFRS 5 Non-current assets held for sale and discontinued operations, 98, 126
Impaired asset, 126
Impairment, 126
Impairment loss, 119
Impairment of development costs, 149
Impracticable, 103
Imputation system, 327
Income, 19
Indirect method, 173
Indirect taxation, 298
Indirect versus direct, 173
Input tax, 316
Intangible asset, 138, 145, **146**
Integrity, 56
Interest, 23
Interest rate implicit in the lease, 156
Interest received, 335
Interest revenue, 334
Interest, royalties and dividends, 25
Internal audit services, 65
Internally generated goodwill, 140
International Accounting Standards Board (IASB), 4
International Organisation of Securities Commissions (IOSCO), 6
International Standards on Auditing 200 Objective and general principles governing an audit of financial statements, 32
Intimidation threat, 67
Intra-group sales of non-current assets, 264
Intra-group trading, 279
Inventories, 202
Investing activities, 169, 171
Investments in associates, 245
Irrecoverable VAT, 316
Issue expenses, 222
Issue of shares for cash, 223
IT services, 65

Joint control, 197

Key management personnel, 197

Lease, 156

Lease term, 156
Legal services, 65
Liability settled, 337
Liability, 18, **186**, 329, 332
Litigation support, 65
Loan payable, 333
Loans and guarantees, 62
Long association of senior personnel with assurance clients, 66
Long life assets, **301**
Long-term asset, 114
Lowballing, 63

Material, 102

Materiality, 17
Measurement of revenue, 23
Measurement, 21
Minimum lease payments, 156

Net basis, 330

Net realisable value (NRV), 202, 204
Non-controlling interest, 270
Non-distributable reserve, 222
Non-registered persons, 316
Normal capacity, 203

Objectivity, 56

Offset, 330
Onerous contract, 189
Opening balance of retained earnings, 330
Operating activities, 169, 171
Operating cycle, 82
Operating lease, 156
Operating segment, 108
Originating timing differences, 333
Other matter paragraph, 46
Other services, 64, 65
Output tax, 316
Overdue fees, 62

Parent, 244

Partly-paid shares, 222
Partner on client board, 61
Percentage or contingent fees, 62
Permanent and temporary differences, 333
Permanent differences, 333
Permanent establishment, 321
Place of management, 319
Preliminary expenses, 222
Preparing a statement of cash flow, 176
Presentation and disclosure of taxation, 338
Presented separately, 338
Principles-based guidance, 54
Prior period errors, 102
Professional behaviour, 56, 57
Professional competence and due care, 56, 57
Profit smoothing, 186
Profit, 21
Property, plant and equipment, 118
Prospective application, 102
Provision, 186
Prudence, 337
Purchased goodwill, 145

Qualified opinion, 42

Qualifying asset, 132
Quality control review, 61

Reasons for altering capital structure, 233

Recent service with an assurance client, 63
Recognition criteria, 336
Recognition, 20
Recover or settle the carrying amount, 331
Recoverable amount, 99, 127
Recruitment, 63
Redemption of shares, 228
Redemption or purchase by a company of its own shares, 230
Related party transaction, 197
Relevance, 17
Reliability, 17
Rendering of services, 24
Reporting entity, 15
Reporting period, 78
Research and development (R&D) costs, 140, 146, 336
Research, 147
Residual value, 115, **118**
Restructuring, 190
Retirement benefit costs, 336
Retrospective application, 102
Retrospective restatement, 102
Revaluation, 20, 121
Revenue, 23
Review of depreciation method, 124
Review of useful life, 123
Rights issue, 222
Rights to information, 37
Royalties, 23
Rule of 78, 160

Sale of goods, 24

Schedular system, 302
Second opinions, 68
Segment reporting, 107
Self-interest threat, 60
Self-review threat, 63
Share premium, 222
Share premium account, 222, 229
Short-term work in progress, 202

Significant influence, 197, 244
Special rate pool, 301
Statements of cash flows, 168
Subsidiary, 244
Sufficient future taxable profits, 337
Sum-of-the-digits method, 159

Tax assets and liabilities, 330
Tax base, 332, 333
Tax collector, 314
Tax expense, 329, 330
Tax liability, 326
Tax payments, 334
Taxable person, 298
Taxable presence, 320
Taxable profit, 299, 326, 333
Taxable profit (tax loss), 329
Taxable temporary differences, 331, 333, 334
Taxation services, 65
Temporary differences, 331, 333, 338
Temporary staff cover, 65
Timing adjustments, 302
Timing differences, 335
Timing of payment, 326
Types of lease, 156

UK GAAP, 13
Underlying assumptions, 16
Understandability, 17
Unit taxes, 314
Unpaid tax, 329
Unrealised profit, 263
Useful life, 114, 115, 147, 157
Users and their information needs, 16
Valuation services, 64

Valuation, 64
Value in use, **99, 127**
Value of purchased goodwill, 145
Variable production overheads, 203
VAT on motor cars, 317

Weighted average cost, 204
Withholding taxes, 302, 320.
Working capital, 83
Writing down allowance (WDA), 300

Review Form & Free Prize Draw – Paper F1 Financial Operations (5/09)

All original review forms from the entire BPP range, completed with genuine comments, will be entered into one of two draws on 31 January 2010 and 31 July 2010. The names on the first four forms picked out on each occasion will be sent a cheque for £50.

Name: ______________________ **Address:** ______________________

____

____

How have you used this Interactive Text?
(Tick one box only)

☐ Home study (book only)

☐ On a course: college ______________

☐ With 'correspondence' package

☐ Other ______________

Why did you decide to purchase this Interactive Text? *(Tick one box only)*

☐ Have used BPP Texts in the past

☐ Recommendation by friend/colleague

☐ Recommendation by a lecturer at college

☐ Saw information on BPP website

☐ Saw advertising

☐ Other ______________

During the past six months do you recall seeing/receiving any of the following?
(Tick as many boxes as are relevant)

☐ Our advertisement in *Financial Management*

☐ Our advertisement in *Pass*

☐ Our advertisement in *PQ*

☐ Our brochure with a letter through the post

☐ Our website www.bpp.com

Which (if any) aspects of our advertising do you find useful?
(Tick as many boxes as are relevant)

☐ Prices and publication dates of new editions

☐ Information on Text content

☐ Facility to order books off-the-page

☐ None of the above

Which BPP products have you used?

Text	☑	*Success CD*	☐
Kit	☐	*i-Pass*	☐
Passcard	☐	*Interactive Passcard*	☐

Your ratings, comments and suggestions would be appreciated on the following areas.

	Very useful	*Useful*	*Not useful*
Introductory section	☐	☐	☐
Chapter introductions	☐	☐	☐
Key terms	☐	☐	☐
Quality of explanations	☐	☐	☐
Case studies and other examples	☐	☐	☐
Exam skills and alerts	☐	☐	☐
Questions and answers in each chapter	☐	☐	☐
Section summaries and chapter roundups	☐	☐	☐
Quick quizzes	☐	☐	☐
Question Bank	☐	☐	☐
Answer Bank	☐	☐	☐
OT Bank	☐	☐	☐
Index	☐	☐	☐

Overall opinion of this Study Text *Excellent* ☐ *Good* ☐ *Adeqate* ☐ *Poor* ☐

Do you intend to continue using BPP products? *Yes* ☐ *No* ☐

On the reverse of this page are noted particular areas of the text about which we would welcome your feedback.

Please return this form to: Nick Weller, CIMA Publishing Manager, BPP Learning Media Ltd, FREEPOST, London, W12 8BR

Review Form & Free Prize Draw (continued)

TELL US WHAT YOU THINK

Please note any further comments and suggestions/errors below

Free Prize Draw Rules

1 Closing date for 31 January 2010 draw is 31 December 2009. Closing date for 31 July 2010 draw is 30 June 2010.

2 Restricted to entries with UK and Eire addresses only. BPP Learning Media Ltd employees, their families and business associates are excluded.

3 No purchase necessary. Entry forms are available upon request from BPP Learning Media Ltd. No more than one entry per title, per person. Draw restricted to persons aged 16 and over.

4 Winners will be notified by post and receive their cheques not later than 6 weeks after the relevant draw date.

5 The decision of the promoter in all matters is final and binding. No correspondence will be entered into.